Matsuo Bashō

TRAVEL WRITINGS

Matsuo Bashō

TRAVEL WRITINGS

Translated and Edited by

Steven D. Carter

Hackett Publishing Company, Inc.
Indianapolis/Cambridge

23 22 21 20   1 2 3 4 5 6 7

For further information, please address
   Hackett Publishing Company, Inc.
   P.O. Box 44937
   Indianapolis, Indiana 46244-0937

   www.hackettpublishing.com

Cover design by Rick Todhunter and E. L. Wilson
Interior design by E. L. Wilson
Composition by Aptara, Inc.
Maps by Kimball Carter

Library of Congress Control Number: 2019952426

ISBN-13: 978-1-62466-884-5 (hardback)
ISBN-13: 978-1-62466-857-9 (paperback)

The paper used in this publication meets the minimum requirements of American
National Standard for Information Sciences—Permanence of Paper for Printed
Library Materials, ANSI Z39.48–1984.

∞

To Benjamin and Ella.

A word is dead
When it is said,
Some say.

I say it just
Begins to live
That day.
      —Emily Dickinson (no. 1212)

ACKNOWLEDGMENTS

As always, I thank my wife Mary for encouragement and support. Three anonymous reviewers offered useful comments, and the staff at Hackett Publishing have been kind and accommodating throughout the editing process.

—S. Carter

CONTENTS

PREFACE

This book presents fully annotated translations of the six texts of Matsuo Bashō that are generally categorized as travel literature. Numerous English translations exist for some of these texts, particularly *Oku no hokumichi*; but earlier translators have not had the benefit of recent developments in Japanese scholarship on Bashō's life and travels, which I have been able to consult. I have also included more annotation than most previous translators.

I present the texts in the following order, which is consistent with the practice of Japanese scholars in virtually all editions of the last half century:

> *Bones Bleaching in the Fields*
> *A Pilgrimage to Kashima*
> *Knapsack Notes*
> *A Journey to Sarashina*
> *The Narrow Road through the Hinterlands*
> *The Saga Diary*

Readers will notice that this order is based on the chronological order of the journeys that formed the background of the texts and not of the publication of the texts themselves. The main reason for this is that none of Bashō's travel writings was published in his lifetime, and most of the manuscripts have such complicated textual histories that deciding the true order of their completion has seemed impossible—especially so in the case of *Nozarashi kikō*, *Oi no kobumi*, and *Oku no hosomichi*. (See the bibliography for further information about publication history.)

The titles now assigned to these writings were probably not all chosen by Bashō, who in particular seems not to have called his travel writings *kikō*, or "travel record," and evidently thought of what he produced as new and different (see the Introduction). For this reason, I have chosen to avoid the word "record" in most contexts, because it can so easily be taken as a quick, crude jotting down of events. Instead I have opted for "writing" or "account" or "text"—a step in the right direction in terms of literary connotations, I hope. The word "memoir" also comes to mind, of course, but that word is so associated in popular discourse with modern conceptions of subjectivity and confession that I hesitate to use it in relation to Bashō.

In my translations of the travel writings and in my introductions and appendices, I have generally not translated place names, except when necessary because of puns and other figures of speech or when the literal meaning of a name is directly relevant to the meaning of the text. The exceptions are most mountains (Mount Fuji, Mount Takao, etc.); moors (Saba Moor, Miyagi Moor, etc.); rivers (Fuji River, Ōi River, etc.); roads (Tōkai Road); islands (Magaki Island), etc., where I have incorporated the English translation of those general terms. Most place names do have meaning—Edo 江戸, meaning "bay door"; Tsuruoka 鶴岡, meaning "crane hill"; Yamura 谷村, meaning "valley village"; and so on—but as is true with place names generally, literal meanings are irrelevant in most contexts. I have also generally not translated personal names but rendered them in romanized form: Sensui 川水 rather than "river water," Isshō 一笑 rather than "one laugh," and Bashō 芭蕉 rather than "plantain cottage."

Bashō and his contemporaries used the lunar calendar, which divided the year into twelve months that closely reflected the phases of the moon, with months being either twenty-nine or thirty days in length. Thus, the Twelfth Month in my translation refers to the twelfth lunar month. Because over time this system did not correlate with the 365 days of the solar year, an intercalary month (*jun-*) was periodically added in.

I have included a glossary of literary terms and notes on important people and places in the back matter of the book, along with short essays intended to supplement the introductions and notes.

INTRODUCTION

The Life

In the winter of 1687, at a farewell party, Matsuo Bashō composed the following first
verse (*hokku*) for a linked-verse gathering:

A traveler—	*tabibito to*
that is what I shall be called.	*waga na yobaren*
First rain showers.[1]	*hatsushigure*

Like so many of his *hokku*, this one ended up doing double duty, appearing later as the
first poem in his *Knapsack Notes*. In the centuries since then, the poem has come to
signify the centrality of travel in his poetic practice, and also to define his commitment to
experiencing the rigors of the road, symbolized in the poem by rain showers. However, as
the journey of 1687–88 would inspire not the first but the *third* of his travel writings, one
must stress that Bashō had become a traveler much earlier. Almost certainly he spent time
on the road while still living in his hometown, which was close to the cultural centers of
Kyoto, Ise, and Nara.[2] We also know that he took the Tōkai Road to Edo in 1672, when
he determined to make a career for himself as a *haikai* poet in that capital city, and that
he traveled back to his hometown and to Kyoto in the summer of 1676, not to mention
the journeys of 1684–85 and autumn of 1687, for which he left accounts.

No one would have predicted this future for a man of Bashō's origins. He was
born the second son of a farmer,[3] and not in one of the great Japanese cities of the

---

1. See p. 50. The party was hosted by Kikaku, evidently at the house of Yoshiyuki, before Bashō
set off for his hometown and points west.
2. Tanaka 2008, 44–45, surmises that while in service to Tōdō Yoshitada in his teens, Bashō
carried messages between Iga Ueno and the scholar-poet Kitamura Kigin in Kyoto. In a *haibun*
piece he also says that before a visit in spring of 1688, he had previously visited Ise four times,
only one of which we can account for (*Ise sangū* 伊勢参宮, 446). He would visit again in 1689.
3. In past generations the Matsuo had been counted among farmers called *musokunin* 無足人,
low-level soldiers who might be called upon to fight in exigent circumstances. As a second son

time—Edo or Kyoto or Osaka. His birthplace was rather Iga Ueno—the customary way of referring to the city of Ueno in Iga Province—a middling-size castle town on one of the roads between the Kansai area and the Grand Shrines at Ise. We know little about his youth except that his father, Matsuo Yozaemon, died when he was just thirteen, leaving his older brother head of a house that could not be described as wealthy.[4] This would spare the younger brother the toil of maintaining and managing a household, perhaps; yet it also meant that he would have to find a way to make his living. It seems certain that he had some schooling—reading, writing, ciphering; but there are indications that he did not have the education received by even low-ranking samurai.[5] Fatefully, though, he somehow came to the attention of one of the lords of the castle, known by his poetic name Sengin, a young man just a few years his senior, whose large town residence was in the same neighborhood.[6] In this way he was taken into service as an attendant, with the name Munefusa. We assume that this happened because the younger man showed talent in linked verse (*haikai renga*), a communal genre that required individual talent but always in the context of a social gathering.[7] Among the literate, skill in such arts was encouraged if not absolutely required, and in this case there were local adherents that provided a ready place for a young man of taste and ability.

Had his patron not died suddenly in 1666, Munefusa's life might have turned out differently. He was already in his mid-twenties and might have continued on in clan service of some kind. True, the stipend of his patron's lineage was just 5,000 *koku* 石 (nothing compared to the nearly 300,000 assigned to the primary domain fortress to the east in Anonotsu),[8] but still Iga Ueno was a place where a man of talent could do well for himself. Instead, though, and for reasons not entirely clear, after Sengin's death

---

who had left his ancestral home in Tsuge District, however, Yozaemon would not have had that status. See Tanaka 2008, 8–23; Inui 1982, 25; Abe Masami 1970, 232–33.

4. See Tanaka 2008, 21–22; Kon 1992, 229–53.

5. See Tanaka 2012 for a discussion of Bashō's childhood education.

6. Sengin's formal name was Tōdō Yoshitada. It would have been Yoshitada's father, Yoshikiyo, who first called Bashō into service. The town residence (*shimoyashiki* 下屋敷) was a large compound of 5000 *tsubo* 坪 (just over four acres) located just minutes from the Matsuo house (Kon 1989, 197).

7. See pp. 191–98 below and appendix, "*Haikai* Poetry in Bashō's Day."

8. *Koku* was the term used to measure stipends or incomes. It refers to a bale of rice of approximately 180 liters in the Edo period. The Lord of Ueno castle was the heir of the Uneme lineage of the Tōdō, boasting a stipend of 7,000 *koku*.

he turned away from a conventional career—a conscious decision, he later wrote.[9] From that time forward he dedicated himself more exclusively to poetry, cultivating a relationship with his former master's Kyoto teacher and participating in local gatherings of poets composing linked verse. By his early thirties he had determined to become a professional *haikai* master, signaling his resolve in 1672 by going up to Edo, the political capital of the nation and a hotbed of activity in the arts.[10] He might have gone to Kyoto, but that was a more staid world and less open to new ways. Edo was a lively place, although a riskier market.

In Edo, Bashō soon launched a poetic practice under the name Tōsei, which was the common name he would use until his death.[11] At first he was dependent on supporters connected with Kitamura Kigin and the Tōdō clan and had a day job,[12] but soon he was serving a sort of internship, acting as a *shuhitsu*, or scribe, for the Danrin poet Yūzan.[13] Before long he was renting rooms in Nihonbashi, a thriving district in downtown Edo, making a living as a *tenja*, a "marker" who corrected and commented on the work of paying students.[14] By all accounts he did well, but as he matured he tired of the tedium of the marker lifestyle and the superficiality of the poetic circles of the day and their obsession with bourgeois competition. In 1680—perhaps for those reasons, perhaps for personal issues not satisfactorily revealed in the historical record—he left Nihonbashi and moved across the Sumida River to a place called Fukagawa, where he gave up his career as a marker and determined to follow a different path.[15] This did

---

9. In *Genjūan no ki* 幻住庵記 (1690) he writes that he once was envious of officials and also considered the priesthood, but instead opted for a life of poetry (504). In *Knapsack Notes* he also says, "For a while I sought to achieve worldly stature." See p. 49.

10. Inui 1982, 36, argues that he traveled back and forth between Iga Ueno and Kyoto during the first two years and did not become a permanent Edo resident until the spring of 1674.

11. See Tanaka 2009, 331–34. The origins of the name Tōsei are unclear, but it appears that Bashō began using it at the death of his patron, Tōdō Yoshikiyo, in 1674 (Takahashi 1993, 42).

12. Takahashi 2002, 58–59; Kon 1989, 198.

13. Ogata 2002, 17. Scribes were basically factotums, assistants responsible for recording verses in linked-verse sessions and other clerical tasks (Takahashi 1993, 43–44).

14. Kon 1989, 199, estimates that the rates for marking were 300 *mon* 文 for a hundred-verse *renku* sequence, 100 *mon* for a thirty-six-verse *kasen*, and 1,000 *mon* for supervision of a gathering and calculates that at 1 *mon* = 15 yen, that would mean 4,500 yen, 1,500 yen, and 15,000 yen, respectively.

15. Shin Ōhashi Bridge and Eitai Bridge were not built until after his death, which meant that he had to use Ryōgoku Bridge or ferries to get across the river. Some scholars, notably Takahashi Shinji, argue that while in Nihonbashi Bashō was a proper householder with a wife but that he moved to Fukagawa to renounce that life. In a letter from the early 1680s, he says he has quit the marking profession due to illness (Tanaka 2005, 60).

not signal a withdrawal from the world but rather, as Horikiri Minoru puts it, a kind of "retreat within the city" (*shiin* 市隠) that still allowed a social life, especially a life of interacting with disciples and other poets.[16] Nor did it signal an end to his literary ambitions; if anything he showed more commitment than he had before, especially when it came to linked verse. By 1680 he had twenty-one disciples (*monjin* 門人) and was publishing New Year's chapbook anthologies (*saitanchō*) for his "school"—using the latter term in the loose sense of disciples who accepted his authority, listened to his counsel, contributed poems to his anthologies (*shū*), and, in many cases, provided financial assistance—and appearing in other publications.

Bashō remained in contact with people in his hometown and took advantage of other hometown contacts in Edo, but he was only able to make a go of it in Fukagawa because of patrons, chiefly a wealthy man named Sugiyama Sanpū, whom he had probably met through the Iga Ueno network.[17] It was in a small cottage[18] donated by that man that Tōsei now lived, and although sources show that he had not given up marking altogether,[19] he was more selective and concentrated on study and attending meetings where full sequences were composed under his direction—the *za* in the vocabulary of the genre. This he found satisfying, although not lucrative. As a literatus, however, he had to support only a small household[20] and could pursue a frugal life-style, and thanks to generous students and fees for his work as a master of ceremonies at linked-verse gatherings, he was able to live in a kind of genteel poverty.[21] Before long, after the gift of a plantain (*bashō* 芭蕉) by a student, his house was dubbed the Bashōan (Bashō Cottage), and he began using that same name—often along with Tōsei—in a thriving poetic practice. He had given up one source of income for a *haikai* master but continued to receive the other three—supervising linked-verse gatherings, gifts from students, and various kinds of writing and copying fees and gratuities.[22]

---

16. Horikiri 2003, 36, 41, 51; Matsubayashi 2012, 21–51.

17. On Bashō's ongoing relationship with the Iga Ueno leadership, see Inoue 1992, 135–41; Takahashi 2002, 58–59. Sanpū had residences in both Nihonbashi and Fukagawa.

18. The lot was about half an acre, but the cottage was small. At first he called the place Hakusendō, Harbor Hall, alluding to a poem by the Chinese poet Du Fu. See Ueno 1989, 178–81.

19. See Danjō 1977, 206.

20. See appendix, "Bashō's Family and Other Relationships."

21. A *haikai* master of ceremonies might receive the equivalent of 80,000–100,000 yen per session in today's money, according to Yamakawa Yasuto 2000, 260, in addition to lodging and food in many cases.

22. Matsubayashi 2012, 81.

Around the time he moved to Fukagawa, Bashō became acquainted with a Zen priest who lived nearby, one Butchō, chief priest of a temple in the town of Kashima in Hitachi Province who was in the city to represent his constituents in a petition before the shogunate.[23] There is much disagreement about the extent of Butchō's influence on the poet, some arguing that under Butchō's tutelage Bashō became a dedicated Zen practitioner, others that he stopped short of that but was inspired by Butchō to make a proper study of Buddhist texts and Chinese poetry and works of Confucian and Daoist philosophy.[24] There can be no doubt that from this time onward Bashō opted for a more frugal lifestyle based on models inherited from literati of the past, began to wear monkish robes, and began to move away from what he saw as the facile comedy of the *haikai* world across the river in Nihonbashi. In time he forged a style informed by his reading of classical texts (Japanese and Chinese) and by critical ideals inspired by the great poets of the past, such as Saigyō and Sōgi.[25]

The other change in his way of life that occurred around this same time involved his dedication to a life of travel. At the end of 1682, when a fire destroyed his house, he took refuge in the home of a patron in Yamura in nearby Kai Province[26] for some months until supporters in Edo began to raise money for a second Bashōan. In the summer of 1683, he moved in. It appears, though, that his new dwelling was not enough to keep him in the city after experiencing a little of what it meant to escape the daily obligations of a householder: now he wanted to go on the road, and as an independent artist with no conventional occupation and few worldly entanglements, he was able to do so. His disciples and family relations in the capital city would miss him, of course; but he would be back.

The rest, as the saying goes, is history. His vita going forward until his death eleven years later would list numerous linked-verse sequences and anthologies, involving works by himself and his many disciples, and it was those texts that he no doubt thought of as his primary legacy.[27] Among his sequences are many with his chief disciples in Edo, but others were direct products of his traveling life, such as one composed at the home of Shōkei of Nagoya in the winter of 1687, from which the following five

---

23. See pp. 25–27 for details.
24. See appendix, "Bashō and 'Religion.'"
25. He was in fact criticized by the Danrin poet Zaishiki for writing *haikai* that was too much like classical *renga*—bad *renga* but still *renga* (Matsubayashi 2012, 78).
26. Takayama Biji was in Edo to supervise repair of buildings owned by his domain when he found out about Bashō's situation and invited him to Yamura. See Kusumoto 2006, 42–53.
27. Kyoriku quotes Bashō as saying that some of his disciples produced *hokku* not inferior to his own but that it was linked verse that was at his core. See *Uda no hōshi* 宇陀法師, 305.

verses—the first of the sequence—are taken. As is always the case in proper linked verse, the poets present us with not a single narrative or description, but rather with scenes that flow into and out of each other, the energy going into pivots between units where new meanings and plots merge and emerge. The frozen dewdrops of Bashō's first verse signify autumn moving into winter and may have alluded directly to the weather of the moment.

1	Dewdrops, frozen.	*tsuyu itete*
	A brush dips the last	*fude ni kumihosu*
	of the clear water.	*shimizu kana*
	Bashō	
2	Ears pick up leaves descending	*mimi ni ochiba o*
	out in the windy night.	*hirou kaze no yo*
	Kyōkei	
3	In dawn's first light	*akatsuki no*
	a flying squirrel gnaws his way	*musasabi tsuki o*
	into the moon.	*mushibamite*
	Ichibu	
4	A *go* master's rain-hat	*gouchi no kasa o*
	fades into autumn mist.	*kakusu akigiri*
	Fuchin	
5	A hairdresser	*kamiyui ga*
	begs a sprig of morning glory	*asagao hitotsu*
	to take along.[28]	*moraiyuku*
	Jūgo	

Except for Bashō and Jūgo (a Nagoya merchant), we know nothing about these provincial participants but their names. Yet they clearly follow the conventions of the genre. The first verse, for instance, obeys the rule of making a complete statement with the inclusion of a *kireji*, or "cutting word," and also indicates the season of the gathering (winter), while containing the auspicious image of a brush dipped in pure water—a way to praise the host of the gathering for the fine venue he has prepared for the purpose of putting the writing brush to work. The following two winter verses give way

---

28. Abe Masami 1965–89, vol. 5, 435–37. Kyōkei may be a mistake for Shōkei.

to another category—in this case, autumn—again according to convention. Moreover, the connections between verses are based on traditionally linked words, such as "wind" and "dew," "dawn" and "night," and "morning glory" and "mist." In this way the verses reveal serious *haikai* practitioners guided by a master's hand. There are no truly obscure references of the sort for which Bashō had little patience, just one cheeky word game ("hair" linking to "hat") and one somewhat forced metaphor (a squirrel "gnawing" at the moon). Finally, all the scenes are taken from everyday life. Thus as readers we move through a chain of *haikai* images from the world of the time: a brush using the last of the ink, ears "picking up" the sound of leaves falling outside, a flying squirrel spotted going past a crescent moon, a *go* master on the road, a hairdresser departing after providing his service. Mixed in, though, are distinctly classical images, such as dewdrops and clear water, leaves on the wind, dawn light and the moon, spreading autumn mist, and morning glories—all items inherited from the courtly tradition of *uta*, the ancient form that had provided the foundation of poetic discourse for nearly eight hundred years. Rather than rhetorical preening, then, we encounter careful links that give us subtle glimpses of human perception and feeling that transcend their immediate context but are embedded in it. The best and most complete link is based on the seasonal connection between the autumn images of spreading mist and morning glories and the juxtaposition of two "traveling" laborers—a *go* master and a hairdresser. Indeed, one may easily imagine the men leaving the same house, the one up at dawn to make for the next town, the other leaving a little later after providing his service—and taking with him a sprig of flowers for a tip.

In these verses from a sequence produced on the road, there are other nods toward travel as topic: those leaves could be on a mountain road; the *go* master could be on a journey. But *renga* sequences were not the only literary works that resulted from Bashō's days on the road. In time—quite a lot of time, as it turned out—he also produced the six travel writings translated in this book. The first of these begins with events in 1684, the last with events in 1691. His early journeys took him to areas clustered around his hometown: the Nagoya area, Kyoto, the mountains of the Kii Peninsula, Ise, Nara, and the coast of Settsu Province; later he went into the northern hinterlands, then returning to the cities around Lake Biwa and back to Kyoto, where he stayed in cottages provided by disciples, sometimes for months at a time.[29] He

---

29. Kyokusui provided the cottage Genjūan (west of the temple of Ishiyama in Ōtsu), where Bashō stayed more than three months in the summer of 1690; Masahide provided the cottage Mumyōan within the precincts of the temple of Gichūji (likewise in Ōtsu, on the southwest shore of Lake Biwa), where Bashō stayed for a time in the autumn of 1690 and in the late summer of 1694.

also spent long periods back in Edo, where he maintained a residence and was always involved in his profession, supervising gatherings and texts for publication.

Now a poet of undisputed prominence, Bashō could have settled into a more sedentary life and foregone the rigors of the road, remaining in Edo or elsewhere. He had chronic ailments, the chief one being some kind of intestinal inflammation,[30] that were a ready excuse to stay home, and he had household obligations, especially involving a nephew whom he had been looking after since 1676 and a mysterious nun known only by her Buddhist name Jutei.[31] But the lure of the road and his many disciples outside the capital city never left him. After returning to Edo at the end of 1691 from the journey that would later produce *The Narrow Road through the Hinterlands*, the most famous of his travel writings, he stayed in Edo for more than two years—first in a rented house in Nihonbashi and then in a newly built Bashōan arranged by Sanpū and a few other disciples.[32] This was a difficult period for him because of the illness of his ailing nephew, who died in the late spring of 1693. For a time, in the early autumn of that same year, he was so disenchanted that he closed his door to callers for a needed rest. Still, the next spring he was planning to see new places. As early as 1690, when he was staying in Zeze on the shores of Lake Biwa, he had written about plans to visit Shikoku and Tsukushi,[33] places he had never seen.

But as time went by, he felt increasingly frail. One is surprised, in fact, that he hazarded a trip west to see his disciples again, but in the Fifth Month of 1694, he set out once more, with Jutei's teenage son, Jirōbei, as his helper. One reason he made the journey was to mediate squabbles among disciples, some of whom were doubtful about his championing of the aesthetic of *karumi*, or "lightness." But it soon became clear that he did not have the physical strength to act as mediator. He no doubt enjoyed seeing friends in his hometown and visiting Kyorai in Kyoto, but after spending five months traveling from place to place—Nagoya, Ōmi, Kyoto, and Nara—he fell prey

---

30. Chronic ailments translates *jibyō* 持病. In a *haibun* of 1681 he complains of his "many maladies" (*Kotsujiki no okina* 乞食の翁, 410) and in letters (see Tanaka 2005) he frequently mentions his illness, most likely intestinal inflammation and hemorrhoids, both aggravated by drinking too much saké and by cold weather or intense heat. Muramatsu 1985, 141, also mentions the possibility of gallstones.

31. The nephew, Tōin, came to Edo to find work at around age sixteen and relied greatly on his uncle. Scholars are divided about just who Jutei was, some arguing that she had been Bashō's mistress years earlier. What is certain is that she died in Bashō's house (while he was on his own final journey) and that her son lived with Bashō for a time and was briefly one of his traveling companions.

32. Kusumoto 2006, 261–63.

33. Tanaka 2005, 225–27, 237.

to a flare-up of his chronic ailment, in Osaka, in the Tenth Month of 1694. He fought for two weeks but lost his battle on the 12th day of that month, leaving behind a poignant final poem—not a death poem (*jisei no ku* 辞世の句), a disciple tells us,[34] but certainly a vivid evocation of his last days.

Ill on a journey,   *tabi ni yande*
I amble in my dreams   *yume wa kareno o*
on withered moors.[35]   *kakemeguru*

His dreams of travels farther west remained unrealized—as did the account (or accounts) that he would doubtless have made of them; but there can be no doubt that he achieved his wish of being called a traveler. Saigyō had died on the road, and so had Sōgi and the Chinese poet Du Fu. Now in that one way at least he could count himself among their number.

THE TRAVELS

Why did Bashō find travel so appealing? For one thing, it should be mentioned that in the late 1600s, tourism was becoming popular. Peace and stable government had made for the establishment and maintenance of an ever-expanding network of roads to famous places, from natural sights such as Mount Fuji or Matsushima to places of historical interest.[36] Likewise, many people used those roads to visit temples and shrines as pilgrims.

It would be disingenuous to argue that Bashō was never and in no way a tourist or a pilgrim, his writings being replete with references to tourist places and to Buddhist temples, Shinto shrines, and sacred mountains.[37] In a letter to a friend in Iga Ueno he reveals that he was not above going out to see the local sights when he and a traveling companion were briefly in Osaka:

---

34. See Imoto 1972, 269.
35. *Bashō kushū* no. 758. Here and throughout the book, *hokku* numbers refer to those in Ōtani 1962 (*NKBT* 45).
36. See appendix, "Travel in Bashō's Day."
37. Yamamoto Satoshi 1994, 167–68, notes that Bashō departed from the typical tourist pattern by staying at hot springs only three times during his journey to the hinterlands, for short times, and that he actually chose to do so himself only once.

We lodged in Kyūzaemon's place, but it turned out to be such a trial, so cramped and noisy, that I lost all of my excitement for visiting Osaka. But I couldn't seem to relax, so I went out to see what there was to see.[38]

Perhaps it is significant that he fails to mention the places he visited: an indication that he was not that impressed? But it seems certain that wherever he went he acted the role of tourist some of the time; indeed, one can only believe that on that matter his hosts often insisted.

But there are a number of other, easily identifiable reasons for Bashō's engagement in travel that have more to do with his personal and professional life. First was his desire to see his family, friends, and disciples and to check in with domain officials in Iga Ueno, a stop that he worked into the itinerary of all his major journeys.[39] Second was the opportunity to meet with poets ("fine people of artistic discernment," he calls them in a letter[40]) in places far from Edo, to recruit more disciples, and to engage in his genre of linked verse with new companions. So much was this true that in a letter to Sanpū in 1689, he writes that he will move on swiftly from Sukagawa to Sendai because he is "told that there are no poets in the area."[41]

A third motive, of at least equal importance, was his desire to walk in the footsteps of worthy monks and literary predecessors such as the *renga* master Sōgi, the medieval poet-monk Saigyō, and even Chinese poets like Du Fu: to see the sights, natural, historical, and religious, that had been the subject of many of their finest poems and experience the road the way they had, "to test his mettle against the demands of the landscape and the poets of the past," as I have noted elsewhere.[42] It was this dimension

---

38. Tanaka 2005, 148. This and all other translations in the book are my own unless otherwise noted.

39. The lords of the Tsu Domain, comprising Iga and Ise, required anyone away from home to check back on a periodic basis, usually every five years. See Satō Katsuaki 2014, 25; Ueno 2008, 91. Bashō remained in close contact with people in his hometown all of his life and was in some sense always classified as an Iga man. Yamamoto Yuiitsu 1994, 146, notes that Bashō used Iga Ueno as his home base for a month or so in 1676, for another month in 1684, for four months in 1687, seven months in 1689, and four months in 1694.

40. *Fūryū keijin* 風流佳人 (Tanaka 2005, 194–95). *Fūryū* is a complex concept, and Bashō is not entirely consistent in his use of the term. Here he seems to imply the artistic sensitivity and refinement of those dedicated to poetry. See Qiu 2005, 94–126, for a full analysis of the term in Bashō's poetics.

41. Tanaka 2005, 200–201. Doubtless it was Tōkyū, with whom he and Sora stayed in Sukagawa, who provided the information.

42. Carter 2000, 193. In *Sanzōshi* 三冊子 (527), Dohō quotes Bashō as saying, "Someone who has no experience of the Tōkai Road will feel uneasy writing poetry."

of travel—travel as poetic practice—that seems to have been crucial to him, as we know from a short tongue-in-cheek note he sent to his disciple Kyoriku in 1693 that defines travel as something to which poets are naturally attracted:

> Here we have a man named Kyoriku, of the Morikawa clan, who is return-
> ing to his hometown by the Kiso Road. Since long ago people of poetic
> feeling have burdened their backs with packs, pained their feet with san-
> dals, and donned tattered rain hats against frost and dew, thus subjecting
> their own hearts to trials—and yet rejoiced withal to learn the truth of
> things. Kyoriku, though, is in service to his lord, and so he traipses off
> with a sword stuck in his belt, a lance bearer trotting along behind his
> loaded horse, followed by young samurai whose dark formal robes billow
> in the wind—a sight that cannot be in keeping with his true feelings.[43]

While making allowances for a disciple, Bashō still asserts that for a poet travel should be more than moving from place to place on worldly errands. The rigors of the road offered engagement with the world and stimulation for the poetic imagination: new places and new people, as well as communion with places and people from his own past. Thus what Bashō sought as a poet might be compared to the Daoist practice of "freewheeling" or the Zen practice of *angya* 行脚, travel as ascetic training.[44] In this way he could play a role that would be more difficult for a city-bound *haikai* marker—namely, the role of a poet chanting "crazy lines," fancy free, so to speak, as he describes himself walking down the road to Nagoya in one of his writings.[45] Since around 1680 he had been wearing Buddhist robes and was dedicated to the literary life as a religious Way. But his Way did not entail obedience to the regulations that bound fully ordained clerics. His commitment was to a religious mode of living while still in the world, and to converting the stuff of everyday experience—an abundance of which could be found on every bend of the road—into poetry.[46] In this sense, as Abe Kimio points out, after completing his errands, he was free in ways that he could not be in his

---

43. *Kyoriku o okuru kotoba* 許六を送る詞, 543.
44. The Chinese term for "freewheeling" is 逍遥遊 (C. *xiaoyaoyou*; J. *shōyōyū*), the title of the first chapter of *Zhuangzi* 荘子. See Shirane 1998, 286–87; Qiu 2005, 75–87. Bashō uses the term *angya* often in reference to his own travels: for instance, at the beginning of *The Narrow Road through the Hinterlands* (see p. 99) and in a letter describing his trip to Yoshino with Tokoku (Tanaka 2005, 125).
45. See p. 17.
46. Kusumoto 2006, 186–87.

Fukagawa cottage.[47] And it was the exercise of that freedom—in his activities in the realm of *haikai* rather than just in physical trials—that challenged him most as a poet. Scholars committed to an otherworldly image of Bashō often see a conflict between his practical motives and his literary ideals.[48] But one can also see the road as a place of practice partially constituted by the tension between the "practical" and the "literary/religious." It was the physical, natural, and social challenges and opportunities of travel that ultimately became the basis of much of his writing in both poetry and prose. Travel for Bashō was a practical means of exercising professional skills in a social arena where such tensions were always in play.[49] In this sense, he made travel a component of his profession.

And what, concretely, did travel entail in his day? His writings show that Bashō had read the great travel writings of the past. But his was a different world: more stable not just politically, but also economically, socially, and even geographically. The establishment of a central government and strong, well-administered domains had changed nearly everything in practical terms. When writing about his trip to Shirakawa Barrier in 1468, the *renga* master Sōgi wrote of being afraid of traveling through the fields of Musashino even with a samurai escort, worried about running into marauders or perhaps armed men going into battle.[50] There were far fewer places on most of the roads in Bashō's day where a traveler—provided that he moved in daylight and used common sense—had occasion for such concerns. And Bashō nearly always traveled with at least one companion, more often two or more, a fact that no doubt brought increased safety and peace of mind.[51]

At various times, Bashō traveled the full length of the Tōkai Road and long stretches of the Nikkōkaidō, the Ōshūkaidō, and the Nakasendō, all thoroughfares in the Five Road System (*gokaidō* 五街道) maintained by the central government. Some of these roads and other roads maintained by domains and businesses went through more remote territories and were perhaps not so well appointed or maintained. But everywhere there were *sekisho* 関所 (Tokugawa-garrisoned checkpoints) or *bansho* 番所 (checkpoints maintained by domain governments, usually on borders), and nearly everywhere there were post stations (*shukuba* 宿場). This meant that he and his companions—the latter

---

47. Abe Kimio 1970, 100–103. For more on Bashō and *angya*, see Shirane 1998, 286–88.

48. For a discussion of the problem, see Yayoshi 1977, 199–211.

49. See Carter 2000, 190–92.

50. *Shirakawa kikō* 白河紀行, 9.

51. Abe Masami 1982, 265–66, argues that often he had two companions. Takahashi 2002, 58–59, notes that even on his first trip to Edo in 1672, he was accompanied by Bokutaku and perhaps Bokuseki as well.

taking care of physical arrangements, money, and logistics—had to have documents (*tegata* 手形) with them. But it made it easier that he was dressed as a monk and thus not subject to all the regulations that applied to people in the four-class system of samurai, farmers, artisans, and merchants. Furthermore, we know that his movements were often planned beforehand, that he often had maps and guidebooks, and that much of the time he stayed with friends or patrons who provided him with all he needed or he stayed at comfortable inns where he could eat well and sleep peacefully. (This was a practical necessity: an exhausted or ill *haikai* master—especially one with a chronic ailment—could not perform his duties.) It appears that in many cases those same friends and patrons actually went to the checkpoints themselves or sent escorts to make for easy passage.[52]

A typical sketch of life in transit is offered by a passage from the diary of Sora, one of his traveling companions. The time was a summer day in 1689, the place the Ushū Road[53] from Ōishida to Shinjō in what is now Yamagata Prefecture:

> Sixth Month, 1st day: Left Ōishida at around 8 in the morning. Ichiei and Sensui saw us as far as Amida Hall and provided two horses as far as Funagata. We received departure documents at Ōishida that provided passage at Nakisawa. When we arrived at Shinjō we received documents and passed inspection at Funagata. We had no trouble at either checkpoint. In Shinjō we lodged with Fūryū.[54]

The journey chronicled here involved just six *li* 里 (about 14.5 miles) on a well-traveled road, running through mountain valleys close to the Mogami River, then up via a well-traveled mountain pass and down into the broad, rich farmlands around the castle town of Shinjō. It might have been taxing had they not been provided horses, been escorted much of the way, and benefited from documents prepared by men (all rich merchants) who were well known in the area.[55] The exit checkpoint for Obanezawa was manned by Tokugawa government officers, while the entry into Shinjō was staffed by samurai of that domain, but neither seems to have posed any problems. Bashō and Sora probably were at Fūryū's house by mid-afternoon.[56] That evening they composed

---

52. See appendix, "Travel in Bashō's Day."
53. 羽州街道. A thoroughfare that began at Ko'ori, a stop on the Ōshū Road, and passed through Yamagata and Shinjō and then all the way to Aomori at the northern tip of Honshū.
54. Ogata 1995, 331. For information about this text, see appendix, "Fact and/or Fiction: The Challenge of Sora's Diary."
55. Bashō had met Fūryū in Obanezawa.
56. See Takatō 1966, 203–6.

a three-verse sequence with their host, then another such sequence the next day at the home of another patron, and a full thirty-six-verse *kasen* the day after that, which helps to emphasize he was almost never "on vacation," so to speak. The road was as much a place of practice as the city, and it was with that in mind that all preparations were made. If travel offered an escape *from* one world, that escape was always *into* another world where Bashō still had obligations. In this sense, one might say that he was more like a business traveler than a tourist. We should not take him too literally when he says a traveler has just two desires each day: "May I find a good place to stay tonight, and may I find good straw sandals for my feet."[57]

Thus the image of Bashō as a mendicant, not sure of finding lodging and often spending the night in the fields or squalid quarters along unknown tracks is an exaggeration at best—that is, the product of poetic conceptions as well as his own reluctance to waste ink on routine matters. A *hokku* composed by his host, Fūryū, in Shinjō does nothing to discourage the illusion:

> For an honored guest
> I have only my cramped house—
> and a frayed mosquito net.[58]

> *otazune ni*
> *waga yado sebashi*
> *yabure kaya*

As is often the case in *hokku*, this scene was intended as an expression of modesty and welcome, aimed specifically at the author's guest. The house where the sequence was composed was most likely a fine structure equal to a samurai dwelling at least and certainly nothing cramped or shabby.[59] And, in the same way, we should take Bashō's representations of himself on the road as rhetorical. True, traveling cannot have been easy, especially when contemplated from the twenty-first century. He was often on foot rather than on horseback or in a palanquin; and there can be no doubt that he encountered nasty weather from time to time, got lost, or had to stay in shabbier lodgings than he wished.[60] Moreover, it cannot have made things any easier that he had a chronic ailment that meant he must be careful about what he ate and drank and where

---

57. *Knapsack Notes*, p. 65. Finding good lodging and sandals was not an insignificant matter, of course; generally speaking, straw sandals lasted no more than a day or two on the road. On the "poetic hyperbole" of Bashō's presentation of himself in his writings, see LaFleur 1983, 159–63.

58. For the full sequence, see Takatō 1966, 207.

59. See Takatō 1966, 205.

60. Horses may have been used more for luggage than for riding. In *Knapsack Notes* he talks about falling off his horse, which was a danger; and in summer horses were stinky and plagued by flies. See Inagaki 1993, 10.

he stayed. But this was a common situation during his era, and physicians—who were often learned men of literary leanings—were usually not far away.

Relying on the kindness of patrons allowed him to travel light. In *Knapsack Notes* he says he made do with "a set of bedclothes for the nights, a rain cloak, an inkstone, brushes, paper, medicines, and a lunchbox"—probably contained in a carryall (*zudabukuro* 頭陀袋) hung around his neck.[61] Other items were probably consigned to his companions: a money pouch, a mirror, a needle and some sort of blade, spare sandals, candles, flints, string, fans, and a supply of paper strips (*tanjaku*) on which to write poems as gifts.[62] As he and Sora both had shaved heads, they would not need a comb or hair oil, but a razor and a nicer suit of clothing might have been necessary, as they would be visiting some important people and wanted to give a good impression.[63] Many of the things travelers carried were available for purchase at post stations, and even in the hinterlands he mostly spent his time in cities or in regional towns like Obanezawa in Yamagata, where provisions were easy to obtain. At such places one could even secure paper, which was essential for the one activity that was central to all he did: practicing the art of *haikai*.

THE TRAVEL WRITINGS

After writing poems, perhaps the most important thing Bashō the *haikai* master gained from his journeys was new disciples or closer relationships with older ones. Giving up his marking practice in Nihonbashi in 1680 meant relying more on face-to-face meetings with students. As noted above, for example, he spent two weeks in the Obanezawa-Ōishida area in the summer of 1689, where he stayed with at least four different patrons and met with more than a dozen *haikai* poets. He undeniably organized his itineraries around visits to such people, many of whom became formal disciples and provided financial assistance as well as support for Bashō's practice.

Equally important were the many *hokku* and *kasen* that he produced along the way, such as the following short travel narrative, which appeared in a *haibun* (*haikai* prose piece) presented to an unidentified patron:

---

61. Such a bag, rectangular in shape and hung around the neck and resting on the chest, used by Bashō on his 1689 journey is preserved in Kanazawa (Yamane 2017, 96).
62. Kanzaki 2004, 14–17. Fans were used not just against the heat but also to beckon from a distance. In a letter to his friend Sōmu, Bashō says tongue in cheek that he carries *tanjaku* that he can write poems on and sell for a few coins when money is in short supply (Fukasawa Shinji 2016, 16).
63. See Kanamori 2000, 35–44.

Pilgrimage to Ise

At the end of the Second Month of 1688, I went on pilgrimage to Ise. This was the fifth time I had trodden the grounds there. On each occasion I was adding a year to my age and growing older, and as I felt the grandeur of the noble light emanating from the place, I was more impressed. I thought fondly of how tears came to the eyes of Saigyō and he wrote, "out of gratitude . . ."[64] Putting down my fan, I did obeisance, bringing my forehead down to the sandy ground.

What tree in flower	*nani no ki no*
it comes from, I do not know.	*hana to wa shirazu*
But, ah, the scent![65]	*nioi kana*
Bashō Tōsei	

Some of the poems he wrote on journeys were written out and given as mementos to patrons or disciples, and those and many others would later end up in anthologies. At the time the *hokku* above was written, for instance, it served as the first verse for a thirty-six-verse dedicatory sequence presented to the shrine, while later it would also appear in a travel piece and in *hokku* collections. Textual products such as these offer us the traces of his practice as a poet.

Whatever the practical demands and distractions of life on the road, poetry was never far from Bashō's mind, as he reveals in a comment about a night spent on the way to Mount Obasute: "Going through *hokku* still in rough form in my mind, I took out my writing things and bent close to the lamp, eyes closed, tapping my hand against my head while I lay there mumbling lines."[66] *Haikai* was the premier challenge that justified all the effort spent on lesser tasks. Of course, not all of the poems he produced on his treks have survived to become part of the canon, but enough remain to show how central composition of *hokku* and sequences with students was to his professional identity.

---

64. A poem attributed to Saigyō, supposedly composed when he was visiting Ise (*Saigyō waka shūi* 西行和歌拾遺, 2109): "Composed on a festival day at the Great Shrine: 'Just what it is / that resides in this place / I do not know, / yet out of gratitude / the tears come flowing down'" (*nanigoto no / owashimasu ka wa / shiranedomo / katajikenasa ni / namida koboruru*).

65. *Ise sangū*, 446–47. The poem was composed as the *hokku* to a sequence at the home of Nakatsu Masumitsu in Ise Yamada.

66. See p. 76.

When it comes to the other chief product of his travels—the six texts translated in this book—we are less sure about the master's intentions. The accounts of his short trips to Kashima in 1687 and Sarashina in 1688 and his diary of his days at the cottage of his disciple Kyorai in Saga in 1691 seem to have been written up very soon after the journeys, mostly as souvenirs to be circulated among members of his poetic network. But the same is not true of the longer works, which came into being only years after the travels they describe and were not published until well after his death. Indeed, as Fukasawa Shinji has recently argued, it seems that Bashō's travel writings derived directly from his practice of carrying *kuchō* (logbooks of poems, often accompanied by notes) as reference and resource, and as primers for students—works in progress that in some ways could never be complete.[67] Nonetheless, his actions vis-à-vis the manuscripts he produced show that he spent considerable time on these writings and must have thought of them as independent works that he wanted to be preserved and read. Firstly, this meant being read by the connoisseurs, disciples, and patrons of his own day who were his first audience.[68] But realizing his prominence in his own day, we cannot but believe that he was also looking further into the future.

Bashō had behind him a long tradition of travel literature, going back at least eight hundred years. He was well acquainted with the travel classics of the past, from Ki no Tsurayuki's *Tosa Diary* (*Tosa nikki* 土佐日記; c. 935) to the works of Sōgi and other *renga* masters. Likewise, he was aware of the travel vignettes in the headnotes to poems by famous figures like Saigyō, as well as folktales in which that poet was a central figure. Travel as a conventional topic (*dai*) in classical poetry was as old as the Japanese poetic tradition itself, and travel motifs were common in classical Chinese poems as well. For the most part, however, travel writings before Bashō's time were diaries that focused on *utamakura* ("pillow words"), famous places where poets felt obligated to add poems of their own to a long, long list of prior offerings. With a few exceptions, these works appear to the modern reader to justify Bashō's characterization of them as formulaic—"seem[ing] to make something too similar—never a new brew."[69] And so at least from 1687 or so, he decided that he would do something different. It is not by accident that the conventional word for "travel records"—*kikō*—in fact appears

---

67. Fukasawa Shinji 2016, 14–17, argues that students would want to see his recent work and that references in various *kasen* and other texts show how his *kuchō* served as sample or pattern books (*mihon* 見本) when he presented gifts of his work to patrons. He also argues (see 16–17) that the versions of his manuscripts show that he seldom actually produced final drafts, explaining why his travel writings were never published before his death.
68. See Carter 2000, 198.
69. A passage from *Knapsack Notes*. See p. 51.

nowhere in the earliest titles of his writings or that some scholars avoid using that term.[70] This does not mean that his writings do not belong in the genre of travel literature, as all of them clearly deal with the subject of travel, indeed, doing so in ways that obviously resonate with travel literature of the past. But it does mean that Bashō was consciously attempting something that departed from old traditions. First of all, this meant discarding some things—consistent references to dates, distances, money, and so on; but it also meant including other things that were within the broader scope of *haikai.* He no doubt would have agreed with his disciple and painting master, Kyoriku, who wrote in his own essay on travel that what Saigyō and Sōgi left out of their travel writing was precisely what was at the heart of Bashō's poetic project: *haikai no nasake* 俳諧の情—that is, the commonplace sentiments proper to *haikai.*[71]

It is also obvious that to Bashō his travel writings did not have the same status as his primary poetic texts, meaning the anthologies of his *hokku* and linked verse. Indeed, a few seem to have been written for specific patrons rather than a broader readership.[72] Moreover, as scholars endlessly note, the earlier ones—before *The Narrow Road through the Hinterlands*—were not, in a general way at least, as polished as his canonical works; perhaps they were even left incomplete. The first of them, *Bones Bleaching in the Fields,* reads like a collection of *hokku* with headnotes that he referred to as "not in the manner of a *kikō,* but just a recording of scenes—here a thought, there a happening—and nothing more."[73] At the same time, however, all of them are artifacts of his practice as a *haikai* master relating his experiences *on the road.* Furthermore, parts of his earlier travel writings and all of *The Narrow Road through the Hinterlands* are highly fashioned works that go far beyond the genre of travel diary (*tabi nikki*), which one might guess from the fact that they were produced so long after the journeys they document. When writing *hokku,* he may have counseled students to act quickly: "You should get words down while the light that illuminates them has not yet faded away."[74] But clearly this was not advice he followed when producing his travel writings, which he thought of

---

70. For this reason, Takahashi 1993, 101–7, eschews *kikō* and calls the works *kobumi* ("short writings") instead.

71. Ueno 1989, 4.

72. See pp. 3, 28.

73. See Ogata 1998, 5. The comment is made in a colophon to Jokushi's illustrated edition. See *Nozarashi kikō emaki batsu* 野ざらし紀行絵巻跋, 424. Many scholars take this as rhetorical posturing, but Takahashi 2002, 183, takes it quite literally, arguing that the phrase *ichinen ichidō* 一念一動 (literally, "here a thought, there a happening") shows Bashō as a Zen mendicant (*kotsujiki angya* 乞食行脚).

74. *Sanzōshi* (1702), 551. Quoted by Horikiri 2003, 44.

as something other than day-by-day records. As Eguchi Takao says, had his purpose been to keep a diary, he would have written a good deal on the road, and polished it up soon after returning, "before his memories began to fade."[75] Instead, he tinkered with his travel texts for years.

It would be an overstatement to say these writings are in any strict sense works of pure imagination or fictions, however. Bashō makes no attempt at creating a recognizable fictional world, to begin with; and corroborating documents make it clear that his accounts follow his actual itineraries fairly closely and that he actually "concocts" events out of whole cloth only rarely.[76] It would be better to say that he shows no hesitation in shaping his material. A comparison of two passages written around the same time and about the same event on his journey from Nagoya to his hometown at the very end of the year 1688 illustrates his methods. The first is a *kaishi* (poem sheet) that he gave to someone during the journey; the second is from *Knapsack Notes*.

> *Kaishi* version: At Saya, a man with a frightful-looking beard who looked to be a courier was on the boat with us, and he was so ill-tempered with the other passengers that we could not enjoy anything, getting no pleasure from the mountain scenes along the way. After a while we arrived at Kuwana, and from there on went by horse some of the way. As I rode my horse going up Tsuetsukizaka, "Walking Staff Slope," my saddle slipped from beneath me and I fell off. All the more so I felt the sadness of traveling alone. When I got up off the ground, the groom scolded me, saying, "You sure you're up to riding?"

> Walking Staff Slope.   *kachi naraba*
> On foot, I would not have toppled   *tsuetsukizaka o*
> from my horse.   *rakuba kana*

> I forgot to include a season word.[77]

> *Knapsack Notes* version: From Kuwana, I came to Hinaga Village—famous for the lines "From Kuwana I came, / without a thing to eat." There I

---

75. Eguchi 1998, 23.
76. See Carter 2000, 191.
77. Kon 2005a, 122. Abe Masami 1965–89, vol. 2, 236, concludes that the *kaishi* dates from the spring of 1688, around the same time that he was writing up *Knapsack Notes*.

rented a horse, but as I climbed Tsuetsukizaka, "Walking Staff Slope," my saddle slipped from beneath me and I fell off.

Walking Staff Slope.	*kachi naraba*
On foot, I would not have toppled	*tsuetsukizaka wo*
from my horse!	*rakuba kana*

I wrote this last *hokku* out of such annoyance that I forgot to include a season word.[78]

As Kusumoto Mutsuo argues, what Bashō does here is more than just eliding details from a scene; nor is it a case of fact versus fiction.[79] Instead, he appears to have pared down the *Knapsack Notes* version in order to make it flow as part of a larger narrative rather than focusing on an incident for its own sake. Specifically, the freestanding *kaishi* contains nods toward two medieval anecdotes—one about rude treatment from a ferryman from *Saigyō monogatari* 西行物語 (mid-thirteenth century) and another about a famous priest losing his temper after falling off his horse in *Essays in Idleness* (*Tsurezuregusa* 徒然草, c. 1331) that if included in *Knapsack Notes* would have detracted from the flow of the narrative at a crucial juncture, just before Bashō arrives home to reunite with his family. The poem he does allude to amplifies his text in poetic terms.[80]

Thus, the works I translate in this book are shaped narratives but still very much travel narratives, each written to commemorate experience while also serving literary purposes. Each text is unique and deserves its own introduction, which I have provided in the pages that follow. Nevertheless, there are a number of features they all share that assist us in understanding Bashō's approach to travel writing.

First and most obviously, all of Bashō's writings are hybrid texts, involving straightforward narration and description, but also short essays and ruminations. Most importantly, they present us with a mixture of poetry and prose and of various levels of diction. In the earliest texts, the prose is more in the way of headnotes or prose introductions to poems, but in the later works he seems to have been attempting to create a form that integrates prose and poetry into a narrative stream. It is tempting to see *The Narrow Road through the Hinterlands* as a final attempt in this process, building upon

---

78. See *Knapsack Notes*, p. 55.
79. See Kusumoto 2006, 110–11.
80. See *Knapsack Notes*, p. 55, n. 79.

the experience of the earlier offerings, although thinking that way may seem too tidy an explanation. Certainly, his most famous travel writing achieves a finely modulated texture that the earlier texts do not consistently achieve.

Second, each text is presented by a narrator—no one who steps forward and identifies himself openly, but still a distinctive speaker, often seeming to be alone, even when we know he had companions, which was almost all the time.[81] Obviously, historical knowledge tells that this narrator is in a fundamental sense Bashō himself: he made the trips, he wrote the accounts, and it is with his own personal experience that he is most concerned. But as many scholars have pointed out, he poses occasionally as a traveler of the past such as Saigyō or Du Fu, or as a true mendicant, while also using lines that remind one of the wandering monks (*wakisō* ワ キ 僧) in Noh drama that announce their arrival at a place in order to learn its past.[82] To this extent, Bashō creates a subjective text of varying textures and referents, going beyond the journalistic style of many other travel works of the past.

Third, while each writing presents descriptions of major famous poetic places, Bashō skips over many of these. Indeed, as Yamamoto Yuiitsu observes, he says not a word about some of the most magnificent sights he encountered on his journeys: for example, the castles in Sendai, Kanazawa, or Nagoya.[83] Instead, he uses his ink to describe obscure places, while at places of great historical importance, he often puts his brush down, sometimes claiming that he cannot come up with a proper poem.[84] Why he adopts such a posture is not obvious. Modesty, perhaps? Or true reverence?

---

81. Sora records, for instance, that when he left Kanazawa he was accompanied by eight men, some only to the city limits, a few more as far as Nonoichi, and then two—Hokushi and another local poet—all the way to Komatsu. His companions carried food and saké to consume along the way. Ueno 1989, 155–73, argues that Bashō sometimes effectively "erases" his companions in order to stress his own private experience. To a certain extent, the way Bashō seems to be alone reflects a feature of the Japanese language, which does not overtly specify singular or plural in most situations.

82. Ogata 1998, 114–15, sees this as early as *Knapsack Notes*, and he and other scholars identify phrases (particularly place name + *ni tsukinikeri*) in *The Narrow Road through the Hinterlands* that are modeled on Noh texts. See Fukasawa and Kusumoto 2009, 68; Hisatomi 2011, 6, n. 7. Bashō was an avid student of *utai* 謡, the chanting of Noh librettos as a hobby.

83. Yamamoto Yuiitsu 1994, 158.

84. Examples are Yoshino in *Knapsack Notes* (p. 63) and Matsushima in *The Narrow Road through the Hinterlands* (p. 119). This feature of his strategy was highlighted by his disciple Dohō in his *Sanzōshi*, 604: "The master said: 'When confronted with peerless views, you may be so overwhelmed that you cannot produce a verse.' At Matsushima he did not write a *hokku*. . . . This was important."

Both explanations are acceptable. There is no reason to assume he is insincere.[85] We can be certain from his own comments, however, that one thing is definitely going on: in trying to produce something different, he wants to elevate places of lesser traditional significance into the realm of artistic representation. He is producing a work of *haikai*, after all, and his method of *haikai* is to focus more on the inconspicuous, the mundane, even the vulgar at times—people and places that, as he says, share only the fact that they "stayed in his mind."[86]

Fourth, while giving attention to important figures of the past—emperors, court ladies, famous priests and poets of China and Japan, warriors of the time of the Genpei Wars and their aftermath, and so on—he also puts a few contemporary characters into the mix: his own traveling companions or hosts, an abandoned child, an obnoxious monk, a little girl in the fields, a colorful innkeeper, to name a few, thus giving his own world and his own experience their due. Again, this is one thing that marks his writings as squarely in the realm of *haikai*. It also allows him to expand his canvas to include people whose existence would never be registered at all in his *hokku* and *kasen*, which by nature involved participation by prominent people most of the time. For him, people were at the heart of the poet's project: "He who does not sympathize with the predicaments of men, who does not respond to human feeling—he is the one first of all that I would say is no poet."[87]

Lastly, all of his writings are elliptical, especially for modern readers. Partly this is because our education does not prepare us to follow hints and make connections that would have been obvious to readers of Bashō's day. Yet this is not enough to explain the loose, sometimes disjointed, nature of his narratives. This is one reason that scholars often characterize his texts as "series of short writings" (*rensaku*), suggesting that for Bashō the most natural model was linked verse—a form of antinarrative that is invested less in overarching structures and themes than in dynamic, dialectic, aesthetic concepts such as *ji* and *mon* (alternating "background" and "design") and *johakyū* (the three-part progression of a *renga* sequence).[88] But surely another, not incompatible, way of looking at the issue is to remember that he is after all writing travel narratives, in which connections are made by moving forward on an itinerary obvious to anyone

---

85. In a letter to his friend Sōshichi, he says about seeing Furu Waterfall, a famous site, "as for the scenery of the waterfall, I have no words." Tanaka 2005, 135.
86. *Wasurenu tokorodokoro.* See *Knapsack Notes*, p. 51.
87. Quoted by Shikō in *Zoku gorin* 続五輪 (1699), 694. See Ueno 1989, 112; Shirane 1998, 249.
88. See Carter 1987, 95–100; Miner 1979, 72–76.

who knew the geography and landscapes of the time. Readers would know, at least vaguely, that after Nikkō would come Shirakawa, after that Nihonmatsu, after that Ko'ori, after that Sendai, and so on, just as they would already know many place names and historical figures—all of which would provide templates or underlays (*shitajiki*) for his later writings. In the minds of readers, the roads themselves could function as a narrative arc, as travel itself could figure as a narrative activity.

A final point is worth making emphatically: even in Bashō's time many of the places he sought out were gone from the landscape, or marked only by memorials off the beaten track, having only a phantom existence of the sort nearly all of the places he evokes must have for us. He was aware of the natural processes by which sites were swallowed up by cityscape or literally erased by expanding or drained marshes or floods or earthquakes. Indeed, it is with this in mind that he very cagily invites us to look over his shoulder at places like the remains of the strongholds of the northern Fujiwara clan at Hiraizumi, asking us to imagine not just the facts or the scenery but also the experience of absence behind poems such as this one, one of his most famous:

> So here it is, I thought: the place where the stalwarts holed up in their fortress and gained an instant of glory—only to end as grassy fields. "The country ravaged, mountains and rivers remain; spring comes to the fortress, covered over in green." Putting my hat beneath me, I sat for quite a while and found myself in tears.

> Summer grasses: *natsukusa ya*
> all that is left to us now   *tsuwamonodomo ga*
> of warrior's dreams.[89]   *yume no ato*

Bashō had traveled nearly 250 miles to get to Hiraizumi, and in this and other passages he gives us considerable detail about how his expectations were rewarded by actually seeing famous sites with his own eyes. But this passage offers travel in time as well as description of the here and now, evoking important human issues such as worldly glory, the inevitable force of historical change, the ongoing and ineluctable power of natural processes, and the ability of poetry—as signified by lines by Du Fu—to move us. We are perhaps not surprised to learn from other documents that he did not indeed have time to stop and sit "for quite a while" and that the famous poem was most likely produced not at Hiraizumi but a few years later, when he was writing up *The Narrow*

---

89. See p. 122.

Road through the Hinterlands.[90] As he said in a letter, "Poems do not come easily while on the road,"[91] suggesting that his poems often emerged in recollection or reflection.

Should we call the passage a fiction, then? Perhaps so, in a limited sense. But we should also understand how unlikely it is that Bashō—who was interested in chronicling what he called the dynamic of "the changing and unchanging" (*fueki ryūkō*) along the way, and in the feel of a place, and in absence as much as presence—thought in those terms at all.[92] Certainly he was not at all like other fiction writers of the day, such as Tomiyama Dōya or Ihara Saikaku. What he wanted was to present his own *poetic* experience, in space and time, of *fūga no makoto,* or poetic truth and honesty.[93] His writings document the struggle to find an adequate form to convert that experience into art.

Yet there is one other thing that must be said: namely, that Bashō was a master of *haikai* first and last and that his travel writings above all showcase poems, while also showing students the process of creating poetry from experience on the road.[94] And not only his own works: for, particularly in *The Narrow Road through the Hinterlands,* he makes references to a broad range of genres, either directly or through allusion. Chinese poetry, *uta, hokku, renga,* rice-planting songs—all are included. Nor does he overlook participation in poetic culture by people of all historical periods and social backgrounds, from Chinese monks to Japanese court poets to merchants to traveling salesmen, or leave out people at the bottom of the social ladder—a little farm girl in the fields, a groom, young monks at a Zen temple. Everywhere he looks, he sees poetry, in landscapes present and absent, in people living and dead. As the prostitutes in Ichiburi say, "The road is a daunting place." But for him it was also a place of poetic practice and possibilities.

---

90. See Fukasawa and Kusumoto 2009, 193; Uozumi 2011, 81–82. Sora says they set out from Ichinoseki at about eight o'clock in the morning and were back at their inn before four o'clock that same day, heading back to Iwateyama early the next day (Ogata 1995, 327). Imoto Nōichi 1970, 328, argues that Bashō's claim that he sat on his hat for quite a while (*toki no utsuru made*) cannot be taken literally but is an expression of Bashō's "protagonist" (*shujinkō*).

91. *Tabi nite wa ku mo idegataki mono nite soro* たびにてハ句も出難きものにて候. The letter is to his disciple Kikaku and was written at the end of 1688. See Tanaka 2005, 170.

92. See the introduction to *The Narrow Road through the Hinterlands* and appendix, "Fact and/ or Fiction: The Challenge of Sora's Diary." For an analysis of these terms in English, see Shirane 1998, 258–59; Qiu 2005, 236–40.

93. See Imoto 1970, 322–23. See also Shirane 1998, 263–68.

94. For more on this topic, see Carter 2000, 197.

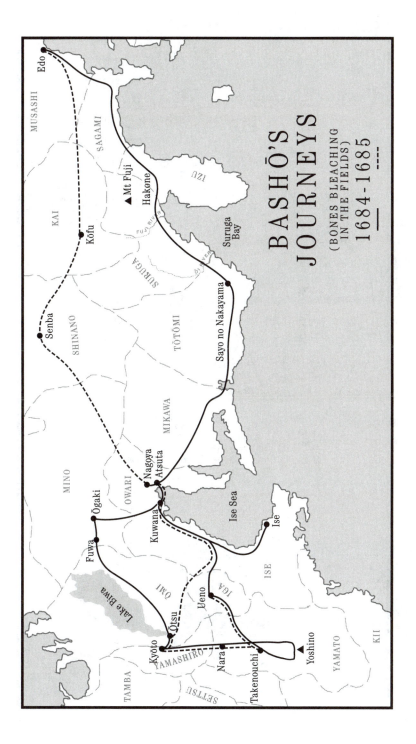

BASHŌ'S
JOURNEYS

(BONES BLEACHING
IN THE FIELDS)
1684-1685

- - - -

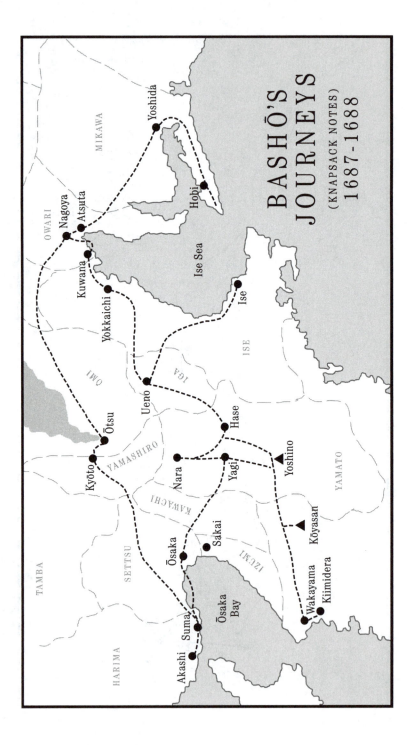

BASHŌ'S JOURNEYS
(KNAPSACK NOTES)
1687-1688

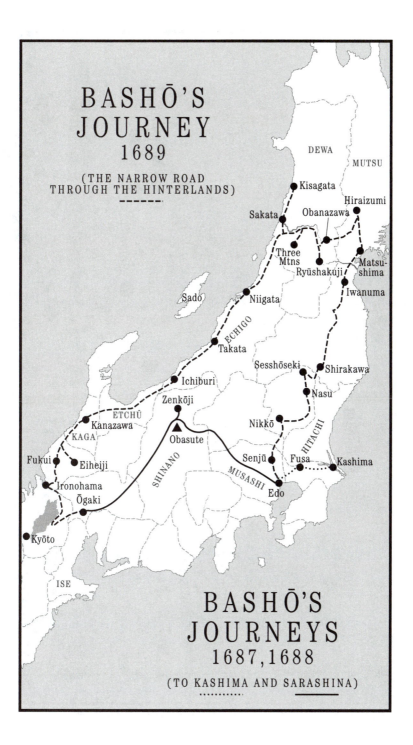

BASHŌ'S
JOURNEY
1689

(THE NARROW ROAD
THROUGH THE HINTERLANDS)
- - - - - -

DEWA

MUTSU

Kisagata

Hiraizumi

Sakata   Obanazawa

Three
Mtns   Matsu-
Ryūshakúji   shima

Sado   Niigata   Iwanuma

ECHIGO

Takata

Sesshōseki   Shirakawa

Ichiburi   Nasu

Zenkōji

ETCHŪ   Nikkō
Kanazawa   Obasute
KAGA

Fukui   SHINANO   Senjū   Fusa   Kashima
Eiheiji   HITACHI
Ironohama   MUSASHI
Ōgaki   Edo

Kyōto

ISE

BASHŌ'S
JOURNEYS
1687, 1688

(TO KASHIMA AND SARASHINA)
············· ————

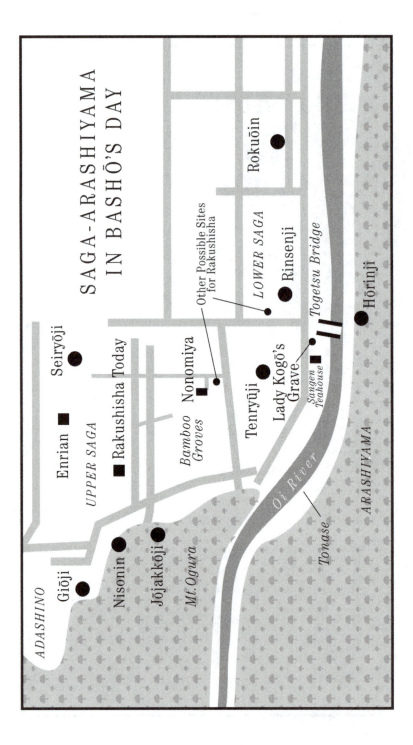

SAGA-ARASHIYAMA
IN BASHŌ'S DAY

ADASHINO

Giōji

Nisonin

Jōjakkōji

Mt. Ogura

UPPER SAGA

Enrian

Seiryōji

Rakushisha Today

Bamboo Groves

Nonomiya

Tenryūji

Lady Kogō's Grave

Sangen Teahouse

Other Possible Sites for Rakushisha

LOWER SAGA

Rinsenji

Rokuōin

Togetsu Bridge

Oi River

Tonase

ARASHIYAMA

Hōrinji

BONES BLEACHING IN THE FIELDS

INTRODUCTION

We know of two immediate reasons for the journey that would become the basis for Bashō's first example of travel writing. Foremost was his desire to visit his hometown in Iga Ueno in order to pay his respects at the grave of his mother, who had died in the summer of 1683; next was his need to report in to clan authorities, as regulations required. But there was another practical reason for the trip: to respond to an invitation by his disciple Bokuin, in the city of Ōgaki, where he had the prospect of leading linked-verse sessions and attracting new students.[1]

Bashō's decision to move out of the Nihonbashi area of Edo and give up his income as a *haikai* marker meant that he was pursuing an eccentric course for a *haikai* poet. Fortunately, his daily needs were mostly met by rich patrons in Edo, but he was also in need of new disciples to support his literary ideals and create a network that would support him in both practical and literary terms. Bokuin had a substantial *haikai* following in Ōgaki, and documents show that there were many *haikai* poets in nearby Nagoya, Atsuta, Narumi, and Gifu as well. In addition, he was in contact with poets in the Ōtsu area, on the southern shores of Lake Biwa.[2] His movements were largely organized around these concentrations of supporters, to whom he offered instruction both in actual linked-verse gatherings and through work submitted for critique by letter.

Bashō and his traveling companion, Chiri,[3] left Edo in the middle of the Eighth Month of 1684 and made it to Bashō's hometown of Iga Ueno on the 8th day of the Ninth Month, having traveled on the Tōkai Road and seen storied sites such as the Hakone Barrier, Mount Fuji, and Sayononakayama. The only place they tarried for any time at all—ten days or so—was Ise, home to one of the most important of all Japanese shrines. While there he stayed with a wealthy merchant disciple

---

1. Uozumi 2011, 42.
2. See Kira 1985 for information about disciples in the Kyoto area.
3. We are not sure whether Chiri left the city with Bashō or met him in Izu (see Ueno 1989, 158), nor do we know whether he continued with Bashō after Takeuchi.

named Matsubaya Fūbaku, a man he knew from Edo who happened to be in his hometown at Ise Yamada. Along with restoring his strength after nearly two weeks on the road, Bashō visited the shrine and sought out the place where Saigyō had lived in a hut in the 1180s.[4] Then he continued on to Iga Ueno, staying on four or five days to visit his mother's grave and visit with his older brother, Hanzaemon; his sisters; and local disciples. After that he headed south into the mountainous areas of Yoshino and Mount Kōya, also important places in the career of Saigyō, and to visit the hometown of Chiri at Takeuchi. The final leg of his itinerary took him north through Yamato Province and on through Ōmi Province to Ōgaki, where he brought the first and major phase of his journey to a conclusion at the end of the Ninth Month of 1684. Ōgaki was a prosperous castle town and center of commerce where his disciples, most of them prominent men of the samurai class, could host him generously.

Bashō stayed on with Bokuin as his primary host until the end of the year before returning to his family in Iga Ueno. He lodged with a number of other people in the cities of Ōgaki, Nagoya, Atsuta, Kuwana, and Narumi, always composing linked verse and *hokku*, in formal and informal settings. Indeed, it was at Nagoya in the Eleventh Month that he participated in the linked-verse gatherings that were memorialized in the first of the anthologies of what later was called the Bashō school—*Fuyu no hi* 冬の日 (Winter Days).[5] Among the seven participants were Kakei and Yasui, who would go on to become major figures in the world of *haikai*.

Headnotes to the collection of twenty-five *hokku* that Bashō would later attach to his account trace his movements in the Ōgaki area, where he pursued his profession as a *haikai* master while also traveling to places such as Yoshino, Nara, Kyoto, and Ōtsu. Scholars tend to see in these *hokku* serenity and tranquility that is less prominent in the first part of the text.[6] But there are hints that show the same pattern of practice: he visits his hometown again to ring in the New Year 1685, and then goes to noted places and composes poems, some independent *hokku* and others as first verses for linked-verse sequences. And he is again recruiting disciples, at least four of whom formally "signed on" in Ōtsu.[7] When he sets off to return to Edo on the 10th day of the Fourth

---

4. Saigyō left Mount Kōya in 1180 and stayed in Ise Yamada until embarking in 1186 on a journey to the East Country to raise money for rebuilding Tōdaiji.
5. Published by Izutsuya in a woodblock edition in Kyoto early in the next year.
6. See Yayoshi 1977, 207–10. Uozumi 2011, 51, uses the phrases "gentle in style" and "bright in tone."
7. Shōhaku, Senna, Seia, and Rotsū.

Month, it is after another layover—this time over a month—in the Atsuta area, where his disciples, old and new, gather to see him safely away.

***

The above background information on the journey of 1684–85 is mostly gleaned from a host of outside sources rather than from the text of *Bones Bleaching in the Fields* itself, which was written up considerably after the events it describes and was published after the poet's death. It is almost certain that writing such a work was not a prime motive for the journey,[8] and the final draft was not finished until perhaps the autumn of 1687.

These details serve to reemphasize that for Bashō travel writing had a different status than composing *hokku* or linked verse. The latter he arranged to have published in anthologies, but not so his travel writings, which circulated only in manuscript, and probably only among intimates, leaving them in a kind of textual limbo. Thus some scholars—a majority—see the work as simply incomplete, a set of fragments not fully integrated into a travel piece that might be seen as an account of Bashō's journeying as a Zen monk, or a collection of *hokku* and *haikai* prose, or *haibun*.[9] A complicating factor is that Bashō commissioned from his disciple Jokushi a fair copy (*seisho* 清書) with illustrations, which seems to have been sent to Bashō's primary patron in Edo, Sanpū, as a gift, sometime between 1688 and 1692.[10] These illustrations, meant as rough drafts from which Jokushi would produce his more sophisticated and expert paintings, have survived, a testament to Bashō's investment in the work that ironically makes it more difficult to understand exactly how he conceived it.[11] There is every possibility that, at least in the beginning, he thought of it as a work specifically for Sanpū, who as a businessman had little time to travel and would enjoy an illustrated account of his master's journey.

Yet none of these conclusions means that Bashō did not approach the creation of his text with some sort of formal, aesthetic goals in mind. He knew that it would circulate

---

8. See Uozumi 2011, 56.

9. See the Introduction, pp. 28–29. Inoue 1992, 53–62, likewise takes the colophon literally, arguing that the text should be seen as a *hokku* collection or a string of *haibun*.

10. See Kusumoto 2009, 333–40, for a summary of the complex textual history alluded to here.

11. Kusumoto 2006, 78, sees evidence that Bashō had studied Chinese-style ink-wash painting in his emphasis on images of mountains, rivers, seas, and lakes. Takahashi 2002, 212, stresses that Bashō's paintings were actually just models (*shitagaki*) to show basic narrative order and the relationship between prose and illustrations and were not meant to survive, but someone must have preserved them, probably Jokushi himself.

among *haikai* poets, and the consistency of the themes he pursues suggests that he meant it to be more than an anthology with longish headnotes. One of these themes is his sense of connection with the numerous celebrated places he encountered on the journey, many of which—Mount Fuji, Hakone, Ise, Yoshino: the list is long—are memorialized with poems. Another is his sense of connection with literary figures of the past, both Japanese and Chinese, which he prepares us for at the beginning of the work with quotes from the Daoist classic *Zhuangzi* and the following poem by the Tang poet Du Mu:

Setting Out Early

Sparing the whip, I let my horse set our pace,
passing several villages and hearing no cock-crows.
Beneath the trees I go, half in a dream-state,
awakened only by leaves scattering on the wind.
The ground is hard with frost, and I hear only one wild goose, far off,
as the dawn moon trails low over far mountains.
Servants, stop complaining that the climb is steep:
all roads are level in a world at peace.[12]

Needless to say, the last line of this poem was directly relevant to his practice as a poet who lived in an age of peace following upon the endemic warfare of the 1500s. It was the Tokugawa peace that quite literally made the sort of traveling he did possible.

Such allusions serve to amplify Bashō's text, connecting him with the past and claiming for himself a host of literary forebears. The most important of these is not Du Mu, however, but Saigyō, whose dwelling places in Ise and Yoshino Bashō visited and who also figures greatly in *Bones Bleaching in the Fields*.[13] As an itinerant poet for whom poetry was a religious Way, Saigyō was a model whose poetry in the ancient *uta* form (the term for traditional 5-7-5-7-7-syllable court poems) Bashō was anxious to claim as an influence on his own *haikai*. Among many poets, these two genres—one associated with elite aristocratic culture and the other with the world of commoners—were thought of as antithetical, but Bashō wanted to bridge that gap.

---

12. See Imoto 1972, 289, n. 18.
13. Bashō explicitly refers a few times to other texts—from *The Tale of Genji* (*Genji monogatari* 源氏物語, early eleventh century) to *Tales of the Heike* (*Heike monogatari* 平家物語, late fourteenth century)—but fully half a dozen times to Saigyō. Only Bashō's references to *Zhuangzi* rival this level of engagement.

The other theme that informs the work is obvious in Bashō's first *hokku*, in which he reveals a preoccupation with transience and death—a perfectly natural preoccupation for a man often stricken with ailments who had recently been burned out of his house and then a few months later received news that his mother had died.[14] No wonder, then, that he imagines himself ending as "bleached bones in a field," or that over and over again he reminds us of the perilous nature of existence: in the image of an abandoned child, his late mother's hair, the tomb of an ancient emperor, the grave of an ancient court lady, and so on, including even the sight of a flower being eaten nonchalantly by a horse.

Yet it is revealing that at the end of the major phase of his journey, Bashō writes, somewhat comically: "Here I am, not dead." Ultimately, *Bones Bleaching in the Fields* is life affirming. The poet's response to his mother's death, which had taken place more than a year before, is thus to shed tears with his siblings—a gesture that reveals a deep humanity unwilling to give in to pessimism, even while admitting that like the abandoned child we are all fated to die. In the grand scheme of things, the tears are of course meaningless; but to not share such a moment with his family would be to fail as a human being. The act of weeping is what makes us human, as does the creation of art. After all, Saigyō is long dead, but we still have his poems, which speak to us across the abyss of time. And that theme is one that animates the collection of *hokku* at the end of the text as well, in which Bashō confronts ephemerality again (in withered grasses, the aging of one old friend, word about the death of another friend, etc.) but nonetheless continues to chant his crazy lines. In this way he provides us with the exquisite sensory delights of *haikai*: a horse on a snowy morning, a dog barking in the rain, the sound of monks running in wooden shoes. His last poem, focused as it is upon the seemingly trivial act of picking lice from summer robes, points us toward a world of consolation in the observation of just such small things. And it is not insignificant that it also gives us a narrative conclusion, showing him back home, at rest, his journeying over.

---

14. Bashō's mother died in Iga Ueno on the 20th of the Sixth Month of 1683.

BONES BLEACHING IN THE FIELDS

Off I went, on a trek of a thousand *li*, with not so much as food prepared for the journey.[15] "Beneath the moon, in the third watch of the night, I enter into the Land of Naught"—so said the sage,[16] and his words were my staff as I left my ramshackle hut at riverside, in the Eighth Month of the year 1684, with the moaning wind blowing cold.

Bones bleaching in a field:	*nozarashi o*
that's what I feel in my heart	*kokoro ni kaze no*
with each blast of wind.[17]	*shimu mi kana*

After ten autumns	*aki totose*
now it's Edo that I mean	*kaette edo o*
when I say *home*.[18]	*sasu kokyō*

On the day I passed through the barrier,[19] rain was falling and the mountains were obscured by clouds.

---

15. Zhuangzi says that a traveler should take three meals for a jaunt in the suburbs, enough food for an overnight stay on a sojourn of one hundred *li*, and three months' worth of meals for a journey of a thousand *li* (Mair 1994, 4).

16. Imoto 1972, 287, n.2, notes an allusion to a poem (偈 C. *ji*; J. *ge*) by the Chinese Zen monk Guangwen: "No food prepared for my journey, I laugh and sing my poems; beneath the moon, in the third watch of the night, I enter the Land of Naught" (路不賷粮笑復歌／三更月下入無何). "Land of Naught" (無何有之郷 C. *wu he you xiang*; J. *mukayū no sato*) refers to another quote from *Zhuangzi*, a metaphor for freedom from worldly concerns (see Mair 1994, 9). The "third watch" equates to between 11 p.m. and 1 a.m.

17. *Bashō kushū* no. 413. Here and throughout the translations, *hokku* numbers refer to those in Ōtani 1962 (*NKBT* 45).

18. *Bashō kushū* no. 648. There is virtual agreement now that Bashō moved to Edo twelve years before, in the spring of 1672. The fact that he alludes to a Chinese poem by Jia Dao that uses the term "ten frosts" in a vague way suggests that he may not mean "ten autumns" precisely. See Imoto 1972, 287, n. 6.

19. The *sekisho*, or checkpoint, at Hakone, at the far western border of the Kantō. I have used the singular here because most scholars argue that Chiri had not joined Bashō at this point.

Misty rain showers.   *kirishigure*
A day *not* seeing Fuji   *fuji o minu hi zo*
has its own allure.[20]   *omoshiroki*

A man called Chiri was my help on the road, and he put his whole heart into attending to my every need. Always we had got along, and he was a trustworthy friend.[21] He composed this:

In Fukagawa   *fukagawa ya*
we leave the *bashō* plant   *bashō o fuji ni*
in Fuji's care.[22]   *azukeyuku*
    Chiri

As we were nearing Fuji River, we came upon an abandoned child of perhaps three years, crying pitifully. Had someone been so overwhelmed by worldly trials as to abandon the child, leaving it to wait for its life to flow away like the river's current? Would it be tonight that the child would die, like dewdrops on the young bush clover; or would it perish tomorrow?[23] I took a little food from my sleeve, tossed it to the child, and continued on my way.

You who grieve at monkeys' cries: *saru o kiku hito*
what of a child cast adrift   *sutego ni aki no*
in the autumn wind?[24]   *kaze ika ni*

---

20. *Bashō kushū* no. 521. Fuji's peak loomed larger at Hakone than from Edo. Bashō's attitude serves as a reinforcement of Zhuangzi's concept of accepting the world as it is. Yuzawa 1982, 23, n. 10, links this technique with the aesthetic of overtones (*yojō*).
21. In the *Analects* the sage says that every day he reflects on whether he has been trustworthy in his relations with friends. See Lau 1983, 3.
22. The *bashō* plant (plantain) refers to the one at Bashō's hut in Fukagawa, from which derives the penname by which he would come to be known. On a clear day Fuji could be seen from Bashō's home.
23. Dew is a symbol of ephemerality. In a poem in *The Tale of Genji*, the emperor laments the fate of the child Genji after his mother's death, in which the bush clover stands for the child: "At the sound of wind / blowing dewdrops hither and yon / on Miyagi Moor, / my heart cannot but go out / to the young bush clover" (*miyagino no / tsuyu fuki musubu / kaze no oto ni / kohagi ga moto o / omoi koso yare*). See *Genji monogatari*, vol. 1, 105. Cf. Tyler 2001, 8.
24. *Bashō kushū* no. 438. First in a string of poems displaying "hypermeter"—meaning more than the standard number of Japanese syllables in the original verse (*jiamari*). In Chinese poetry the cries of monkeys are depicted as particularly heart-wrenching. Bashō may also be alluding

So, child: Did your father despise you? Had your mother no pity? No, I cannot think that your father hated you or that your mother was heartless. This is Heaven's work, and you can do no more than bemoan your sad state.[25]

The day we crossed the Ōi River it rained all day long.

Rain on an autumn day.	*aki no hi no ame*
In Edo the count will put us	*edo ni yubi oran*
at Ōi River.[26]	*ōikawa*
Chiri	

Composed on horseback:

Beside the road,	*michinobe no*
a rose-marrow flower—	*mukuge wa uma ni*
gobbled by my horse![27]	*kuwarekeri*

---

to a line from the Noh play *Kurama Tengu* 鞍馬天狗, 455, that describes the gut-wrenching effects of hearing monkeys crying at the clouds and to *Wakan rōeishū* 和漢朗詠集 (1012), nn. 454–61. Kusumoto 2006, 198, following Ogata 1998, 48–50, indicates this poem was written later, near Kakegawa, but that Bashō placed it here because Fujikawa was an *utamakura* and as a way to evoke poems by Chinese poets alluded to by the author of *Kaidōki* 海道記 at Fuji River. See *Kaidōki*, 99. There is much debate about who "you who grieve at monkeys' cries" refers to. Usually, the answer is Chinese poets. Kusumoto 2006, 202–6, says that the phrase refers to Chinese Zen monks but that the statement is directed at Bashō himself, evoking Zen-style self-questioning that leads to the conclusion that all must accept the decrees of Heaven.

25. Some scholars argue that this episode is a fiction meant to represent accepting fate. However, Imoto argues that the episode has the ring of truth and says that such sights were not unusual in Bashō's day. See Imoto and Yayoshi 1968, 154, n. 4. Uozumi 2011, 44–45, identifies an allusion to a passage of *Zhuangzi* in which a starving man opines that "surely my father and mother would not wish for me to be so poor" and concludes that the cause of his plight is simply destiny. See Mair 1994, 53, 64–65. The word *ten* ("heaven") is an elastic concept translated variously as "destiny" or "the will of Heaven" or "nature." There is also the possibility that Bashō has in mind an episode from *Senjūshō* 撰集抄 (mid-thirteenth century), 107–11, a text attributed to Saigyō in Bashō's day—about an abandoned child. See Inoue 1992, 43–48.

26. Another *jiamari*. Chiri imagines friends in Edo counting up on their fingers the days since the travelers left.

27. *Bashō kushū* no. 598. Yonetani 1985b, 80–81, notes that in some texts the headnote reads just *ganzen*, "right in front of my eyes." He also notes that "rose marrow" is a frequent topic in Chinese poetry and that in the Noh play *Atsumori* 敦盛 it is used as a metaphor for ephemerality and suggests that the first line alludes to a poem by Saigyō (*SKKS* 262): "Beside the road / where pure waters flow by / beneath a willow / I thought to rest a moment / but ended up lingering on"

With the late-month moon shining only faintly in the sky,[28] our path beneath the mountain slope was dark, but I put the whip aside and passed by a number of villages, still hearing no cockcrows. Feeling halfway in the sort of lingering dream Du Mu describes in his "Setting Out Early," I did not awaken until we arrived at Sayononakayama.[29]

Asleep on my horse,	*uma ni nete*
half dreaming, I see the far moon	*zanmu tsuki tōshi*
and smoke from tea fires.[30]	*cha no keburi*

Matsubaya Fūbaku happened to be home in Ise, so we sought him out and stayed on for about ten days. I have no weapon, not even a dagger at my waist, carrying only a monk's hold-all hanging on my collar and prayer beads—eighteen of them on a string—in my hand.[31] Thus I look like a monk but live in the world of dust, look like a layman but have no hair. Here, though, they took anyone with a shaved head as a cleric, and I was not allowed to go before the God.[32] At dusk I went up to the Outer

---

(*michinobe ni /shimizu nagaruru / yanagikage / shibashi tote koso / tachidomaritsure*). Ogata 1998, 61–64, mentions a saying—*kinka ichijitsu no ei* 槿花一日之栄, "For the rose marrow flower, just one day of glory"—but also sees the poem as a parody of a poem by Kinoshita Chōshōshi, the central phrase being *asakusa kuwamu o muma*—"a horse at Asakusa grazing in short grass [*asakusa*]. "On the way home, I came to a placed called Asakusa Kannon, a temple gifted to the province, and came up with a poem off the cuff: 'How can it be / that among the short grasses / grown for grazing / the horses are not fed / here at Asakusa?'" (*ika nare ya / nobe ni karikau / asakusa no / kuwamu o muma no / haminokoshitsuru*).

28. At the end of the lunar month, the moon would be just a sliver in the sky.

29. See the introduction, p. 4. The last phrase, about not wakening till Sayononakayama, refers to a poem by Saigyō (*SKKS* 987): "That in old age / I again should cross here— / I never imagined. / Life's decree has brought me / to Sayononakayama" (*toshi takete / mata koyu beshi to / omoiki ya / inochi narikeri / sayononakayama*). Thus what finally awakens Bashō is the voice of the ancient poet at an *utamakura*.

30. *Bashō kushū* no. 488. The first version of this poem read, "Asleep on my horse, / lingering dream, lingering moon— / and smoke from tea fires" (*uma ni nete / zanmu zangetsu / cha no keburi*), which he rejected because of the repetitive syntax (*Sanzōshi*, 554). Bashō went through several other versions before deciding on the one included in *Bones Bleaching in the Fields*.

31. "Monk's hold all" translates *ichinō* 一嚢, otherwise called a *zudabukuro*, used to carry scriptures, money for alms, etc. Zen monks generally used eighteen-bead rosaries.

32. The most sacred places in Shinto shrines forbade entry to Buddhist monks, obliging them to worship from a special facility located some distance away.

Shrine,[33] just as darkness was obscuring the first *torii* gate,[34] and lamps could be seen here and there. The words "Loftiest of all are these—pine winds on the mountain"[35] struck me with the force of the winds themselves, and I was profoundly moved.

At month's end—no moon.	*misoka tsuki nashi*
Ageless cedars embraced	*chitose no sugi o*
by storm winds.[36]	*daku arashi*

At the base of Saigyōdani ran a stream where we saw women washing potatoes.[37]

Women scrubbing potatoes.	*imo arau onna*
Were I Saigyō, I would write	*saigyō naraba*
a proper *uta*.[38]	*uta yomamu*

---

33. The Grand Shrine at Ise was a large complex of buildings, the most sacred of which was the Naikū 内宮, or Inner Shrine. The Outer Shrine (Gekū 外宮), dedicated to the gods of agriculture and the harvest, was located some five or six kilometers from the Naikū.

34. The first formal gateway into the shrine complex. Yonetani 1985b, 83, posits an allusion to Saigyō's visit to the shrine complex recorded in *Saigyō monogatari* (89), a medieval text treating Saigyō's life, although not produced by the poet himself. There the poet, likewise wearing Buddhist robes, stayed around the first *torii* and only gazed at the buildings inside.

35. See another poem by Saigyō, *SZS* 1278: "At loose ends after living at Kōya, I was staying at a mountain temple near Futami Bay in Ise. The holy mountain of the Great Shrine was called Kamiji Mountain, which made me think of how our Sun Goddess was the incarnation of Dainichi Nyorai: 'Into the recesses / I make my pilgrimage / along the God's Pathway. / Loftiest of all are these— / pine winds on the mountain'" (*fukaku irite / kamiji no oku o / tazunureba / mata ue mo naki / mine no matsukaze*). Thus Bashō quotes a poem by Saigyō that brings Shinto and Buddhism together after referring to shrine policy that insists on keeping them separate.

36. *Bashō kushū* no. 489. Another *jiamari*. Bashō sees irony in the way moonlight is not shining brightly on the abode of the Sun Goddess while the winds Saigyō had described half a millennium before still blow. With the verb *daku* (literally, "to embrace"), Bashō suggests that the power of the wind protects the sacred mountain.

37. An earlier version of this sentence indicates that the following *hokku* was written "on the spot" (*sokuji*). See Yuzawa 1982, 25, no. 43.

38. *Bashō kushū* no. 630. Another *jiamari*. Saigyō addressed a poem to a prostitute at Eguchi, asking for a place to spend the night. The elegant—and moralistic—way she turned him away became the basis for the Noh play *Eguchi* 江口, which Bashō doubtless had in mind. Needless to say, no proper *uta* would describe women scrubbing potatoes.

On our way back, we stopped by a teahouse where there was a woman named Chō, "Butterfly." She handed me a piece of white cloth and said, "Put my name in a poem," so I wrote this:

Orchid scent—	*ran no ka ya*
perfume burnt into the wings	*chō no tsubasa ni*
of a butterfly.[39]	*takimono su*

We visited the cottage of a certain recluse:[40]

Vines planted,	*tsuta uete*
and four or five bamboos—	*take shigohon no*
in blustery winds.[41]	*arashi kana*

It was the beginning of the Long Month[42] when we arrived at my hometown. Around the north hall little remained of the forgetting grasses,[43] already stricken by frost. Everything had changed utterly, down to my siblings, who

---

39. *Bashō kushū* no. 605. *Takimono su* refers to the practice of scenting robes. In *Sanzōshi*, 570, Bashō's disciple Dohō says that Bashō told him that the woman in question told him a story about how at the same place, the *haikai* master Sōin was once asked for a poem by a woman who had been a prostitute before becoming the wife of the proprietor. The practice of scenting robes was an old one, calling up images of ancient times. Dohō's version of the story says the woman handed Bashō paper, not cloth. See Hori and Imoto 1972, 77, n. 84.

40. Probably Roboku. See Abe Masami 1982, 95. Toyama 1978, 29, n. 11, assumes he was a professional *haikai* poet who had gone into seclusion. Bashō's verse is a compliment, praising the beauties of the autumn leaves on the vines and the swaying bamboos as an ideal setting for reclusive life.

41. *Bashō kushū* no. 620. Bashō probably has in mind this poem by Fujiwara no Ietaka (*SKKS* 959): "Written for a fifty-poem sequence commissioned by the Reverend Prince Shukaku: 'At Utsuyama / not even moonlight shines through / to my vine-bound hut; / and my dreams cannot withstand / the sound of the storm winds'" (*utsunoyama / tsuki dani morenu / tsuta no io ni / yumeji taetaru / kaze no oto kana*). Both vines and bamboo are associated with the reclusive life because of the way they quickly take over any spot where they are planted, representing the forces of nature and discouraging visitors.

42. *Nagatsuki*, the Ninth Lunar Month.

43. *Wasuregusa* or *kensō* 萱草, a kind of lily. In ancient China, women typically lived in the northernmost building or wing of a house, a practice that continued among aristocrats in Japan. *Wasuregusa* was often planted in the gardens around the hall. In the *Shijing* 詩経 (*The Book of Songs*), a woman missing her husband who is serving in the army asks, "Where am I to get forgetting grass? I would plant it by my North Hall" (I.5.62; see Waley 1960, 50). One is left asking, "If even the forgetting grass disappears, how will memories be kept alive?"

were all gray hair and wrinkled brows. "Well, here we are, still among the living"—that was all my brother could manage to say. He opened up the memento pouch[44] and said, "Here's some of Mother's white hair—pay your respects. You're like Urashima looking at the jeweled case,[45] the way your eyebrows show your age." We wept for a few minutes.

In my hand, it would melt	*te ni toraba kien*
in the warm tears I'm shedding—	*namida zo atsuki*
this autumn frost.[46]	*aki no shimo*

We trekked on into Yamato Province, to a place called Takenouchi in Katsuge District, which was Chiri's hometown, where we rested our legs for a while.

Twanging bowstrings:	*watayumi ya*
as soothing as lute music	*biwa ni nagusamu*
back in bamboos.[47]	*take no oku*

We went to worship at Taimadera at Mount Futagami.[48] Seeing the pine in the garden, I thought it must have stood there a thousand years. Its trunk had girth enough to hide oxen, as the saying goes, and however lacking in human emotion, its connection to the Buddha had saved it from the woodsman's ax—a most holy fate.[49]

---

44. *Mamoribukuro* 守袋. A small pouch carried as a kind of talisman. In this case it contains relics of Bashō's deceased mother.

45. A folktale about a fisherman who is rewarded for saving the life of a turtle by a journey to the Dragon Palace beneath the sea. Returning to the world, he discovers that centuries have passed in his absence. When he opens a jeweled box, a parting gift that he was told never to open, he turns into an old man.

46. *Bashō kushū* no. 522. Another *jiamari*, this one containing eight syllables in the first line. Just as Urashima suddenly ages after opening the box, the mother's hair suddenly melts away in the son's tears.

47. *Bashō kushū* no. 542. A bow-like device used to make native cotton yarn. Twanging the bowstring against the cotton created a ball from which thread could be spun. Although the text makes it seem as if this *hokku* was written during a visit to Chiri's, it was written for the village head of Takenouchi as a gift. See Abe Masami 1982, 97–98; Ogata 1998, 96. Some texts include a headnote: "There was a house far back in a grove of bamboos."

48. Abe Masami 1982, 98, argues that Chiri accompanied Bashō on the visit.

49. *Zhuangzi* tells of a carpenter coming on an old pine tree so huge it could hide thousands of oxen who concludes that it has stood so long because its wood is useless. See Mair 1994, 37.

Monks, morning glories: *sō asagao*
how many have passed away   *iku shinikaeru*
by Buddha's pines?[50]   *nori no matsu*

Alone, I went deep into Yoshino, far back into mountains where white clouds
piled up on the peaks and rainy mists buried the gorges. Here and there
were the houses of mountain folk, looking small. I heard the sound of wood
cutters in the west echoing off toward the east, while the tolling of bells from
temples all around struck deep into my heart. Since long ago, people have
left the world to enter these mountains, many of them escaping into Chinese
poetry or hiding themselves in *uta*.[51] A place that could fairly be compared
to Mount Lu in China.

I spent a night in the sleeping quarters at a certain temple.[52]

Wield that mallet,   *kinuta uchite*
let me hear it strike—   *ware ni kikase yo ya*
temple wife![53]   *bō ga tsuma*

To get to the remains of Saigyō Shōnin's hut, you make your way a few hundred meters from the hindmost of the shrine buildings,[54] bearing right, and
then go down a faint path used only by wood gatherers—which brings you to

---

50. *Bashō kushū* no. 600. Bashō's poem suggests that it is Buddhism that protects the tree rather
than inferior wood or girth.

51. No doubt Bashō has Saigyō chiefly in mind, along with Emperor Go-Daigo and his court.
See p. 14 below.

52. Imoto 1972, 293, n. 15, notes that an early source offers Kizōin 喜蔵院 and Nanyōin
南陽院 as possibilities, both temples where wives were permitted.

53. *Bashō kushū* no. 535. *Kinuta* refers to cleansing and removing the wrinkles from robes by
placing them on a rock or wooden block and beating them with a wooden mallet. In poetry,
the sound of the *kinuta* is associated with autumn and thought of as forlorn, echoing with the
loneliness of a woman doing the annual cleaning of the robes of an absent man. Bashō's request
implies that he wants to experience the fullness of his time in the depths of the mountains.
The "common" image of the temple wife and the colloquial diction distinguish his poem from
formal *uta*. Bashō probably has in mind a poem by Fujiwara no Masatsune (*SKKS* 483): "In fair
Yoshino, / autumn winds on the mountains / late into night— / and cold in the old capital, /
the sound of mallet on block" (*miyoshino no / yama no akikaze / sayo fukete / furusato samuku /
koromo utsu nari*).

54. Hori and Imoto 1972, 78, poem 87, n. 2, identify this as the Kinbu Shrine.

a hut that stands facing the mountain opposite across a steep gorge. A sight to inspire awe! The pure flowing waters appear to flow as they did of old, making the same drip-drip sound as they trickle down.

Drip, drip goes the water.	*tsuyu tokutoku*
How I wish I could use it	*kokoromi ni ukiyo*
to wash the world away.[55]	*susugabaya*

If Boyi had lived in Japan, he would surely have washed his mouth with these waters; and had Xu You been told of them, he would have used them to cleanse his ears.

In the time it took for me to climb up one mountain slope and down another, the autumn sun had already started to set, so I had to forgo seeing some famous places and just worship at the tomb of Emperor Go-Daigo.[56]

After ages at this shrine,	*gobyō toshi hete*
what might they remember still—	*shinobu wa nani o*
these memory ferns?[57]	*shinobugusa*

Through Yamato and then Yamashiro I passed, and then took the Ōmi Road to Mino. Passing by Imasu and Yamanaka, I came to the grave of Tokiwa. It was Moritake of Ise who wrote, "It's like Lord Yoshitomo, / this autumn wind."[58] I wondered where he saw the resemblance.

---

55. *Bashō kushū* no. 517. See a poem attributed to Saigyō: "Drip, drip flows water, / barely trickling down from boulders / onto the moss /—still, more than I can use / in my brief stay in this hut" (*tokutoku to / otsuru iwama no / koke shimizu / kumihosu hodo mo / naki sumai kana*). Hori and Imoto 1972, 78, poem 87, n. 3. Daiyasu 1994, 207, notes that Bashō is probably relying on a guidebook, *Yoshinosan hitori anai* よしの山ひとりあない (1671), which attributes the poem to Saigyō.

56. Go-Daigo led rebellions against the leaders of the shogunal government in 1324 and 1331. He escaped from exile and ended up forming his own government, called the Southern Court, in Yoshino. The memorial was located at Nyoirinji.

57. *Bashō kushū* no. 646. Another *jiamari*. *Shinobu* ("hare's-foot fern") appears in poetry often because it is homophonous with the verb *shinobu*, meaning "keep secret" or "yearn for." The Tokugawa government was particularly harsh in its treatment of Yoshino, withdrawing support to maintain the structures there. See Daiyasu 1994, 213.

58. From a solo thousand-verse sequence (*Moritake senku* 守武千句, 75), the previous verse of which reads, "Gazing at the moon, / we approach the village / of Tokiwa" (*tsuki mite ya / tokiwa no sato e / kakaruran*). Minamoto no Yoshitomo bore three sons by Tokiwa Gozen, one of them

Surely it was like   *yoshitomo no*
the *heart* of Yoshitomo—   *kokoro ni nitari*
the autumn wind.[59]   *aki no kaze*

At Fuwa Barrier:

That autumn wind—   *akikaze ya*
blows now in thickets and farmlands   *yabu mo hatake mo*
by Fuwa Barrier.[60]   *fuwanoseki*

Bokuin was the host for my night in Ōgaki.[61] When I left Musashino as I set out on my journey, I had thought I might end as bleached bones in a field.

Here I am, not dead   *shini mo senu*
after many nights on the road—   *tabine no hate yo*
at autumn's end.[62]   *aki no kure*

Composed at Hontōji[63] in Kuwana:

---

being Yoshitsune. She was captured by the Taira and forced to serve as a concubine to the Minamoto clan's enemy, Taira no Kiyomori.

59. *Bashō kushū* no. 439. No doubt Bashō sees the cold autumn wind as a fine symbol of Yoshitomo's desolate feelings at the time.

60. *Bashō kushū* no. 440. See a poem by Fujiwara no Yoshitsune (*SKKS* 1601): "On 'Autumn Wind at a Barrier,' composed for a poem contest held at the Poetry Bureau: 'No one lives now / beneath the deep eaves / at Fuwa Gatehouse— / long a ruin, visited / only by autumn wind'" (*hito sumanu / fuwa no sekiya no / itabisashi / arenishi nochi wa / tada aki no kaze*). Even the ruin of Yoshitsune's poem was of course long gone in Bashō's time, when the place was nothing but thickets and farmer's fields (Yuzawa 1982, 28, n. 82). Yonetani 1985b, 86, points out that the word *yabu* ("thickets") usually refers to trees around houses.

61. See the introduction p. 2. Bashō arrived in Ōgaki late in the Ninth Month and stayed on until early in the Eleventh Month, when Bokuin accompanied him to Kuwana in Ise, after which Bashō went on to spend the New Year in Iga Ueno.

62. *Bashō kushū* no. 418. This wry comment marks the conclusion of Bashō's original travel plan. See the introduction p. 5. He stayed through the Tenth Month and well into the Eleventh, and traveled in the area until leaving for his hometown in Iga Ueno. Yuzawa 1982, 28, n. 85, notes that *aki no kure* can mean either "autumn evening" or "autumn's end," and argues for the latter. The Japanese allows for both at the same time.

63. The chief priest of the temple was Takue.

Winter peonies.	*fuyubotan*
These plovers, they are cuckoos	*chidori yo yuki no*
in the snow.[64]	*hototogisu*

Tired of sleeping on the road, I got up while it was still mostly dark and went out to the beach.

In faint dawn light,	*akebono ya*
the white of a white fish—	*shirauo shiroki*
an inch of it.[65]	*koto issun*

We went on pilgrimage to Atsuta.[66]

The main shrine was in poor repair, its earthen walls crumbling and half hidden in clumps of grass.[67] Some distance away, a holy rope marked the spot where there had been a small shrine, and nearer by a stone was placed that

---

64. *Bashō kushū* no. 819. Just as summer peonies bloom when cuckoos sing, plovers play the same role in winter. Yonetani 1985b, 87, notes two allusions: the first to a poem attributed to Fujiwara no Teika: "Deep in the mountains / they sing even in winter— / the cuckoos. / Seeing jewels of falling snow / as deutzia blossoms" (*miyama ni wa / fuyu mo nakuran / hototogisu / tama chiru yuki o / unohan to mite*); and the second to a poem by Kinoshita Chōshōshi (*Chōshōshi zenshū*, vol. 2, 200): "A gourd beater / calls out a single time / as dawn is coming. / Even on a summer night / a cuckoo is calling" (*hachi tataki / akatsukigata no / hitokoe wa / fuyu no yo sae mo / naku hototogisu*). "Gourd beaters" refers to followers of Pure Land founder Kūya, who went through the streets in the last months of the year, beating on bells and gourds and chanting prayers.

65. *Bashō kushū* no. 74. Bokuin records that on this day he took Bashō to the beach, where they dug clams and then went out on a boat and scooped up *shirauo*, the "white fish" of the poem. In *haikai*, the fish are more associated with spring; in winter they would be smaller and more translucent, giving off a bluish-white sheen (Yonetani 1985b, 88–89). An earlier version of the poem had the first line as *yuki usushi* ("A thin snowfall"), which Bashō emended later (*Sanzōshi*, 566). The revised form would seem to have been written early in the day, whereas in actuality it was probably written after the boat trip—an example of "artistic fashioning." See Abe Masami 1982, 104–5. Toyama 1978, 35, n. 8, identifies an allusion to lines from a poem by Du Fu, "Just a bit of white, but here is life, nature's offer of a two-inch fish" (白小群分命 / 天然二寸魚).

66. Bashō traveled by boat from Kuwana to Atsuta, where he stayed at the house of Tōyō, who served as his guide in the area. Abe Masami 1982, 101–10, argues based on documentary evidence that Bokuin accompanied Bashō at this time.

67. In *Knapsack Notes*, Bashō describes how after repairs in 1686 the shrine is sparkling again. See p. 53.

bore the name of the god. Mugwort and memory fern had their run of the
place, a sight that moved me more than would a finer display.

All is withered—	*shinobu sae*
even roadside memory ferns	*karete mochi kau*
where I buy rice cakes.[68]	*yadori kana*

Chanted as we headed down the road toward Nagoya:[69]

Ah, the crazy lines I chant	*kyōku kogarashi no*
as I wither in harsh winds—	*mi wa chikusai ni*
like Chikusai![70]	*nitaru kana*

Pillow of grass.	*kusamakura*
Is that dog rained on too?	*inu mo shigururu ka*
Barking in the night.[71]	*yoru no koe*

---

68. *Bashō kushū* no. 817. Just as the withered "memory fern" (see p. 000, n. 82) preserves no
sign of spring, so the place where he stops to rest can offer only rice cakes. Another text tells us
that the *yadori*, usually a "house" or an "inn," was in fact a teahouse. See Hori and Imoto 1972,
84, n. 100; Ogata 1998, 164–65. The withered state of the flower is no doubt meant as a comment on the ruined state of the shrine.
69. In Nagoya, Bashō stayed with his disciple Kakei. He participated in the linked-
verse sequences that were included in *Fuyu no hi*, for which he served as compiler. See
p. 2. Abe Masami 1982, 109–10, again reasons that Bokuin accompanied Bashō as far as
Nagoya.
70. *Bashō kushū* no. 747. Another *jiamari* in the first line. Chikusai—like Kakei, a physician—
was the name of the protagonist of an eponymous fiction about the travels of a quack doctor
on the Tōkai Road, written by the physician Tomiyama Dōya. This poem served as the *hokku*
for a thirty-six-verse linked-verse sequence composed with Yasui, Kakei, Tokoku, and several
other Nagoya disciples. Some scholars argue that the first word of the poem belongs in the prose
introduction, introducing the poem as a "crazy verse" (*kyōku*). For a summary of the arguments,
see Abe Masami 1965–89, vol. 4, 48–50. Narukawa 1999, 241–47, explains that the preface to
the *hokku* in *Fuyu no hi*, an anthology of *kasen* by Bashō and Nagoya poets, is designed to under-
line affinities with Chikusai as a castaway and an outsider: "My rain hat shredded by rains along
the long road, my paper robe bent and worn by storm winds, I was the most pitiful of pitiful
souls, a sad case even to myself. Suddenly I thought of that old master of madcap verse when he
arrived in the same place." See also Ogata 1998, 175–78.
71. *Bashō kushū* no. 690. Sleeplessness is a common theme in travel poems. Here, rather than
blaming the dog for keeping him awake, Bashō asserts a kinship with the animal.

Walking around looking at the snow:

You merchants—   *ichibito yo*
let me sell you this hat,   *kono kasa urō*
my snow-covered hat!⁷²   *yuki no kasa*

Seeing a traveler:

Even a horse   *uma o sae*
is something to gaze upon   *nagamuru yuki no*
on a snowy morning.⁷³   *ashita kana*

At the end of a day spent at seaside:

The sea darkens   *umi kurete*
and I hear ducks—   *kamo no koe*
their far voices faintly white.⁷⁴   *honoka ni shiroshi*

I untied my sandals, cast my staff aside, and went to bed, still on the road as the year came to an end:

---

72. *Bashō kushū* no. 719. Another document notes that this *hokku* was composed for a sequence at the home of one Hōgetsu in Nagoya. In the version appearing there, the first line ends with the directional particle *ni* rather than the interjection *yo*, and the last line reads *kasa no yuki* ("the snow on my hat") rather than *yuki no kasa* ("my snow-covered hat").

73. *Bashō kushū* no. 720. He used this poem as the *hokku* for a short sequence at the home of Tōyō. Abe Masami 1965–89, vol. 4, 40, notes differing opinions on whether *yuki no ashita* means that snow is on the ground after a storm in the night or still falling, opting for the latter.

74. *Bashō kushū* no. 801. The second line of this *hokku* contains just five syllables rather than the standard seven, while the last line contains seven rather than the standard five. In a headnote to this poem, Bashō says that he and the people with him at the time went out on a boat. He used this poem as the *hokku* for a sequence with Tōyō and an unidentified man named Kōzan. See *Kōhon Bashō zenshū*, vol. 3, 277–81. Many modern scholars and critics offer this poem as an example of synesthesia, but a note in the *Kōhon Bashō zenshū* text (vol. 3, 277, n. 9) edited by Ōtani Tokuzō, Kon Eizō, Toyama Susumu, et al., states emphatically that Bashō "is not saying that the voice of the ducks is white." Instead, the editors contend that he means that he hears the ducks calling off over the ocean, where the sky is white as dusk comes on: "The sea darkens / and I hear ducks voices / sound faint in the whiteness." Sugiura and Miyamoto 1959, 42, n. 42, equivocate, saying that "there is a white feel to light remaining at dusk off where the ducks cry." However, Abe 1965–89, vol. 4, 292–93, argues to the contrary that saying the voices are "white" is an example of Bashō's genius and quotes Kōda Rohan and Imoto Nōichi in his defense.

The year ends.   *toshi kurenu*
Still I wear my traveler's hat,   *kasa kite zōri*
my walking sandals.[75]   *hakinagara*

Coming up with such lines, I greeted the New Year in a house in the mountains:

Whose new husband   *ta ga muko zo*
loads an ox with ferns and *mochi*   *shida ni mochi ou*
this Year of the Ox?[76]   *ushi no toshi*

On the road into Nara:

Must be spring!   *haru nare ya*
Over nameless mountains,   *na mo naki yama no*
a thin swath of haze.[77]   *usugasumi*

When in seclusion at Nigatsudō:

Ice-cold monks   *mizutori ya*
run with water for the rite.   *kōri no sō no*
The sound of shoes.[78]   *kutsu no oto*

---

75. *Bashō kushū* no. 676. Composed at his hometown in Iga Ueno at the end of 1684. Yonetani 1985b, 94, suggests that the setting of the poem is not at home but on the road as he travels toward home and notes the mediating influence of poem 624 in Saigyō's personal anthology, *Sankashū* 山家集 (precise date unknown): "Written in Michinoku, as the year came to an end: 'Even more so / do I find my heart / feeling forlorn— / beneath traveler's skies / as the year comes to an end'" (*tsune yori mo / kokorobosoku zo / omohoyuru / tabi no sora nite / toshi no kurenuru*).

76. *Bashō kushū* no. 18. Again, composed in Ueno. It was customary for a new son-in-law to bring gifts—*shida* ferns for New Year's decorations and rice cakes—to his wife's family at New Year's. According to the twelve-year cycle of the Chinese zodiac, 1685 was a "Year of the Ox."

77. *Bashō kushū* no. 33. Sometime in the middle of the Second Month, Bashō traveled to Nara, where he saw a Noh performance at night on the grounds of Kōfukuji. *Kasumi* ("haze") was a harbinger of spring.

78. *Bashō kushū* no. 50. The "Second-Month Service" (*shunigatsue* 修二月会) was held during two weeks of the Second Month. Bashō describes the rite, which he probably witnessed sitting in the porticos of the Kannon Hall with scores of other visitors, on the 12th day. The rite involved monks carrying water from the well up a long stone stairway lit by pine torches, and then going into the Kannon Hall, walking briskly around the image dais, and finally running around the hall on the outside. During the rite the monks first wore sandals, then, inside the hall, put on flat shoes (*kutsu*) with wooden soles, which were taken off for the final run, when they wore only split-toe socks (*tabi*). Given the time of year, the metaphor "ice-cold monks" may actually be taken as literal. See Daiyasu 1994, 48–49.

I went up to Kyoto and called on Mitsui Shūfū at his mountain home in Narutaki:

Plum blossoms of white.   *ume shiroshi*
Was the crane stolen   *kinō ya tsuru o*
just yesterday?[79]   *nusumareshi*

The oak tree   *kashi no ki no*
appears to have no interest   *hana ni kamawanu*
in flowers.[80]   *sugata kana*

Meeting Ninkō Shōnin at Saiganji[81] in Fushimi:

For my robes   *waga kinu ni*
I ask from Fushimi's peach trees *fushimi no momo no*
drops of water, please.[82]   *shizuku seyo*

Along the road to Ōtsu we crossed a mountain pass:

On a mountain path   *yamaji kite*
they are somehow more charming— *naniyara yukashi*
clumps of violets.[83]   *sumiregusa*

---

79. *Bashō kushū* no. 88. Shūfū's villa was in the Narutaki area (Satō Nobi 2014, 30). The Sung dynasty poet Lin Hejing, disenchanted with service in a corrupt regime, withdrew to the mountains in Hangzhou with a crane as his child and plum blossoms as his wife. He spent forty years at Gu Shan. Bashō's poem compares Shūfū, his host, with the Chinese poet, asking where his attendant crane could be. It appears that Bashō was accompanied by Koshun, the son of his old master, Kitamura Kigin, who provided an introduction (Yonetani 1985b, 96). Bashō stayed for several weeks with Shūfū. See Abe Masami 1965–89, vol. 4, 324. After Bashō's death, Kyorai would write as if his master had little use for the rich man, but Abe Masami 1982, 119, disputes the accuracy of his conclusions.

80. *Bashō kushū* no. 144. Another nod by Bashō to his host, an aging oak that stands above the worldly display symbolized by the flowers.

81. Ninkō was head priest there.

82. *Bashō kushū* no. 176. Bashō praises the area as akin to the Chinese abode of sages, Peach Blossom Spring—appropriately so, the Fushimi area being known for its peach groves. A few drops of dew from the flowers were believed to confer good health.

83. *Bashō kushū* no. 192. Another version of this *hokku*— "For some reason / they are charming, somehow— / clumps of violets" (*nani to wa nashi ni / nani yara yukashi / sumiregusa*)— served to begin a sequence composed by Bashō, Tōyō, and Kōtan on the 27th day of the

Looking out on the vista of the lake:

At Karasaki,	*karasaki no*
more misty is the pine	*matsu wa hana yori*
than the flowers.[84]	*oboro nite*

At Minakuchi I met up with an old friend after twenty years:

Two separate lives,	*inochi futatsu no*
together just hanging on—	*naka ni ikitaru*
amidst cherry blossoms.[85]	*sakura kana*

Another monk, this one from Hirugakojima in Izu, who had been trekking since autumn the year before, heard about me, and came looking for me all the way into Owari, hoping that we might go on the road together.[86]

Let's be off, then—	*iza tomo ni*
though we must eat young barley,	*homugi kurawan*
grass for our pillows.[87]	*kusamakura*

Third Month of 1685. See Abe Masami 1965–89, vol. 4, 339. Kon 2005b, 50, assumes that this is Bashō taking literary liberties, but another possibility is that he came up with the idea on the road and then revised the poem at the *haikai* gathering later. See Imoto and Yayoshi 1968, 157, n. 13. Yonetani 1985b, 97–99, argues that Bashō ended up changing the headnote from "At Hakuchōsan," referring to Hōjiji, a temple in Atsuta, to "On the road to Ōtsu" in order to "bracket" the text with references to two mountain passes, Hakone near the beginning and Ōtsu near the end.

84. *Bashō kushū* no. 34. See an envoy written by Kakinomoto no Hitomaro (*MYS* 2930), attached to a long poem (*chōka*) written when he visited the ruins of the old capital nearby. "At Kara Cape / in Shiga of the rippling waves, / all is as it was. / But those who wait for courtier's boats / surely do so in vain" (*sasanami no / shiga no karasaki / sakiku aredo / ōmiyabito no / fune machikanetsu*).

85. *Bashō kushū* no. 124. The old friend was Dohō from Iga Ueno, Bashō's hometown. Yonetani 1985b, 100, notes an allusion to a line from the Noh play *Shichikiochi* 七騎落: "Parent and child—one body, two lives."

86. Yonetani 1985b, 100–101, identifies this man as Rotsū, an itinerant monk and disciple.

87. *Bashō kushū* no. 343. *Homugi* is green barley, not yet ready for eating, standing metaphorically for meager fare. The poem reminds the reader of the beginning of the text, where Bashō admits to leaving without even preparing food for the journey.

This monk informed me that Reverend Daiten of Engakuji had passed away at the beginning of the First Month of the current year. Life is truly a dream, I thought, and before anything else sent a letter off to Kikaku.

Missing plum blossoms,	*ume koite*
I offer my mourning tears—	*unohana ogamu*
to deutzia flowers.[88]	*namida kana*

Sent to Tokoku:

To the white poppies,	*shirageshi ni*
this butterfly leaves a keepsake—	*hane mogu chō no*
a torn wing.[89]	*katami kana*

Again I stayed with Tōyō, and wrote this as I was about to head back to the East Country:[90]

A bee makes its way out,	*botanshibe fukaku*
from deep in the peony flower—	*wakeizuru hachi no*
but with regrets.[91]	*nagori kana*

Composed when I was approaching Yamanaka in Kai Province:

For my fine pony—	*yuku koma no*
a house where he is treated	*mugi ni nagusamu*
to barley ears.[92]	*yadori kana*

---

88. *Bashō kushū* no. 340. The poem compares the priest to the most high-class of flowers, the plum, but laments that he did not know about the man's passing—when the plums were coming into bloom—until later, in the season of *unohana*.

89. *Bashō kushū* no. 368. Tokoku would become one of Bashō's closest friends and companions. Bashō's *hokku* expresses his sadness at having to depart from his friend, symbolized by the poppies. A butterfly's wings would blend in with white poppies until it flew away.

90. Azuma 東, a somewhat antique term for the area northeast of Hakone.

91. *Bashō kushū* no. 359. The peony represents Tōyō, from whom the bee—Bashō—has received courtesy and sustenance. This *hokku* served as the first verse of a sequence.

92. *Bashō kushū* no. 344. It appears that here Bashō was visiting his old patron, Biji. Scholars debate about whether Bashō went back to Edo via the Kiso Road, which would have taken him fairly close to Biji's place, or the Tōkai Road. In a letter, he expressed worry about taking the Kiso Road, although saying that he was planning to do so. See Tanaka 2005, 73. Grazing in a

Composed at the end of the Fourth Month, when I was back in my hut still recovering from my time on the road:

Not yet, I admit,   *natsugoromo*
have I rid my summer robes   *imada shirami o*
of all their lice.[93]   *toritsukusazu*

---

field of "barley ears" would have been a treat for the horse—more than could be expected at an inn—and thus symbolizes Biji's generosity. Kai Province was known for its horses.

93. *Bashō kushū* no. 289. An oblique way of saying that it took a while to gain his strength for even the most mundane of tasks. Yonetani 1985b, 103, notes that lice are associated with the reclusive lifestyle.

A PILGRIMAGE TO KASHIMA

Introduction

In the last decade of his life, Bashō seems always to have been on a journey or preparing for one. It was in the Fourth Month of 1685 that he returned to Edo after the trip that resulted in *Bones Bleaching in the Fields*, and by the late spring of 1686, he was already planning another stay in the Kyoto area.[1] As it turned out, he had to postpone his plans until the next year, but still he kept in contact by letter with his disciples, particularly Bokuin, Chisoku, Kyorai, and Jokushi, the last two of whom visited him in Edo as well. Partly the postponement may have been due to a busy schedule with disciples and patrons in Edo; partly it may have been because of episodes of ill health.[2] Yet he did not stop planning, and he would keep his promise to reunite with supporters in the Kyoto area in the Eleventh Month of 1687. Before then, however, in the middle of the Eighth Month of that same year, he went on a short trip of just ten days or so to Kashima on the northeast coast of Honshū, which he wrote about in the form of his *A Pilgrimage to Kashima*.

Bashō's stated purpose for this journey was to see the moon at Kashima, which would be at the full on the 15th day of the lunar month, the very day he arrived. However, we know that Kashima was hardly renowned as a moon-viewing site,[3] and we also know that he had another motive—namely, to answer an invitation to see his friend and teacher, Butchō, at Konponji, a Zen temple in Kashima, in order to say goodbye before heading out on a journey to the west again a few months later. Perhaps the scholar Kusumoto Mutsuo is correct in joining those two purposes together: "In the end, what he did was to convene an elegant moon-viewing gathering at Konponji."[4]

---

1. See Kon 2005a, 92–99, 102. In the spring of 1686, he wrote to Kyorai saying that he was planning to have a peaceful stay at Rakushisha and asks Kyorai not to let his visit be known (Tanaka 2005, 88).
2. Another possible reason is that he was involved in Zen training at the time that he did not want to interrupt. See n. 10 below.
3. He states the same purpose for his journeys to places that were indeed celebrated for moon viewing: Sarashina (see pp. 77–78) and Matsushima (see pp. 97–98, 118–19). Danjō 1970, 243, argues that visiting Butchō was Bashō's primary motive.
4. Kusumoto 2009, 342.

If Butchō is known today, it is mostly because of his association with Bashō. Yet he appears to have been a dedicated and gifted monk of some reputation in his day.[5] Born in the Kashima area in 1642, he entered Konponji, located on the outskirts of Kashima Shrine, at the age of eight and proved a serious student, going on to do *zazen* (meditation exercises) and rigorous training on the road from the age of fourteen. His talent and commitment are evidenced by the fact that when the abbot of the temple, Reizan, died in 1674, Butchō ascended to that position. Almost immediately, however, his devotions were interrupted, when the leadership at Kashima Shrine filed a claim against the temple's stipend, which had been granted by Tokugawa Ieyasu early in the seventeenth century. This resulted in Konponji losing half its annual income of 100 *koku* and left it in danger of being reduced to a sort of annex of Kashima Shrine rather than an independent institution. Probably feeling it his duty to present a countersuit before the commissioner of shrines and temples in Edo, Butchō traveled to the shogunal capital and took up residence, first living in Kaizenji[6] and then moving into Rinsenan,[7] a cottage in Fukagawa established as a residence by his predecessor as abbot. He was there in a kind of limbo for nine years, although probably traveling back to Kashima from time to time.

It was during these years in Fukagawa that Butchō became acquainted with his neighbor, a *haikai* poet then known as Tōsei, who moved into a nearby hut in the winter of 1680, a place that would later be called Bashōan, or "Plantain Cottage."[8] Scholars agree that this was a turning point in the *haikai* master's life. Having left his thriving practice as a marker in Nihonbashi, for reasons not completely certain, Bashō determined over time to practice *haikai* less as a worldly profession than as a spiritual Way. There can be little doubt that his study with Butchō, who evidently introduced him not just to Zen but to Daoist texts and Chinese poetry, provided a necessary foundation for the development of his mature poetics.[9]

---

5. Tanaka 2008, 94–95, cites evidence that Butchō was one of the renowned Zen monks of his time.
6. See Yamamoto Satoshi 1994, 90. Kaizenji 海禅寺, located in Asakusa, was affiliated with the Myōshinji branch of Zen, as was Rinsenan.
7. Only later, in 1713, did the place became a full-fledged temple, called Rinsenji, the name by which it is still known today.
8. The later name came about after one of Tōsei's disciples, Rika, presented him with a gift of plantains that thrived in his grounds.
9. Records do not indicate how the men came in contact with one another. Some texts say that it was through a common acquaintance in the Zen community. Tanaka 2008, 95, assumes that Bashō heard of Butchō, who was well known through his proselytizing activities, and just called

In 1682 Butchō finally prevailed in his suit and returned triumphantly to Kashima, where he showed his spiritual sincerity by promptly resigning as abbot and withdrawing into a cottage on the grounds of Konponji.[10] It seems almost certain that he invited Bashō to visit him in his hometown, perhaps even suggesting as a time the midpoint of the Eighth Month, renowned nationwide as the most beautiful moon of the entire year. For whatever reason, it was at that time, in 1687, that Bashō made the trip, accompanied by two companions, both disciples who often helped him with chores: Sora, a man of samurai origins, and a Zen monk named Sōha.[11]

The journey to Kashima was not a long or arduous one, really nothing compared to any of Bashō's other treks. From Bashō's home the men went by boat on the Konagi River west to the city of Gyōtoku (now in Ichikawa City), and from there they walked the thirty-two kilometers to the town of Fusa (modern Abiko City in Chiba Prefecture) on the Tone River. At Fusa they chose to press on by night boat to Sawara, finishing the journey by canals through the towns of Ushibori and Itako and arriving finally at Ōfuna Harbor near Kashima—another forty-four kilometers.[12] Going by boat made for a swift trip, just two days. From the harbor the threesome went directly to Konponji, located just to the west of Kashima Shrine, where Butchō was expecting them at his cottage in the temple grounds.

In his later account Bashō writes that he was somewhat disappointed that rain spoiled the moon viewing on the night of his arrival, but at the same time he says in a poem that staying in the temple, he was able to "attain tranquility" and see "the true face of the moon" through the rain—this suggesting that he had a religious experience as Butchō's guest. Although not producing a *hokku*, the retired abbot did compose a classical *uta* in which he contrasted the rain with the light of the moon, suggesting a similar contrast between worldly perceptions and Buddha's steady, unwavering light.

We are not sure of the precise itinerary of the threesome after their first night at Butchō's, but from the *hokku* at the end of the text, we know they did visit Kashima

---

on him; he also argues (94–99) that Butchō's "teaching" probably amounted to reading texts—aloud—and brief discussions, as well as friendly chats.

10. The place was called Chōkōan. The standard account (see Tanaka 2008, 2012) of Butchō's movements is that he left Edo soon after the government decision was handed down in 1682. Takahashi Shōji, who treats Bashō as a Zen monk, dissents, arguing that Butchō spent time in Edo until the spring of 1687, and that the reason Bashō postponed his trip to the west was that he was undergoing intensive Zen training with Butchō. See Takahashi 2002, 207–12.

11. Both men lived nearby and were disciples. Takahashi 2002, 126, notes that Sōha was also a student of Butchō.

12. Danjō 1970, 228.

Shrine[13] and that during their return journey they stopped in Gyōtoku at the home of Bashō's disciple, Jijun,[14] where they composed a linked-verse sequence, the first three verses of which, by Jijun, Bashō, and Sora, Bashō included in his account. A few days later they were back in Edo.

***

The account based on the journey to Kashima seems to have been written up just after the poet's return to Edo and soon given to Bashō's chief patron, Sanpū, just as was done in the case of *Bones Bleaching in the Fields*.[15] The journey had been a short one, and so is the text, just two pages of prose and eighteen poems (an *uta*, fourteen *hokku*, and a *mitsumono*), organized by topic in four thematic groups but not offered in strict order of composition.[16] While some scholars argue that this two-part structure—first prose, then poems—constitutes an aesthetic misstep, others see it as an attempt to forge a new form of travel writing.[17]

The copy of the text given to Sanpū was titled *A Record of Kashima* (*Kashima no ki* 鹿島の記), but another early text in Bashō's hand is titled *A Pilgrimage to Kashima* (*Kashima mōde* 鹿島詣)—the latter clearly denoting a devotional purpose. From this fact Danjō Masataka argues that Bashō ultimately saw religious instincts behind his journey, which he thought of as a kind of pilgrimage, and that the focus of it was the visit to his mentor Butchō, whom he looked to as a model of the same sort as Saigyō.[18]

---

13. Although the text includes three *hokku* composed at the shrine, the prose section of the text says nothing about such a visit. One wonders if Butchō's recent history might have made a proper guided tour difficult.

14. Many modern editions identify this man as Dōetsu, a physician who was originally from Ōgaki but in the 1680s lived in Itako. But consensus now (see *Sōgō Bashō jiten* and *Haibungaku daijiten*, Kon 2005a, 107; Satō Katsuaki 2014, 37) identifies him as Konishi Jijun. For a discussion of the relevant texts and issues involved, see Abe Masami 1965–89, vol. 5, 175–77.

15. Kon 2005a, 108, says Bashō wrote the text up on the 25th day of the Eighth Month. Inoue argues that Bashō's *hokku* collection *Atsumeku* あつめ句 was compiled about the same time and that the two texts—presented to Sanpū in one box—were meant as companion pieces. See also Inoue 1992, 65–90.

16. Danjō 1970, 233–34, argues that some *hokku* that were evidently written on the way to Kashima appear after those written on the way back. The themes are all common poetic topics (*dai*).

17. See Kusumoto 2009, 345–46.

18. Danjō 1970. Inoue 1992, 117–22, sees the description of Butchō "living in seclusion near a temple at the foot of Mount Kashima" as modeled on a description of Saigyō in *Saigyō waka shugyō* 西行和歌修行 and on the Chinese poet Du Fu.

And Danjō also argues that the Buddha statue that Sōha carried in a portable shrine on his back was brought along so that it could be used for the first time in a ritual setting (*kaigen* 開眼) by the Zen monk.[19] On the other hand, Kusumoto Mutsuo speaks for those impatient with the idea of the text as something other than what to him it obviously is: a literary text, an early example, that is, of *haibun*, or *haikai* prose, that focuses in literary fashion on two things—the travel experience, reinforced with abundant reference to famous places, and the moon.[20]

Nothing in the text helps us resolve these diverging views. The truth is that Bashō alludes to a broad array of literary and religious texts, from classical poems of both Japan and China and Zen works to *The Pillow Book of Sei Shōnagon* (*Makura no sōshi* 枕草子, early eleventh century) of Heian times and medieval Noh dramas. Furthermore, it is undeniable that the moon—clearly a central image of the text—can function in either realm, the aesthetic or the Buddhistic. Indeed, it is perhaps best to say that the dichotomy in the minds of these scholars is actually one of the discursive tensions that produces the text. Bashō, a professional poet, again as in *Bones Bleaching in the Fields*, defines himself early in the text as somewhere between a monk and a layman ("something between *b*ird and *r*at, a *bat*" as he puts it): a man in limbo, operating in a liminal space because that is where he wants to be. Some see *A Pilgrimage to Kashima* as a halting step toward the supposed formal "perfection" of *The Narrow Road through the Hinterlands*, and thus as an "imperfect" work in a fundamental sense. But one need not go that far to admit that it is a text that refuses easy categorization—unless one takes it straightforwardly as a brief prose account of a journey, followed by *hokku* that emerged from it.[21] Again one must remember that at this point in his career, Bashō did not publish his travel writings, but distributed them among disciples and friends, thus making them something less than canonical, neither this nor that.

A few themes should be identified that emerge in the prose and the poetry. One is the universal appeal of the moon, whether regarded in aesthetic or religious terms, or both. While not the only seasonal image the text puts forth (we see in the prose also bush clover and other autumn flowers, ponies grazing, fishing weirs, and in the poems bamboo, pines, deer, and a crane, to give a partial list), it is the dominant one. And another theme, also seen in *Bones Bleaching in the Fields*, is the poet's seeming inability to compose poems at the most renowned places: Mount Fuji in the earlier

---

19. Danjō 1970, 242.
20. Kusumoto 2009, 340–46.
21. In this sense, the text reads easily as an example of *haibun* in both style and format. On Bashō's focus on *haibun* at around this time, see Inoue 1992, 127–29.

work, Mount Tsukuba in *A Pilgrimage to Kashima*. (One should add that in the latter he also says in the prose section that he is too overwhelmed by the beauty of the moon seen through the rain to come up with a poem—although, ever the trickster, he then includes a poem on the moon among the list of poems at the end.[22]) Imperfection over perfection, indirect over direct. I take these feints as a rhetorical strategy that is often at the heart of Bashō's method as a *haikai* poet: a cagey way to play his role of a challenger to tradition while at the same time persisting within it.

---

22. Scholars often see this kind of rhetorical stance as part and parcel of Bashō's method as a *haikai* poet. See Inoue 1992, 18–19.

A PILGRIMAGE TO KASHIMA

Gazing at the moon at Suma Bay, Teishitsu of the Capital wrote something like "Beneath pines, I see / the full moon at mid-month. / Ah, Middle Counselor!"[23] It was of that same madcap poet[24] of the past that I was thinking when this autumn I decided to go see the moon at Mount Kashima.[25] Accompanying me were two men, one a samurai rover, the other a Zen monk wandering like rivers or clouds.[26] The monk wore ink-dark robes, black as a crow, with a sundry pouch hanging round his neck[27] and a box altar strapped to his back in which he had placed an image of Buddha leaving the mountain,[28] and it was thus that he went forward, jangling the rings on his staff,[29] finding nothing to block the Gateless Gate, "traveling alone in the universe."[30]

---

23. Bashō slightly misquotes the poem, which should read, "Clear in the pines— / the full moon at mid-month. / Ah, Middle Counselor" (*matsu ni sume / tsuki mo sangoya / chūnagon*). Suma is where the eponymous hero of *The Tale of Genji* went into exile, as had Middle Counselor Ariwara no Yukihira before him. Teishitsu's poem alludes to a Chinese poem by Bai Juyi that includes the line "At midmonth, in the new light of the moon in the night" (三五夜中新付月色). See Imoto and Yayoshi 1968, 158, n. 1 and Kusumoto 2009, 345.

24. *Kyōfu* 狂夫. Bashō uses the term *kyō* ("zany, eccentric, unconventional") to describe his own verses in *Nozarashi kikō* (see p. 17). The ideal is associated with Zen and Daoism.

25. In this declarative statement of the poet's identity and purpose in traveling, Danjō 1970, 230–31, sees the influence of the typical openings encountered in Noh dramas.

26. "Samurai rover" translates *rōkaku* 浪客, a samurai without official assignment, while "Zen monk wandering like rivers and clouds" translates *suiun no sō* 水雲の僧 (more commonly reversed, *unsui no sō*), a metaphor usually applied to Zen priests.

27. *Sane no fukuro* 三衣の袋. Originally, a pouch for Buddhist robes but by this time simply a carrying pouch, or *zudabukuro* (Imoto 1972, 303, n. 8).

28. Sugiura and Miyamoto 1959, 46, n. 11; Nakamura 1971, 55, n. 10; and Toyama 1978, 55, n. 10, believe that this refers to a painting, while Imoto and Yayoshi 1968, 159, n. 3 argue that it is a small statue, basing their contention on an early text describing a statue Bashō kept on his altar and the phrase *zushi ni agameirete*, that he "put in his portable altar." "Buddha leaving the mountain" refers to when the historical Buddha, after six years of rigors with other ascetics in the mountain forest, realized that he must leave and seek his enlightenment in another way and departed. Such statues show Buddha leaning on a staff and taking a step forward.

29. One kind of staff employed by Zen priests had rings around its top that jingled. Yonetani 1985a, 109, notes that the sound was believed to ward off noxious insects.

30. See *Mumonkan* 無門関 (C. *Wumen guan*, *The Gateless Gate*), a thirteenth-century Zen *kōan* collection by the Chan (J. Zen) monk Wumen Huihai that says in typical madcap fashion that the gate has no gate and that those who pass through it walk on through the universe independent (Aitken 1991, 4).

As for the other member of our threesome—myself: I am neither monk nor layman, but something between *b*ird and r*at*, a *bat*, one might call me,[31] heading off toward "an island without birds," as the saying goes.[32] We boarded a boat just outside my gate[33] and went as far as Gyōtoku but did not proceed from there on horseback, thinking to test our shins by going on foot.

Donning hats of cypress provided by a certain man of Kai Province,[34] we passed through the village of Yawata and arrived at Kamagainohara, a place of broad fields. It was like looking out a thousand leagues and more over the plains of Qin, so far ahead could our eyes range.[35] Before us rose Mount Tsukuba, its two peaks standing side by side. I had heard of twin peaks in China, near Mount Lu.

> Fine under snow, surely,   *yuki wa mōsazu*
> but better still in purplish-red: *mazu murasaki no*
> Mount Tsukuba.[36]   *tsukuba kana*

It was my disciple Ransetsu that composed this verse.[37] Tsukuba is connected to the words of Prince Yamatodake[38] as passed down to us, and those who compose linked verse relate it to their origins and use the name in referring to their Way.[39] It won't do,

---

31. *Chōso no aida* 鳥鼠の間, meaning "neither bird nor rat." An old expression used in much the same way as the English expression "neither fish nor fowl." The question of whether the bat should be classified as bird or rat was an old one.

32. An adage: *tori naki shima no kōmori*, the sense of which is that in a place where there was no person of prominence, even a person of no importance stands out. Bashō puns on the name Kashima, "Deer Island," although Kashima is actually on a peninsula.

33. Bashō's hut was near the Sumida River and a canal. Commercial boats carrying passengers operated in the area at the time, and it is likely that the threesome traveled together in that way as far as Gyōtoku. See Imoto and Yayoshi 1968, 160, n. 6.

34. Yonetani 1985a, 111, suggests that the man was Biji.

35. See a Chinese couplet in *Wakan rōeishū* (no. 240). Imoto and Yayoshi 1968, 136, see a more immediate source in *Tōkan kikō* 東関紀行 (c. 1242), an anonymous travel record that Bashō knew well. See also McCullough 1990a, 430.

36. In spring the slopes would appear reddish purple.

37. Confusingly, the *hokku* appears in the Winter book of Ransetsu's anthology, *Genpōshū* 玄峰集 (precise date unknown). See Imoto and Yayoshi 1968, 161, n. 8.

38. Commonly known as Yamato Takeru, a son of Emperor Keikō credited with many heroic exploits in subduing frontier lands.

39. Tsukuba boasts two peaks, the taller figured as male and the shorter as female. *Renga* (linked verse) was known as the Way of Tsukuba because of a legend that relates how Prince Yamato-dake and an attendant composed a dialogue couplet (*katauta mondō* 片歌問答) that referred to Mount Tsukuba. See *Tsukuba mondō* 筑波問答 (c. 1372), 19; Heldt 2014, 103–4.

then, to not compose a court poem, to pass by without a *hokku*. So fine a sight do the peaks provide!

The bush clover lay like a brocade spread over the ground, reminding me of how Tamenaka showed his fine taste by sending a long box of those flowers back to the Capital as a gift.[40] Before us the fields offered a patchwork of bell flowers, maiden flowers, *karukaya* grasses,[41] and miscanthus, and these, along with the sound of a stag calling for its mate,[42] moved me deeply. It was also a delight to see ponies grazing freely in the fields, strutting around in groups as if they owned the place.[43]

Near sundown we arrived at a village near the Tone River called Fusa. The people there put weirs in the river to catch salmon that are popular in the Shogun's City.[44] As night came on, we stopped to rest in the house of a fisherman, a night-lodging that truly reeked of fish.[45] The moon was clear and unobscured, so we took a boat by night and arrived at Kashima.

From noon the next day the rainfall was so unrelenting that we could not hope to see the moon. But knowing that His Reverence,[46] the former chief priest of Konponji, was living in seclusion near a temple at the foot of Mount Kashima, we went to call on

---

40. In his *Mumyōshō* 無明抄 (precise date unknown), Kamo no Chōmei relates how Tachibana no Tamenaka took twelve boxes with bush clover from Miyagino (in modern Sendai) back with him to Kyoto, where crowds gathered to see the cargo paraded through the streets. See Yonetani 1985a, 114; *Mumyōshō*, 95.

41. "Thatching grass" (*Themeda triandra* var. *japonica*).

42. In classical poetry, the deer's call was considered particularly poignant and was often figured as a call to an absent mate.

43. The area was well known for its horses.

44. In classical poetry, weirs—stakes set in a river current to trap fish and make them easy to net—usually appear in a winter context and are associated with *hiuo* 氷魚 (literally, "ice fish"), a variety of trout. Doubtless the same device was used in other seasons, to catch salmon, as in this case, or other river fish. The Shogun's City (Bukō) refers to Edo, seat of the Tokugawa regime.

45. An allusion to a similarly described fisherman's house in *Tōkan kikō* (148–49; see McCullough 1990a, 441), which in turn alludes to a poem by Bai Juyi titled "Captive Barbarians of the West." The latter speaks of prisoners lying in the filth and stench at night rather than fish odor. See Imoto and Yayoshi 1968, 163, n. 10; Yonetani 1985a, 116. The stench was bad enough that Bashō and his companions decided to travel on by night rather than stay on amidst the stench. Inoue 1992, 115–17, sees allusions to other sources, Chinese and Japanese, as well, and argues that Bashō and his companions went out of their way to have this experience, as part of what it meant to travel.

46. His Reverence, *oshō* 和尚, is an honorific term usually synonymous with *hōgen,* "dharma eye." Here referring to Butchō.

him and stayed the night. A poet once wrote of a place "that caused a man to reflect,"[47] as I recall, and that was true here: for, briefly, at least, I was able to attain a pure state of mind. As the dawn skies cleared a little, His Reverence woke us and we all got up. The profound feelings I had then, inspired by the moonlight and the sound of the rain, filled my breast more than words could express.[48] I was disappointed at not seeing the moon at its fullness after so long a journey, of course; but then, did I not have a confederate in a certain woman who felt low having to go home without composing a poem on the cuckoo?[49]

<table>
<tr><td>At all times
the moon shines unchanging
in the sky above.
The many vistas before us
are the work of passing clouds.[50]

Reverend Butchō</td><td>oriori ni
kawaranu sora no
tsukikage mo
chiji no nagame wa
kumo no ma ni ma ni</td></tr>
</table>

<table>
<tr><td>So swift the moon!
—above branches holding on
to raindrops.[51]

Tōsei</td><td>tsuki hayashi
kozue wa ame o
mochinagara</td></tr>
</table>

---

47. A line from a poem by Du Fu about visiting the Longmen area, titled "A Visit to the Temple of Fengxian at Dragon Gate," in which he describes the bell at sunrise inspiring reflection. See Yonetani 1985a, 118.

48. Yonetani 1985a, 119, notes that usually people would enjoy saké while viewing the moon, but here a spirit of seriousness prevailed. "More than words could express" no doubt means "in a poem," offering an excuse for why he does not offer a *hokku* here—although he does so below.

49. In *The Pillow Book*, Sei Shōnagon writes of being unable to produce a poem for the empress about the cuckoo (*hototogisu*) she heard at Kamo in Kyoto. See *Makura no sōshi*, 137–34; Morris 1967, vol. 1, 109.

50. On the surface, this poem simply describes how our view of the unchanging moon is affected by moving clouds, but the deeper meaning is how the distractions of human perception and understanding can conceal the true light of the Buddhist Law.

51. *Bashō kushū* no. 490. Written at Konponji. A later collection in which this *hokku* appears notes a *dai* (conventional topic), "Rain at a mountain home, and later the moon," and the following three *hokku* are on the same topic. Bashō's poem obviously resonates with the idea at the heart of Butchō's *uta*, offering a momentary misperception in which the moving clouds of a storm just breaking up make it appear as if the moon is racing by. Needless to say, the poem is evidence that Bashō did get glimpses of the moon, although not in its full glory.

Staying in a temple—
where we see the true face
of the moon.[52]

    The Same

tera ni nete
makotogao naru
tsukimi kana

Amidst rain, to bed—
till bamboos bouncing back
wake us to the moon.[53]

    Sora

ame ni nete
take okikaeru
tsukimi kana

The moon, lonèly.
Down from the temple eaves
raindrops fall.

    Sōha

tsuki sabishi
dō no nokiba no
ame shizuku

Before the shrine:

It was long ago
that these pines first flowered.
Autumn of the gods.[54]

    Tōsei

kono matsu no
mibae seshi yo ya
kami no aki

From God's Stone
I would brush them away—
dewdrops on moss.[55]

    Sōha

nuguwabaya
ishi no omashi no
koke no tsuyu

---

52. *Bashō kushū* no. 474. Written at Konponji. The "true face" appears because the poet has been able to "attain tranquility" and see beyond the surface of things.

53. As raindrops fall from the bamboos in the wake of a storm, the stalks tap against each other when bouncing back to their natural posture.

54. *Bashō kushū* no. 649. Written during his visit to Kashima Shrine (see n. 3 above). "Autumn of the gods" has a double meaning referring to both the shrine in the present and that ancient autumn when the pines first "flowered," or grew from seedlings.

55. "The stone of the God" (*ishi no omashi* 石のおまし) refers to a stone mostly buried in the ground where according to legend the god Takemikazuchi once stood to prevent forces below—figured as a huge catfish—from causing earthquakes. Sōha's intent is to in some way show his respect, if only by brushing the raindrops away.

In respect   *hiza oru ya*
even they are on their knees—   *kashikomarinaku*
those lowing deer.[56]   *shika no koe*
    Sora

"House in the paddies"

Out in paddies   *karikakeshi*
half-harvested—stands a crane.   *tazura no tsuru ya*
Village autumn.[57]   *sato no aki*
    Tōsei

For night harvest   *yodakari ni*
I would help, if asked!   *ware ya towaren*
Village moon.[58]   *sato no tsuki*
    Sōha

A farmer's child   *shizu no ko ya*
takes a break from husking rice   *ine surikakete*
to look at the moon.[59]   *tsuki o miru*
    Tōsei

Potato leaves: *imo no ha ya*
in parched fields by a village   *tsuki matsu sato no*
waiting for the moon.[60]   *yakebatake*
    Tōsei

---

56. As at other Shinto shrines, deer roamed free within the Kashima compound. Sora sees their prostrate forms as expressions of faith.

57. *Bashō kushū* no. 650. The crane, always a symbol of peace and good fortune, adds to the already auspicious image of a rice field where harvesting has begun. It also adds a note of color to the landscape. This and the next three *hokku* are all written on the same traditional topic, "House in the paddies" (*denka* 田家).

58. Seeing the farmers out working even at night, Sōha says that on such a lovely moonlit night, he would not mind joining them.

59. *Bashō kushū* no. 475. At harvest time, even children must work, but this one takes a moment's rest to enjoy the full moon. Yonetani 1985a, 123, takes *shizu no ko* to mean "a farmer's son."

60. *Bashō kushū* no. 491. Yonetani 1985a, 123, explains that potatoes generally were ready to harvest at the time of the full moon in the Eighth Month, but in drought there is always a question of how good the crop will be and whether the potatoes will be hard and bitter to the taste.

"Fields"

See my leggings!	*momohiki ya*
Robes dyed by just one pass	*hitohanazuri no*
through bush clover.[61]	*hagigoromo*
Sora	

They've had their fill	*hana no aki*
among flowering fall grasses—	*kusa ni kuiaku*
grazing horses.[62]	*nouma kana*
The Same	

You fields of bush clover—	*hagihara ya*
won't you lend night lodging	*hitoyo wa yadose*
to the mountain dogs?[63]	*yama no inu*
Tōsei	

Composed on the way home when we stayed with Jijun:[64]

This drying straw—	*negura seyo*
let it be your nest tonight,	*wara hosu yado no*
comrade sparrows![65]	*tomosuzume*
The Host	

---

61. After walking through a field of bush clover heavy with dew, the poet offers a conceit, comparing his leggings to robes dyed the color of bush clover flowers after one single treatment. This and the next three *hokku* are written on the traditional topic, "Fields" (*no* 野).

62. Another scene of prosperity, showing horses frolicking, their bellies full of grass.

63. *Bashō kushū* no. 562. In *waka*, wild boar often bed down in the bush clover. Bashō—a *haikai* poet committed to expanding the canon—takes that as a precedent and says, why not mountain dogs, too? (Yonetani 1985a, 124) *yama no inu* 山のいぬ ("mountain dogs") probably refers not to wolves, but to smaller wild dogs that roamed in the hills.

64. See n. 14 above. This and the following two poems are the first three verses of a linked-verse sequence (*mitsumono*).

65. Jijun welcomes his guests, using the image of "comrade sparrows" (*tomosuzume* 友すずめ, birds thought of as fond of human company), to whom he offers straw drying in his house as a nest for the night.

Full in autumn is the fence—   *aki o kometaru*
lined with cedar saplings.[66]   *kune no sashisugi*
    The Guest

For moon gazing   *tsuki min to*
men pull a boat from midriver   *shio hikinoboru*
into shore.[67]   *fune tomete*
    Sora

The year 1687, midway through autumn, the 25th day of the Eighth Month.

---

66. In this 7-7-syllable link to Jijun's *hokku*, Bashō offers praise for the beauty of the house and grounds, where cedar saplings—planted by the owner—are flourishing around a garden fence.
67. Most scholars imagine men on a boat going upriver from a harbor pulling the boat to the bank to take a break to enjoy the moon. Sugiura and Miyamoto 1959, 49, n. 26, and Abe Masami 1965–89, vol. 5, 178, say the better interpretation is that someone calls the boat to shore so that they can get on and enjoy the moon from the water.

KNAPSACK NOTES

Introduction

After returning from Kashima to Edo in the Eighth Month of 1687, Bashō was ready to make good on his promise to travel west once more. Again, he had both personal and artistic motives. Though scholars tend to stress the latter, a headnote to a poem composed when he arrived home some months later makes his emotional connections to Iga Ueno clear:

> It appears that even the sages of the past could not forget their home-towns. As for me, now four years into old age,[1] I find myself nostalgic about everything and cannot bear to ignore my siblings in their declining years. And so beneath skies wet with autumn's first showers, I set out and made my way through snow and frost, arriving in the mountains of Iyō at the end of the Twelfth Month. If only my mother and father were still alive, I thought, feeling overcome with sadness as I remembered their loving-kindness in the past.

In my hometown	*furusato ya*
I weep to see my navel cord	*heso no o ni naku*
at year's end.[2]	*toshi no kure*

First among the poet's priorities, then, was probably his desire to greet the New Year with his siblings, celebrate the thirty-third anniversary of his father's death date,

---

1. Bashō was in his forty-fourth year in 1687.
2. *Bashō kushū* no. 679. See p. 55. The headnote comes from a poetry collection compiled by Chisoku and published in 1716. See Muramatsu 1972, 444–45. Muramatsu also explains that Bashō refers to his hometown not as Iga but as Iyō 伊陽, a Chinese compound meaning "south of the mountains." The umbilical cord reminds him of time gone by, juxtaposing his own birth with his mother's death.

attend to other family problems, and respond to requests from the domain leadership.[3] Next was doubtless his obligation to reply to the countless invitations of disciples to visit Narumi, Atsuta, Ōgaki, and Nagoya, which were now major centers of the Bashō school. Yet one cannot discount the allure of the poetic sights along his route, which would eventually involve the seacoast on Osaka Bay and the mountains of Yoshino, where, we know from the beginning of *Knapsack Notes*, he hoped to see the cherry blossoms in the spring of the following year.[4] The previous autumn, he had postponed his travel plans because of what he called "impediments" and "worries" that he did not specify, along with a flare-up of his chronic illness that made him wary of venturing out in cold weather.[5] Now, however, he seems to have been confident that he was up to the challenges of the road.

The account that would come from the journeying he did for about six months beginning in the Tenth Month of 1687 is perhaps the most problematic of Bashō's travel writings. Indeed, many call it no more than a series of fragments loosely organized and perhaps not even organized by Bashō himself. But other sources, including letters, *haikai* prose pieces, and information from headnotes to poems, make it possible to trace his movements with relative confidence. Before he left, for instance, we know that he was feted at five different going-away parties, most of which involved linked-verse sessions; that he received various gifts to assist him on the road; and that he left care of his cottage to one of his Edo disciples, Kyohaku.[6] Leaving on the 25th day of the Tenth Month, he made good time and arrived in Narumi on the 4th day of the next month.

During the next month or so until he pressed on to his hometown of Iga Ueno, Bashō stayed with men who had been disciples since his journey to the Nagoya area

---

3. The headnote to a poem written at a farewell party reads, "Written to send the Old Master off as he left to return to his hometown" (see Danjō 1968, 70), showing that that is how the journey was thought of by his disciples in Edo, who evidently believed that Bashō would have to be home for some time—perhaps because of the illness of one of his sisters. Bashō's father had died on the 18th day of the Second Month of 1656. Death-anniversary memorial services were held on set years at temples until the fiftieth anniversary. The thirty-third was particularly important because at that time the deceased joined the company of ancestral spirits (*kamisama*). Inoue 1992, 135–41, surmises that Bashō had been invited back to Iga Ueno by Tomoda Ryōbon, a high-ranking samurai in Iga Ueno, probably representing the domain leadership.

4. See below, pp. 51.

5. These concerns emerge in letters to disciples. The words he uses in a letter to Chisoku are *nani ka to shinchū sawaru kotodomo* 何角心中障る事共. See Tanaka 2005, 100.

6. Danjō 1968, 70. The hosts were Rosen (see n. 52 below), Yoshiyuki (n. 51 below), Jokushi, Matsue (otherwise known as Honma Dōetsu), and Kyohaku. See Kon 2005a, 109–10.

two years before. In Narumi, his host was Chisoku, with whom he had been in frequent correspondence. People had waited anxiously for him to arrive, and he attended linked-verse gatherings at various places for three nights running—the 5th, 6th, and 7th. Then he was escorted by Tōyō to the latter's inn near the Atsuta Shrine, just to the north. On the 10th, however, he was off again, escorted by a disciple, a Nagoya dyer named Etsujin.[7] This time he went back up the seacoast to visit his disciple Tokoku, whom he had met in Nagoya two years earlier and with whom he may have had a romantic relationship.[8] In Edo he had heard that Tokoku, a rice dealer in Nagoya, had been banished because of improper speculation and was now living in exile near Irago Point in Mikawa Province, in a village called Hobi.[9] Bashō stayed with Tokoku several days, cheering him up as best he could.[10] The men enjoyed the local sights, touring the area around the cape on horseback. Before leaving, Bashō made arrangements for Tokoku to come to Iga Ueno the next spring, planning to take him along on his journey to Yoshino and other sites on the Kii Peninsula.

Bashō returned to Narumi on the 16th and stayed in the area, having meetings, paying his respects at several temples and shrines, until the middle of the Twelfth Month. Poetry gatherings were the order of his nights, not just in Narumi but also in Atsuta and Nagoya proper, other places where disciples had been waiting impatiently for his appearance. Around the 24th of the Eleventh Month, he suffered a flare-up of his illness and was attended to by a physician—something that seems to have been commonplace on his journeys—but was not deterred from doing his duty. The next day he made the journey to Nagoya and, after meetings with well-wishers, attended a poetry gathering at the home of a prominent literatus.[11] Then he returned to Atsuta and the comfort of Tōyō's inn, where he became ill again, but not so ill that he had

---

7. The reason Etsujin went to Hobi with Bashō was probably because he had done jobs for Tokoku before (Yamakawa 2000, 273). That he went on the Sarashina trip with Bashō also indicates that he was, like Sora, a helper.

8. Traditionally scholars have been ambiguous on this issue. See appendix, "Bashō's Family and Other Relationships."

9. Some studies suggest that Bashō only heard of Tokoku's situation after arriving in Narumi, but Abe Masami shows that he knew about his friend's punishment before leaving Edo. See Danjō 1968, 75. Exactly why Tokoku ended up in Hobi is not known, but it is perhaps significant that the area was under the jurisdiction of a direct vassal of the Edo government rather than the Owari Domain that had jurisdiction in Nagoya.

10. The motives of Bashō's journey to see Tokoku and his attitude are the subject of debate. Inoue 1992, 205–7, argues against Ogata's treatment of Bashō as entirely sympathetic, seeing Bashō as perhaps rather critical of Tokoku's recent offenses.

11. Shōheki.

to forgo another visit to Nagoya several days later, even though it had started snowing. Thus we see the degree of his dedication to disciples, whose visits and invitations clearly outweighed other considerations. By the end of the Twelfth Month, when he arrived at his brother's house in Iga Ueno after a few more days on the road, he was barely well enough to engage in the obligatory drinking at a banquet on New Year's Eve. He greeted the New Year in bed, catching up on sleep, apologizing with a poem the next day.

> As Day Two begins—
> I vow to miss no more
> of flowering spring.[12]

> *futsuka ni mo*
> *nukari wa seji na*
> *hana no haru*

His many send-off parties had shown how prominent Bashō had become in Edo. In Ueno he was treated like a minor celebrity and no longer just the younger brother of a local farmer. For much of his stay, he was put up at the home of local samurai, most conspicuously Ryōbon and Taisō. On the evening of the 9th day of the New Year, his disciple Fūbaku, a samurai of the Tōdō Domain, hosted a banquet and poetry gathering in his honor, and no doubt he was greeted by other people of his hometown in similar ways. Letters show that he had many friends and disciples in the area and also maintained contact with family not only in Ueno proper but in other towns nearby.[13] He stayed in Ueno until the 19th day of the Third Month, during which time he made a three-day trip to Ise Shrine, where he saw disciples[14] and traveled to see Futamigaura on the coast, as well as participating in the thirty-third anniversary services for his father.

The day after his father's memorial services, Tokoku arrived from Irago and the two men, sleeping under the same roof, began enjoying time together and making plans for their journey to Yoshino, the plan being, we learn in a letter, to go as soon as the weather began to warm up.[15] By this time Bashō was staying in Taisō's cottage, called Hyōchikuan, "The Cottage of Gourds and Bamboo," on the southeastern edge of Ueno, while also spending time at the new cottage of his old friend Dohō.[16] Finally,

---

12. *Bashō kushū* no. 8.
13. See the letter to his brother in Kon 2005b, 116–17.
14. In a letter to a disciple named Heian, Bashō notes that he stayed in Ise Yamada with his disciple Ranchō and, thanks to an introduction from Heian, was able to call on Ajiro Hirokazu, a high-ranking shrine official and *haikai* poet. At Hirokazu's house he provided a *hokku* for a *haikai renga* sequence involving eight poets from the area. Tanaka 2005, 122–24.
15. Okada 1972, *kaisetsu*, 53; Tanaka 2005, 122.
16. Dohō called his cottage Minomushian ("Bagworm Cottage"), taking the title from a *hokku* Bashō had composed the previous autumn. See Danjō 1968, 90.

it was around this time that he was invited to visit Tōdō Yoshinaga, the heir of his early patron and *haikai* master Sengin. It was there that he composed one of his most famous *hokku*, looking out on the cherry blossoms.

Ah, the many things   *samazama no*
they call back to mind: *koto omoidasu*
cherry blossoms.[17]   *sakura kana*

What went through Bashō's mind as he sat with the heir of his departed patron, dead now more than two decades, we cannot know, but certainly looking out at the blossoms put him in a reflective mood as he departed just a few days later, for Yoshino, which in all of Japan was the most famous place for cherry blossoms. On the journey described in *Bones Bleaching in the Fields*, he had experienced the rugged mountains of that area alone and in autumn. This time he was with his companion Tokoku and could anticipate seeing the storied trees at the height of their glory. In honor of the occasion, Tokoku adopted an elegant sobriquet with somewhat erotic connotations, Mangikumaru 万菊丸, or "Lad of Ten Thousand Chrysanthemums."[18]

Assisted by a servant named Roku,[19] Bashō and Tokoku then embarked, on the 19th day of the Third Month of 1688, on a tour of important poetic and historic sites on the Kii Peninsula. Their route took them to visit the grave of the medieval poet Kenkō,[20] and then on to Yoshino, Mount Kōya, Waka Bay, Nara, and Osaka, where they spent six days, probably because Bashō needed to rest.[21] Then they headed to Suma and Akashi on the coast just to the west. In Nara, a group of supporters from Iga Ueno came to visit,[22] and in Naniwa he visited with one disciple, Isshō, an old friend likewise from his hometown; but for the most part the companions stayed in more rustic accommodations and did not face the sort of professional duties that had so preoccupied Bashō the previous autumn. Instead, all through the trip he spent his time at temples, shrines, and famous sites, many of which he memorialized in *hokku*,

---

17. *Bashō kushū* no. 127.
18. See appendix, "Bashō's Family and Other Relationships."
19. Danjō 1968, 91, notes that Roku accompanied the travelers for more than a month, until they arrived in Nara.
20. A later source identifies the place as at the foot of Mount Kunimi on the eastern edge of Yoshino. Tradition identifies it as Kenkō's home in his later years, but hard evidence for the contention is lacking.
21. Danjō 1968, 100.
22. At least five men came, including his staunch supporters Ensui and Takutai, both merchants.

although he claimed again to be too overwhelmed for words at the most famous of places, Yoshino—once again pursuing the rhetoric of reverent silence.[23]

The journey ended on the 21st day of the Fourth Month, in Akashi, with Bashō looking out on the sea and imagining scenes from centuries before, preeminently the frantic escape of the Taira forces after their defeat at the temporary imperial palace at Ichinotani.[24] A short list left by Tokoku summing up the journey in a catalog betrays no such emotions but does give us a useful overview of the trek the men had enjoyed together. First, he says they had traveled 130 *li* from Iga in thirty-four days, by boat and palanquin and on foot, and then he gives us more numbers, writing that they had encountered rain fourteen days, seen seven waterfalls and thirteen graves of famous people, crossed six passes, climbed seven slopes, and seen six mountain peaks.[25] One cannot avoid the impression that the trek must have been physically demanding for Bashō, who was forty-five years old and not in robust health.

And that was of course not all: the text would end in Akashi, but the traveling could not. Other sources tell us that Bashō and Tokoku in fact journeyed northeast to see other places in Settsu Province, arriving in Kyoto on the 23rd. There they spent nearly three weeks, enjoying the pleasures of the city (including a Kabuki performance), and visiting Bashō's disciple Kyorai and the calligrapher Unchiku. It was at this time that Bashō parted with Tokoku, who returned to his place of exile in Hobi. The master himself left Kyoto midway through the Fifth Month, with a Gifu disciple named Kihaku as guide, and traveled to visit disciples in Ōtsu and then on to the Nagoya area, where countless *haikai* gatherings awaited him. It need hardly be noted that he was once again planning a journey, on which he would embark from Gifu in the Eighth Month. This time he would go to see a famous moon-viewing site in Shinano Province, before turning his steps toward Edo.

***

We know less than we would like to about how *Knapsack Notes* came to be, although the text that is universally used by scholars was published in Kyoto by Bashō's disciple Otokuni in 1709. One common theory is that after fiddling with the account of his travels of 1687–88 for some years, Bashō finally lost interest in making it into a

---

23. In fact, he seems to have composed a number of poems. See p. 47.
24. A daring assault by Minamoto forces down a steep mountainside surprised the Taira in their encampment on the beach and left them no option but to flee to boats through heavy surf.
25. The memo was attached to a letter from Bashō to Sōshichi. See Tanaka 2005, 137–38.

tightly coherent narrative, instead putting all of his energy into the work that is widely acknowledged as his masterpiece, *The Narrow Road through the Hinterlands*.[26] Another is that it was intended as a tribute to Tokoku, who died in the Third Month of 1690, and therefore something Bashō worked on seriously after that date.[27] More recently, Hama Moritarō has done a detailed analysis arguing that *Knapsack Notes* as we have it now was in fact among the last of Bashō's writings to be written, during his final months.[28] External evidence shows conclusively that many of the poems in *Knapsack Notes* were written or at least greatly revised much later, and it is clear that the sections at the beginning and end of the text were written independently and added on.

Moreover, the issue of how much editing Otokuni did is also contested, although it seems certain that he was working from a less than coherent text, which he allowed to go out into the world retaining that quality.[29] As Hama argues, the duty that Otokuni felt as the one entrusted with the master's behest must have been immense, motivating him to make it available, in some form consistent with Bashō's wishes.[30] By 1709 three of the master's travel writings, including *The Narrow Road through the Hinterlands*, had been published, after all, and Otokuni no doubt felt it was time for the text left with him to circulate more broadly, whether it seemed polished and complete or not.

But it is too easy to endlessly focus on perceived "imperfections" of the text, for the fact is that it does cohere as an independent work of literature. To begin with, after an initial essay that is not unrelated to the rest of the text thematically, *Knapsack Notes* proceeds in a basically chronological manner through the poet's departure from Edo, his time in the Narumi area, his visit to Tokoku back up the coast in Mikawa, his sojourns in Iga and Ise, and then on to Yoshino and other important sites, ending with his highly nostalgic encounter with historic sites on the coast near Suma. What's

---

26. See Okada 1972, *kaisetsu*, 60.

27. Ogata Tsutomu in fact argues that the text was written as a *chinkon* 鎮魂, a sort of requiem praying for the repose of Tokoku's soul. See Ogata 1977. Inoue 1992, 206–7, characterizes Ogata's reading as highly subjective.

28. Specifically, Hama 2016, 112, determines that Bashō probably entrusted the text to Otokuni in the Fifth or Sixth Month of 1694, when he was in Ōmi.

29. Writing about Bashō's travel writing, Kusumoto 2009, 347, concludes that "one simply cannot take the entire structure of the text as a product of Bashō's own fashioning." However, Akabane 1970, 262, 268–69, 280–84, speaking for many other scholars, argues that *Knapsack Notes* is no more fragmented that *Bones Bleaching in the Fields* and that its pattern of allusions and constant evocation of the spirit of travel shows enough subtle fashioning by Bashō that it cannot be dismissed as a mere collection of fragments.

30. See Hama 2016, 112, 143–44. Possession of such an object in the master's hand came with a certain cachet, which improved Otokuni's standing in his area.

more, we know enough about the genesis of the text to conclude that Bashō was doing his tinkering within the context of another example of travel writing, following on *Bones Bleaching in the Fields*. The text began as a number of separate pieces—what Inoue Toshiyuki calls *tampen kikō*, "short travel accounts"[31]—focusing first on his persona and his approach to travel writing, and then on dimensions of his experience in Iga Ueno, Ise, Yoshino, Kōya, Wakayama, Nara, and the coast at Suma. But when put together, those pieces, all by Bashō, and probably joined together by him before his death, do present a basic narrative.

Indeed, I would argue that the text presents two consecutive narratives loosely joined together. The first begins in the autumn of 1687 with a famous self-portrait of the poet, who uses a paragraph to describe himself as one Fūrabō 風羅坊, "Master Gauze in the Wind," no doubt alluding to his rather frail state, both professionally and physically, and then goes on to offer the poet's thoughts on travel writing, finally fleshing out his theories by offering a very slight account of Bashō's journeying in Narumi, Mikawa, and Iga, in both prose and poetry—the latter covering the time he was intensely involved in linked-verse sessions with disciples, and not "traveling" in a strict sense. The second account is more akin to *Bones Bleaching in the Fields*, focusing on the independent journey he took with Tokoku, beginning with a sentence that sounds like a new beginning because that is what it is, quite literally: "Halfway through the Third Month, my heart grew restless, and I let that feeling be my guide, with the blossoms of Yoshino as my goal." Bashō has a new companion and is setting out to explore a specific region known particularly for its abundance of famous sites.[32]

The latter of these two accounts, while offering a less thorough treatment than we might desire, presents a better balance of poetry and prose, while also giving us a better picture of the poet's encounters with celebrated sites. For, as in his other travel writing, Bashō here gives us glimpses of the present and the past—of places where Saigyō had walked, where the Heike had camped, fought, and fallen. In this sense, however imperfect it may be, *Knapsack Notes* does show us Bashō at work on his poetic project. If we are left wanting a less disjointed text, especially about his days in Yoshino, for instance, we could do worse than remember what he said near the beginning of *Knapsack Notes* as we have it, where he pointedly criticizes conventional travel journals and hints that his attempt would be something different:

---

31. Inoue 1982, 79–81; 1992, 183.

32. This argument is strengthened by the fact that Otokuni published *A Journey to Sarashina* with *Knapsack Notes*, thus putting both Bashō texts of 1687–88 in one edition. See p. 248.

Here I have assembled, not always in strict order, jottings about places that have remained in my memory, saying to you, reader: don't hear what I say too seriously; take it as you would the ramblings of a drunk or the nonsense of a man talking in his sleep.[33]

It is too easy to dismiss this statement as false modesty. Rather, I take it that Bashō is announcing his work as a work of imagination and art in which he presents himself as a *hyōhakusha* 漂白者, a poetic wanderer in the tradition of Saigyō and Sōgi.[34] Textual study has proven that he has indeed not kept strictly to the order in which he experienced sites, and it is also clear that his account cannot be taken literally in every particular. We know, for example, that he concocted some episodes,[35] and despite claiming that he was too overawed to produce a proper *hokku* at Yoshino, he probably did produce the following poem at the time.

Cherries in full bloom.   *hanazakari*
Yet how everyday a scene   *yama wa higoro no*
in murky dawn light.[36]   *asaborake*

In the face of such evidence—which is to be found elsewhere in Bashō's travel writings, too—one must agree with Akabane that in Bashō's approach to travel writing, "revising became necessary."[37] And this leads inevitably to the conclusion that what Otokuni was working with was not just raw notes, but a text or group of linked texts that had been structured to a certain extent before he received it and therefore can properly be called a work of travel writing by Bashō.[38] To be sure, the text was not

---

33. Yayoshi and Nishimura 1968, 38.
34. Here I follow Inoue 1992, 247–60, who analyzes the close relationship between the final revision of *Genjūan no ki* (1690–91) and the genesis of *Knapsack Notes*, concluding that those final revisions involved excising a number of images related to Bashō's identity as a wanderer and instead creating an image of the poet informed by the example of Kamo no Chōmei in his *Hōjōki* 方丈記 (1212).
35. See Akabane 1970, 279, 286, 295.
36. *Bashō kushū* no. 158. Noted by Sugiura and Miyamoto 1959, 60, n. 10; Imoto 1972, 323, n. 19; Kon 2005a, 132. See also Danjō 1968, 95. Danjō also notes one case of what he terms "pure fictionalizing" in one instance and in general argues that Bashō's account is highly fashioned.
37. Akabane 1970, 283. "Revising" translates *suikō* 推敲, which might also be rendered as "polishing" or "fashioning." In this passage Akabane is focusing on the *hokku*, but it is clear that he believes the same kind of fashioning characterized *Knapsack Notes* as a whole.
38. Akabane 1970, 299.

fully realized and included gaps, and remained in that sense incomplete.[39] But it is hard to believe that it was just a sheaf of papers left to Otokuni to organize all by himself. For one thing, the journey that produced the text already existed in the minds of those who knew the master—a narrative frame that was inevitably already there in the background.

What were Bashō's preoccupations, as revealed in his writing? That question is easily answered because at the beginning of *Knapsack Notes* he addresses it directly, stating his resolve "to be called a traveler," embracing a role that he understands in Daoist terms amply suggested by the metaphor of being tossed like "a leaf on the wind" and the idea of drawing closer to "the world of wind and clouds." For it is in order to live that way that he tells us he has cast aside worldly ambition and embraced *haikai* as his Way. Among other things, this attitude meant that, as I have argued elsewhere, the road was for Bashō a place to test his mastery of poetry and his professional talents as a master working with disciples.[40] But it is important not to stop our analysis there, for, as noted above, Bashō goes on to commit himself not just to travel but to a new and different kind of *travel writing*. This is not to negate the characterization of *Knapsack Notes* as largely fragmentary (might episodic be a better word?) or even to suggest that he thought of it as a completely finished work, but it is to again shift our focus to what the text *is* rather than what it is not. One need not agree completely with Akabane's contention that a skein of allusions and the spirit of travel provide the text with a subtle unity to admit that even as it is, the text presents the experience of sojourning through a particular time and place. And at the heart of it, especially in the accounts of his time in storied places like Yoshino, Kōya, and Suma, is an account of his encounter with landscapes imprinted in his mind with history—focusing not just on natural scenes, but on the people, past and present, in those scenes. In this sense, *Knapsack Notes* establishes an important pattern that would culminate in *The Narrow Road through the Hinterlands*.

---

39. For a concise statement of the state of the text, see Kusumoto 1994, 34–51. Hama gives us our most complete argument about the genesis of the text, which he sees as going through three stages before Bashō's death, and then another stage in the hands of Otokuni.
40. See Carter 1997, 67.

KNAPSACK NOTES

Within the hundred bones and nine orifices of my body[41] is a certain being; here I shall call him Fūrabō, "Master Gauze in the Wind"—by which I mean a thin fabric easily torn by the wind.[42] Since long ago this Fūrabō has loved mad verses, so much so that in the end I made them my livelihood. Sometimes I grew tired of poetry and nearly cast it aside; other times I prided myself in triumphing over others. In my breast a conflict raged, for which my body suffered. For a while I sought to achieve worldly stature, but was prevented by Fūrabō; then I set myself to studying to achieve enlightenment, only to be defeated by him again and end up following—without ability, without skill—this one lone path.[43] The *waka* of Saigyō, the *renga* of Sōgi, the paintings of Sesshū, the tea of Rikyū—there is one thread that runs through them all.[44] For it is the essence of art to follow the Way of creation,[45] taking the four seasons as a companion. Do that, and what you see will never *not* be a flower; what you ponder will never *not* be the moon. To not see the form before you as a flower is to be like a

---

41. Zhuangzi describes the human body as made up of "the hundred bones, the nine orifices, and the six viscera." See Mair 1994, 15. The statement appears in the chapter titled "On the Equality of Things," which presents a critique of ordinary distinctions and the mutual dependence of opposites.

42. This compound is made up of the characters for "wind," "gauze," and the word for "temple dormitory," which in this case is a synecdoche for "priest."

43. The pronoun references in this passage (from "Since long ago" to "this lone path") are ambiguous at best. I follow Ueno 2008, 3–4, in making Furabō the rhetorical personification of *haikai*, a force within Bashō that "prevents" and "defeats" Bashō whenever he tries to stray from his commitment to *haikai*. In *Genjūan no ki* (504), Bashō says that he once was indeed envious of those who worked as officials, and also considered entering the priesthood, but instead opted for a life of poetry.

44. Here Bashō refers to four different artistic discourses: the traditional court poetry of Saigyō, the classical linked verse of Sōgi, the ink-wash paintings of Sesshū, and the tea ceremony of Sen no Rikyū, all artist-monks who pursued their arts as a religious Way. The "one thread" (貫道する物) that runs through all their work remains vague, but one must assume that all shared a commitment to *zōka*, the "creative." "There is one thread that runs through them all" is almost a direct quote from book four, item fifteen, of the Confucian *Analects*. See Lau 1983, 32–33. Inoue 1992, 154–260, also draws attention to a passage of Sōgi's *Tsukushi no michi no ki*.

45. The "essence of art" translates *fūga*, a term that Bashō often uses to mean *haikai* but here means art more generally.

barbarian; to not have a flower in your mind is to be like the birds and the beasts.[46] So, I say, go out from among the barbarians, separate yourself from the birds and beasts: follow the creative, get back to the creative![47]

The Godless Month[48] began with unsettled skies, and I felt myself a leaf on the wind, destination unknown.

A traveler—	*tabibito to*
that is what I shall be called.	*waga na yobaren*
First rain showers.	*hatsushigure*

Again, sasanqua flowers	*mata sazanka o*
for lodging, night after night.[49]	*yadoyado ni shite*

Chōtarō[50] of Iwaki Province kindly provided this second verse at a farewell gathering at the house of Kikaku.

The season—winter.	*toki wa fuyu*
But it is from Yoshino	*yoshino o komen*
we expect a gift.[51]	*tabi no tsuto*

---

46. These two sentences seem to mean that what one looks at as a flower becomes a flower, and what one ponders as the moon becomes the moon, the conclusion being that not to see the beauty and creative energy in things is to be a barbarian or beast.

47. For the Daoist reverberations of the "creative" (J. *zōka*; C. *zaohua*) in Bashō's poetics, see Qiu 2005, 82–88.

48. *Kannazuki*, a shortened form of *Kaminazuki* 神無月, the Tenth Month in the lunar calendar, when according to legend all the gods left their home shrines to gather at Izumo Shrine.

49. The *hokku* is *Bashō kushū* no. 684. The full sequence is not extant. The headnote to the two-verse link in the *haikai* collection *Zoku minashiguri* 続虚栗, and later in several other works, reads exactly as the sentence before the poem here. The date was the 11th day of the Tenth Month, 1687, a week or so prior to his departure. Bashō and nine disciples, including his most prominent supporters, Kikaku and Ransetsu, composed a forty-four-verse sequence (*yoyoshi*) with *tabibito to* as the first verse.

50. Also known by his *haikai* name, Yoshiyuki. A samurai retainer serving the Naitō clan of Iwaki Province.

51. Originally, this *hokku* began with the line "The season—autumn," which was in keeping with the time it was composed, the Ninth Month. Bashō evidently made the revision to be consistent with his statement at the beginning of his narrative, i.e., that it was in the Tenth Month—the first month of winter—that he felt the urge to set out on the road. Asking for a

This *hokku* was provided by Lord Rosen,[52] but it was just the first of the parting gifts I received from old friends, from people well known to me and not so well known, along with disciples. Some brought me poems or bits of prose, others packets of coins for buying sandals, all showing their regard. Hence it needed no labor for me to prepare my three months' worth of food for the road.[53] Paper robes, padded coat, caps, stockings for my feet, all these, thanks to the kindness of many, I gathered in, leaving me no worries about suffering in the cold of frost and snow. People invited me onto boats or to villas, or brought me gifts of saké and food to offer as prayers for my journey. So many showed concern at my parting that I began to feel a little awkward, as if I were a person of real consequence going out on the road.

Now then: when it comes to travel diaries,[54] Lord Ki,[55] Chōmei,[56] and the Nun Abutsu wrote with such style and feeling that all who followed them seemed to make something too similar—never a new brew. Much less could someone of my shallow understanding and meager talent with the brush take on such a task. Almost anyone can write, "That day it rained, clearing at noon; in this place was a pine tree, in that place So-and-So River flowed by," after all—which leads one to think, if you are aren't up to Huang's wonders or Su's novelties,[57] then you'd best say nothing!

Yet the fact is that the scenes one saw at this place or that *do* stay in one's mind, and the pains one suffered spending the night at lodgings in the mountains and fields— well, they may provide things to chat about later on. So, then, as a gesture toward the world of wind and clouds,[58] here I have assembled, not always in strict order, jottings

---

gift "from Yoshino" indicates that Bashō was planning to visit there—and not in the winter, but in spring, the time of the cherry blossoms for which it was famous. Abe Masami 1965–89, vol. 5, 180, argues that *tsuto* does not mean "gift" here, but rather "travel pack," which would make the last two lines read something like, "Thinking of Yoshino you go, / travel pack on your back."

52. Rosenkō. With the exception of Bashō and Kikaku, all of the other participants in this sequence were students of Rosen. Kusumoto 2006, 60, argues that Bashō probably became acquainted with the samurai leaders of the Naitō clan through the Tōdō in Iga Ueno. Kusumoto 2006, 344, notes that the gathering was held at Rosen's house.

53. See p. 6, n. 15, above.

54. The term he uses is *michi no nikki*.

55. Ki no Tsurayuki, author of *Tosa nikki*.

56. Kamo no Chōmei. In Bashō's time it was believed that he was the author of the medieval travel record *Tōkan kikō* (1252?).

57. Huang Tingjian and Su Dongpo, Chinese scholars, poets, and painters that were both known for their creativity.

58. Meaning ever-changing natural phenomena, an articulation of what he calls *zōka*, the creative force.

about places that have remained in my memory, saying to you, reader: don't hear what I say too seriously, no, take it as you would the babbling of a drunk[59] or the nonsense of a man talking in his sleep.

Written when I stayed at Narumi:

Cape of Stars.	*hoshizaki no*
"Gaze out into the gloom!"	*yami o miyo to ya*
cry the plovers.[60]	*naku chidori*

I learned that Lord Asukai Masaaki had stayed at this house, honoring them with a poem that reads, ". . . at the Strand of Narumi / Kyoto seems far away— / off there in the distance, / with the sea in between."[61] When they told me His Lordship had written a copy out in his own hand, I gave them this:

Only halfway	*kyō made wa*
to the capital, and yet—	*mada nakazora ya*
snow clouds.[62]	*yuki no kumo*

I was planning to visit Tokoku,[63] where he was hidden away in a place called Hobi in Mikawa, so I sent a message to Etsujin, and we headed back down the road twenty-five *li* from Narumi, staying one night at Yoshida.

So cold a night!	*samukeredo*
Two sleeping side by side—	*futari nuru yo zo*
that works out fine.[64]	*tanomoshiki*

---

59. Scholars take the garbled character in the text here as a mistake or transcription error for *mōgo* 妄語, "falsehoods," and suggest a passage in *Zhuangzi* where Zhang Wuzi says to Qu Quezi, "Let me say a few careless things to you and you listen carelessly, all right?" (Tr. Mair 1994, 22).

60. *Bashō kushū* no. 803. Composed on the 7th day of the Eleventh Month as the first verse of a thirty-six-verse sequence at the home of Yasunobu in Narumi. Hoshizaki was located on the coast just northwest of Narumi and was famous for its plovers. On a gloomy night, when the poet cannot hope for a view of the stars that the place is famous for, the plovers seem to be calling, "Search for us instead."

61. The house was Bokugen's. Masaaki was a poet in the traditional *uta* form and scion of an important court lineage. The first line of the poem is, "Here, today" (*kyō wa nao / miyako mo tōku / narumigata / harukeki umi o / naka ni hedatete*). See Ueno 2008, 10, n. 4.

62. *Bashō kushū* no. 723. Composed on the 5th day of the Eleventh Month for a thirty-six-verse sequence at the home of Bokugen.

63. See above, p. 4.

64. *Bashō kushū* no. 664. Composed on the way to Hobi on the 11th day of the Eleventh Month.

At Amatsunawate a narrow path runs straight through the paddies, and the wind blowing up from the sea is cold.

Winter day.   *fuyu no hi ya*
I, frozen on my horse—   *bashō ni kōru*
like my shadow.[65]   *kagebōshi*

From the village at Hobi it is just one *li* or so to Irago Point. The point is connected to Mikawa and separated from Ise by the sea, yet for some reason it is listed as one of the famous sites of Ise in *Man'yōshū*.[66] It is on the beaches here that they collect *go* stones—what are called Iragojiro,[67] I think. Kotsuyama[68] is a place where they take hawks. On the south it juts out into the sea and is the place where migrating hawks come first, so they say.[69] Thinking of *uta* about the hawks of Irago, I felt even more moved by the place.

Just one hawk—   *taka hitotsu*
but I'm glad I found it   *mitsukete ureshi*
at Irago Point.[70]   *iragozaki*

The refurbishing of Atsuta Shrine:

So clear the glow   *toginaosu*
of a mirror newly polished!   *kagami mo kiyoshi*
Petals of snow.[71]   *yuki no hana*

---

65. *Bashō kushū* no. 752. The shadow is cast on the water in the rice paddies.
66. "The Collection of Ten Thousand Years," c. 759, the first great anthology of Japanese poetry. In that work, Irago Point is sometimes treated as an island off the coast of Ise. See Imoto 1972, 315, n. 20; Imoto and Yayoshi 1968, 168, n. 17.
67. 伊良湖白, "Irago Whites." It appears that the *go* stones were made from seashells rather than stones. See Imoto 1972, 316, n. 1.
68. 骨山, "Bone Hill." Now known as Koyama. See Ueno 2008, 13, n. 3.
69. The area was known as a stop for hawks migrating from the continent.
70. *Bashō kushū* no. 799. Composed on the 12th day of the Eleventh Month. On the surface, this *hokku* means that the poet was happy to see at least one of the hawks for which the area was famous, but Imoto 1972, 316, n. 4, voices the opinion of most scholars in taking the lone hawk as a metaphor for Tokoku, although it is puzzling that he does not mention his friend by name but instead harks back to old poetic traditions. See Kusumoto 2006, 104–7. Bashō probably has in mind two poems from *Man'yōshū* (vol. 1, nn. 23–24) associated with the cheerless life of Prince Omi, who legend says was exiled to Irago, and poems on hawks by Saigyō.
71. *Bashō kushū* no. 725. Composed for a thirty-six-verse duo sequence with Tōyō sometime between the 21st and the 25th of the Twelfth Month, at the latter's home in Atsuta. On his

I wrote the following when I was taken care of by people from Hōsa[72] who came to see me and I was able to rest for a time.

There will be people	*hakone kosu*
at the pass at Hakone.	*hito mo arurashi*
This morning—snow.[73]	*kesa no yuki*

At the gathering of a certain person:

I tidy it up	*tametsukete*
to do some snow-viewing—	*yukimi ni makaru*
my wrinkled robe.[74]	*kamiko kana*

I'm off, then:	*iza yukamu*
out to enjoy the snow	*yuki ni korobu*
till I drop.[75]	*tokoro made*

At a *haikai* gathering held by a certain person:

---

earlier visit, Bashō had found the shrine in great need of repair. See p. 16. Renovation had taken place between the Fourth and Seventh Months of 1687. The snowfall—purifying the scene—seems like nature's acceptance of the renovation. Bashō had left Chisoku's place in Narumi, where he had been for a week or so before moving to Tōyō's place in Atsuta on the 21st of the Eleventh Month.

72. 蓬左. The area west of Atsuta Shrine, i.e., Nagoya. Literally, it means "left of Hō," the latter being an abbreviation of Hōraikyū 蓬莱宮, an alternative name for Atsuta Shrine. The name Hōrai was based on a legend telling how a Chinese emissary visited there, searching the east for an island of immortals (C. Peng lai; J. Hōrai).

73. *Bashō kushū* no. 726. This poem was the first verse of a full thirty-six-verse sequence held on the 4th day of the Twelfth Month at the Atsuta villa of a man named Chōsetsu of the Minoya, who appears to have come from Nagoya along with the other four participants in the event, Jokō, Yasui, Etsujin, and Kakei. Now safely with his supporters, in comfortable accommodations, the poet can enjoy the beauty of a morning snowfall, but he also thinks of other travelers facing an ordeal back up the Tōkai Road at Hakone Pass, which he had traversed just a month or so before.

74. *Bashō kushū* no. 781. From a thirty-six-verse sequence involving Kakei, Yasui, Etsujin, and other Nagoya poets composed on the 28th day of the Eleventh Month. "Certain person" refers to Shōheki of Nagoya, where Bashō had arrived on the 26th.

75. *Bashō kushū* no. 737. Composed in Nagoya on the 3rd day of the Twelfth Month at the home of Sekidō, and therefore not in proper order.

For plum scent	*ka o saguru*
I searched, and found the eaves	*ume ni kura miru*
of your storehouse.[76]	*nokiba kana*

During this time I had visits from connoisseurs from Ōgaki and Gifu in Mino and we composed *haikai* sequences, some of thirty-six verses and some of just one sheet.[77]

On the 10th day of the Twelfth Month, I left Nagoya, making for my hometown.

Nights on the road	*tabine shite*
bring me to a sight I know:	*mishi ya ukiyo no*
year-end cleaning.[78]	*susuharai*

From Kuwana, I came to Hinaga Village—famous for the lines "From Kuwana I came, / without a thing to eat."[79] There I rented a horse, but as I climbed Tsuetsukizaka, "Walking Staff Slope," my saddle slipped from beneath me and I fell off.

Walking Staff Slope.	*kachi naraba*
On foot, I would not have toppled	*tsuetsukizaka wo*
from my horse![80]	*rakuba kana*

I wrote this last *hokku* out of such annoyance that I forgot to include a season word.

In my hometown	*furusato ya*
I weep to see my navel cord	*heso no o ni naku*
at year's end.[81]	*toshi no kure*

---

76. *Bashō kushū* no. 825. Composed around this same time in Nagoya. In this case the "certain person" has not been identified but was probably a *haikai* poet living in Nagoya. Another document calls him the resident of the Bōsentei 防川亭.

77. *Hitoori*, the first eighteen verses.

78. *Bashō kushū* no. 787. Year-end cleaning—literally "brushing the soot away"—took place in this era on the 13th day of the Twelfth Month. A letter from Bashō, in Nagoya, to Sanpū in Edo on that day quotes this poem (Tanaka 2005, 119).

79. The remaining lines of the anonymous poem are "passing Star River / as night gave way to dawn / at Hinaga Village" (*kuwana yori / kuwade kinureba / hoshikawa no / asaki wa suginu / hinaga narikeri*). Imoto 1972, 317, n. 17, identifies this as an *uta* quoted in various contemporary travel guides, including *Meisho hōgakushō* 名所方角鈔.

80. *Bashō kushū* no. 836. Bashō traveled by boat from Nagoya to Kuwana and then by palanquin and by horse. In a preface to this same poem given to someone, he says that the groom leading the horse scolded him for falling off. See Kon 2005a, 122.

81. *Bashō kushū* no. 679. In *Bones Bleaching in the Fields* (see p. 12), when Bashō arrived home, his brother had shown him locks of his mother's hair kept as a memento. See n. 2 above.

On the last day of the year, we drank till late at night, drowning our sorrows over the past year, and I slept through New Year's Day.

As Day Two begins—	*futsuka ni mo*
I vow to miss no more	*nukari wa seji na*
of flowering spring.[82]	*hana no haru*

T he beginning of spring"

Spring arrives	*haru tachite*
and on the 9th, already—	*mada kokonoka no*
these fields and hills.[83]	*noyama kana*

On leafless scrub	*kareshiba ya*
a low shimmer of warmth—	*yaya kagerou no*
an inch or two.[84]	*ichini sun*

In Iga Province, in a place called Awanoshō, stands a remnant from the time of Shunjō Shōnin that people call Gohōzan Shindaibutsuji, "Temple of the New Great Buddha at Mount Gohō." The name will stand in memory for a millennium, but the tile roofs have collapsed, leaving only foundation stones, while the monks' quarters have quite vanished, now just a name lingering in fields and orchards. The Buddha statue, once sixteen feet tall, is covered in green moss, leaving only its head as an object of worship. Still erect, however, is the image of Shunjō, an undeniable witness of ages past that brings tears to one's eyes. The lotus base of the statue and the seats of the lion guardians protrude from the weeds that have taken the place over, making one feel as if one is beholding that famous withered grove.[85]

---

82. *Bashō kushū* no. 8. See p. 42.
83. *Bashō kushū* no. 9. Composed on the 9th day of the New Year, at the house of Bashō's disciple Fūbaku, a samurai in service to the Tōdō clan.
84. *Bashō kushū* no. 35. Also composed at the house of Fūbaku. "Shimmer of warmth" translates the verb *kagerou*, referring to the shimmer of heated air meeting the colder air of the sky above.
85. The precise dating of this episode is uncertain, but Kon 2005a, 124, places it on Bashō's way to Ise. His old friends from Iga Ueno, Sōmu, and Ensui (see Danjō 1968, 89), went along. "That famous withered grove" refers to the grove where the Buddha died.

That tall statue—
now a shimmering pillar
above a stone.[86]

jōroku ni
kagerou takashi
ishi no ue

Ah, the many things
they call back to mind:
cherry blossoms.[87]

samazama no
koto omoidasu
sakura kana

At Ise Yamada:

What tree in flower
produces it, I do not know.
But, ah, such a scent![88]

nani no ki no
hana to wa shirazu
nioi kana

But, to go *naked*—
still in the Second Month
amidst storm winds![89]

hadaka ni wa
mada kisaragi no
arashi kana

---

86. *Bashō kushū* no. 36. Kon 2005a, 124, states that this *hokku* and an account of the trip to Gohōzan Shindaibutsuji were written in Iga Ueno after the poet's return from Ise.
87. *Bashō kushū* no. 127. Composed in Iga Ueno at the town house of Tanganshi, heir of Sengin, the patron of Bashō's youth. See p. 43. Yuzawa 1982, 51, n. 88, sees this verse functioning as a conclusion to Bashō's time at home, which might explain why Bashō doesn't include a headnote about the specific occasion.
88. *Bashō kushū* no. 151. Composed at the Outer Shrine at Ise on the 4th day of the Second Month of 1688, the first of his thirteen days in the area; first verse for a thirty-six-verse dedicatory sequence presented to the shrine. Among the participants were Masumitsu, the shrine guide who was Bashō's host; some Ise poets; and Tokoku, who had come from Hobi. Bashō probably alludes to a poem by Saigyō that may not be authentic but was widely believed to be so. It was supposedly composed when he was visiting Ise (*Saigyō waka shūi* 2109): "Composed on a festival day at the Great Shrine: 'Just what it is / that resides in this place / I do not know / yet out of gratitude / the tears come flowing down'" (*nanigoto no / owashimasu ka wa / shiranedomo / katajikenasa ni / namida koboruru*).
89. *Bashō kushū* no. 24. Composed when Bashō was on his way back to Iga Ueno from Ise on the 17th of the Second Month. The allusion is to an incident in the life of the monk Zōga Shōnin in which, while on pilgrimage to Ise, he removed his clothes and gave them to a beggar in order to rid himself of all signs of high status (*Senjūshō*, 28).

At Bodai Temple:

Please tell me	*kono yama no*
the sad tale of this mountain—	*kanashisa tsugeyo*
you, digging potatoes.[90]	*tokorohori*

At Ryūno Shōsha:

First, I must ask:	*mono no na o*
what do you call these reeds,	*mazu tou ashi no*
green with new leaves?[91]	*wakaba kana*

At a gathering held at the Setsudō of Ajiro Minbu:

From a plum tree	*ume no ki ni*
a new shoot is rising forth—	*nao yadorigi ya*
in full flower.[92]	*ume no hana*

At a gathering at a cottage:

Planted potatoes	*imo uete*
and weeds around the gate,	*kado wa mugura no*
green with new leaves.[93]	*wakaba kana*

---

90. *Bashō kushū* no. 198. Composed at Bodaisen Jingūdera near the end of Bashō's time in Ise, when he was visiting Futami Bay and other places. The temple burned down in the 1260s, and Imoto 1972, 129, n. 200, notes that the place was in a state of ruin when Bashō visited, hence his question to farmers there. He echoes a famous *Hyakunin isshu* 百人一首 (no. 11) poem composed by Ono no Takamura on his way into exile: "That I pass now / through the eighty islands / of the broad sea— / could you tell that to my family, / you fishermen in your boats?" (*watanohara / yasoshima kakete / kogiidenu to / hito ni wa tsuge yo / ama no tsuribune*).

91. *Bashō kushū* no. 190. Ryūno Shōsha refers to the residence of Ryūno Hirochika. The first verse of a famous *renga* link from *Tsukubashū* 筑波集, 1333, reads, "The names of things— / they can be different / from place to place; the reeds of Naniwa / are beach grasses in Ise" (*kusa no na wa / tokoro ni yorite / kawaru nari; naniwa no ashi wa / ise no hamaogi*). Bashō's *hokku* is meant as humor but also as a compliment to his scholar host.

92. *Bashō kushū* no. 96. Setsudō ("Snow Hall") was a sobriquet and probably refers to the name of his villa (Yuzawa 1982, 52, n. 95).

93. *Bashō kushū* no. 188. Composed for a poetry gathering at a place called Nijōken 二乗軒, located in the precincts of Taikōji.

Within the sacred fence there was not a single plum tree. When I asked the priest why, he told me there was no special reason, it was just that no tree had ever grown there, but that there was one behind the maiden's chambers.[94]

So charming: by the maiden's house, one tree of flowering plum.[95]	*okorago no* *hitomoto yukashi* *ume no hana*
In sacred precincts, something unexpected: a Reclining Buddha.[96]	*kamigaki ya* *omoi mo kakezu* *nehanzō*

Midway through the Third Month, my heart grew restless, like a blossom set to bud, and I let that feeling lead me on, taking the blossoms of Yoshino as my goal. Before leaving, the man that had made me a promise at Irago to go along met up with me in Ise. "I will share with you the sadness of nights on the road, and act as your servant boy and your helper along the way," he said—"and I shall take the name Mangikumaru." A most amusing name, I thought, the sort by which a boy might be known. As time came to depart, we got a little silly and wrote this inside our traveler's hats.[97]

In the wide universe, we tarry nowhere, we travelers two.[98]

In Yoshino I will show you some blossoms— cypress hat![99]	*yoshino nite* *sakura mishō zo* *hinokigasa*

---

94. *Kora no tachi*, the quarters of young women working at the shrine.

95. *Bashō kushū* no. 97.

96. *Bashō kushū* no. 48. Also composed on the 15th day of the Second Month at an unidentified temple in Ise. That day was celebrated at temples as the birthday of Buddha. Bashō alludes to an *uta* from *KYS* (no. 548) by the wife of the Rokujō minister of the right, Fujiwara Takako: "In the precincts / of a shrine decked with streamers— / so I thought— / the unexpected sound / of a temple bell" (*kamigaki no / atari to omou / yūdasuki / omoi mo kakenu / kane no koe kana*). The "Reclining Buddha" represents Buddha in his last illness, waiting for Nirvana.

97. Takahashi 1993, 183–85, argues that here Bashō is mimicking the beginning of a Noh play, in which Bashō as wandering monk and Mangiku as his servant boy and helper (*dōji* 童子) exchange lines (*kakeai* 掛け合い).

98. Pilgrims would write the Chinese phrase *kenkon mujū dōgyō ninin* 乾坤無住同行二人 ("In the wide universe, we tarry nowhere, Buddha and me") inside their hats. Bashō alters the last words to refer to he and Tokoku, who are on a poetic mission (Ueno 2008, 25, n. 4).

99. *Bashō kushū* no. 128.

In Yoshino   *yoshino nite*
I will show you some, too—   *ware mo mishō zo*
cypress hat!   *hinokigasa*
    Mangiku

Carrying too much hinders one's progress on the road, I knew, so I tossed most things aside. But still I was left with a bundle containing a set of bedclothes for the nights,[100] a rain cloak, an inkstone, brushes, paper, medicines, and a lunchbox, all hoisted onto my back. With such a burden on my feeble legs and frail body I felt as if I were leaning backwards and made slow progress. Nothing but trouble and pain.[101]

How weary I am   *kutabirete*
by the time I seek lodging.   *yado karu koro ya*
Flowering wisteria.[102]   *fuji no hana*

At Hatsuse:

On a spring night,   *haru no yo ya*
how charming to see someone   *komorido yukashi*
in a hall corner.[103]   *dō no sumi*

Some priests   *ashida haku*
walk by in wooden clogs.   *sō mo mietari*
Flowers in the rain.[104]   *hana no ame*
    Mangiku

---

100. Imoto 1972, 321, n. 5, explains that at the time most lodgings did not provide bedclothes.
101. Ueno 1989, 170, notes that Bashō writes here as if he were bearing his burdens alone, when we know he was not, presenting a conception of travel writing emphasizing how one traveler suffers on the road. See the Introduction pp. xxi–xxiv.
102. *Bashō kushū* no. 178. Imoto 1972, 321, n. 10, notes that the first version of this *hokku* appears to date from the 10th day of the Fourth Month and begins with the line *hototogisu*, "cuckoo." Bashō probably changed the line in order to emphasize late spring, closer to the time the travelers set out.
103. *Bashō kushū* no. 25. Referring to Hatsusedera, a Shingon-sect temple just south of Nara. Bashō's *hokku* gestures toward a number of classical works that describe supplicants praying to the Kannon there, often for solace or success in love. In particular, Bashō probably has in mind an incident recorded in *Senjūshō*, 302–4, about Saigyō encountering his former wife, now a nun, praying in the Kannon Hall.
104. Tokoku's poem, focusing on the rather inelegant sight of monks wearing wooden clogs to avoid the mud, is more humorous than Bashō's. Probably he alludes to *The Pillow Book* (*Makura no sōshi*, 155), where Sei Shōnagon speaks of seeing monks wearing clogs at Hase Temple (some texts have Kiyomizu Temple instead).

At Mount Kazuraki:

Still I'd like to see it	*nao mitashi*
as dawn breaks in the blossoms—	*hana ni akeyuku*
the face of the god![105]	*kami no kao*

M ount Miwa
Tōnomine
Hoso Pass, crossing from Tōnomine to Ryūmon[106]

As I take a break,	*hibari yori*
a lark rises in the sky below	*sora ni yasurau*
the mountain pass.[107]	*tōge kana*

At Ryūmon Falls:

From Ryūmon,	*ryūmon no*
I shall send a gift of flowers	*hana ya jōgo no*
to that tippler![108]	*tsuto ni sen*

To saké lovers,	*sakenomi ni*
yes, to them shall I tell	*kataran kakaru*
of Dragon Flowers.[109]	*taki no hana*

---

105. *Bashō kushū* no. 154. According to legend, the god of Mount Kazuraki, Hitokotonushi no kami, was so ashamed of his ugly face that he appeared only at night. Bashō implies that even the ugly god would be beautiful surrounded by blossoming cherry trees.

106. That these places are only listed, without accompanying poems, is one fact that makes it seem Bashō had not finished his account. They were all places between Sakurai and Yoshino.

107. *Bashō kushū* no. 64. The path the travelers were walking was steep and rose so high into the mountains that high-flying larks could be seen rising from the valley below. The pass was probably Hoso Pass. See Okada 1972, *kaisetsu*, 56.

108. *Bashō kushū* no. 155. Here the poet probably has in mind the Chinese poet Li Bai, a legendary imbiber, who wrote a poem about a waterfall of the same name in China. A painting by Kanō Tsunenobu depicts him viewing a waterfall. See Imoto 1972, 322, n. 2. Ryūmonnotaki, "Dragon Gate Falls," was located at the foot of Dragon Gate Cliff.

109. *Bashō kushū* no. 156. Here the poet thinks of describing the beauties of the place during blossom season to his saké-loving friends, still with stories of Li Bai in mind.

At Nijikō:

Why so slowly   *horohoro to*
do the kerria flowers fall?   *yamabuki chiru ka*
Water echoing down.[110]   *taki no oto*

Seimei Falls

Furu Falls, located far back in the mountains, twenty blocks from Furu Shrine
Nunobiki Falls at the headwaters of the Ikuta River in Tsu Province
Mino'o Falls, located on the road that passes to Katsuodera in Yamato[111]

Cherry blossoms"

Seeking blossoms,   *sakuragari*
I go on, dazzled, every day,   *kidoku ya hibi ni*
five *li*, six *li*.[112]   *gori rokuri*

Blossoms all day,   *hi wa hana ni*
then dusk and the lonely look   *kurete sabishi ya*
of *asu* cypress.[113]   *asunarau*

---

110. *Bashō kushū* no. 179. The association of *yamabuki* ("globe flowers" or "yellow mountain roses") and Yoshino goes back to a famous *KKS* poem (no. 124) by Ki no Tsurayuki: "On kerria blooming by the Yoshino River: 'On the Yoshino's banks / kerria flowers are carried off / by passing wind: / even their images scattering / on the water flowing by'" (*yoshinogawa / kishi no yamabuki / fuku kaze ni / soko no kage sae / utsuroinikeri*). Bashō attributes the scattering not to wind but to the sound of the water. Other sources tell us that Bashō and his companions stayed in a farmhouse for the night at this point and were treated very well. See Danjō 1968, 93. Scholars disagree about whether the *hokku* describes Nijikō—not really a waterfall, but rapids—or Seimei Falls. Okada 1972, *kaisetsu*, 57, opts for the latter, while most others favor the former.
111. Imoto 1972, 322, n. 6, notes that these items do not appear in the order in which the travelers would have visited them. Thus we have a categorical list rather than a narrative, presenting more justification for seeing *Knapsack Notes*, in this section at least, as closer to a collection of *hokku* than a travel narrative. Mino'o Falls is actually located north in Settsu Province and not Yamato.
112. *Bashō kushū* no. 130. This *hokku* gives us a sense of how far the companions traveled in Yoshino over the three days they spent there. One *li* amounted to almost four kilometers.
113. *Bashō kushū* no. 157. *Asunarau* (翌檜; also pronounced *asuwahinoki*) is a kind of cypress, but with larger, coarser leaves than the standard variety. The name means literally, "tomorrow I shall become a cypress"—a pathetic sort of name, given that that tomorrow will never come. Bashō evidently thought the trees looked particularly forlorn next to cherry blossoms.

Beneath cherries,	*ōgi nite*
a fan poised to pour saké—	*sake kumu kage ya*
as blossoms fall.[114]	*chiru sakura*

"Pure water on moss"

Spring raindrops:	*harusame no*
flowing down from the trees	*koshita ni tsutau*
to make pure water.[115]	*shimizu kana*

For three days we tarried among the cherry blossoms of Yoshino, gazing at the sights at dawn and dusk, moved by the beauty of the lingering moon at dawn—all of which filled my heart and mind to overflowing. Already that poem of the Lord Regent[116] had left me overwhelmed, and Saigyō and his path markers[117] had left me bewildered. And then I remembered the poem dashed off by Teishitsu that starts, "Look—look!"[118] and found myself without words, so cowed that I just shut my mouth, regretting it all the while. Thus though the grand impressions I had at the place had made me hope for a fine poem, when it came down to it, I felt only disappointment.

At Mount Kōya:

Father and Mother,	*chichi haha no*
how I miss them, each time	*shikiri ni koishi*
the pheasants cry.[119]	*kiji no koe*

---

114. *Bashō kushū* no. 129. An allusion to a use of the fan meant to mimic pouring saké in Noh drama. Whether Bashō is casting himself in an imagined Noh play or to someone viewed at a picnic beneath the blossoms is unclear.

115. *Bashō kushū* no. 42. This *hokku* alludes to the area around Saigyō's hut, already described in *Bones Bleaching in the Fields*. See p. 13.

116. Sesshōkō 摂政公. Fujiwara no Yoshitsune. See *SCSS* 58: "Who might it have been / that planted seeds that grew / into these cherry trees— / making fair Yoshino / into mountains of flowers?" (*mukashi tare / kakaru sakura no / tane o uete / yoshino o hana no / yama to nashikemu*).

117. See *SKKS* 86: "The path I marked / when last year I entered / into Yoshino / I now abandon to search for / blossoms I have not yet seen" (*yoshinoyama / kozo no shiori / no michi kaete / mada minu kata no / hana o tazunen*).

118. Teishitsu was the chief disciple of Matsunaga Teitoku. The full poem reads, "Look—look at these! / that's all you can find to say / in flowery Yoshino" (*kore wa kore wa / to bakari hana no / yoshino kana*). See Imoto 1972, 323, n. 17.

119. *Bashō kushū* no. 66. Kōya refers to the Kongōbuji temple complex. Bashō alludes to *GYS* 2627, written at Kōya by Gyōki Bosatsu: "On hearing a pheasant cry: 'A pheasant cries— /

As blossoms fall   *chiru hana ni*
I feel shame still having hair.   *tabusa hazukashi*
Forest temples.[120]   *oku no in*
    Mangiku

    At Waka Bay:

Departing spring.   *yuku haru ni*
Finally I catch up with it   *wakanoura nite*
at Waka Bay.[121]   *oitsuketari*

    Kimiidera[122]

With heels cracked and sore, I felt like Saigyō, remembering him at Tenryū Crossing,[123] and as I hired a horse, I saw in my mind that other monk who lost his temper.[124] In the fine vistas of mountains and fields, the seas and beaches, I had seen the wonders of creation,[125] and by seeking out the remains of men of the Way who had no attachments[126] I had glimpsed the truth of those who pursue art to the

---

horohoro, horohoro—/ and each time / I wonder, is it Father? / Is it Mother?'" (*yamadori no / horohoro to naku / koe kikeba / chichi ka to zo omou / haha ka to zo omou*). The pheasant's cry was figured as calling to its young, hence the association with parents.

120. "Still having hair" refers to having not yet taken the tonsure, which he regrets when presented with the example of devout monks in the forest and in the midst of cherry blossoms that teach the Buddhist principle of transience. See Yuzawa 1982, 55, no. 143. "Forest temples" refers to small residential temples far back in the mountains, where those who had truly left all worldly ties behind might live.

121. *Bashō kushū* no. 29. A *jiamari* (in the last line). Waka Bay literally means "poetry bay." In the mountains, the poet had been surrounded by cherry blossoms, but now that he feels the warming air and the fine vistas of haze out on the water, he catches up with seasonal change.

122. Another example of a headnote with no following poem, suggesting that one had perhaps been planned but for some reason not realized. The formal name was Kongōhōji gokokuin. See Imoto and Yayoshi 1968, 173, n. 30.

123. The third chapter of *Saigyō monogatari* (114–15) relates how at the Tenryū River, Saigyō was driven off an overloaded boat with a whip but showed no anger whatsoever—an example of devout Buddhist behavior.

124. *Essays in Idleness* (*Tsurezuregusa*, circa 1333;180) tells an incident from the life of Shōkū Shōnin, who lost his temper upon falling from a horse into a ditch but later ran off in embarrassment.

125. *Zōka*. See pp. 49–50 above.

126. An allusion to a passage in the *Linji lu* 臨済録, a collection of Zen *kōan* 公案 put together by the Chinese monk Linji Yixuan. See Watson 1993, 36.

fullest.[127] One who leaves all dwellings behind, desires nothing; owning nothing, he has no fear along the way. Forgoing palanquins, he goes on foot and finds a late meal sweeter than proper evening fare.[128] Aiming for no destination, he has no time in the morning by which he must get away, and each day he has just two hopes. "May I find a good place to stay tonight, and may I find good straw sandals for my feet"—that is all he need think about. Now and then his mood will change, from day to day his feelings will shift. And if he happens on someone who has even a little taste for poetry, his joy knows no bounds. Even the sort of stodgy, stubborn person that he would normally have nothing to do with he will chat with when out in the wilds, and any person of feeling he comes upon in a rundown, weed-choked house will seem like a jewel found amidst broken roof tiles, or coins found in the mud—something to write about or save for conversation. This is one of the boons of travel.[129]

Changing into summer robes"

Off goes one layer	*hitotsu nuide*
and into my backpack.	*ushiro ni oinu*
My change of robes.[130]	*koromogae*

Leaving Yoshino,	*yoshino idete*
I should sell it as I change—	*nunoko uritashi*
my padded robe.[131]	*koromogae*
Mangiku	

---

127. "I had glimpsed the truth of those who pursue art to the fullest" translates J. *fuzei no hito no jitsu o ukagau* 風情の人の実をうかがふ. *Fuzei* is a synonym of *fūga*, by which Bashō often means *haikai*. Here I take it to have a broader frame of reference.

128. Referring to a passage in *Zhan guo ce* 戦国策 ("Strategies among the Warring States"), an anonymous Chinese work dating from the fifth to the third century BCE. See Imoto 1972, 324, n. 7.

129. More literally, "this is one of the facets of travel," although certainly the implication is that it is a benefit.

130. *Bashō kushū* no. 260. The 1st day of the Fourth Month was the day designated for changing from spring into summer clothing.

131. In a letter to Sōshichi in Iga Ueno dated the 25th day of the Fourth Month, Bashō writes that in fact Tokoku took off his robe, sold it, and gave it to a woman named Ima that they visited in Takeuchi on the way to Kyoto. See Imoto 1972, 325, n. 13; Tanaka 2005, 135. Ima was a woman famous for her filial piety, whose story was later written up in various collections.

On the day of Buddha's birth celebration, I was in Nara and I saw a deer give birth, amused that it should happen on that day.

On Buddha's Day	*kanbutsu no*
he just happens to be born:	*hi ni umareau*
a baby deer.[132]	*ka no ko kana*

I worshipped before the statue of Reverend Ganjin of Shōdaiji, who endured a boat trip to our shores at past seventy and then ended up losing his sight because of the salty sea wind blowing into his eyes.

With these young leaves	*wakaba shite*
I would wipe away the drops	*onme no shizuku*
from his holy eyes.[133]	*nuguwaba ya*

When I parted from old friends in Nara:

A deer's horns—	*shika no tsuno*
just starting to show themselves	*mazu hitofushi no*
as we part.[134]	*wakare kana*

At the home of a certain person in Osaka:

To talk of irises—	*kakitsubata*
this too is one of the boons	*kataru mo tabi no*
of travel.[135]	*hitotsu kana*

---

132. *Bashō kushū* no. 261. Buddha's birthday was the 8th day of the Fourth Month. Traditionally temples set up a temporary shrine decorated lavishly with flowers. It is not by chance that it was on this day that Bashō's disciples from home came to visit him in Nara. See p. 43.

133. *Bashō kushū* no. 350. In response to requests from believers in Japan, the Chinese monk Jianzhen (J. Ganjin) made many attempts to travel to Japan between 743 and 753, being impeded by everything from political trouble to shipwreck. He finally arrived in Nara in 754, and established Shōdaiji in 759, having gone blind due to an infection. A statue of him, rendered as blind, stands in the founding hall of the temple to this day. Bashō's "young leaves" represent the beauty and restorative power of nature, while the tears represent the monk's purity. The *hokku* echoes the poem alluded to in *Bones Bleaching in the Fields* as well. See p. 14.

134. *Bashō kushū* no. 297. The growth of horns represented new life and prosperity and was thus a good omen. It also signals the transition from late spring to summer.

135. *Bashō kushū* no. 363. Composed when visiting his old friend Isshō in Osaka, on the way to Suma. Bashō, Tokoku, and Isshō composed twenty-four verses of a linked-verse sequence at

At Suma:

The moon is there—	*tsuki wa aredo*
yet somehow seems not at home.	*rusu no yō nari*
Summer in Suma.[136]	*suma no natsu*

I see the moon—	*tsuki mite mo*
but it seems to lack something.	*mono tarawazu ya*
Summer in Suma.[137]	*suma no natsu*

It was midway through the Fourth Month,[138] the skies hazy, the fickle moon lovely despite the shortness of the night. On the mountains the young leaves were getting darker in hue,[139] and as night ended it seemed the right time for a cuckoo to sing. But it was in the whitening over the sea that day started to show. Then off at what seemed to be the Ueno area,[140] waves of wheat began to glow, and poppy flowers could be seen here and there at the eaves of fishermen's huts.

Fishermen's faces—	*ama no kao*
those are first to appear.	*mazu miraruru ya*
Poppy flowers.[141]	*keshi no hana*

---

the time, one of the few such gatherings we know of after they left Iga Ueno for Yoshino and parts west. Evidently Isshō lived in a place whose name reminded Bashō of Yatsuhashi, a place in Mikawa that is the setting for a famous episode in *Tales of Ise* (*Ise monogatari*, c. 947; 140–42). At the heart of the story is an acrostic poem written by Ariwara no Narihira in which the first syllables of the five successive lines spell out *kakitsubata*, "iris"—hence Bashō's *hokku*. The implication is that both visiting famous places and composing poetry with friends are treasured aspects of travel.

136. *Bashō kushū* no. 247. A *jiamari* (in the first line). As the prose says more directly, since at least the time of *The Tale of Genji*, Suma has been associated with autumn, so somehow the vistas in summer are less impressive.

137. *Bashō kushū* no. 248. Virtually a restatement of the previous *hokku*, which makes both seem like drafts that perhaps needed revision.

138. Documents indicate that the traveling party arrived in Suma on the 20th day of the Fourth Month.

139. Imoto 1972, 326, n. 6, notes that the change is the result of growing dawn light.

140. 上野. The name of a small butte where Sumadera stood.

141. *Bashō kushū* no. 370. Seeing the white poppy flowers in the growing light makes him think of the faces of the fishermen as they leave their homes for the day.

East Suma, West Suma, Suma Strand—Suma is divided up into those three areas. It is hard to see how the people there must make their living. In the old *uta* people hauled seaweed to extract salt,[142] but now one doesn't see them doing that kind of work. Now what one sees is fish—what they call whiting, caught with nets—laid out on the sand to dry, where crows sweep down and carry them away. To prevent this, the men use bows and arrows to frighten the birds, which is hardly what one expects to see among fishermen. Indeed, when I thought that perhaps this was the legacy of warfare that took place there in the past, what they were doing seemed downright sinful.[143] Yet it was while imagining those same ancient days that I decided I must climb to the top of Tekkai Peak.[144] The boy we had hired to guide us thought the task too hard and said all he could to dissuade us, even suggesting that he would treat us to something to eat in a tea house at the foot of the mountain; but in the end he had to give in. In the old story, the village boy was sixteen,[145] while this boy was four years younger; nevertheless, off he struck, leading us several hundred yards up a path both winding and steep. We stumbled and almost fell a number of times, clinging to azaleas and clumps of bamboo grass, and were struggling for breath and drenched with sweat by the time we reached the peak up in the clouds. And all thanks to the same Holy Guide[146] in whom we had had so little confidence.

> Suma fishermen.   *suma no ama no*
> What was that, where the arrow flew—   *yasaki ni naku ka*
> a cuckoo's cry?[147]   *hototogisu*

---

142. An allusion to *KKS* 962, written by Ariwara no Yukihira when he was in exile at Suma: "If by any chance, / someone should ask about me, / tell them I suffer— / like those here at Suma / who haul seaweed to make salt" (*wakuraba ni / tou hito araba / suma no ura ni / moshio taretsutsu / wabu to kotae yo*). Suma was known as the place of exile for Yukihira, an important poet, and Genji, the eponymous hero of *The Tale of Genji*, and as the place where the Heike forces were overcome by the Minamoto, led by the warrior Minamoto no Yoshitsune in a decisive battle.

143. Buddhism teaches that the shedding of blood, human or animal, is sinful. Here the poet is thinking of the human blood shed at the battle waged in the place five hundred years before as well as the frustrated peasants shooting arrows at crows.

144. Tekkaigamine てつかひが峯. Evidently located inland and north of the beach.

145. Yoshitsune, leader of the Minamoto forces at the battle of Ichinotani, used a boy—actually eighteen years old, not sixteen—to guide him up onto the hill behind the Heike encampment. Imoto 1972, 328, n. 2, suggests that Bashō may be confusing the guide for the son of Kumagae Naozane, who was wounded that day at the young age of sixteen.

146. Referring tongue-in-cheek to a *dōshi* 導師, a title given to a priest lecturing believers.

147. *Bashō kushū* no. 305. A *jiamari* (in the first line). Referring back to the fishermen shooting arrows at crows, with the suggestion that they might hit an innocent cuckoo.

A cuckoo passes

and where it fades from view,

a single island.[148]

hototogisu

kieyuku kata ya

shima hitotsu

Suma Temple.

A flute, though not truly heard

in the dark of the trees.[149]

sumadera ya

fukanu fue kiku

koshitayami

Staying the night in Akashi:

In octopus traps,

a brief dream fades away.

Summer moon.[150]

takotsubo ya

hakanaki yume o

natsu no tsuki

"Autumn is matchless in places like this," the tale says,[151] and it must be that autumn is when its true character comes through. Myself, I felt sadness and loneliness beyond

---

148. *Bashō kushū* no. 306. The single island is Awaji, a large island extending from the coast off Suma almost to the shores at Naruto on Shikoku. Yuzawa 1982, 57, n. 176, notes an allusion to a famous poem (*KKS* 409) by Kakinomoto no Hitomaro: "In the dim dawn light / of the morning haze spreading / over Akashi Bay / a boat fades behind the isle— / my thoughts following it away" (*honobono to / akashi no ura no / asagiri ni / shimagakureyuku / fune o shi zo omou*).

149. *Bashō kushū* no. 110. Other sources show that Bashō and Tokoku visited the Sumadera grave of Taira no Atsumori, a young Heike courtier-warrior killed at Ichinotani in an episode of *Tales of the Heike* that also became the basis for a Noh play, but decided not to pay the viewing fee to see the relics stored there, including Atsumori's famous flute that figures in the story. Danjō 1968, 103–4, says that Bashō's *hokku* teasingly hints that they did not get to even see the flute, let alone hear it.

150. *Bashō kushū* no. 246. Yuzawa 1982, 57, n. 178, says that the headnote, "Staying the night in Akashi," echoes the famous Chinese poem "Staying the Night at Maple Bridge" by the mid-eighth-century poet Zhang Ji, which describes a man unable to sleep on a journey, hearing crows and a temple bell in the night. Most scholars argue that this poem was not composed while Bashō was at Akashi (or Suma), but later on, and that it was inserted into the text later, perhaps by Otokuni. See Imoto 1972, 270, poem 472; Ueno 2008, 43. Furthermore, we know from a letter that Bashō and his companions did not spend the night in question—the night of the 22nd day—in Akashi, but in Suma. Danjō 1968, 104, says that the headnote, "Staying the night in Akashi," seems to be a fiction intended to heighten the impact of the poem." Akashi was famous for its seafood, in particular its octopus. Traps were put in the water near shore at evening and hauled out by ropes in the morning, which meant that an octopus thinking to have found refuge would in fact die the next day, its brief dream of life over.

151. A line from a description in the *The Tale of Genji* (*Genji monogatari*, vol. 2, 190) of the shore near Genji's place of exile. Cf. Tyler 2001, 244.

words. Perhaps if it had been autumn, I thought, I might have been able to say a little of what I felt; but that was only me failing to realize my own shortcomings as a poet.

Awaji Island seemed close enough to touch, dividing the sea off Suma and Akashi into left and right, and I had to wonder if the sight before me must be like "Wu and Chu, divided east and south."[152] A person of true learning might have compared the spot to many places. In the mountains behind us, in an area called Tainohata, was the village where they say Matsukaze and Murasame were from,[153] and also a ridgeline path that connects to the Tanba Road.[154]

Up there were places with frightful names like Hachibuse Nozoki and Sakaotoshi,[155] and the pine where Yoshitsune hung his battle gong, from whence one gets a glimpse of the site of the temporary imperial palace at Ichinotani[156] far below.

The upheavals of that age, the violence of those times, all rose up as images crowding my mind: the Nun of Second Rank[157] with the prince in her arms; Kenreimon'in struggling along, her legs so tangled in skirts that she stumbled and fell getting into the boat cabin; the handmaids and other such ladies and servants[158] laboring to carry palace furnishings; lutes and zithers wrapped only in cushions and bedding and then just tossed into the boat; the royal stores falling overboard to become food for the fishes; the royal makeup boxes scattered into the sea like so much cast-off seaweed. For a thousand years the grief of those times will remain in this bay, echoing in the sound of waves that break sadly on the shore.

---

152. A line from a Chinese poem by Du Fu titled "Climbing Yueyang Tower" (登岳陽楼) in reference to a place in Hunan Province.

153. Matsukaze 松風 and Murasame 村雨 are characters in Zeami Motokiyo's Noh play *Matsukaze* 松風 (Pining Wind), sisters whose names were Pining Wind and Passing Showers. The plot tells of how they had loved Yukihira when he was there in exile.

154. The road into Tanba Province (now western Kyoto).

155. 鉢伏のぞき ("Hachibuse View") and 逆落 ("Headlong Slope"). Hachibuse was the mountain just west of Tekkai, while Sakatoshi refers to the steep slope leading down to the area of the Heike encampment.

156. The name of the Heike encampment, with its temporary palace for the boy emperor Antoku, whom Bashō refers to as prince, probably because of his young age.

157. Nii no ama, Taira no Tokiko.

158. Palace ladies of various titles and ranks.

A JOURNEY TO SARASHINA

Introduction

The area of Sarashina, deep in the mountains of Shinano Province (now Nagano Prefecture), was as renowned for its autumn moon as Yoshino was for its cherry blossoms. It comes as no surprise, therefore, that Bashō decided to take the Kiso Road to Sarashina on his way back to Edo in the Eighth Month of 1688. As early as the Second Month of that year, he had written of his plan to his patron Sanpū back in Edo, although at that time he was thinking of returning earlier.[1]

As already noted, after his trip to Yoshino and the Settsu coast, Bashō spent nearly four months in Kyoto and then the Nagoya area. In those places he was hosted by disciples, allowing him time to rest after his journeying. But there was no rest from poetic activities, which took him to the same cities he had visited earlier the year before: Nagoya itself, Gifu, Narumi, Atsuta, and Ōtsu. Many of his hosts were men of considerable wealth who could provide lodging above the level he had sometimes experienced on the road.

Yet he of course had to make the trip back to Edo, and as autumn began he determined to view the full moon of the Eighth Month—the prime time for moon viewing according to tradition—in the mountains on the way. The place he chose was Mount Obasute, notorious as a site where old people were in ancient times abandoned to die. Such mountains existed all over Japan, but the one in Sarashina was perhaps the best known because of a story in the tenth-century poem tale *Yamato monogatari* や ま と 物語 (c. 947–57). It is a short piece about how a man gives in to pleadings from his weary wife to take his aged aunt up onto the mountainside and leave her there to die, which he does. But back home, as he looks up at the moon, he cannot live with what he has done and expresses his feelings in a poem, before going to get her back.

---

1. Tanaka 2005, 125. At the time he seems to have been thinking of returning in the summer.

This heart of mine	*waga kokoro*
can look nowhere for comfort—	*nagusamekanetsu*
at Sarashina,	*sarashina ya*
where above Mount Obasute	*obasuteyama ni*
I see the moon shining bright.[2]	*teru tsuki o mite*

Bashō of course knew this story and planned to see that bright moon for himself. He left on the 11th day of the month, evidently from East Mino.[3] Accompanying him was Etsujin, the same disciple that had been his guide on his brief trip to see Tokoku in Hobi. Accompanying them was a servant provided by Bashō's student and patron Kakei, who was concerned about the rigors his friends would face.

Bashō had traveled the Kiso Road in the early summer of 1685, but then he had gone only as far as Seba, where he took the road on to Kōfu in Kai Province; now he continued north, deeper into the mountains, through more rugged terrain. Still the men were able to make the trip to Sarashina in five days and four nights, traveling on the average thirteen kilometers or so per day (about eight miles). Along the way they encountered steep paths, deep gorges, and dizzying heights, and they stayed in rustic lodgings, the names and locations of which do not appear in his text. But their efforts were rewarded, and Bashō was able to realize his dream of seeing the moon at Obasute for three clear nights, from the 15th to the 17th. Then he pushed on to Zenkōji, a great temple complex just to the north, and from there took the Nakasen Road back toward Edo. At some point the servant sent by Kakei returned to Nagoya on his own,[4] but Etsujin stayed with Bashō all the way to his hut in Fukagawa. By the 3rd day of the Ninth Month, Bashō was able to write to Kakei that Etsujin was spending his time napping and that many people were coming to welcome him back.[5] He had been in the west for nearly a full year.

***

Records mention no meeting with disciples on his journey through Shinano, not even in sizable places such as Zenkōji; nor was he traveling to visit someone like Butchō. In that

---

2. *Yamato monogatari*, 406.
3. Using documentary evidence, Inoue 1992, 324–31, summarizes the itinerary this way: from Tōyō's place in Atsuta, Bashō traveled to Nagoya on the 6th day of the Eighth Month, left Nagoya on the 8th or 9th, and began his trek at the East Mino post station. A group of Owari disciples accompanied him from Nagoya for the first three *li*.
4. Akabane 1968, 123.
5. Tanaka 2005, 153.

sense his purposes were focused more on the road itself: famous places, most prominently Sarashina. And, as always, he was set on converting his experience into *hokku*. Partially for that reason, *A Journey to Sarashina*, the account he left of his trip, is even briefer than *A Pilgrimage to Kashima*, amounting to just a few paragraphs of prose describing the trip, along with a collection of thirteen *hokku*, two by Etsujin and the rest by Bashō.

A Journey to Sarashina is so short that it gets little attention from scholars, but it is interesting as travel writing for two reasons. For one thing, just as he did in *A Pilgrimage to Kashima*, Bashō in the prose section of the work collapses the experiences of several days into what seems one day and one night—a clear example of fashioning.[6] Furthermore, he gives descriptions of a true "character" similar to those that will appear in *The Narrow Road through the Hinterlands*—in this case an elderly traveling monk that Bashō and his companions assist and who ends up sharing their sleeping quarters at night.[7] Thus the account has considerable human interest, providing an example of the sort of person he had imagined happening upon "out in the hinterlands," as he put it in *Knapsack Notes*.[8] As scholars commonly note, however, Bashō does not offer a straightforward narrative of events, but a boiling down of the experience of travel, including everything from the fear of high mountain passes to interactions with people met along the way.[9] Once again, one is reminded of how travel allowed Bashō to experience times of aimless wandering of the sort held up as an ideal by Zhuangzi.

The prose account ends with a passage that presents classical allusions to autumn but then goes on to describe a contrasting scene and a contrasting aesthetic, in which the moon floats in saké poured into clumsily decorated and oversized cups. It is significant that in the end these things charm the poet rather than putting him off, which is no doubt a point he wanted to make, related both to his lifestyle and his artistic ideals. In other words, Bashō makes it clear that the efforts and dangers he faced along the way serve as preparation for an epiphany. His is labor expended for emotional, spiritual, and artistic rewards.

The first *hokku* of the coda relates directly to the end of the prose section of the work, but thereafter Bashō puts the poems in rough chronological order, beginning with those composed on the Kiso Road, moving on to Mount Obasute, and

---

6. Inoue 1992, 336, uses the word *sakkaku* 錯覚 ("illusion") rather than *fashioning* (*kyokō* 虚構) but is obviously making the same point. Inoue argues that Bashō does this to be consistent with the method he established in *A Pilgrimage to Kashima*.
7. The "collapsed" account does not make it clear whether they are together for more than one night.
8. See *Knapsack Notes*, p. 65; Kusumoto 2009, 349.
9. See, e.g., Kusumoto 2009, 347–54, who on the same and related points alludes to Inoue Toshiyuki, Akabane Manabu, Ueno Yōzō, and others.

concluding with poems about Zenkōji and Mount Asama, with no substantial head-notes. As always, some poems seem to have been revised later; a few in fact being recycled from earlier versions composed before the trip. But together they do present sketches of places, some not mentioned at all in the prose introduction. What emerges from them is a description of emotions felt on the journey, from physical struggle to fear to amusement and elation. True to the *haikai* spirit, Bashō even includes references to things classical poems would not, such as spicy daikon radishes, gesturing toward a whole world of tactile human experience.[10]

The next to last of Bashō's poems, on how the moon shining down on Zenkōji erases all sectarian differences, gets more attention than the other poems, and justly so, as it is important formalistically, as a conclusion to the narrative, and philosophically. For the way the moonlight makes the sects represented at the temple "all one" can be thought of as a conclusion to what is after all a narrative of moon viewing first of all. Perhaps it is not going too far to conclude that the poem also represents a realization: that all of the poet's experiences, those with classical resonances but also those of contemporary relevance, could be circumscribed into a whole. In Yoshino he had seen cherry blossoms in all their glory; now in Sarashina he saw that the bright orb of the full moon accommodated all.

A letter by Bashō to Sōshichi in Iga Ueno dating from the intercalary First Month of 1689 shows that his journey to Sarashina had left a truly lasting impression.

> This last autumn I traveled the Kiso Road with that fool friend of mine,[11] Etsujin. There—risking our lives at Kakehashi, finding no comfort at Mount Obasute, hearing fulling blocks and bird clappers and voices scaring away the deer—we experienced the limits of deep feeling, as I think you will remember. As this New Year begins, my desire to travel has not abated.[12]

It was with this kind of "deep feeling"—*aware* is the Japanese word—that the poet adds that he is planning on heading out again in a few months' time, referring to the journey that would become the basis for *The Narrow Road through the Hinterlands*. Hence the frequent claim of scholars that *A Journey to Sarashina*—undeniably a sort of appendix to *Knapsack Notes*—was also preparation for the challenges soon to come.

---

10. It is in features like this that one sees the growing influence of Bashō's aesthetic of *karumi*, or "lightness." See Fukasawa and Kusumoto 2009, 353–54.

11. *Shiremono*. Here used tongue-in-cheek as a term of endearment.

12. Tanaka 2005, 181. Tanaka, 185, notes that the addressee of the letter is tentative. Other possibilities are Takutai and Ensui.

A JOURNEY TO SARASHINA

To go and see the moon at Mount Obasute in the village of Sarashina—that is what the autumn wind had been urging me to do, incessantly; and I had a companion likewise driven to distraction by winds and clouds, a man named Etsujin.[13] Then came a servant, dispatched by Master Kakei, who knew that the Kiso Road[14] was a steep climb through deep mountains and was worried that we might need help on the way. These two expended every effort, but they appeared to know little about the road[15] and in all seemed unsure of themselves, and so we just blundered along, taking things as they came, which made for an amusing journey. That is, until at a certain place[16] we came upon a Buddhist monk[17] of about sixty years, who seemed not at all amused as he just trudged along in grim silence, bent over with the weight of the things on his back, breathing heavily, his strides short and halting. My companion felt such pity for the man that we bound everything up in a single bundle—what was on our backs, what was on his—and hoisted it onto the horse, with me perched on top of it all. And so away we went, the high mountain bearing down from above us, a great river flowing by on our left, and the cliffs descending into what seemed truly fathomless depths.[18] There was not a single stretch of level ground, and I was nervous in the saddle, feeling fear every moment.

---

13. Akabane 1968, 116, notes that Etsujin decided to go along very late in the planning process. The idea of being excited by "wind and clouds" also appears in *Knapsack Notes* (p. 51). For Bashō the term refers less to natural landscapes than to energies active in the natural world.

14. As Imoto and Yayoshi 1968, 174, n. 3, explain, the Kiso Road is a somewhat elastic term sometimes used synonymously with Nakasen Road, the road going all the way from Ōtsu to Edo. Bashō seems to use it to mean the road through Mino to Zenkōji.

15. "The road" translates *ekiryo* 駅旅. Imoto 1972, 333, and Toyama 1978, 94, take this to mean the stations and inns along the way.

16. Ueno 1985b, 177, notes that it is unusual for Bashō to leave the place vague in this way and hazards that maybe he intended to fill the name in later—an evidence that the manuscript was dashed off rather quickly and perhaps without much revision.

17. *Dōshin no sō* 道心の僧, an itinerant monk, perhaps going on pilgrimage to Zenkōji, a major center of Amida worship.

18. "Fathomless depths" translates *senjin* 千尋 (alternatively *chihiro*), a hyperbolic expression applied to high mountains and deep gorges.

We passed by Kakehashi[19] and Nezamenotoko,[20] then Sarugababa[21] and Tachi Pass[22] with its forty-eight twists,[23] curving so—like spreading vines—that we felt as if we were making our way through the clouds. I was on foot then, and the heights were so dizzying that I nearly lost my courage and my footing. Yet there was our servant, showing no fear, up on the horse, dozing off and on, while I walked along behind, cringing every time it looked like he might fall and in a state of constant trepidation. This must be what the Buddha felt when he looked down on people in the cruel world, I thought. Then I pondered my own life, caught up in the bustle of uncertainty and change,[24] and realized that "those winds and waves at Naruto in Awa"—they *are* truly nothing at all.[25]

At night we sought out pillows of grass,[26] and I considered the scenes I had seen during the day. Going through *hokku* still in rough form in my mind, I took out my writing things and bent close to the lamp, eyes closed, tapping my hand against my head while I lay there mumbling lines.[27] Seeing this, the monk must have supposed I was upset by the day's experiences on the road—for he attempted to console me.

---

19. 桟はし ("Hanging Bridge"), a bridge of planks supported by stakes driven into a cliff face. Imoto and Yayoshi 1968, 175, n. 6, and Inoue 1992, 334, note that Bashō is in fact referring to a place known by that name, between Agematsu and Fukushima, although it was probably the presence of such a bridge that gave the place its name.

20. 寝覚の床 ("Wakeful Bed") describes a rock surface made flat by the elements over time (Ueno 1985b, 179). The order of place names is wrong here: Nezame comes before Kakehashi on the road.

21. 猿がばば ("Gibbon Pass").

22. たち峠 ("Standing Pass"). Here the order of places on the road is again reversed.

23. Another hyperbolic expression. Here Bashō gets the referents wrong. This phrase is usually applied to another place nearby. See Akabane 1968, 120.

24. *Mujō jinsoku* 無常迅速, a Buddhist term referring to the rapid pace of change in the phenomenal world.

25. See section 41 of *Essays in Idleness* (*Tsurezuregusa*, 117–19). There the sight of a monk dozing off on a tree limb leads Kenkō to ponder the perilous state of all human existence. The reference to the straits at Naruto also alludes to a poem attributed to the same author: "As I see people / struggling to make it in life / I realize this: / they are nothing, those winds and waves / at Naruto in Awa" (*yo no naka o / watarikurabete / ima zo shiru / awa no naruto wa / kazenami mo nashi*). See Hori and Imoto 1972, 335, nn. 11–12; Ueno 1985b, 179. According to a headnote in his personal poetry anthology (*Kenkō hōshi shū* 兼好法師集, poem 51), Kenkō traveled the Kiso Road after taking the tonsure. Imoto and Yayoshi 1968, 176, n. 13, also see an allusion to a passage in the medieval travel record, *Tōkan kikō*, 140.

26. *Kusamakura* 草枕, a poetic word for lodging.

27. Ueno 1985b, 180, notes that the verb *umeku* in this case means quietly chanting lines of poetry in a soft voice.

Pilgrimages he had undertaken in his youth, the holy mercies of Lord Amida—about such things he rambled on and on, telling me of the wonders he had witnessed, all of which kept me from calling on my artistic feelings[28] to come up with even a single poem. But just then, I saw rays of moonlight that I had been too preoccupied to notice coming in through cracks in the walls, shining down from between the trees outside, and I heard from here and there the sound of clappers and the voices of people scaring deer away.[29] That was when I felt in my heart the true sadness of autumn.[30] "Come now," I said, "let's have some saké, in honor of the moon."[31] The cups brought out were larger than the usual size and decorated rather clumsily in lacquer. People in Kyoto would have thought them too lacking in artistry to even pick up, but I got in the spirit of things and thought of them as fine blue bowls and jeweled cups.[32]

Into that circle	*ano naka ni*
I would put a lacquer sketch.	*makie kakitashi*
Moon at my lodging.[33]	*yado no tsuki*
Hanging Bridge.	*kakehashi ya*
All around it, creeping vines	*inochi o karamu*
clinging for life.[34]	*tsutakazura*

---

28. J. *fuzei* 風情. Toyama 1978, 96, and Imoto 1972, 335, take the word to mean "ideas for poems," while Ueno 2008, 56, n. 3, equates it with feelings associated with the synonym *fūga* and the winds and clouds mentioned at the beginning of the text. Inoue 1992, 344, argues that Bashō's tolerant reaction to the old man shows his human side and ultimately leads to a feeling of refreshment rather than world-weariness.

29. *Hita*—sticks of wood clapped together by pulling on a string—were used to scare off deer and other animals disturbing people's crops.

30. As Ueno 1985b, 181, notes, Bashō feels the essence of autumn when he notices things referred to in classical poems such as Saigyō's (*Sankashū* 334): "Truly forlorn— / this moonlight spilling down / into my hut. / While all I hear is clappers / sounding in the mountain paddies" (*io ni moru / tsuki no kage koso / sabishikere / yamada wa hita no / oto bakari shite*).

31. Bashō offers saké as a treat to the owner of the inn, who quickly has things brought in.

32. *Seiwan gyokushi* 瑆碗玉卮, an obscure term that must mean something like "the finest saké bowls and cups." Scholars argue that Bashō used mistaken characters. Toyama 1978, 96, n. 5, suggests Bashō meant *hekiwan gyokushi* 碧碗玉卮, "bowls of blue stone and cups made of jewels."

33. *Bashō kushū* no. 492. Ueno 1985b, 181, takes this *hokku* to mean that the unusually large saké cups are right beneath such a large, full moon, and that in honor of the occasion, Bashō offers, wittily, to do a sketch in lacquer in the circle of the moon above.

34. *Bashō kushū* no. 622. The suggestion is that not only the vines are clinging for dear life. Far below was the Kiso River. Hori and Imoto 1972, 148, n. 239, note that by Bashō's time the old bridge had been replaced by a more substantial structure.

At Hanging Bridge
my first thought is of horses
awaited in Kyoto.[35]

kakehashi ya
mazu omoiizu
komamukae

The mists clear—
and my eyes refuse to close
at Hanging Bridge.[36]
  Etsujin

kiri harete
kakehashi wa me mo
fusagarezu

At Mount Obasute:

Her image I see,
that old crone weeping alone.
Friends beneath the moon.[37]

omokage ya
oba hitori naku
tsuki no tomo

The 16th day—
and still I linger on
at Sarashina.[38]

izayoi mo
mada sarashina no
kōri kana

At Sarashina:
three nights of moon-viewing,
not a cloud in sight.[39]
  Etsujin

sarashina ya
miyosa no tsukimi
kumo mo nashi

---

35. *Bashō kushū* no. 534. Anciently tribute horses had been sent to the imperial government on this same route, each year in the middle of the Eighth Month. The horses of Shinano—known as *mochitsuki no koma*, "full-moon horses"—were particularly well known. Imperial messengers came from the capital to meet those bringing the horses at Ausaka Gate, east of Kyoto.

36. Two possible interpretations: either the poet is so scared at the sight of the deep gorge that he cannot get his eyes to shut, or he cannot close his eyes safely as he makes his way across the bridge.

37. *Bashō kushū* no. 493. Hori and Imoto 1972, 149, n. 240, see the influence of the Noh play *Obasute* 姨捨, where the phrase *tsuki no tomo*, "friends beneath the moon" appears. They argue that Bashō puts himself in the role of the traveler in the play, who visits the place and has a vision of the abandoned crone. Another interpretation, not necessarily incompatible with the first, is that the speaker is the son in the *Yamato monogatari* story.

38. *Bashō kushū* no. 483. A headnote in another source says this *hokku* was composed at Sakaki, just east of Sarashina, providing a different view of Mount Obasute. The fullest moon shone on the 15th day of the month, but as this *hokku* and the following one by Etsujin attest, the travelers lingered through the 17th, relishing the beauties of the area.

39. *Miyosa* refers to the three nights of the full moon, the 15th through the 17th. The travelers were able to view the moon at Sarashina for three nights in a row, apparently from different vantage points.

Still looking fresh
though near to toppling with dew—
maiden flowers.[40]

hyorohyoro to
nao tsuyukeshi ya
ominaeshi

It cuts to the quick,
so spicy is this daikon!
Autumn wind.[41]

mi ni shimite
daikon karashi
aki no kaze

Kiso chestnuts:
a gift for those who must cope
with life in the world.[42]

kiso no tochi
ukiyo no hito no
miyage kana

All those send-offs,
those partings, come to this end:
autumn in Kiso.[43]

okuraretsu
wakaretsu hate wa
kiso no aki

---

40. *Bashō kushū* no. 609. An earlier version was composed when some disciples accompanied the travelers into the suburbs of Gifu, seeing them off on their journey to Sarashina. See Akabane 1968, 116. "So dew-laden / that some drops topple and fall: / maiden flowers" (*hyorohyoro to / kokete tsuyukeshi /ominaeshi*). Bashō probably has in mind lines from the Noh play *Obasute*, which builds on the legend. In the play, the wraith of the old crone, still haunting the slopes of the mountain, describes herself as a maiden flower whose glory has passed (421).

41. *Bashō kushū* no. 442. Daikon radish, still a staple in Japanese cooking, was too plebeian an image for poets writing in the classical *uta* form. In Bashō's conception it is both the autumn wind and the Kiso daikon—notoriously spicy—that cut to the quick (*mi ni shimite*).

42. *Bashō kushū* no. 644. Bashō sent this *hokku* and a gift of chestnuts to Kakei back in Nagoya, perhaps by the servant when he went back (Akabane 1968, 120). Hori and Imoto 1972, 150, note a poem by Saigyō (*Sankashū* 1290) that Bashō may have had in mind: "Would that I could stop / this water dripping onto rocks / deep in the mountains— / long enough to pick up / chestnuts that keep dropping down" (*yama fukami / iwa ni shitatataru / mizu tomemu / katsukatsu otsuru / tochi hirou hodo*). They stress that while Bashō makes a distinction between himself and "those" in the world, he does not imply criticism of Kakei. The gift suggests that Kakei would derive strength from the chestnuts in the manner of a mountain hermit.

43. *Bashō kushū* no. 651. An earlier version of this *hokku* was written in Gifu as Bashō was planning his Kiso trip: "Being sent off / and seeing off, these will end / in autumn, in Kiso" (*okuraretsu / okuritsu hate wa / kiso no aki*). The version in *Journey to Sarashina* obviously looks backward rather than forward, serving as a conclusion to the trip that was planned. As Akabane 1968, 116, explains, the *hokku* has in that sense been recycled, a not uncommon practice in *haikai*.

At Zenkōji:

In the moonlight,	*tsukikage ya*
the four gates, the four sects—	*shimon shishū mo*
they're all one.[44]	*tada hitotsu*

Can it be true?	*fukitobasu*
Rocks tossed aloft by the gales	*ishi wa asama no*
at Mount Asama.[45]	*nowaki kana*

---

44. *Bashō kushū* no. 494. There are various interpretations of the "four gates" and the "four sects." See Hori and Imoto 1972, 150–51, n. 243. On the basis of sources associated with the temple itself, Akabane 1968, 122, suggests that the four sects were Tendai 天台, Pure Land 浄土, Ritsu 律, and Kusha 倶舎, and that the "four gates" refers to the four gates to the temple, one in each cardinal direction; and Ueno 1985b, 186, agrees. Bashō's *hokku* suggests that the light of enlightenment—represented by the moon—recognizes no sectarian boundaries in any case.

45. *Bashō kushū* no. 436. Bashō passed by the mountain on his way from Shinano back to Edo. *Nowaki* refers to an autumn typhoon. Asama is known for its rocky slopes and relative lack of forest, and Bashō may actually have seen small stones lifted in the air by strong winds, although that image is so conventional that one cannot be sure. Asama is a partial homophone of *asamashi*, "amazing" or "hard to believe." Why the text ends with this *hokku* rather than the one composed about Zenkōji, which would provide a neater conclusion, as noted above, is anyone's guess. Perhaps Bashō wanted to end with a major *utamakura*. In this sense it is safe to say that he thought of all his travel writings as in a real sense poetry collections.

THE NARROW ROAD THROUGH
THE HINTERLANDS

INTRODUCTION

The autumn of 1688 was a busy time at Bashō's Fukagawa cottage. As always, he was meeting with students, conducting linked-verse sessions, keeping up with correspondence, and attending to family duties. But the tug of the road persisted. Late in the First Month of 1689 he wrote his old friend Sōshichi in Iga Ueno of his plan to tax his legs again, this time not going west down the Tōkai Road but into the hinterlands (Ōshū) beyond the Shirakawa Barrier to the north.

> In the Third Month, I will fulfill my long-held desire to see the cherry blossoms at Shiogama and the murky moon at Matsushima; then from around the time the *katsumi* bloom in the marshes at Asaka, I will make a circuit of the northern provinces, arriving in Mino and Owari in late autumn, before winter. If I survive the journey, I comfort myself thinking that I may meet you again, even if it's only to drop by a moment and say hello at your door.[1]

As this passage indicates, he had wanted to travel north for a long time, probably for many reasons. To begin with, after seeing many of the *utamakura* and historic sites in his travels on the Tōkai Road and in the old home provinces, he no doubt wanted to visit such places in the north.[2] ("There were regions I had heard of but not seen," he said when he later wrote about the 1689 trip.) Furthermore, he had disciples in the territories to which he would travel, as well as potential disciples waiting to be introduced. As to why he chose 1689 rather than giving himself a little more rest, one possible motive was that he wanted to commemorate the five-hundredth anniversary of the

---

1. Tanaka 2005, 181. See note 13, p. 85. The identity of the *katsumi* (*hanagatsumi* in modern Japanese) is uncertain. See n. 138 below.
2. Imoto Nōichi stresses this more general motive over a desire to honor Saigyō's death anniversary. See Imoto 1970, 309–11.

death of the Japanese poet that he revered above all others: the poet-priest Saigyō. More than five centuries before, his poetic forebear had visited the hinterlands, and Bashō wanted to honor his memory and test his own mettle on the same roads—or at least on roads in the same areas.[3] The gap in time could not be spanned in any but figurative ways, but experiencing the same geography was something.

Reports of lingering cold weather in the Shirakawa area made Bashō postpone his departure for a few days, but at the end of the Second Month, he took the step of relinquishing his house. From then on, living in a nearby villa provided by his patron Sanpū,[4] he dedicated himself to preparing for the trek. His first task was to secure a companion, which would be even more necessary on this journey than on his previous ones.[5] Initially, it appears that two men, both neighbors in Fukagawa, would be going along: the monk Rotsū, whom he called a "fine traveling companion, a begging-monk dedicated to *haikai* and trained in Buddhist rigors"; and Sora, a reliable, stalwart disciple used to helping the master with mundane tasks. In the end, Rotsū was unable or unwilling to go,[6] but Sora committed to the task. His contributions would be more logistical than literary: someone was needed to literally take the weight off Bashō's shoulders, carrying gear and documents, preparing and following an itinerary, arranging for transport and lodging, and handling correspondence, not to mention providing basic protection and security. Most of the roads in the west where Bashō had traveled before were well established and maintained, but the northern territories—especially the areas of Honshū moving west from Sendai and down along the coast of the Japan Sea—were more off the beaten track, and unknown to either man. To prepare, Sora even compiled a guidebook of sorts,

---

3. See Uozumi 2011, 71. Yamamoto Yuiitsu 1994, 130–31, notes that going on a trek (*angya*) on death anniversaries was a practice at the time. Takahashi 2002, 310–25, suggests another reason behind the trip: that Bashō left to escape family problems involving Tōin and Jutei. Fukasawa Shinji, 2009, 371, adds the name of another model: "In Bashō's consciousness, travel meant following in the footsteps of Nōin and Saigyō."

4. Bessho Saitōan (or Saitaan), probably a fine cottage far above the level of Bashō's hut. Takahashi 2002, 309, describes the place as Sanpū's *shimoyashiki*, a secondary residence.

5. His traveling companions were usually disciples who knew the rules of linked verse and could serve as scribes and take care of travel correspondence and arrangements, as well as providing support when the master was ill. See Kanamori 2013, 274–75.

6. See Abe Masami 1982, 263–66. Tanaka 2009, 416–19, surmises that Rotsū had not truly wanted to go and left without informing Bashō at the last minute. However, Rotsū's appearance in Fukui at the end of the journey would seem to indicate that there had been no ill feeling. Later, in 1691, Rotsū committed some offense that resulted in him being ostracized by Bashō's disciples. Tanaka 2009, 420.

including lists of the shrines they intended to visit as well as background on other likely destinations.[7]

As they set out at the end of the Third Month, the road stretching before Bashō and Sora—actually the series of roads—was a long one that would amount to as much as 1,500 miles, a distance they would cover in 156 days, mostly on foot, horseback, or palanquin, and occasionally by boat. What's more, it was for them virtually all new territory. Some main stops on their route were doubtless set before departure after research by Sora: population centers, such as the Nikkō-Kurobane area, Shirakawa, Fukushima, Sendai, Obanezawa, Tsuruoka, Sakata, Kanazawa, Fukui, and Tsuruga; but at various times they made unscheduled stops, sometimes in response to the invitations of patrons and poets, sometimes to look for poetic sites.[8] More than half their nights they spent with patrons and friends who saw to all their needs, often assisting with documents, transport, and men to guide and assist them on their way. Sora doubtless carried money (for horses, bearers, ferries and boat passage, inns, food, and miscellaneous needs, such as sandals) and passport documents (*tegata*). He also seems to have taken charge of most of the letters of introduction—some written by people back home, others by his hosts on the road—that were necessary to secure lodging and get through the checkpoints (*sekisho* and *bansho*). Some disciples actually traveled to meet them and provided all kinds of assistance. Like all travelers, the men carried passport documents, but it did not hurt that in many cases they had letters from wealthy, powerful men who would be hosting them.

The tradeoff with these hosts was literary: students were anxious for their master to practice his profession while under their sponsorship, meeting old disciples and attracting new ones. Although there are only hints of it in his own writings, other sources show that he fulfilled these obligations, usually with unstinting devotion. Various sources indicate that by 1689 Bashō had to deal with frequent callers, many of them poets wanting to make his formal acquaintance and apply to be disciples. It was the size of his constituencies and perhaps the quality of available lodging that explains his lengthy stays in a number of areas: Kurobane (nearly two weeks); Sukagawa (a week); Obanezawa (ten days); Sakata (a week); and Kanazawa (a week). As a *haikai* master, he

7. See Kanamori 2000, 59; Uozumi 2011, 73. Ueno 1989, 176, notes that Sora's travel record mentions more than 130 *utamakura*.

8. A letter to Sanpū written in the Fourth Month of 1689, from Sukagawa, reveals that the travelers planned to arrive in Kaga at the beginning of the Sixth Month, rather than the middle of the Seventh Month, which is when they actually arrived. Tanaka 2005, 199–204.

was of course compensated for his labors, receiving money and gifts (including lots of scraps of paper, mostly containing poems) as well as room, board, transportation, and so forth, though we have only hints at such matters, which were probably taken care of by Sora.[9] There were a few places where he was not very well received or not pleased with accommodations, as for example in Niigata and Kashiwazaki on the coast road.[10] In general the road from Sakata to Kanazawa—which ended up being in the worst of the summer heat—seems to have been the least pleasant part of the journey, which is perhaps why Bashō writes little about it.

Needless to say, he composed linked verse at many places along the way[11] and wrote independent *hokku* in various settings. To maintain contact with his poetic network, friends, and family, he kept runners going back and forth with letters, sometimes to people he had visited or was planning to visit but also to friends in Edo or the Nagoya area. He also gave away many literary gifts: *tanjaku*[12] (poem strips, a supply of which he carried with him) and other samples of his writing, many of which have survived and are now preserved in museums. Already there was a culture of connoisseurship, even in the hinterlands.

But his journey was not only a way to engage people in his poetic network and fulfill social obligations. Besides interaction with disciples, the other priority for Bashō during his journey, as noted in the Introduction, was seeking out *utamakura* and other famous places. Indeed, it is no overstatement to say that he and Sora aimed to travel in time as well as space. Places like Nasunokurobane, Unganji, Shinobu, Miyagino, Kisagata, and Tada Shrine may not be major tourist attractions today, but because of their literary or historical associations, he went out of his way to visit these and places even more obscure, usually recording poems that were the result of his encounters. And although he doubtless enjoyed beautiful vistas, it is fair to say that he was not a conventional tourist: as Uozumi Takashi stresses, the men went out in the spirit of religious training (*shugyō* 修行), to experience what forebears—in both Japan and

---

9. Kanamori 2000, 45–50. Needless to say, it was the payment and support he received as a master that financed most of the trip. See Kanamori 2013, 4–6.

10. Kanamori 2000, 298–310.

11. Takatō 1966 gives fully annotated versions of fifteen of the sequences, the first at Kurobane, the last at Ōgaki.

12. In a letter, he writes that he is taking one hundred *tanjaku*, to sell for money if the travelers are starving; he even specifies the anticipated reward: five or ten copper coins (*mon*). He also mentions begging bowls, a rush mat to use against the rain, a walking staff—all of these being the sort of things used by wandering Zen monks. See Tanaka 2005, 190–92.

China—had experienced on their journeys.[13] Later he would quote the great Buddhist teacher Kūkai to his disciple Kyoriku: "Don't mimic what the masters left behind; rather seek what they sought."[14] In this sense their journey had a spiritual dimension— something that Sora, a devotee of the Way of the gods and Japanese ancient history and mythology—probably did everything to encourage.

Yet if we look at the day-to-day itinerary of the men, we discover something unexpected: for it appears that in his journeying Bashō was often more interested in exploring out-of-the-way places than in the big cities and religious centers and truly famous places, which is to say the stops on the grand tour of the time.[15] At the great mausoleum of the Tokugawa at Nikkō, for instance, he spent just a day or so, and spent no more time at Matsushima, just as he used much more daylight and energy looking for obscure places around the home of his friend Tōkyū at Sukagawa than at Shirakawa Barrier. And at Hiraizumi, which he would later describe at some length in his travel account, he spent only a few hours before returning to his inn, where a hot bath was waiting.[16] In this context the labor he expended looking for *katsumi* flowers near Mount Asaka or doubling back to visit Ryūshakuji (up a stairway of seven hundred steps) seems incongruous. Incongruous, that is, unless one takes it as a revelation of his priorities, among which were a desire for this kind of searching and chance experience and encounters on the road of the sort that he included in all his travel writings. His fascination with the idea of "the changing and the unchanging" (*fueki ryūkō*) was clearly at work in his journey through the hinterlands, as it would be in the travel account that would be based on it.[17] Moreover, this same fascination carried over into his encounters with people—which included not just those of secure station (*fueki*), but anonymous souls in the endless flow of life (*ryūkō*) happened upon in the fields—grass cutters, farm children, servants, recluses, and so on.

---

13. Uozumi 2011, 72. In the letter to Sōshichi quoted above, Bashō uses that term in describing Rotsū, who was at that time going to be his companion, and alludes to going on the road as a beggar monk (*kotsujiki* 乞食) living by his begging bowl (Tanaka 2005, 181–82), and in another later to the same man in the Second Month, he refers to himself that way again (190).

14. *Kyoriku ribetsu no kotoba* 許六離別詞, 542, presents it as a quote from Kūkai.

15. See the Introduction, pp. xxxi–xxxii. Imoto 1970, 315, points out that Bashō persisted in searching out less important spots because he was not just a tourist but a believer and seeker committed to the journey: "As he busily walked about, searching . . . Bashō was able to hear the voices of the ancients."

16. See the Introduction, n. 90.

17. In *Kyoraishō* 去来抄, 518–20, Rochō says that it was when he was on his trip through the north country that Bashō first explicated the concept of *fueki ryūkō*. Imoto 1970, 316, narrows the location down to the travelers' time at Mount Haguro.

Bashō knew when he left that such a long journey was not without its risks.[18] Choosing to risk such an ordeal at all meant that he must have had confidence in his general health. However, he was troubled by flare-ups of his chronic illness during his journey on several occasions; and a few times he was held up by weather or logistical troubles.[19] In all, though, the journeying of the two men went as smoothly as could be expected. So far as we know, Bashō connected with all the people he had hoped to, with the exception of a disciple in Kanazawa who had recently died; and he saw most of the sites he had hoped to see, forgoing just a few fairly minor ones because of rain, heat, uncertain directions, or fatigue. Along the way, he seems to have kept notes for himself—*hokku* and sequences and a few descriptions of places—which we can assume, judging from his past habits, that he would later rely on in creating his text. Being able to rely on Sora for logistics was not just a fortunate factor but a necessary one if he was to concentrate on the practice of his art. Indeed, the only substantial time in his trek that he was left to his own devices at all was when Sora became ill and went on ahead to Ise, leaving Bashō to go on alone to the last leg of his planned journey— from Yamanaka Hot Springs and on through Tsuruga to Ōgaki. Scholars quickly point out, however, that at the most it was for a day or so that Bashō was truly on his own, if at all.[20] After that, various local disciples and then Rotsū and Etsujin, who had come to welcome him back to Mino, took up Sora's mantle.[21]

Bashō arrived in Ōgaki on the 21st day of the Eighth Month of 1689. Although in a certain sense the journey was over—that place being the terminus he had indicated in his letters—the pattern of his life changed little. Still he was put up by disciples, still he was meeting poets and supervising gatherings, and was in that sense "on the road." From Ōgaki he traveled to Ise, and then to his hometown in Iga Ueno. He would spend nearly two full years in various places around Lake Biwa and in Kyoto, Nara, and his hometown, visiting disciples and following the same routines. In a letter

---

18. A document from late in the Second Month of 1689 (Kon 2005a, 167) says that news of cold weather in Shirakawa made him push his departure forward because of his "apprehensions about his frequent illnesses" (*tabyō kokoromotonashi*).

19. Sora gives more details about illness (his own and Bashō's) and weather than Bashō does. We know that Bashō was ill in Sendai, on the Hokuroku Road, and at Iizuka. He saw physicians at various places and received medicine occasionally. Sora was ill in Kurobane and again during the stay in Kanazawa, finally leaving for home at Yamanaka.

20. Kanamori 2000, 417, calculates the distance that he traveled alone at six *li*. See n. 336 below.

21. As he went ahead, Sora stopped at places where he knew Bashō would stop and made arrangements in advance, often paying for Bashō's lodging and leaving letters with explanations and instructions.

he complained that he had been worn out by his trek through the hinterlands, not feeling well a single day through the following winter.[22] The summer of 1690 he spent in relative seclusion in a hut called Genjūan, west of Ishiyamadera in Ōtsu, and in the summer of the next year, he stayed in the cottage of his Kyoto disciple Kyorai in Saga—the stay that would become the basis for the last of his travel writings.

***

His own words tell us that Bashō carried ink and brushes on his journey through the hinterlands. As he was a poet who had to write poems in preparation for meetings or as gifts, such things were simply necessary, as much so as proper clothing to wear when meeting people of social stature.[23] But we can also assume that along with *hokku* and *kasen*[24] he jotted down notes that would assist him in writing *The Narrow Road through the Hinterlands*. Many scholars conclude that he took the title from a place name (near Sendai) mentioned in the text, arguing that he cannot have been unaware of a phrase from his own notes.[25] Uozumi demurs, contending that the more relevant allusion is to Bashō's 1693 prose piece written for Kyoriku about the essence of poetry, where he quotes Retired Emperor Go-Toba's definition of poetry as "sincerity with a touch of sadness."[26] It is in that context that Bashō writes, "Follow that one narrow thread—and do not lose it."[27] Whatever the case, scholars are unanimous in concluding that the title is a metaphor gesturing toward something much larger: the deepest realms of *haikai* or art in general, thus not just a physical journey but a search into the depths of poetic experience.

The process of creating the account took a long time, which scholars interpret as a sign that he thought of it as important. It began, one can only conclude, with notes

---

22. Tanaka 2005, 242.

23. Kanamori 2000, 38, notes that for this reason nice robes were probably carried by Sora or by a pack animal.

24. Ogata Tsutomu puts the number of *hokku* composed by Bashō on the journey at ninety-three, only forty-one of which made their way into *The Narrow Road through the Hinterlands* (see Eguchi 1998, 222).

25. See p. 115.

26. Uozumi 2011, 200. "Sincerity" translates *makoto. Kyoriku ribetsu no kotoba*, 542. This exact quote does not appear in Go-Toba's *Go-Toba no in gokuden* 後鳥羽の院御口伝, but Muramatsu 1972, 542, n. 9 refers to a passage that is similar.

27. *Kyoriku ribetsu no kotoba*, 542. The Japanese phrase is *sono hosoki hitosuji o tadori, ushinau koto nakare.*

he penned in 1689 during the journey, along with copies of poems and prefaces he had given to people along the way. But it appears that he began serious work on it in the latter half of 1692 and that it reached full form in the late autumn and early winter of 1693.[28] Documents indicate that this was a time of seclusion for the poet in his new Bashōan in Edo, and it seems that a causal relationship must be assumed.[29] Creating what would become his masterwork demanded uninterrupted time. Yet the complex manuscript history of the work reveals that he continued to tinker with it for months, not arriving at a "final" version until the Fourth Month of 1694, just before he set off for what would become the last of his trips to his hometown.[30] He carried the text with him during his final journey and provided fair copies to his brother in Iga Ueno and Sanpū in Edo.[31]

Why did he write it? The most obvious answer is that doing so had become a habit: he had left texts of his other major journeys—and often after a gap in time—and was simply following his routine, perhaps trying to improve on earlier attempts, as all scholars agree that he succeeded in doing. Indeed, in terms of varying stylistic textures, formal cohesion, and integration of prose and poetry, Bashō seems in *The Narrow Road through the Hinterlands* to have achieved a realization of what he had perhaps been striving for in his earlier works. But one should not discount another reason for the labor he put into his text: to enter his name in the lineage of past traveler-writers, from Ki no Tsurayuki to Saigyō and Sōgi, all of whom he alludes to in various contexts—to join the "elite fraternity of poetic practitioners for whom travel was the ultimate professional challenge," as I have argued elsewhere.[32] By the 1690s, Bashō was a poet of substantial reputation, and no doubt his many friends, disciples, and patrons looked forward to a distillation of his experience on the road in the form of a written account—at least of the *hokku* he wrote along the way, along with headnotes that together would make up a narrative. As Kusumoto Mutsuo has argued, it is important to remember that while *The Narrow Road through the Hinterlands* has over time gained a canonical status as a literary work, in the beginning it was a handwritten manuscript (*shahon* 写本) circulated among his friends to give them a glimpse of his travel experience and his evolving poetics.[33]

---

28. Ogata 1989, 192–93.

29. Uozumi 2011, 197–200, summarizes the arguments concerning the text's evolution.

30. A letter from Isui addressed to Sora on the 7th day of the Third Month of 1694 says: "I went to attend the old master at his cottage and got a peek at *The Narrow Road through the Hinterlands*, his collection of *hokku* written on the road." See Kon 2005a, 400.

31. See Uozumi 2011, 200; Sakurai and Ueno 1997, 114–16. A woodblock edition of the text was published by Izutsuya in Kyoto nearly a decade later.

32. Carter 2000, 193.

33. Kusumoto 2009, 361–64.

In that sense, *The Narrow Road through the Hinterlands* was another artifact of practice, a by-product of his work as a poet. Whatever else one could say about it, it was connected to an actual journey, which inevitably made his account into a narrative—a travel narrative. The journey had begun in Edo, and the text did the same; then he had gone to Nikkō, Shirakawa, Sendai, across Honshū to Sakata, and down the coast of the Japan Sea to Kanazawa and on to Mino, just as the text describes—and on the real roads that Bashō and his companions traveled, where he encountered real people and wrote poems arising mostly out of real-world contexts. In other words, as a travel account, *The Narrow Road through the Hinterlands* presented readers with a *duality* that no one could deny: actual, historical experience and the representation of that experience, and all grounded in details of everyday life that cannot be described as anything but realistic.

For a long time, it was the historical dimensions of this dichotomy that dominated scholarly studies of *The Narrow Road through the Hinterlands*. Scholars discovered corroboration everywhere they looked, making it possible to literally chart Bashō's course with documented people and places and contextualize the poems he wrote. But things changed upon the discovery in 1943 of a travel journal kept by Sora—titled *Sora tabi nikki* 曽良旅日記, or "Sora's Travel Journal"—which made it apparent that Bashō's account involved considerable aesthetic fashioning.[34]

What sort of fashioning? This is a question that has exercised scholars for nearly eight decades and produced a huge volume of commentary and analysis. Yet summary is possible. It is clear that scholars tend to concentrate on certain dimensions of the text that mark it as literary work rather than reportage: narrative design; style and texture; formal organization and structure; artifice; and literary purposes.

Narrative design. Literary works always involve a speaking voice not coincidental with their authors, and *The Narrow Road through the Hinterlands* is no exception. Historically, of course, the narrator of that text is undeniably Bashō the man and not some fanciful construct, but a close reading of the text reveals that he is not *simply* so. For instance, in his preamble he speaks as a solitary figure, and even after he is joined by Sora, he seldom shows interactions between the two men or involves his companion in episodes, instead focusing overwhelmingly on his own personal, subjective experience.[35] Furthermore, there are times when, as noted in the Introduction, Bashō adopts

---

34. See appendix, "Fact and/or Fiction: The Challenge of Sora's Diary." "Aesthetic fashioning" translates *kyokō* 虚構.

35. For instance, whether Sora is there or not, when he sits down to rest beneath Saigyō's willow, it is as an individual, as it is when he hears the Buddhist message in the cicadas at Ryūshakuji.

personas, the most noteworthy example being when he uses formulaic phrases deriving from Noh drama that invite comparison with "witness monks" (*wakisō*) who in many plays introduce viewers (or readers) into realms of history and myth—which is precisely what Bashō's text is doing, in a different medium.[36] What's more, and ironically, there are times when we *expect* Bashō to adopt a persona that he does not: the most obvious example being the persona of a *haikai* master, making critical comments on poems or interpretive asides, or doing things we know that he did during his journey, such as supervising gatherings, instructing students, and so on. In this sense, he maintains the pose of a literati traveler from the first word to the last, pursuing what one has to call a narrative strategy.

Style and texture. Long before the discovery of Sora's diary, scholars had remarked on Bashō's persistent mixing of genres, including most obviously poems and prose, but also long prose pieces and short; passages dense with Chinese characters and passages flowing smoothly with Japanese *kana*; narrative passages and offerings of natural description or exposition; and snippets from a broad variety of texts, in Chinese and Japanese. In all of this, scholars see Bashō the artist consciously creating a texture of linguistic, imagistic, thematic, and discursive variety that can only be a product of careful fashioning. Part and parcel of this are his scores of allusions to historical events, to works of Chinese philosophy and poetry, to Japanese poems and tales. And that is to say nothing of the many "characters" that appear in a random pattern in the text—children in the fields, an innkeeper, a mountain guide, prostitutes, and a host of historical figures from warriors to wandering monks, and so on—together making for a rich weave of reference and allusion. The total effect of Bashō's method is described in a postface by Soryū:

> The austere and the rich, the sturdy and the frail—all of these appear as *The Narrow Road through the Hinterlands* unfolds, impressing you so much that, without thinking, you get up and clap your hands, or lie prostrate, struck to the core. One moment you want to put on a travel cloak and go out on the road like he does, another you feel like stopping to rest and enjoy the sights before your eyes.[37]

Formal organization and structure. Since the discovery of Sora's account, most scholars have come to see Bashō's text not as a literal account but as a work of art. Some signs of

---

36. Fukasawa Shinji 2009, 372–82, argues that the *katarite*, or narrator, is a traveler modeled on Saigyō, who is presented as the narrator in *Senjūshō*.

37. *Kōhon Bashō zenshū*, vol. 6, 138.

organization are obvious. What else if not conscious "framing" can explain, for instance, why Bashō begins with a poem that includes the phrase *yuku haru*, or "departing spring," and ends with a poem that includes the phrase *yuku aki*, or "departing autumn"—the former actually composed only years later as he wrote up the final version of his narrative?[38] Such elements are of course not natural but constructed, betraying an organizing author and not a mere record-keeper. The full effect of the structuring makes for a sense of a fully realized work of verbal art that contrasts with his earlier travel writings in not dwindling to a final list of *hokku* but maintaining a carefully modulated mix of poetry and prose to the end.[39] Significantly, he offers no independent headnotes for many of the *hokku* in the text, not even in the case of poems that were obviously written for specific occasions; instead he makes the poems appear to emerge organically from within his narrative.

As one might expect, many scholars also see Bashō as creating more expansive architecture. In an attempt to suggest its highly polished and articulated effects, one scholar describes the work as a symphonic prose poem.[40] Other scholars break it down into three parts (or two), in concepts that focus on differing rhetorical treatments of geographic regions—the road to Sendai, the road down the Japan Sea coast, and so forth.[41] Needless to say, these analyses see various thematic purposes at work, usually involving dichotomies, such as civilization versus the outback, the present and the past, man versus nature, humans and their dwellings, archaic versus modern, immediate experience versus mediated experience, exterior versus interior, and so on. However, there are other, less reductive approaches that see Bashō as drawing on the resources of two subgenres of *haikai* discourse that he knew well—and from the inside, as part of his daily practice. One is the genre of *haibun*, or *haikai* prose, a form largely of Bashō's creation that in many cases consists of a prose preface and a *hokku* that can easily be seen as a model for the discrete sections of *The Narrow Road through the Hinterlands*, making it read like a series of *haibun*.[42] The other is *haikai renga*, or linked verse, the

---

38. See Imoto 1970, 333; Eguchi 1998, 213.

39. See Satō Katsuaki 2018, 15.

40. Imoto 1970, 332–33.

41. For a summary, see Kusumoto 1994, 53–55. He mentions structural analyses (*kōseiron* 構成論) by Ogata Tsutomu, Ueno Yōzō, Imoto Nōichi, Shiraishi Teizō, and Horikiri Minoru, but the list could be much longer. More recently, Satō Katsuaki 2018, 11–13, sees the *johakyū* dynamic (prelude, breakaway, and presto*)* of a linked-verse sequence at work in Bashō's text: Edo to Shirakawa Barrier serving as *jo*, Shirakawa Barrier to Nezu Barrier as *ha*, and Nezu Barrier to Ōgaki as *kyū*, with Shitomae Barrier as a center point in the *ha* section.

42. For treatment of this general topic, see Millett 1997. Eguchi 1998, 234–40, documents that Bashō's experiments with *haibun* as a new genre correspond with the period of his travel writings.

rules and conventions of which by long habit must have been hardwired into any *haikai* master's brain and can serve as a template to analyze what he offers us: an elastic text, an interweaving of categories in a scheme committed to modulation and variety above all else.[43]

It should come as no surprise, then, that the dynamics of linked-verse can so easily be seen to relate to elements of Bashō's writing: his inclusion of images from all the main categories of linked verse—each of the four seasons, love, and miscellaneous topics, such as Buddhism, Shinto, and travel; his careful alternation of elements mundane and distinctive (*ji* and *mon* in the aesthetic vocabulary of linked verse); his use of ellipsis and "asides" that seem to draw attention away from the main narrative momentarily; his employment of various styles in order to either slow down or speed up the reading progress. *The Narrow Road through the Hinterlands* in that sense presents readers with a flow of images and experiences of precisely the sort that any linked-verse sequence was designed to represent. And in order to sustain that sense of flow and a sense of randomness, Bashō constantly toys with any sense of a steady, linear plotline, offering no *hokku* on major sites, such as Shirakawa and Matsushima, while memorializing more obscure places, such as a small checkpoint on the way into Dewa that he remembers with a poem about fleas, lice, and a pissing horse.[44] As we follow the travelers, bits and pieces of history pop up in the geography or on memorials or in the narrator's mind— always fragmentary, never whole, always present only in a surrounding absence, always alternating with human encounters that must have the same temporal fate—and we thus experience something like what poets do together in the *za*.

Artifice. Attention to schemes of narration, texture, and organization inevitably leads scholars back to the central question arising from Sora's journal: How much of *The Narrow Road through the Hinterlands* is fact, and how much fiction? This is not an easy question to answer, because discrepancies can in so many cases be explained by arguing that Bashō—or Sora, in some cases—had a faulty memory, or by other things of no significance to modern readers, such as social relationships or station.[45] But a close comparison shows that such explanations do not always suffice. To begin with, it is clear that Bashō has omitted a great deal, including an interesting episode like the

---

43. As early as the 1850s, the *haikai* poet Baba Kinkō analyzed the Ichinoburi episode of the text in terms of *renga* categories. See Ueno 2005, 290–92.
44. As Eguchi 1998, 92, points out, the poem would surely have given offense if used to begin a linked-verse sequence. In this way Bashō is making creative use of an independent *hokku* in order to provide local color and show the less seemly aspects of travel.
45. Fukasawa and Kusumoto 2009, 116, see this as evidence of fashioning. See also Muramatsu 1977, 193–94.

following that he neglects to even allude to but which Sora records. It took place on the coastal road between Niigata and Kanazawa, on the 5th day of the Seventh Month:

> Rained 'til morning, letting up between seven and eight. Rain started again just after we left Izumozaki. Arrived at Kashiwazaki and delivered letter from Yasaburō to Ten'ya Yasōbei about arranging lodging, but Bashō was out of sorts and left. People came running two or three times to stop us, but he would not have it and left. Light rain off and on. Arrived at Hatsusaki around five o'clock. For lodging, stayed at the inn of Tawaraya Rokurōbei.[46]

Scholars are divided about why Bashō chose not to stay in Kashiwazaki, some arguing that the owner offended him somehow, others that the rooms were not adequate. For whatever reason, Bashō became angry and chose not to stay at the place arranged by his disciple Teiji (here identified as Yasaburō), instead going down the road to another town, despite persistent rain showers. And Sora does not gloss over that this happened because the master was "out of sorts" (*fukai* 不快), and continued so the next day, perhaps a fact that the master did not want to make part of his "literary" text.

This is not all: for as well as omissions, the text also contains additions or enhancements—sections of the work that Bashō has almost certainly concocted.[47] Moreover, evidence of artistic fashioning is also apparent in episodes that, while not entirely fictional, are exaggerated or embellished, suggesting that it was part and parcel of his method. This is obvious, for instance, when we compare the two accounts of Bashō and Sora of the night spent at Iizuka, an obscure place about which Sora says next to nothing, whereas Bashō gives us one of his longer descriptions of lodging on the road, as well as some details about his own state of mind—and body.

> Bashō: That night we spent in Iizuka. There being a hot spring, we bathed first and then took lodging in a wretched house where we had only straw mats on a dirt floor. With no lamps, we did our best to make up our beds by the light of the hearth fire. In the night there were claps of thunder and

---

46. Ogata 1995, 339. Yasaburō refers to Teiji. Ten'ya Yasōbei was known by the *haikai* name Shōya and Rokurōbei by the *haikai* name Shōsai.

47. See appendix, "Fact and/or Fiction: The Challenge of Sora's Diary," for details. Sections scholars deem fictional or at least highly embellished are the encounter with prostitutes at Ichiburi, the episode with the little girl Kasane at Nasu no Kurobane, and the description of his visit to the recluse Tōsai in Fukui.

constant squalls of rain, and there was a leak in the roof right over where I lay and so many fleas and mosquitoes biting me that I couldn't get to sleep. Then, to top it all off, I had a flare-up of my chronic ailment, so intense that I nearly passed out. The short summer night passed slowly as I waited for the sky to brighten. When it did, we hit the road again.

Sora: Across the river and ten *chō* toward the east was a place called Iizuka that had a hot spring. . . . The road up went from Fukushima to Sawano, Iizuka, and Ko'ori, and we were told that the road down went through Ko'ori, Iizuka, Sawano, coming out at Fukushima. The skies clouded up at midday, and rain began to fall that evening, coming down hard that night. We stayed in Iizuka and went to the bath. On the 3rd we rose at about eight and left Iizuka. It was two *li* to Ko'ori. Light rain fell from time to time.

Is it possible that Bashō remembered this level of detail long after the events, while Sora writing at the time did not? Perhaps. But scholars think it more likely that the master embellished his account for dramatic effect—that he was more interested in *affective* than in journalistic detail.

In a letter to Kyorai, Bashō explicitly condoned changing facts in a travel account for artistic reasons,[48] and it appears that he meant it. Muramatsu Tomotsugu, in an article on the way Bashō plays with certain names, sums up the matter amusingly by imagining what Sora must have thought of the account when he first read it:

It was probably Sora who was the first reader of *The Narrow Road through the Hinterlands*. Right off, he must have been surprised to read a parting verse (*yuku haru ya*) composed at the time the travelers set off that he did not remember at all from that time, and surprised again to find woven into the account verses by himself that he had no recollection of composing; then he must have been even more surprised to encounter unexpectedly a number of episodes (such as the Ichiburi story) that had never happened. At that point he must have realized that what Bashō had produced was not a literal or true-to-life record, but something largely fashioned: that

---

48. Among comments on Kyorai's *Ise kikō* 伊勢紀行 (1686) Bashō suggests switching the attribution of poems by the author and his sister. See Ōuchi and Wakaki 1986, 39.

the Sora that appeared in its lines was not his real-world self and that the "I" of the text was not just the real-world Bashō.[49]

Literary purposes. Of course, all of this had to be justified in terms of some goal or goals. If Bashō is offering not a day-by-day record of a journey, or a collection of poems with headnotes, but a fully articulated literary effort, then its literary features—narrative approach, style and texture, organization and structure, and artificial qualities—should serve a larger purpose or purposes. Here scholars offer a host of possibilities (some of which I have already listed above in relation to formal organization and structure). Not surprisingly, the most common and expansive theory is that Bashō is using travel as a metaphor for the vagaries of human existence. Related to this are theories that see it as a Buddhist meditation on the struggle of life and the inevitability of death, or as a historical meditation on the vanity of human ambition. Then there are theories that see the work as a contemplation of other large categories of human meaning—man and nature, for instance, or temporality. Finally, there are those that see it, in more strictly literary terms, as a statement of the ideals of the Japanese *haikai* tradition, an illustration of Bashō's budding poetics of *karumi* ("lightness"), or a dynamic treatment of Bashō's idea of the unchanging and the changing.[50]

Little in the text itself helps us choose one of these theories—which are not necessarily mutually incompatible—over another. But one may summarize by saying that nearly all scholars agree that Bashō had in mind big issues—whether philosophical, historical, religious, poetic, or aesthetic, in any order, in any combination. From the beginning he signals that he is not just giving a day-to-day account of any actual journey. As one reads the celebrated words of his preamble, "The moon, the sun—these are wayfarers down the generations; so too the years are travelers that come and go." One cannot but remember his commitment in an earlier account to going beyond the usual, "That day it rained, clearing at noon; in this place was a pine tree, in that place

---

49. Muramatsu 1977, 194.
50. To name a few examples: Ogata and Uozumi see it as a contemplation of life and death inspired by the passing of people close to its author: first Isshō, in 1688; then his beloved disciple, Tokoku, in 1690; and then four people dear to him in succession in 1693—Rogan, Tōin, Ranran, and Tōjun, father of Bashō's chief disciple, Kikaku. Takahashi Shōji is foremost among those who analyze the work in terms of Zen practice and Yamamoto Kenkichi among those who analyze it as an articulation of Bashō's *karumi*. Horikiri Minoru is one of many scholars associated with analyses based on linked-verse dynamics and *fueki ryūkō*. For more on *karumi*, see Miner 1979, 120–23; Ueda 1965, 59–63; 1967, 165–67; Qiu 2005, 152–59.

So-and-So River flowed by."[51] His ambitions were greater, which is perhaps why he was careful to be comprehensive in so many ways, including references to historical events of all periods of Japanese history; men and women of all ages; a broad representation of social classes and levels of wealth; all poetic forms, in both Chinese and Japanese; and indeed all other forms of literature—classical tales, folktales, Noh plays, shrine and temple records, sutras, gazetteers, histories, philosophical works, and so on. None of these features—except perhaps poetry itself, which he is careful to present in all its forms, beginning with rice-planting songs and going all the way to erudite poems from poets such as Du Fu—is allowed to dominate, but each is presented as part of a broad picture of literary culture in Bashō's day.

What did Bashō think of *The Narrow Road through the Hinterlands*? We cannot know, of course, but he left a hint in a chat he had with Hattori Dohō, a childhood friend from Iga and staunch disciple.

> He mentioned that he had written up an account of his travels of a certain year, but when I asked to see it, he replied, "Oh, it's really nothing special; but if you take a look at it after I die, you might think, 'Ah, so even something like this can be moving and contain things worth reading about.'" Impressive words, I think. I haven't seen the work, but still I am moved.[52]

We cannot be certain that he alludes here to *The Narrow Road through the Hinterlands* and not another travel work, of course. But we can be certain about the centrality of the old ideal of *aware*—said of experiences that were moving, touching, often tinged with the sadness inherent in ephemeral experience but also somehow beautiful—in his poetics. And if he felt that any of his travel writings found such a response in readers, he would doubtless have been content. However modest, he was well aware of his reputation and knew that the works he left behind with family and disciples would be published and that for some time—no author ever knows how long—his travel writing would be read.

---

51. The quotation is from *Knapsack Notes*. See p. 51.
52. *Sanzōshi*, 606–7. Quoted in Ogata 1989, 193.

THE NARROW ROAD THROUGH
THE HINTERLANDS

The moon, the sun—these are wayfarers down the generations; so too the years are travelers that come and go.[53] For those who bob their lives away on boats or lead horses as old age approaches, travel is daily life, travel is home.[54] Many among the ancients died on the road,[55] and I, too, for some years past had felt the tug of winds that tatter the clouds, unable to put rambling from my mind. So it was that after a jaunt on ocean shores,[56] I cleared the cobwebs from my broken-down hut last autumn, and as the year drew to a close set my heart on making for Shirakawa Barrier as soon as the skies turned hazy with spring.[57] Lured by the god of wanderlust, I could not keep my mind on anything; beckoned by the god of the road, I could not hold my hand to any task.[58] After mending the holes in my trousers, putting a new cord on my rain hat, and bracing my kneecaps with moxa treatments,[59] I was thinking of the moon at

---

53. Fukasawa and Kusumoto 2009, 58, reference a prose piece by Li Bai, "Feast in a Garden of Peach and Plum Blossoms on a Spring Night" (春夜宴桃李園序): "All things in Heaven and earth are in travelers' lodgings; the sun and the moon are wayfarers down the generations, and our lives—they are dreams, phantoms" (夫天地者、万物之逆旅、光隠者、百代之過客、而浮生若夢). In an abstract sense, the word *tsukihi* (meaning "the moon and the sun" and/or "months and days") in Bashō's introduction means "time."

54. *Fusō in'itsuden* 扶桑隠逸伝 (1664) notes a reference to the *renga* master Sōgi by Gensei in his: "Sōgi made travel his home, the wind and the moon his life." See Fukasawa and Kusumoto 2009, 59.

55. Among the people he had in mind were probably Saigyō, the *renga* master Sōgi, and the Chinese poets Li Bai and Du Fu. See Yokosawa 1995, 173.

56. A reference to his time at Suma and Akashi the previous year, as noted in *Knapsack Notes.* See pp. 67–70.

57. See *GSIS* 518 by Nōin about visiting the Shirakawa Barrier: "From the capital / I set out on the road / with the spreading haze. / Now autumn winds are blowing / at Shirakawa Barrier" *(miyako o ba / kasumi to tomo ni / tachishikado / akikaze zo fuku / shirakawa no seki)*. See p. 107.

58. *Sozorogami* そぞろ神 was evidently a folk god believed to drive people to distraction; "god of the road" translates Dōsojin 道祖神.

59. Treatments involved burning powder made from mugwort on specific points on the skin to stimulate and restore the proper flow of vital energy.

Matsushima and feeling restless. Giving up the place where I had been living, I moved into a retreat owned by Sanpū.[60]

My grass hut, too,	*kusa no to mo*
now home to someone else.	*sumikawaru yo zo*
A doll's house.[61]	*hina no ie*

This and the seven other verses of a first linked-verse sheet I left hanging on the pillar of the hut.[62]

It was at the end of the Third Month, on the final 7th day, in the second year of the Genroku era,[63] as I recall. The sky was murky with dawn light that dulled the glow of the lingering moon, but Fuji's peak appeared faintly in the distance.[64] "When will I see the cherry blossoms at Ueno and Yanaka again?" I had to wonder, saddened by the thought.[65] My closest friends had all gathered the night before and rode along in the boat to see us on our way. It was at a place called Senju that we got off the boat, and my heart was heavy with the thought of the three thousand *li* before us. In this fleeting world we are always at a crossroads, but still at this one I shed a few tears.

---

60. See n. 4 above. Sanpū was an important disciple and patron.

61. *Bashō kushū* no. 52. The next tenant—a man named Hiraemon—had a wife, a daughter, and a grandchild (Tanaka 2005, 195; Takahashi 2002, 310) and would likely celebrate the *hina matsuri*, or Dolls' Festival, held on the 3rd day of the Third Month, which was around the time Bashō turned over the house.

62. A common custom. Bashō may have in mind a scene in *The Tale of Genji* when a young woman leaves a poem expressing her grief in the crack of a pillar as she leaves her father's home because of a divorce between her parents (*Genji monogatari*, vol. 3, 364–65; Cf. Tyler 2001, 533–35). Some scholars argue that the "hut" (*iori*) refers to Sanpū's retreat, but most take it to mean Bashō's Fukagawa cottage.

63. The second year of the Genroku era corresponded to 1689 in the Western calendar. The three days that end in 7 are the 7th, the 17th, and the 27th.

64. See two passages: one from Kinoshita Chōshōshi's *Sanka no ki* 山家の記: "Near and far the mountains were murky in spreading mist, a captivating sight . . . and how elegant was the faint moon lingering in the misty sky of dawn" (*Chōshōshi zenshū* 2, 9); and another from *The Tale of Genji*: "The sky was murky with dawn light, but the moon still glowed faintly, making for a most charming scene" (translation mine). See *Genji monogatari*, vol. 1, 180; Cf. Tyler 2001, 41. My translation follows the interpretation of Kon 2004, 38–42.

65. Places known for their cherry blossoms, located northwest of Bashō's cottage. See Kon 2004, 42–46, for a discussion of the contentious question of whether the cherry trees were actually in bloom when Bashō left.

As spring moves on	*yuku haru ya*
birds weep, and fishes' eyes	*tori naki uo no*
brim with tears.[66]	*me wa namida*

I meant this to be the first use of my writing kit,[67] but we could not get going. The people who had come to see us off stood in a line in the road—thinking to stay there until our backs faded from view, I suppose.

When this time I made up my mind, almost on a whim, to trek the long road through the hinterlands,[68] I remembered those lines about lamenting "white hairs added to my head beneath Wu's skies."[69] Yet there were regions I had heard of but not seen,[70] and I thought how happy I would be if I made the trip and returned home alive. So it was with that frail hope that I set out, getting as far as Sōka the first day and taking lodging there.[71] My skinny bones suffered under the weight of what I bore on my shoulders. I had wanted only my body for baggage, but still I carried a paper robe[72] to use lying down at night, a bathing garment, rain gear, ink, and brushes; and then there were the gifts I had been reluctant to accept but could not throw away. There they were, burdens I had to bear.

---

66. *Bashō kushū* no. 30.

67. *Yatate* 矢立て is a small writing kit holding ink and brushes. Keeping a log of *hokku* composed on the way, along with perhaps notes on places visited, was a conventional practice of travelers. Here the word functions symbolically, meaning the first step of his journey. Many scholars believe this poem was written much later, when Bashō was writing up his account. See Hori and Imoto, 272, n. 475.

68. "Trek" here translates the word *angya*, originally meaning a kind of ascetic pilgrimage undertaken by Zen monks but by Bashō's time also meaning just going on the road.

69. Fukasawa and Kusumoto 2009, 68, note sources for this line in Chinese poems by Li Dong in *San ti shi* and a Zen poem from *Shi ren yu xie* 詩人玉屑 by a priest named Keshi of Fujian. Bashō probably had in mind a line from the Noh play *Katsuragi* 葛城, 344, "a hat heavy with the snows of Wu" (*kasa wa omoshi gosan no yuki* 笠は重し呉山の雪).

70. Hisatomi 2011, 5, n. 3, points out that Bashō echoes the openings of various Noh plays, such as *Nishikigi* 錦木: "Having never seen the eastern provinces, I made up my mind to go in pilgrimage to the far edges of Michinoku." The wording *karisome ni omoitachite* suggests that he had been thinking about making the trip for some time before finally—on the spur of the moment—he determined to go ahead. See Fukasawa and Kusumoto 2009, 67.

71. Sora's text makes it clear that the two went farther, to Kasukabe. The structure "This time I made up my mind . . . getting as far as . . ." (*kono tabi . . . omoitachite . . . ni tadoritsukinikeri*) is again reminiscent of the early lines of many Noh plays, including *Atsumori, Eguchi, Nishikigi,* and *Katsuragi.* See Yamamoto Yuiitsu 1994, 143–44.

72. J. *kamiko* 紙子, a short, sleeved jacket made of thick paper treated with persimmon juice to make it softer and more pliable.

We paid our respects at Muronoyashima. My companion, Sora,[73] said, "The god honored here is called Konohanasakuyabime, the same as the god at Mount Fuji.[74] After holing up in a doorless chamber, she set it on fire, vowing to prove her purity, and through that ordeal gave birth to Hohodemi no Mikoto.[75] That is why the place is called Muronoyashima and why people mention smoke in poems they write here."[76] Also, it is known from shrine writings that this is a place where eating the fish called *konoshiro* is forbidden.[77]

On the 30th we lodged at the foot of Mount Nikkō. The proprietor of the place said this: "I'm called Buddha Gozaemon—because my aim is to be forthright in all things.[78] So relax, be my guest: lie down on your pillows of grass and spend the night at your ease." What Buddha might it be, I wondered, who reveals himself thus in our world of dust, assisting men who are like beggar priests on pilgrimage?[79] Observing him, I saw that he was without guile, straightforward to a fault. Indeed, he was "close to benevolence—strong, unyielding, simple, discreet,"[80] a man one could praise for his purity of disposition.[81]

---

73. Since this is the first mention of Sora, some scholars argue that he only joined Bashō on the road at or after Sōka, having left in advance in order to make travel arrangements. I follow Ueno 1989, 162, and many other scholars in concluding that the two men departed Edo together.

74. The same god is worshipped at Sengen Shrine at the foot of Mount Fuji.

75. The story is that when she became pregnant after one night with Ninigi no Mikoto, she vowed that she would give birth in the midst of the fire, thus proving her purity. Aston 1972, 71–73. Her son's complete name is Hikohohodemi no Mikoto.

76. *Utsumuro* 無戸室, "doorless chamber," is a partial homophone with Muronoyashima. Yokosawa 1995, 181, notes that the story about Konohanasakuyabime is in fact not connected to the name of Muronoyashima. See also Fukasawa and Kusumoto 2009, 71.

77. As a ruse to deceive a suitor into thinking his daughter had died, a man substituted *konoshiro* for her body at the cremation ceremony, because it smelled like burning human flesh. Yokosawa 1995, 182.

78. Fukasawa and Kusumoto 2009, 73, note an allusion to a story in *Senjūshō* (78) about an obscure monk named Gōsai associated with Hatsusedera who is "so honest in all things that the people around him named him Master Honesty." Fukasawa and Kusumoto 2009, 73, note that in Shinto teaching honesty was considered to be the most fundamental virtue.

79. Sora did have a begging bowl and went out at least once (Yokosawa 1995, 315). Hisatomi 2011, 9, n. 4, notes that Bashō uses the word *gotoki* ("like") because he is not truly tonsured.

80. From the Confucian *Analects*. For the original text and another translation, see Lau 1983, 130–31. Sora (see Ogata 1995, 313), notes that the men stayed in the house of a man named Gozaemon in the town outside the gates of the shrine.

81. "Purity of disposition" translates *seishitsu* 清質, a neologism. See Tanaka 2009, 58–59.

On the 1st day of the Fourth Month, we offered obeisance at Oyama.[82] Anciently, the name was written with the characters 二荒山 Futarasan,[83] until the Great Teacher Kūkai changed it to 日光 Nikkō.[84] He must have seen a thousand years into the future, I muse: for now the light from this place shines throughout the heavens, its beneficence overflowing in all eight directions, where peace prevails in the homes of all four classes of people. Overwhelmed, I put down my writing brush.

Awesome sight:	*ana tōto*
green leaves and young leaves	*aoba wakaba no*
glowing in the sun.[85]	*hi no hikari*

Haze hung on Mount Kurokami, where the snow still shone white.[86]

Head now shaved,	*sorisutete*
I am at Mount Kurokami—	*kurokamiyama ni*
on robe-changing-day.[87]	*koromogae*
Sora	

As to my fellow traveler, Sora: he is of the Kawai lineage and had been called Sōgorō. His eaves being next to the eaves of Bashōan, he had helped me with chores, gathering wood and

---

82. J. Oyama 御山 ("honored mountain"), the common name of the place at the time, which was highly venerated because of its status as the family temple of the Tokugawa lineage. "Offered obeisance" translates *keihai su* 詣拝, another neologism. See Tanaka 2009, 59–60.

83. Nikkō is the Sinified reading of the characters 日光, meaning "light of the sun." It was Kūkai who chose Fudaraku 普陀落山 (Skt. Potalaka, meaning "brilliance"), a sacred mountain in India, for the "naming text" (記文) of the shrine. See Yokosawa 1995, 184. The characters Bashō uses are phonetic equivalents which could be read as Futarasan or Nikōsan.

84. While it was believed in Bashō's time that Kūkai was the founder of the shrine (Fukasawa and Kusumoto 2009, 76), it appears that actually Shōdō, who visited the place a number of times, established Shihonryūji and later, in 784, the shrine.

85. *Bashō kushū* no. 351. I follow the *Nakaobon* here, which has *ana* rather than the later *ara*, which was the version composed on the spot at Nikkō. Ogata points out that in poetry handbooks "young leaves" (*wakaba*) denotes the Fourth Month, whereas "green leaves" (*aoba*) is in the miscellaneous category and implies no particular season (Fukasawa and Kusumoto 2009, 77). The contrast is between deeper greens of evergreens and the light green of new growth on deciduous trees.

86. Fukasawa and Kusumoto 2009, 79, note an allusion to a sentence in section nine of *Tales of Ise*, which tells of the travels of a man from Kyoto to the East Country: "I look up at Mount Fuji, where here at the end of the Fifth Month, white snow is falling" (*Ise monogatari*, 141).

87. Some scholars argue that this poem is by Bashō rather than Sora. See Fukasawa and Kusumoto 2009, 79–80.

hauling water.[88] Happy to think of being by my side to see the vistas of Matsushima and Kisagata,[89] and determined to help me with the trials of the road, he had shaved his head and put on dark robes at dawn on the day we set out, changing the characters of his name, Sōgo, from 惣五 to 宗悟.[90] That is why he composed the *hokku* at Kurokamiyama, "Mount of Dark Robes." The words "robe-changing" have power and work well.[91]

Just over half a *li* away, up a mountain, was a waterfall. Water fell a hundred feet from high on an outcropping of rock, ending in a pool formed by countless stones. One squeezes oneself into the depression in the rock behind the falls to see the water descending, which is why the name has been passed down—Uraminotaki, "Waterfall Viewed from Behind."

> For a moment   *shibaraku wa*
> I go behind a waterfall.   *taki ni komoru ya*
> First summer rigor.[92]   *ge no hajime*

I knew someone[93] at Nasunokurobane, so we set off across the moors, hoping to find a direct path. As we moved along, our eyes on a village in the distance,[94] rain started

---

88. A standard phrase describing devout monks who go into service as part of their devotions. Fukasawa and Kusumoto 2009, 80. Tanisawa Shōichi notes (see Sakurai 2006, 133–34) that there was a townhouse of a samurai lineage that Sora was associated with in Fukagawa.

89. Both places were among the most renowned sights in Japan. The scholar-educator Kaibara Ekiken ranked the two sights as numbers one and two in all of Japan (Fukasawa and Kusumoto 2009, 81).

90. Many scholars believe Sora actually took the tonsure at the end of 1688, fully a year and a half before. However, a document from the Third Month of 1689 indicates that he had not taken that step yet and that the *Narrow Road through the Hinterlands* account may be accurate (Fukasawa and Kusumoto 2009, 81). The new characters carried symbolic meanings: the first gesturing toward a long lineage of poet-priests, the second meaning "enlightenment."

91. "Robe-changing" refers to changing into lighter robes at the beginning of summer, the 1st day of the Fourth Month. In Sora's case, there is the added meaning of having just changed from lay robes to religious attire.

92. *Bashō kushū* no. 262. There is considerable agreement that this poem was written much later and inserted into the narrative in place of another (Fukasawa and Kusumoto 2009, 85). *Ge no hajime* 夏の初 refers to the practice among Buddhist priests of going into retreat in the summer, concentrating on sutra reading and copying and other devotional activities. The waterfall was associated with Fudō Myō'ō, a protector deity. That they stopped even briefly was no doubt indication of reverence and of Sora's recent tonsure (Fukasawa and Kusumoto 2009, 85).

93. Jōbōji Zusho or his brother, Tōsui, or both (Fukasawa and Kusumoto 2009, 87).

94. Most likely a village named Tamanyū 玉生 (or Tamau).

to fall and the sun was setting, which sent us to a farmer's house for lodging,[95] but the next morning we got up and headed off through the fields again. Coming upon a horse grazing, we begged help from its owner, who was there cutting grass, and found that—wouldn't you know—he was not without feeling, peasant though he was. "You're new to the place, and the paths here go so many ways—east, west, straight across, and off to the side—that I fear you'd take the wrong one; so, you just take my horse and send him back when he stops,"[96] he said. Two little children came running along behind the horse. One was a little miss[97] who said her name was Kasane. It was an unusual name and seemed very refined.

> "Layers" is her name: kasane to wa
> not after the common pink yaenadeshiko no
> but the multi-petaled.[98] na naru beshi
>   Sora

When we got to a group of dwellings, we tied a small gift to the horse's saddle and sent him back.

At Kurobane we called on a certain Jōbōji, the lord deputy of the mansion.[99] Though not expecting us, he was delighted and kept us visiting for days.[100] His younger brother,

---

95. Fukasawa and Kusumoto 2009, 88, point out that other sources identify the "farmer's house" as the house of the village headman of Tamau, evidence that Bashō is taking liberties. Sora also says the skies were clear.

96. Fukasawa and Kusumoto 2009, 90, note a story from China about Qi Huagong, a king in the Spring and Autumn era who, when lost in a field, followed an old horse to find the way.

97. *Kohime*, literally, "little maiden," a term of endearment.

98. The *nadeshiko* (*dianthus*, "pink") flower appears in poems going back to earliest times, often serving as a metaphor for a beautiful young woman. The suffix *yae*, literally "eight layered," means many. Fukasawa and Kusumoto 2009, 91–92, point out that *yaenadeshiko* were not wild but planted and were popular in fine gardens in Edo and Kyoto. Sora's poem suggests that the common pinks (*kawara nadeshiko*) growing in the fields are not elegant enough to represent the little girl. Many commentators follow the Kikaku text in attributing this poem to Bashō. Even those who are dubious about Kikaku's text believe (rather ungenerously) that the poem is too well done to be by Sora and was probably written by Bashō and "given" to Sora (Yokosawa 1995, 189).

99. Kanokohata Takakatsu, otherwise known as Jōbōji Zusho. *Kandai* 館代 ("lord deputy of the mansion") is a neologism. Normally, one would expect the word *jōdai* 城代 ("castle deputy"), but Kurobane evidently lacked a proper castle. Tanaka 2009, 60–61.

100. He spent nearly two weeks in Kurobane and Tōsui's house in nearby Yoze. The grammatical subject of *omoigakenu* ("to not expect") is unclear. Another interpretation (see Fukasawa and

a man named Tōsui,[101] waited on us morn and night, inviting us to his own house and even arranging for us to visit some of his relatives.[102] And so the time went by. One day we went out to take a look at the site where there had once been a dog shoot,[103] and also walked through the bamboo grasses of Nasu[104] and visited the tomb of Lady Tamamo.[105] Then we paid our respects at the Hachiman Shrine,[106] learning that it was that shrine Yoichi Munetaka had spoken of when he made his vow, "above all to the God Hachiman of my lineage and native land"[107]—a story that I found especially moving. As the sun was going down, we returned to Tōsui's house.

There was a temple called Shugen Kōmyōji.[108] We were invited to visit and worshipped at the Gyōjadō.[109]

Kusumoto 2009, 95) is that Bashō is surprised to find that Zusho has succeeded his father and is now *kandai*. Ogata (see Fukasawa and Kusumoto 2009, 95) argues that it is unlikely Bashō was unexpected and that this is an example of aesthetic fashioning.

101. Younger brother of Jōbōji Zusho, who lived nearby in Yoze. Sora indicates that Bashō visited at his house first, going to see Zusho later, because he was thinking in terms of social status. Scholars argue about whether the name is Tōsui or Suitō, the characters reversed (Fukasawa and Kusumoto 2009, 95). Muramatsu 1977, 192–95, argues that it is out of deference that Bashō uses contrived names for Tōkyū, Tōsai, and Tōsui because they were friends rather than disciples. See nn. 132 and 352 below.

102. While there, they visited Kōmyōji, where the wife of the head priest was the sister of Takakatsu and Tōsui.

103. An area where dogs were penned in and shot for sport.

104. See poem 348 in Minamoto no Sanetomo's *Kinkaishū* 金槐集 (1213). "A fighting man / reaches to straighten arrows / in his quiver— / hail glancing from his wrist guard / down onto Nasu Moor" (*mononofu no / yanami tsukurou / kote no ue ni / arare tabashiru / nasu no shinohara*).

105. A story that Bashō probably knew through the Noh play *Sesshōseki* 殺生石. In the story Lady Tamamo, a fox spirit, seduces the emperor and, when she is found out, flees into the fields, where she is shot and dies in a stony area that thereafter exudes poisonous fumes. See p. 106 below.

106. The shrine visited this day, the Kanamaru Hachiman, ancestral shrine of the Nasu and Ōzeki clans, is not the one alluded to in the story of Nasu no Yoichi from *Tales of the Heike*. See Fukasawa and Kusumoto 2009, 97. Yokosawa 1995, 190, says that Bashō probably wrote down what he was told by his guide.

107. An episode in *Tales of the Heike* about how Nasu no Yoichi Munetaka, a young Minamoto warrior, rides into the surf to shoot at a fan placed on a pole on one of the Taira boats on a dare, and succeeds in knocking it into the sea after praying to the God Hachiman of the shrine of his native land. *Heike monogatari*, 369–73; McCullough 1988, 366–68.

108. Shugen refers to an eclectic religious movement with roots in both esoteric Buddhist rites and Shinto mountain worship. Mountain ascetics are again important later when the men visit the Three Mountains of Dewa.

109. Gyōjadō 行者堂, "The Hall of Devouts," is a generic term for a small temple honoring devouts of the past. This structure honored En no Ozuno, also known as En no Gyōja. The clogs

In summer mountains	*natsuyama ni*
we bow before wooden clogs	*ashida o ogamu*
and go out the gate.[110]	*kadode kana*

In this same province, back behind Unganji, is what remains of the mountain retreat of Reverend Butchō.[111]

How it pains me	*tateyoko no*
to have for my abode	*goshaku ni taranu*
even this grass hut,	*kusa no io*
not even five feet square!	*musubu mo kuyashi*
If not for the rains . . .[112]	*ame nakariseba*

Sometime in the past he told me that he wrote these lines on a rock there with charcoal from a pine torch.[113] I decided to go and see the place, and headed off, staff in hand. Lots of people went along, encouraging me on my way—young people talking loudly and making a lot of noise; and it wasn't long before we reached the foot of the mountain. The valley gave an impression of great depth, and the path leading into it and off into the distance was dark with pines and cryptomeria. Water dropping onto the moss made the way slippery, and it was chilly beneath the skies, Fourth Month though it was. Just as we saw the last of the ten sights,[114] we came to a bridge and passed through the temple gate.

"Now then, where would his place have been?" I wondered to myself as I clambered up the path behind the temple, and then there it was, his little hut built on stone, right

---

were one-tooth, high clogs, for walking in rain. Fukasawa and Kusumoto 2009, 98–99, say "worship" implies not just honoring En no Ozuno but also praying for good health on the road and against rain as they prepared to enter the "outback" beyond Shirakawa Barrier.

110. *Bashō kushū* no. 255.

111. In the Zen sect, *oshō* ("reverend") was an honorific title that probably did not imply a particular rank. Butchō was not living there when Bashō visited but outlived him by two decades.

112. Just as in *A Pilgrimage to Kashima* (see p. 79), Butchō's poem is an *uta*. Living in a place barely half the size of the usual ten-foot-square hut is meant as an indication of Butchō's dedication. Leaving a poem upon leaving a residence—as Bashō had in Edo (p. 98)—was an old custom. Bashō may have had in mind a reference to the practice in section 69 of *Tales of Ise*.

113. *Matsu no hai*, in other words, a piece of charcoal from a *tsuimatsu* or pine torch—i.e., a torch made up of pine boughs, usually put in a long holder and held aloft. That Butchō used so rude a substance rather than ink is a measure of his rustic lifestyle.

114. A list that included groves of bamboo and plum trees, peaks, rocks, and buildings.

up against a hollow in the rock face.[115] It felt like I was seeing the Death Gate of Zen Master Yuanmiao or the Rock Chamber of Fayun.[116]

> Even woodpeckers　　　　　　*kitsutsuki mo*
> do no harm to this hut.　　　　*io wa yaburazu*
> Summer grove.[117]　　　　　　*natsukodachi*

Just a poem I dashed off and left there on a pillar.[118]

Next we went to Sesshōseki, "Killer Rock," I on a horse sent by the deputy. The man leading it[119] asked me for a poem strip,[120] and I thought, "What a fine thing to ask."

> Angle our horse　　　　　　　*no o yoko ni*
> your way, across the fields—　　*uma hikimuke yo*
> calling cuckoo.[121]　　　　　　*hototogisu*

Sesshōseki was at a hot spring in the shadow of a mountain.[122] The poison vapors had not ceased, and there were bees and butterflies dead on top of each other on the ground, so many that you could not see the color of the sand.

The willow "by a clear flowing stream"[123] was in an area called Ashino, and it was still standing on a path between rice paddies. The lord of the district, the late

---

115. A place up the mountain slope, behind the main temple, marked as the site of Butchō's hut at the temple today.

116. Both Zen monks who withdrew from the world into mountain retreats.

117. *Bashō kushū* 355. As a season word *kitsutsuki* ("woodpecker") would indicate autumn rather than summer, indicating that Bashō is thinking in broader terms that transcend the season (Fukasawa and Kusumoto 2009, 103). Colloquially, woodpeckers were called *teratsutsuki*, "temple peckers."

118. In response to Butchō's poem scribbled on a rock, as noted above. Bashō had left a poem on a pillar at his house in Fukagawa and here does the same just before crossing the barrier at Shirakawa, traditional gateway to the hinterlands.

119. Sora writes that the man assigned to assist the travelers was Danzō 弾蔵, a *kerai*, or samurai retainer of Zusho, indicating that they were not simply handed over to a groom. See Kanamori 2000, 112.

120. *Tanjaku*. A strip of paper on which poems were recorded. Just like medieval travelers such as Sōgi, Bashō traveled with poem strips on which to record poems and dispense as gifts.

121. *Bashō kushū* no. 310.

122. Noxious vapors rising from the ground around the stone killed insects and even small rodents. Legend links the place to Lady Tamamo.

123. See a poem (*SKKS* 262) by Saigyō: "At roadside, / by a clear flowing stream / beneath a willow / I thought to stop just a moment / but ended up lingering on" (*michinobe ni / shimizu*

Kohō,[124] had said many times that he would like me to see the tree, and I had wondered where it might be. Today, there I was, stopping for a moment in its shade.

One paddy planted—	*ta ichimai*
before I left the shade	*uete tachisaru*
of the willow tree.[125]	*yanagi kana*

Though the days were piling up I had yet not settled down, and only as we approached Shirakawa Barrier[126] did my heart find the rhythm of the road. I understood how the poet felt when he said, "Ah, to get word to the capital!"[127] Shirakawa is one of the Three Great Barriers,[128] a place where poets expressed their feelings. With autumn wind in my ears and the image of colored leaves in my eyes, the green leaves on the trees were somehow more moving.[129] Against deutzia flowers spread like white hempen sleeves, wild white roses were also in bloom, seeming even whiter than snow. As I recall, Kiyosuke wrote of a man of long ago who had paused here to straighten his cap and his robes.[130]

---

nagaruru / yanagikage / shibashi tote koso / tachidomaritsure). The headnote to this poem in *Saigyō monogatari*, 38, says it was written in Kyoto for a screen painting.

124. Ashino Suketoshi. It appears that he was not home at the time and Bashō did not visit him. The words *kohō* 戸部 ("domain chief") and *gunshū* 群守 ("lord of the district") are both Chinese and thus have an antique and honorific feel. Scholars suggest that Bashō may have felt some sensitivity about identifying high officials.

125. *Bashō kushū* no. 265.

126. Bashō visited the site where the old gate was supposedly located before moving on into the castle town of Shirakawa. A new road had been established even before the Edo period, passing through a different area of Shirakawa. Bashō and Sora also visited two shrines in the area, one on each side of the border.

127. *SIS* 339, by Taira no Kanemori. "Written when he passed through the Shirakawa Barrier in Michinoku: 'If only I could, / I would somehow get word / to the capital! / That today I passed / Shirakawa Barrier'" (*tayori araba / ikade miyako e / tsugeyaramu / kyō shirakawa o / seki koenu to*).

128. The other two of the three barriers of the hinterlands were Nakoso Barrier, on the border between Hitachi and Mutsu provinces, and Nezu Barrier, between Echigo and Dewa.

129. Bashō probably has in mind a poem by Minamoto no Yorimasa from *SZS* (no. 365): "In the capital / it was new leaves of green / that I gazed upon. / Fallen leaves cover the ground / at Shirakawa Barrier" (*miyako ni wa / mada aoba nite / mishikadomo / momichirishiku / shirakawa no seki*).

130. In *Fukuro sōshi* 袋草子 (c. 1158), Fujiwara no Kiyosuke tells the story of Takeda Kuniyuki straightening his cap and robe before passing through the Shirakawa Barrier, in honor of Nōin, who wrote the most well-known poem associated with the place (*GSIS* 518), "Written at Shirakawa, when he was on a trip to Michinoku: 'From the capital / I set out on the road / with the spreading

> At the barrier
> deutzia adorns our heads—
> our formal attire.
> > Sora

> *unohana o*
> *kazashi ni seki no*
> *haregi kana*

Proceeding on, we crossed Abukuma River. To the left were the peaks of the Aizu range, to the right, the lands of Iwaki, Sōma, and Miharu; and a mountain range stretched along the border between Hitachi and Shimotsuke. We passed through a place called Kagenuma, "Reflecting Marsh," but the skies were cloudy and we saw no reflections.[131] In the post station of Sukagawa we called on a man named Tōkyū and stayed there four or five days.[132] The first thing he asked me was, "What did you come up with, passing through Shirakawa Barrier?" "After so long on the road," I said, "I was drained, body and soul; and then I had such keen feelings seeing the scenes along the way that I lost myself in thoughts of the past and came up with nothing—but this."

> Our poetry—
> begins with rice-planting songs
> in the hinterlands.[133]

> *fūryū no*
> *hajime ya oku no*
> *taueuta*

"After all," I said, "I couldn't pass without saying something." We went on to a second verse, and a third, until we had a whole sequence.[134]

---

haze. / Now autumn wind is blowing / at Shirakawa Barrier'" (*miyako o ba / kasumi to tomo ni / tachishikado / akikaze zo fuku / shirakawa no seki*). *Fukuro sōshi*, 89, says that Nōin actually wrote the poem in Kyoto, but other sources indicate that he did visit the hinterlands twice.

131. Another name for the place was "Mirror Marsh" (Kagaminuma 鏡沼). According to legend the wife of a man banished to the far north heard of his fate at the site and threw her mirror and then herself into the swamp. The light reflected from the mirror was supposedly visible beneath the water.

132. Bashō uses the wrong character for *kyū*, 窮 instead of 躬, a pattern also seen in his rendering of Tōsui (see n. 101) above.

133. *Bashō kushū* no. 266. Scholars point out that here Bashō is fashioning. In truth, he did compose a *hokku* at Shirakawa Barrier (see Yamamoto Kenkichi 2012, 389), which he chose not to use—possibly because he wanted to stress how the experience was truly overwhelming (see Fukasawa and Kusumoto 2009, 113). There are two ways of interpreting the phrase *fūryū no hajime*: as the beginning of Bashō's poetic experience in the hinterlands, or as something broader—the foundation of all Japanese poetry. See Fukasawa and Kusumoto 2009, 116–17.

134. Other texts have not one sequence (*maki* 巻), but three. For the text of the *fūryū no hajime* sequence, see Takatō 1966, 67–92.

Next to our lodging there was a big chestnut tree, and beneath it lived a recluse monk. I quietly thought to myself, I wonder if it was like this in those deep mountains, "where he picked up chestnuts,"[135] and jotted down these words:

> Reasoning that the word chestnut—written with the characters for "west" and "tree"—had a connection to the Pure Land of the West, Gyōki Bosatsu used only chestnut wood for his walking sticks and pillars his whole life, so it is said.[136]

People in the world— yo no hito no
never see the chestnut flowers mitsukenu hana ya
beneath these eaves.[137] noki no kuri

We left Tōkyū's house and after about five *li*, beyond Hiwada, came to Mount Asaka. It was close to the road. There were many marshes in the area, and since it was getting close to the season for harvesting *katsumi*,[138] I asked people, "Which of these flowers is called *katsumi*?" But no one knew, so I trotted along through the marshes, asking everyone to point out the *katsumi*, until the sun had sunk down to the rim of the mountains. We bore right at Nihonmatsu, had a look at the cave at Kurozuka,[139] and took lodging at Fukushima. With the new day we went to see the rock used for rubbings, at Shinobu. It was just a little village, located off in a mountain's shadow, and

---

135. See a poem by Saigyō (*Sankashū* 1290): "Would that I could stop / this water dripping onto rocks / deep in the mountains— / long enough to pick up / chestnuts that keep dropping down" (*yama fukami / iwa ni shitatataru / mizu tomemu / katsukatsu otsuru / tochi hirou hodo*).
136. The characters for "west" (西) and "tree" (木) combine to make the character for *kuri* 栗, "chestnut." The source of this story about the great Nara-era priest Gyōki Bosatsu is unknown.
137. *Bashō kushū* no. 377.
138. Some scholars identify the plant as a variety of iris (*ayame*), others as water oat (*makomo*). In *Mumyōshō*, 95, Kamo no Chōmei tells the story of how Fujiwara Sanekata when in exile found there was no proper *ayame* in the area to decorate eaves for a summer festival and had people use *katsumi* instead. See *KKS* 677, an anonymous love poem: "Like *katsumi* / glimpsed in bloom at Asaka / in Michinoku, / I saw you but once— / yet my love continues on" (*michinoku no / asaka no numa no / hanakatsumi / katsu miru hito ni / koi ya wataramu*).
139. The verb "have a look" (J. *ikken su*) comes up frequently in the introductory sections of Noh plays. Kusumoto suggests that here Bashō has in mind the Noh play *Kurozuka* 黒塚 (also called *Adachigahara* 安達ヶ原), about a group of men searching for lodging who end up at the home of an old woman who turns out to be an ogre who eats passing travelers. See Fukasawa and Kusumoto 2009, 122.

the rock was half buried in the ground.[140] Some village children came and showed us where it was. "It used to be up on the mountain top," they said, "but the people here got sick of how travelers would make a mess of the grain fields trying the rock out, so they pushed it down into the valley. The topside is underneath now," they said. It was a story one could believe.

> Planting hands
> call to mind the rubbings
> of ancient days.[141]

> *sanae toru*
> *temoto ya mukashi*
> *shinobuzuri*

Crossing the river at Tsukinowa Ford, we came out at the post station of Senoue. The site of Satō Shōji's place was to the left, up against the mountain, no more than a *li* and a half away.[142] We continued on, heading for a place called Sabano in Iizuka, asking for directions along the way, until we ended up at Maruyama—the place where Shōji's dwelling had been.[143] Tears came to my eyes as the guide showed us the location of the main gate and an old temple next to it where there were stone monuments to the family.[144] Most moving to me were the monuments to the two young wives.[145] Women though they were, their devotion has survived down to today, I thought, wiping my eyes with my sleeves. We had no need to travel afar, to that Tablet of Tears.[146] In the

---

140. The story was that the surface of a rock at the site was anciently used to imprint a random pattern—like tangled hair—by rubbing the juices of *shinobugusa* (hare fern) onto cloth draped over a stone. Evidently this process was widely practiced, and there were many such rocks in the area. See Hisatomi 2011, 29. See *KKS* 724 by Minamoto no Tōru: "As confused / as those *shinobu* patterns / of Michinoku— / such are my feelings now / and if not for you, then who?" (*michinoku no / shinobu mojizuri / tare yue ni / midaremu to omou / ware naranaku ni*).
141. *Bashō kushū* no. 272. The word *shinobu* in the poem is a *kakekotoba* meaning to "yearn for" or "remember" and also figures in the compound *shinobuzuri*, "rubbing *shinobu* grass."
142. Satō Shōji refers to Satō Motoharu, estate manager of the Shinobu area. His sons, Tsugunobu and Tadanobu, served Minamoto no Yoshitsune and died in his cause.
143. Maruyama castle, also known as Ōtori castle.
144. Probably a reference to grave markers. See Fukasawa and Kusumoto 2009, 126. The temple was the family temple of the Satō.
145. According to legend, after their husbands died, the wives of Tsugunobu and Tadanobu would put on their armor and visit their mother-in-law as a sign of their continuing devotion. The monument has not survived.
146. Referring to the grave marker of the Chinese official Yanghu, who was so loved by his people that they shed tears whenever seeing it.

temple grounds we asked for tea.[147] Yoshitsune's great sword and Benkei's backpack are preserved there as heirlooms.[148]

Benkei's knapsack—	*benkei ga*
why not show that off too!	*oi o mo kazare*
With the paper carp.[149]	*kaminobori*

This was on the 1st day of the Fifth Month.[150] That night we spent in Iizuka. There being a hot spring, we bathed first and then took lodging in a wretched house where we had only straw mats on a dirt floor. With no lamps, we did our best to make up our beds by the light of the hearth fire. In the night there were claps of thunder and constant rainsqualls, and there was a leak in the roof right over where I lay and so many fleas and mosquitoes biting me that I couldn't get to sleep. Then, to top it all off, I had a flare-up of my chronic ailment, so intense that I nearly passed out. The short summer night passed slowly as I waited for the sky to brighten. When it did, we hit the road again.[151] Still worn out from the night before, I was feeling downcast, so we hired a horse and made our way to Ko'ori Station. Taking ill with such a long journey ahead was worrisome, I thought, nearly despairing; but then I reminded myself that when I had set out to trek through remote regions I had abandoned myself to the uncertainties of the world,[152] knowing that "whether I died on the road—that was up to the Decree of Heaven."[153] This restored my spirits enough

---

147. Sora indicates that in fact the travelers were not allowed to enter the temple, and most scholars argue that he did not actually see the heirlooms there (Fukasawa and Kusumoto 2009, 127; Satō Katsuaki 2014, 72).

148. Minamoto no Yoshitsune and his samurai attendant, Musashino Benkei, were the subject of many stories that worked their way into Noh plays and folk narratives.

149. *Bashō kushū* no. 263. The 5th day of the Fifth Month was a festival popularly known as Boys' Day. Families raised carp-shaped paper kites, praying for the welfare of their sons. Some scholars see this as Bashō's complaint about not being able to see the heirlooms. See Fukasawa and Kusumoto 2009, 128.

150. According to Sora, it was actually the 2nd day of the month.

151. For discrepancies between Sora's account and Bashō's, see p. 94. Yamamoto Satoshi 1994, 167, notes that Bashō stayed at hot springs just three times: Nasu Yumoto, Yamanaka, and Iizuka.

152. Fukasawa and Kusumoto 2009, 134, note Hasui Tetsu's identification of the story of Han'en Shōnin in *Senjūshō*, 114–17, which sees "abandoning oneself" to uncertainty (*mujō* 無常) as a positive step toward enlightenment, as an allusion.

153. Bashō probably has in mind two passages from the Confucian *Analects* about "understanding the Decree of Heaven" and "dying by the roadside" (Lau 1983, 11, 81), although the latter treats dying by the roadside as unfortunate.

that I could stagger on[154] as we passed through the Great Gate of the Date clan.[155] We passed by Abumizuri and Shiroishi Castle and entered the district of Kasajima, "Rain Hat Isle."[156] When we asked where the grave of the Fujiwara Middle Captain Sanekata was, this was the reply:

"It's a ways from here. On your right you'll see villages up against a mountain— Minowa and Kasajima, 'Rain Cloak Ring' and 'Rain Hat Isle,' they're called. The Dōsojin Shrine and the 'memento miscanthus' are still there."[157] That time of year, with all the rain coming down, the roads were awful, and I was worn out, so we just looked at the places from afar and went on. Seeing it raining at these places whose names contained words related to rain,[158] I wrote this:

Rain Hat Isle—	*kasajima wa*
where is it, down a muddy road	*izuko satsuki no*
in constant rain?[159]	*nukarimichi*

Iwanuma Post Station.[160]

---

154. There are basically two schools of thought about the phrase *jūō ni fumu* 縦横に踏む (which I have translated as "stagger on"). One takes it to mean "stagger along" and the other to "stride forward with confidence." I follow Fukasawa and Kusumoto 2009, 134–35, in opting for the former, because it seems more consistent with Bashō's previous description of himself as worn out and downcast at the time.

155. *Date no ōkido*, literally, "the great wooden door of the Date." In the past a major checkpoint at the entry into the hinterlands. The Date clan, which originated in the 1100s, was granted the Sendai Domain, with a stipend of over 600,000 *koku*, in the mid-1600s and was a powerful political force.

156. Scholars point out that the area was actually called Natori (Fukasawa and Kusumoto 2009, 137).

157. See a poem by Saigyō (*Sankashū* 872), written when he visited Sanekata's grave: "Giving honor / to a name that will go on / and never decay: / I see it as a memento— / this miscanthus in withered fields" (*kuchi mo senu / sono na bakari o / todomeokite / kareno no susuki / katami ni zo miru*). As punishment for striking another courtier, Sanekata was ordered to seek out and write poems about *utamakura* in the north country and died there, never seeing the capital again. Legend had it that he fell from his horse and died because he did not dismount to show proper respect at Dōsojin Shrine, which was dedicated to the god of travelers.

158. Minowa contains the word *mino* 蓑, "rain cloak," and Kasajima the word *kasa* 笠, "rain hat."

159. *Bashō kushū* no. 205.

160. This fragment is indented and separated both from the Kasajima and Takekuma sections of the text in the *Nakaobon* and *Sorabon*. Sora notes that they did not stay at Iwanuma but went on into Sendai for lodging (Sakurai 2006, 61). Scholarly explanations stress that Bashō's fashioning in this case allows him to give more attention to the Takekuma account.

The pine of Takekuma brought me back to myself.[161] I'd heard that the trunk divided in two just at ground level[162] remained as of old, and I saw that was true. The first thing I thought of was the Lay Monk Nōin. I wondered why he said in a poem, "Now nothing remains" of the pine.[163] Had he perhaps heard that long ago, a man who came from Kyoto to serve as governor of Mutsu cut down the tree to make pillars for a bridge across the Natori River?[164] I learned that over the ages, the tree has been cut down and replanted many times, but now it looked in such fine shape that it could last a thousand years. I thought it a fine specimen of a pine.

A man named Kyohaku had written this poem by way of farewell,

Pray, show my lord	*takekuma no*
the Takekuma Pine—	*matsu misemōse*
late cherry blossoms![165]	*osozakura*

Now I replied:

Since cherry time	*sakura yori*
I've waited through three months—	*matsu wa futaki o*
to see the two-trunked pine.[166]	*mitsukigoshi*

---

161. See *Essays in Idleness* (*Tsurezuregusa*, 92): "No matter where you are, if you pause for a moment traveling, you feel as if you awaken to something new."

162. Bashō probably has in mind a number of poems, among them one by Tachibana no Norimitsu (*GSIS* 1041): "At Takekuma / the pine *does* have two trunks. / But how can I tell / people wondering in the capital / that I've seen it with my own eyes" (*takekuma no / matsu wa futagi o / miyakobito / ikaga to towaba / miki to kotaemu*).

163. Nōin visited the place twice. The second time, he wrote a poem that appears immediately after the one by Norimitsu (*GSIS* 1042): "He came twice to Michinoku, and wrote this poem when, on the second occasion, the pine was gone. 'At Takekuma / nothing remains now / of that pine tree. / Can it be a thousand years / since I came the first time?'" (*takekuma no / matsu wa kono tabi / ato mo nashi / chitose o hete ya / ware wa kitsuran*).

164. Various medieval sources say that when Fujiwara no Takayoshi was appointed governor of Mutsu Province he cut down two pines—planted by a previous governor—to use as pillars for a bridge across the Natori River. See Hisatomi 2002, 83.

165. This *hokku* is recorded in the spring section of Kyohaku's collection, *Shiki senku* 四季千句 (Fukasawa and Kusumoto 2009, 144). The poem is obviously an example of apostrophe, but opinions vary as to whom it is addressed: to the cherry trees blossoming in the north country at the time it was written or when Bashō eventually visits, to the people of the north country, or to the natural world of the area in a general sense. See Fukasawa and Kusumoto 2009, 144.

166. *Bashō kushū* no. 406. Here *mitsuki* means not "three months in duration," but "within the scope of three calendar months." Bashō's journey so far has entailed a few days in the Third Month, all of the Fourth Month, and a few days in the Fifth Month.

We crossed the Natori River and entered Sendai, on the day for decorating the eaves with sweet flag.[167] We sought out a place to stay and were there four or five days.[168] In the area lived a painter named Kaemon. I had heard that he was a man of some refinement, and was acquainted with him.[169] "For some years I've made a study of famous places of uncertain whereabouts," he said, and spent a day guiding us around. On the Miyagi Moors the bush clover grew so thick that it made me imagine the scene in autumn.[170] Then came Tamada, Yokono—and Tsutsujigaoka, where the *asebi* was in bloom.[171] We went into a pine grove so dense that the sunlight couldn't get through. He said the place was named Konoshita, "Beneath the Trees."[172] It must have been because the dews were just so deep that the poet wrote, "You attendants—tell your lord to don his cap."[173] We did obeisance at the Yakushi Hall, Tenjin Shrine, and continued on till the sun went down. When we departed he sent us off with sketches he drew for us of Matsushima, and Shiogama and other places. Nor was that all: he also sent me off

---

167. *Ayame* あやめ. An old practice, usually observed on the 4th day of the Fifth Month. The plant was believed to ward off evil spirits, disease, and fire.

168. Sora's journal reveals that the men stayed at an inn in Kokubunmachi. According to Bashō's disciple Jōshibō, while there, Bashō became ill and visited a doctor. See Kanamori 2000, 185.

169. Sora's journal also reveals that Bashō's letter of introduction to a prominent samurai *haikai* poet named Hashimoto Zen'emon, with whom he probably expected to stay, accomplished nothing. Eventually—probably through the offices of their innkeeper (Fukasawa and Kusumoto 2009, 147)—they were introduced to Kaemon, an artist specializing in *haikai* and a disciple of Ōyodo Michikaze with a shop called Kitanoya, who stepped in to serve as their guide. For a long time scholars believed the man to be proprietor of the Yamadaya and not the Kitanoya, but consensus now is that Kitanoya is correct. See Fukasawa and Kusumoto 2009, 147. Whether Bashō was acquainted with Kaemon before this journey is not clear.

170. Miyagino, a prominent *utamakura*, that was celebrated for its bush clover (*hagi*) and thus was associated with autumn.

171. *Asebi* (also pronounced *ashibi*) is a variety of pieris, probably not actually in bloom at the time Bashō visited. Yokosawa 1995, 216, notes an allusion to a poem by Minamoto no Shunrai from his personal anthology: "Tether them— / ponies roaming at Tamada / and Yokono. / The *asebi* is in bloom / at Tsutsuji Hill" (*toritsunage / tamada yokono no / hanaregoma / tsutsuji no oka ni / asemi saku nari*). Eating the leaves of *asebi* (sometimes written with the characters 馬酔木, "tree that makes horses drunk") made horses sick. As *utamakura*, Tamada and Yokono are usually associated with Kawachi Province, but it appears that places with the same names existed in the Sendai area. See Fukasawa and Kusumoto 2009, 148. Bashō's information probably came from Kaemon.

172. A word from *KKS* 1091, noted in n. 173 below.

173. See an anonymous Michinoku song recorded in *KKS* 1091: "You attendants— / tell your master to don his cap! / On Miyagino / the dewfall beneath these trees / is heavier than rain" (*misaburai / mikasa to mōse / miyagino no / ko no shitatsuyu wa / ame ni masareri*).

with two pairs of sandals with cords died indigo as a parting gift.[174] That was when he showed himself truly a man of refinement.[175]

> With sweet flag   *ayamegusa*
> I'll bind sandals to my feet.   *ashi ni musuban*
> Cords of indigo.[176]   *waraji no o*

Trusting to our sketches, we traveled along the Narrow Path[177] and ended up against a mountain where ten-strand sedge was growing. Even now, it is said that the people here prepare mats of ten-strand sedge and present them to the governor of the province.[178]

The Courtyard Stele[179] is located at Tagajō, in Ichikawa Village.

The Courtyard Stele is over six feet tall and about three feet across. Scraping the moss away, we were just able to make out the characters.[180] Distances to the four

---

174. New sandals were nearly a daily necessity on the road. The indigo cords were thought to keep insects away. Kaemon also gave them food—dried rice balls; and on the morning of their departure, he brought dried seaweed. The area was famous for a particular kind of dried rice balls, which was a classy gift.

175. "Refinement" translates *furyū* 風流.

176. *Bashō kushū* no. 367. As a traveler, Bashō could not ward off evil by putting sweet flag on his eaves, but thanks to the gift is able to do so by using indigo cords—the color of sweet flag flowers—on his sandals. See Satō Katsuaki 2014, 74.

177. *Oku no hosomichi* おくの細道. Another name for the Shiogama Road. Researchers have identified one stretch of the road in the area in front of Tōkōji in Sendai City. The same path is noted in *Miyako no tsuto* 都のつと (1372), 358, and other medieval travel records. See Fukasawa and Kusumoto 2009, 152.

178. *Sugagomo* 菅菰 is the name of the plant. A special pattern involved weaving ten strands into a mat. In the Edo period, the Date daimyo, lords of Sendai Domain, were given the ancient and now honorary title of governor of Mutsu Province.

179. *Tsubo no ishibumi* (壺碑). *Tsubo* here means "inner garden" or "courtyard," which is probably where the stele stood originally. Scholars agree that what Bashō saw was doubtless not the *tsubo no ishibumi* referred to in old poems (an *utamakura* place somewhere in Michinoku, modern Aomori Prefecture) but another memorial stele that had been discovered during a restoration of the Taga Fortress between 1658 and 1672. In his day the two were assumed to be one and the same. See Satō Katsuaki 2014, 74.

180. There are various interpretations of the phrase *koke o ugachite*, some arguing that the moss itself has made the characters visible or that Bashō and Sora are able to see the characters by examining the moss carefully. I follow Kon 2004, 50–53, who draws on the commentary of Yamazaki Kiyoshi, in taking the phrases to mean they scraped the moss away.

borders of the province are inscribed there, and also this: "This fortress was founded in the first year of the Jinki era, by Imperial Inspector and Shogun of the Garrison, Lord Ōno Azumahito.[181] In the sixth year of the Tempyō-Hōji era repairs on the site were undertaken by Consultant-Imperial Messenger to the Eastern Seas and Mountains and likewise Shogun, Lord Emino Asakari.[182] First Day, Twelfth Month." This would date it to the age of Emperor Shōmu.[183] Sources going back to ancient times speak of many *utamakura* in the area; but mountains crumble, rivers change course, roadways are altered, rocks are covered over with earth, and trees grow old, die, and are replaced by new ones. Thus time goes by, one era gives way to another, and the whereabouts of those places becomes uncertain. Yet here before my very eyes was a sure relic from a thousand years in the past, speaking to me the feelings of people of old.[184] This is one of the virtues of going on the road. Rejoicing that I had lived so long, I forgot the toils of traveling and shed a few tears.

We continued on to Nodanotamagawa and visited the Okinoishi.[185] At Suenomatsuyama a temple had been built, called Masshōzan, where there was a field of graves among the pines.[186] "This is what it is like for those who have exchanged vows, to love

---

181. The first year of the Jinki era corresponds to 724. Azumahito was an imperial general who led campaigns against the *emishi*, a name given to eastern peoples who resisted the authority of the imperial government, into the late 730s.

182. The sixth year of the Tempyō-Hōji era corresponds to 762. Asakari (precise dates unknown) was a court official—he attained the high appointment of consultant—who was sent east to subdue the *emishi* in the early 760s.

183. Shōmu reigned from 724 to 749. The year in question would actually have been in the era of Emperor Junnin.

184. Fukasawa and Kusumoto 2009, 156, posit an allusion to a poem by Saigyō (*Sankashū* 1096): "How alluring / are the hinterlands / of Mutsunoku: / the Courtyard Stele, / the winds at Soto Shore" (*mutsunoku no / okuyukashiku zo / omohoyuru / tsubo no ishibumi / soto no hamakaze*). Sotonohama was evidently located near the *tsubo no ishibumi*.

185. The travelers actually visited the Tama River and Okinoishi *after* Suenomatsuyama. Ogata argues that Bashō changed the order so as to treat the *utamakura* in the same order as the medieval travel record *Miyako no tsuto*—Taga, Oku no Hosomichi, Sue no Matsuyama, and Shiogama (Fukasawa and Kusumoto 2009, 162–63).

186. An *utamakura*. The place was associated with pledges of love because of a number of classical poems, including *Hyakunin isshu* 42, by Kiyowara no Motosuke: "Have you forgotten / how we wrung tears from our sleeves / as we pledged a love / that would stand above the waves / at Pine Mountain in Sue?" (*chigiriki na / katami ni sode o / shiboritsutsu / sue no matsuyama / nami kosaji to wa*).

as if 'on shared wings, neighboring branches,'"[187] I thought, and it was with growing sadness that I heard the evening temple bells ring as we came into Shiogama Bay. The rainy skies of the Fifth Month cleared slightly, and there was the evening moon, barely visible, as we grew closer to Magaki Island. The small boats of fishermen were coming in to shore, and as I listened to their voices as they divided up the catch, I understood what the poet must have felt when he said, "How moving / to see ropes . . ."[188] That night a blind monk-minstrel chanted in a manner called *jōruri* of the Hinterlands,[189] accompanying himself on the lute. This was different from Heike chanting, nor was it *kowakamai*; it was something more rustic, chanted with dramatic flourishes in high tones.[190] It was noisy to have it so close to where I slept,[191] but still I was impressed that such strange old ways had not been forgotten. Early that next morning, we did obeisance at Shiogama Myōjin. The governor of the province[192] having done restoration work, the shrine pillars stood fresh and firm, their paint sparkling, while the stone steps rose flight after lofty flight and the rays of the morning sun made the jeweled

187. An allusion to "The Song of Everlasting Sorrow," a poem by Bai Juyi, in which Emperor Xuan Song and Yang Guifei promise to be like birds with shared wings in Heaven, and on earth like trees with neighboring branches. The poem is alluded to frequently in classical Japanese texts, especially *The Tale of Genji*. Fukasawa and Kusumoto 2009, 160, suggest that Bashō had in mind a reference to Bai Juyi's story in a chapter of *Senjūshō*, 64–65, about a recluse living in a placed called Hirano in Harima Province who left the world after the loss of his wife.

188. Here Bashō quotes a line that appears in two classical poems. The first is an anonymous eastern song, *KKS* 1088: "Of other places / in Michinoku / I cannot say. / But how moving / to see ropes pulling fishing boats / along Shiogama strand" (*michinoku wa / izuku wa aredo / shiogama no / ura kogu fune / tsunade kanashi mo*). The second poem (no. 93 in *Hyakunin isshu*), which obviously alludes to the first, is a travel poem by Minamoto no Sanetomo: "Ah, if in this world, / things could always be like this! / How moving / to see ropes pulling fishing boats / along the strand" (*yo no naka wa / tsune ni mogamo na / nagisa kogu / ama no obune no / tsunade kanashi mo*). Scholars argue about how to interpret the *kanashi* in Sanetomo's poem, as either "sad" or as "engaging." Fukasawa and Kusumoto 2009, 162, argue that Bashō probably saw the scene as an example of ephemerality (*mujō*) and therefore opted for *kanashi*, meaning "sad," in the context of his own description. My "how moving" is a compromise.

189. *Oku jōruri* 奥浄るり; also called *Sendai jōruri*. Narrative song performed to instrumental accompaniment, particularly a shamisen or lute (*biwa*), or perhaps a shamisen that Bashō mistook for a lute. See Fukasawa and Kusumoto 2009, 164.

190. Heike chanting involved the recitation of stories from the era of the Genpei Wars by a minstrel, to the accompaniment of a lute. Similarly, *mai* (short for *kōwakamai* 幸若舞, a performing art closely related to Noh drama) were recitations of tales to the beat of a fan or drum and music by a flute, usually involving three men and sometimes a chorus.

191. This indicates that Bashō did not actually see the performance but only heard it through doors or walls.

192. Date Masamune undertook the restoration in 1607.

fences glow. This is the way of things in our land; that the spirit of the gods should extend so far into out-of-the-way places, I thought, feeling a sense of awe. In front of the shrine was a fine old lantern on whose iron door was inscribed: "An offering from Izumi Saburō, in the third year of the Bunji era."[193] What a rare thing, I thought, as images from five hundred years before floated up before my eyes. He was a warrior of courage and honor, loyalty and filial virtue. Down to this very time, his name is honored, never unremembered. How true is the statement: "Be a proper man, pursue the Way and uphold the right, and maintain a good reputation; then fame will follow as a matter of course."[194]

The sun was already high in the sky. We hired a boat and crossed to Matsushima. After just over two *li* on the water, we pulled in at the shore at Ojima. It's been said before, but Matsushima truly offers the finest vistas[195] in all of Japan: a place not inferior to the lakes of Dongting or Xihu.[196] The sea flowing in from the southeast makes a bay three *li* square, its waters overspread with breakers like those at Zhejiang.[197] And so many islands!—tall ones looming into the heavens, low ones crawling over the waves. Some have two layers, others three; appearing separate from the left, connected to the right. One island carries another on its back, others seem to embrace, like parents or grandparents with their young.[198] The pines are of the richest green,

---

193. 1187. Fujiwara Tadahira, third son of Hidehira, died protecting Minamoto no Yoshitsune in battle against his own brother, Yasuhira, who was acting at the insistence of Minamoto no Yoritomo.

194. The source of this pronouncement is unclear. Some argue that only the last part of it—"fame will follow as a matter of course"—is meant as a citation. One possibility for the source of that phrase is Han Yu's *Jinxuexie* 進学解. See Fukasawa and Kusumoto 2009, 168. Yokosawa 1995, 225, notes that the mid-Edo period commentary on *The Narrow Road through the Hinterlands* (*Sugagomo* 菅菰) traces the exact phrase to an ancient work on military strategy, but adds that our texts of that work do not contain the phrase.

195. In many contexts the word *kōfū* 好風 means "pleasant wind," but Bashō uses it to mean "fine scenery." See Tanaka 2009, 62.

196. A number of works described Matsushima as the finest vista in Japan. See Date Masamune's *Zuiganji Hōjōki* 瑞巌寺方丈記: "This Matsushima—it is the finest sight in all of Japan" (Fukasawa and Kusumoto 2009, 171). The word used here for Japan—Fusō 扶桑 —was used in China to refer to Japan. The whole passage is written in what is called *kanbunchō* 漢文調 that uses Chinese vocabulary and parallelism.

197. A place renowned for its pounding surf.

198. I have followed the first of two possible interpretations; that the larger islands seem to be caring for the smaller ones, as parents and grandparents take care of children, and that the children and grandchildren are taking care of each other. See Fukasawa and Kusumoto 2009, 172.

their branches molded by salt spray into natural shapes that seem as if man-made. So fine is the beauty of the scene that one envisions a woman just finished applying her makeup,[199] or a landscape crafted by Ōyamazumi in the age of the mighty gods.[200] To capture with the brush the work of Heaven's creation—why, no one could do it, not with paint, not with words.

O̲jima is an island that juts from the land out into the sea.[201] There we found the remains of Ungo Zenji's retreat and the stone where he sat in meditation.[202] And more: for here and there were souls who had fled the world to lodge beneath the pines. At one place smoke from a fire of withered rice stalks and pine cones rose from a hut of grass where someone lived in peace and solitude.[203] We knew nothing of what sort of man might be dwelling there, but still we approached, anxious to see more. And there was the moonlight, shimmering on the waters, a scene unlike what we saw in the daytime. From there we returned to the bay shore and sought out an inn, staying in a second-story room with so fine a window view that we felt like travelers spending a night amidst wind and clouds. It was an unaccountable sensation, almost too wonderful to believe.

> Matsushima.   *matsushima ya*
> Change your form for a crane's,   *tsuru ni mi o kare*
> calling cuckoo!   *hototogisu*
>   Sora

I kept silent[204] and tried to go to sleep, though sleep wouldn't come. But Sodō had given me a Chinese poem when I left my old cottage, and Hara Anteki had sent me

---

199. Fukasawa and Kusumoto 2009, 173, note a reference to a passage from a poem by Su Shi about Xi Shi, a legendary beauty of the Spring and Autumn Period. The poem compares the beauty to West Lake wearing makeup. It was believed that West Lake was a reincarnation of the legendary beauty, Xi Shi.

200. The god of mountains, offspring of the god Izanagi and the goddess Izanami.

201. In fact, the island is not connected to land, although it may have appeared so from some vantage points.

202. The name of the cottage was Hafujūken (把不住軒). It is possible that Kenbutsu lived on the same site earlier.

203. See *Essays in Idleness* (*Tsurezuregusa*, 86): "At the house where a man of breeding lives in quietude, even the moonlight seems to shine down with greater effect."

204. In other words, he stopped trying to come up with a fine poem.

a *waka*, so I opened my bag and made them my companions for the night. I also had *hokku* by Sanpū and Jokushi.[205]

On the 11th we went on pilgrimage to Zuiganji. This temple was established by Makabe no Heishirō thirty-two generations back, after he took the tonsure and traveled to the Tang Kingdom. Later, through the virtuous acts of Ungo Zenji, the roofs of the seven halls were tiled again, and the light of its gold walls now shines brilliantly, one of the great Buddhist conclaves—a paradise here and now.[206] I was anxious to see where the temple of that holy man Kenbutsu was.[207]

On the 12th,[208] we set out with Hiraizumi as our goal. We had been told of a path going by the Aneha Pine and Odae Bridge, used by no one but hunters of pheasants and hares and woodcutters,[209] but we couldn't make it out. In the end we took the wrong path and came out at a port town called Ishinomaki. Looking out over the sea, we spied the gold mountain the poem is written about—"flowers of gold blossom forth."[210] Several hundred boats bobbed together in the bay, and the shore was

---

205. The poems from his friends alluded to here are unidentified.

206. *Butsudo jōju* 仏土成就. A Buddhist heaven realized in this world.

207. The Buddhist ascetic Kenbutsu. A story in *Senjūshō*, 83–85, has Saigyō come upon a monk while traveling in the Noto area who introduces himself as the man people call *tsuki matsushima no shōnin*—"the priest who waits for the moon at Matsushima"—and explains about his trips to see the moon there. Saigyō concludes that he is in fact the man people call Kenbutsu no shōnin. By introducing the monk as *that* (*kano* 彼) monk, Bashō is assuming everyone will have heard of him, probably from *Senjūshō*. There was a hut in Ojima that was traditionally believed to be Kenbutsu's, but it may have been Ungo Zenji's.

208. Sora's record says they set out from Ishinomaki on the 11th, staying at Toima that night and at Ichinoseki on the 12th, and heading for Hiraizumi on the 13th. Fukasawa and Kusumoto 2009, 183–84, 188–89, suggest that Bashō has doctored the dates of his visits to Shiogama, Zuiganji, and Hiraizumi, "fashioning" his text in order to be in Hiraizumi on the 12th day, the day of the month on which Saigyō visited Hiraizumi according to his personal anthology.

209. *Chito sūjō* 雉兎蒭蕘, a phrase from a passage in Mencius about a king who had a park seventy *li* square (Lau 1984, 29). The places mentioned here are in the opposite direction from Ishinomaki.

210. The poem is an envoy to a *chōka* in the *MYS* (no. 4121) by Ōtomo no Yakamochi on the discovery of gold in Michinoku Province: "May the reign / of our Sovereign now flourish! / In the East Land, / in Michinoku's mountains— / flowers of gold blossom forth" (*sumeroki no / miyo sakaemu to / azuma naru / michinokuyama ni / koganehana saku*). Although Bashō probably believed that Yakamochi's poem referred to Kinkasan, an island off the coast near Ishinomaki, it was actually at a mountain in another area of Michinoku that gold was discovered. Fukasawa and Kusumoto 2009, 186–87, note that it was not possible to see the island from the bay where Bashō would have been standing and therefore conclude that his memory was faulty, that he was

crowded with dwellings where smoke from hearth fires was rising. "This is unexpected, I thought—finding ourselves in a place like this,"[211] and when we tried to get lodging for the night, no one would take us in. Finally, we spent the night in a poor little house, and the next day wandered along more unknown roads. Walking on a levee, we saw in the distance Sodenowatari, Obuchinomaki, the Manonokayahara. It was after walking alongside a long, forlorn stretch of marshland that we stopped for the night at a place called Toima,[212] arriving at Hiraizumi the next day. I think we had gone over twenty *li*.

The glory of three generations,[213] gone in the space of a sleep. The place where the main gate stood was one *li* this side of the site. Hidehira's fort was fields now, leaving only Mount Kinkei as it was. First I climbed up to the Takadachi, "High Residence," where I had a view of the Kitakami, a large river flowing from Nanbu. And also there was the Koromo River that skirts Izumi Fortress and flows into the larger river below the Takadachi. What remains of Yasuhira's fortress is on the other side of the Koromo Barrier, put there to protect against Ezo[214] who might attack via the road in from Nanbu—so it looked to me. So here it is, I thought: the place where the stalwarts[215] holed up in their fortress and gained their instant of glory—only to end as grassy fields. "The country ravaged, mountains and rivers remain; spring comes to the fortress, covered over in green."[216] Putting my hat beneath me, I sat for quite a while and found myself in tears.[217]

---

seeing a different island, or that he is again fashioning. Another possibility is that writing on the basis of notes, he simply combined memories of vistas seen from a number of vantage points.

211. The sense of "unexpected" in this passage is unclear. The most likely meaning is that the poets had expected grand views at places like Matsushima but not at a lively port town like Ishinomaki. See Fukasawa and Kusumoto 2009, 187.

212. Sora notes that they were unable to get lodging where they had intended, and imposed on the *kendan* 検断 (station head, the man in charge of dealing with travelers' problems and the transport of goods), one Shōzaemon.

213. The "three generations" refers to the heads of the northern Fujiwara lineage in the late twelfth century: Kiyohira, Motohira, and Hidehira.

214. General term for the peoples of the north country.

215. Probably meaning those who died defending Minamoto no Yoshitsune, although some scholars take the term more generally to refer to all those who defied the Minamoto.

216. *Kuni yaburete sansen ari, jō haru ni shite aomitari* 国破れて山河あり／城春にして清たり. Bashō's slightly variant version of a poem titled "Spring View" (春望) by Du Fu, about the futility of human endeavor: "The country ravaged, mountains and rivers remain / in spring at the fortress, the grasses and bushes grow thick" (国破山河在／城春草木深). See Fukasawa and Kusumoto 2009, 191–92.

217. Fuji Masaharu 1989, 137, notes an allusion to another poem by Du Fu, written about an abandoned palace (Yuhua Gong 玉華宮) north of Chang'an, that contains the line: "Grieving, I came and spread grass and sat down (忧来藉草坐)."

Summer grasses:
all that is left to us now
of warrior's dreams.[218]

natsukusa ya
tsuwamonodomo ga
yume no ato

Deutzia blossoms—
looking like Kanefusa
in white hair.[219]
 Sora

unohana ni
kanefusa miyuru
shiraga kana

The doors of the two halls I had heard praised so highly were open.[220] The Sutra Hall holds images of the three commanders,[221] and the Shining Hall[222] preserves the three coffins and shelters the three Buddhas.[223] Once the seven treasures[224] were all but lost, the jeweled door so battered by wind, the golden pillars so ruined by frost and snow that all was on the brink of collapse and desolation, ready to sink into the grass. But then new walls were erected all around and a cover placed over the roof tiles to protect against wind and rain.[225] Thus—for now, at least—it stands as a reminder of a thousand years ago.

Fifth Month Rains.
Year after year they've fallen,
five hundred times.[226]

samidare ya
toshidoshi furite
gobyakutabi

---

218. *Bashō kushū* no. 404.
219. Kanefusa was the retainer of one of Yoshitsune's women who died at Hiraizumi. The white of the blossoms calls to mind the aging warrior in his final battle.
220. Chūsonji's Sutra Hall (Kyōdō) and Shining Hall (Hikaridō).
221. We know from Sora's account that the travelers were not able to go inside the Sutra Hall. The three images were actually of the Buddhist deities Monju Bosatsu 文殊菩薩 (Skt. Manjushri), Uten Daiō 優闐大王 (Skt. Udayana), and Zenzai Dōji 善哉童子 (Skt. Sudhana-sresthi-daraka).
222. Hikaridō. The Hiraizumi area was well known for its gold mines, and the temple housed many objects made of gold and precious metals and jewels.
223. The three coffins were for Kiyohira, Motohira, and Hidehira. The three bodhisattvas were Amida 阿弥陀 (Skt. Amitabha) and his attendants, Seishi 勢至 (Skt. Mahasthamaprapta) and Kannon 観音 (Skt. Avalokiteshvara). See Yokosawa 1995, 237.
224. The list includes gold, silver, and other precious substances. Here the term probably means just "many" precious substances.
225. The shogun-prince Koreyasu had the canopy built over the structure in 1288.
226. *Bashō kushū* no. 220. This poem was probably written not on the spot but in the course of writing up his account. See Fukasawa and Kusumoto 2009, 197–98. Another, probably later version of the *hokku* (used in the Sora text) reads: "Fifth Month Rains / have left only this

Firefly's light:	*hotarubi no*
almost gone in the daytime	*hiru wa kietsutsu*
'round the pillars.[227]	*hashira kana*

Gazing at the Nanbu Road going off into the distance, we traveled on,[228] stopping at Iwade Village for the night. We came to Ogurozaki and Mizunokojima, and then from Narugo Springs we made toward Shitomae Barrier,[229] where we would cross over into the province of Dewa. But few travelers pass this way, and the border guards were suspicious and kept us for questioning a while before we were allowed through.[230] As we climbed a mountain slope, the sun was already going down, but we spotted the house of the barrier guard[231] and asked for lodging. Hard wind and rain kept us in those cheerless mountains for three days.[232]

The fleas, the lice—	*nomi shirami*
and a horse pissing	*uma no bari suru*
by my pillow.[233]	*makuramoto*

---

untouched: / the Shining Hall" (*samidare no / furinokoshite ya / hikaridō*). The earlier version puts the emphasis on *mujō* and the passage of time, the latter the light of the Buddha's message.

227. This *hokku* does not appear in some manuscripts. See Kon 2005a, 185. It alludes to SKS 225 by Ōnakatomi Yoshinobu: "Topic unknown: 'Like the fires / tended by the gate guards / around the palace— / so my love burns in the night, / nearly perishing in the day'" (*mikakimori / eji no takubi no / yoru wa moe / hiru wa kietsutsu / mono o koso omoe*). The light of the fireflies in the structure is faint in the daytime, partly because of the brightness of the pillars. Behind the poem, as in the prose (*shibaraku*, "for now") is the idea of ephemerality. The hall remains, but only as a monument to death and decline.

228. In other words, returning south rather than continuing on to the north.

229. Literally, "Pee-Front Barrier." Bashō's *hokku* obviously plays off the name.

230. It is not clear why the travelers encountered this trouble. Kanamori 2013, 33–46, suggests a range of possibilities: that documents had been lost, or that they stayed longer in the domain than anticipated, or that entry documents noted a different exit—probably the barrier at Karuizawa. The barrier at Shitomae was guarded by farmers in a small village of only a dozen homes or so who probably seldom encountered travelers whose purpose was stated as viewing old poetic sights. Finally, it is clear that Bashō had no close friends or disciples in the Sendai area to rely upon for arranging passage.

231. Sora makes it clear that they stayed at the house of the local village headman, Shin'emon, the elder brother of Izumishōya in Sakaida. See Kanamori 2013, 49–52.

232. The travelers actually spent just two nights at Sakaida. See Ogata 1995, 328–29; Kanamori 2013, 50.

233. *Bashō kushū* no. 339. Eguchi 1998, 84–92, notes that based on what we know of architecture at the time, this poem must be an exaggeration. The travelers would have been some

Our host told us, "From here into Dewa you go high into the mountains, and the pathway isn't easy to make out; you'd best hire a man to guide you across." "Of course," I replied, and asked his help. Our guide was a sturdy-looking young man with a long-ish dagger stuck in his belt and an oak staff in his hand, and he struck right out, going in front. "We're sure to face some perils today," he said, and we were a little hesitant; but we fell in behind him all the same. And it was just as our host had said. We went high into the mountains, through forests where silence prevailed,[234] hearing not so much as a bird singing. Moving along through the dark beneath a thick canopy of trees was like walking at night. It felt as if dust were being scooped up and then rained down on us from the clouds.[235] As we pressed on through fields of bamboo grass, crossing streams and stumbling over outcroppings of rock, I felt cold sweat on my body, until finally we came out into Mogami Estate. Our guide then said, "Something's always happening along that path, but we've come through unscathed—so we can be happy" and headed off, in good spirits. Even after the fact, hearing that made my heart beat hard in my chest.

At Obanezawa[236] we called on a man called Seifū. He was a wealthy sort but for all that a man of fine inclinations and no mean taste.[237] Having traveled to Kyoto now and again, he knew something of how one feels on the road. He put us up for some days and helped us recover from the fatigue of a long journey.[238]

---

distance from where the animals were kept, albeit under the same roof. The poem was probably not written at the time but later, when he wrote up his text (Fukasawa and Kusumoto 2009, 201). See also Kanamori 2013, 49–51.

234. Fukasawa and Kusumoto 2009, 204, point out possible allusions here to poems by Du Fu and Li Bai.

235. The idea of dust being blown up into the clouds and then falling as rain comes from a phrase in a Du Fu poem: "Taken up into the wind on a stairway, dust falls from the edge of the clouds" (已風燈霾雲端). See Fukasawa and Kusumoto 2009, 204.

236. This was the pronunciation in Bashō's day. Later it became Oba*na*zawa. See Fukasawa and Kusumoto 2009, 207.

237. See *Essays in Idleness* (*Tsurezuregusa*, 94).

238. According to Sora's account, the travelers arrived in Obanezawa on the 17th day of the Fifth Month and left on the 27th. He stayed with Seifū only three nights, and in the past scholars tended to see Seifū as less than hospitable toward Bashō. More recent scholarship disputes that contention and argues that Yōsenji, the place where Seifū put them up, was a less hectic place where the travelers could rest. See Fukasawa and Kusumoto 2009, 210–11.

This coolness:
it shall be my lodging,
a place to rest.[239]

suzushisa o
waga yado ni shite
nemaru nari

Come out, now!
Beneath the silkworm greenhouse,
a croaking toad.[240]

haiideyo
kaiya ga shita no
hiki no koe

An eyebrow brush:
that is what they call to mind,
these safflower blossoms.[241]

mayuhaki o
omokage ni shite
beni no hana

Silkworm tenders:
the very image of people
of long ago.[242]
    Sora

kogai suru
hito wa kodai no
sugata kana

In Yamagata Domain is a temple called Ryūshakuji.[243] It was founded by the Great Teacher Jikaku,[244] and is a place of pure tranquility[245] that people urged me to go see,[246] so we backtracked from Obanezawa, a distance of about seven *li*. As there was some daylight left, we hurriedly arranged to stay the night in the monks' lodge[247] at

---

239. *Bashō kushū* no. 236. *Nemaru* means to sit down and rest. This verse served as the *hokku* for a sequence involving Seifū and other local poets. See Kanamori 2013, 61–63.
240. *Bashō kushū* no. 324.
241. *Bashō kushū* no. 380.
242. Fukasawa and Kusumoto 2009, 210, point out that Sora's poem reveals his interest in all things ancient. Sericulture was believed to have started in the age of the gods.
243. Ryūshakuji was independent of the Yamagata Domain, with its own stipend of 1420 *koku*. See Fukasawa and Kusumoto 2009, 212. The temple is now a major tourist attraction but in Bashō's time was frequented mostly by locals (Kanamori 2013, 67–69).
244. Also known as Ennin.
245. *Seikan* 清閑. This is the first of a series of allusions to phrases from the *Cold Mountain Poems* (*Hanshanji* 寒山詩), Daoist and Zen poems dating to the Tang dynasty. The others are "slippery moss" (*koke nameraka ni* 苔滑に) and "fine views . . . secluded and serene" (*kakei jakumaku* 佳景寂寞). See Fukasawa and Kusumoto 2009, 212–14.
246. It appears that Bashō's visit to Ryūshakuji was unscheduled and that he went at the encouragement of Seifū and others.
247. Sora identifies the place as Azukaribō 預り坊, a proper name that no doubt developed from the function of the place—to "take care of" belongings and guests. See Fukasawa and Kusumoto 2009, 213.

the foot of the mountain and climbed up to the halls on top.[248] The mountain is a mound of boulder and rock, covered with hoary pine and cypress and old rocks and earth slippery with moss. The doors of the temple buildings were all shut fast, and there was no noise, not a human sound, as we worked our way along the cliff face and clambered over the rocks to the temples to pay our respects. So fine were the views and the place so secluded, so serene that I felt my heart being cleansed of all worldly concerns.[249]

> Such stillness!   *shizukasa ya*
> The very rocks are pierced   *iwa ni shimiiru*
> by cicadas' drone.[250]   *semi no koe*

Planning to go by boat down the Mogami River, we traveled on to a place called Ōishida and waited for good weather.[251] The seeds of old *haikai*[252] had fallen on this ground, and there were people who had not forgotten that first flowering,[253] which softened hearts that knew only reed flutes[254] and inspired them to pursue the Way. But with no guide they were uncertain of the Way and wandering between new styles and

---

248. Records from several decades later show at least six halls (*dō* 堂) on the top of the mountain (Fukasawa and Kusumoto 2009, 213). Kanamori 2013, 66–67, says that there were twelve.

249. The last phrase used here—*kokoro sumiyuku nomi oboyu*—suggests a moment of Buddhist enlightenment.

250. *Bashō kushū* no. 329. Shida Yoshihide (see Fukasawa and Kusumoto 2009, 215) posits an allusion to a poem by Wang Wei titled "Entering Ruoye Stream" (*Ru Ruoye Xi* 入若耶溪): "Noisy cicadas make the groves more quiet; birdsong makes the mountains more still" (蝉噪林逾静 / 鳥鳴山更幽). Ruoye Stream runs along the border of Ruoye Mountain in Zhejiang Province.

251. The original plan was to go from Ryūshakuji to Yamagata and then to the Three Mountains of Dewa. The choice to backtrack and visit Ōishida, where they spent two nights, came about because poets in that area sent a message pleading with them to come. From there they went by land to Motoaikai, where they got on the boat (Kanamori 2000, 241).

252. The meaning of "old *haikai*" (*furuki haikai*) in this passage is much debated by scholars, some arguing that it is meant in a very general way, others that it refers to the efforts of Michikaze in the area, others that it is meant to contrast with Bashō's new style, etc. See Fukasawa and Kusumoto 2009, 217–18.

253. Again, a controversial passage, dividing scholars on whether the first flowering refers specifically to the Teimon and Danrin schools or to something less definite.

254. Perhaps referring to *Wakan rōeishū* no. 701 by Ōe no Asatsuna, in which "the single sound of a horn" is said to wake people from cold dreams. Fukasawa and Kusumoto 2009, 218, conclude that the meaning must be that *haikai* opens the poetic hearts of people in the hinterlands.

old,[255] which obliged me to lead them in a sequence.[256] It was here in our journey that we reached a poetic high point.[257]

The Mogami River comes in from Michinoku, its headwaters in Yamagata. Upriver are fearsome rapids, Goten and Hayabusa and other places; then it flows north of Mount Itajiki, finally entering the sea at Sakata. With mountains looming left and right, boats stacked with rice plants—they call them Rice-Plant Boats—come downriver through dense forest.[258] The falls at Shiraito cascade down through gaps in the greenery and Sennindō[259] stands facing the river bank. The waters were running high and were dangerous for boats.[260]

It gathers	*samidare o*
summer rains—flowing fast!	*atsumete hayashi*
Mogami River.[261]	*mogamigawa*

---

255. Most likely a contrast between various "old" styles, such as the Danrin, and Bashō's new style.

256. Fuji Masaharu 1989, 141, says in this sequence Ichiei and Sensui were old, Bashō and Sora new. Neither local man was a major disciple.

257. The meaning of this sentence (この た び の 風流爰 に 至 れ り *kono tabi no furyū koko ni itareri*) is much debated. I follow Yokosawa 1995, 248, in taking it to mean that the *kasen* composed at this time among poets committed to *haikai* but lacking leadership—the sequence that began with the *hokku* recorded in the next section (*samidare o*)—was a high point in terms of the poetry composed during the journey. See also Horikiri 2003, 140. Takatō 1966, 176, quotes Abe Kimio as taking it to mean, "In the end, our poetic journey brought us to creating this." It is obviously ironic that the poetic high point came when he was "obliged" to direct a gathering among provincials.

258. Kanamori 2013, 80–82, notes that Bashō and Sora would not have traveled on such a boat but on something more substantial, arranged for by patrons in Ōishida.

259. Both Shiraito no taki and Sennindō were on the north shore of the river. Sennindō was a shrine erected in honor of Hitachinobō Kaison, one of Yoshitsune's samurai attendants. Legend has it that Yoshitsune stopped in that area during his flight to Hiraizumi.

260. The author of the medieval travel record *Tōkan kikō*, 140, describes the hazards of crossing the river when the water is running high in autumn and admits to "feeling in peril" in his boat, which is probably the source of Bashō's "dangerous for boats"—intended as a general statement. Although Bashō does not mention it, Sora records that despite letters from locals they again had document trouble at the checkpoint where they planned to leave the river and were denied entry. The boat captain took them downriver and dropped them off, where they went off as illegals for a time, until patrons in Sakata intervened. See Kanamori 2013, 85, 112–13.

261. *Bashō kushū* no. 221. Another version of this *hokku* was the first verse in a sequence composed at the house of Ichiei in Ōishida over two days. See Uozumi 2011, 83–87 and Carter 1997. See poem 116, "Summer Rains," from *Kenkō Hōshi shū* (c. 1352): "In Mogami River / waters rise,

On the 3rd day of the Sixth Month we climbed up to Mount Haguro. After calling on a man named Zushi Sakichi, we were granted an audience with Egaku Ajari, deputy abbot.[262] He provided lodging in the annex at Minamidani[263] and was a careful host, attending kindly to our needs.

On the 4th we participated in a linked-verse gathering at the abbot's residence.[264]

A happy wind	*arigata ya*
brings us the scent of snow	*yuki o kaorasu*
in South Valley.[265]	*minamidani*

On the 5th we paid our respects at the Gongen Shrine.[266] When the Great Teacher Nōjo, founder of the place, lived, is unknown. In the *Engi Regulations* there is mention of "the shrine at Satoyama 里山 in the province of Dewa."[267] Probably a copyist wrote the character for "village" (里 *sato*) instead of the character for "black" (黒 *kuro*) by mistake. It seems people use a shorter version of the name: "Mount Haguro," rather than "Mount Haguro in the province of Dewa."[268] Mounts Haguro,

---

flowing fast / as rainclouds / climb upriver, then come down / in summer rains" (*mogamigawa / hayaku zo masaru / amagumo no / noboreba kudaru / samidare no koro*).

262. It appears that it was Zushi Sakichi (also known by his *haikai* name, Rogan) that introduced Bashō to Egaku Ajari (the latter term coming from Sanskrit *acarya*, an honorific term for a teacher), a priest representing Tōeizan Kan'eiji, a prominent temple of the Tendai sect in Edo. Sakichi lived in Tōge Village, near Mount Haguro. During Bashō's time in the area, it was Sakichi who served as guide and host, going so far as to accompany the travelers to Tsuruoka on the next leg of the journey and probably paying all the fees involved in the mountain rituals.

263. Traditionally identified as Kōyōin Shionji located in Minamidani. See Fukasawa and Kusumoto 2009, 226–27. Yamamoto Satoshi 1994, 328, says Shionji burned in 1672 and Genyōin was moved there. It was a place used by Egaku for elite guests.

264. Only the first six verses of the sequence were composed on the 4th. It was finished in the coming days.

265. *Bashō kushū* no. 230. Here "brings us the scent" (*kaorasu*) is thus figurative, although surely the phrase might also mean carrying "fresh air" from the peaks down to the valleys. The *hokku* also expresses gratitude to Egaku, their host.

266. Located on Mount Haguro. Buddhist deities that appeared in the world as Shinto gods were called Gongen.

267. No surviving text of *Engishiki* 延喜式 (c. 927), a compendium of government regulations, including those involving shrines and festivals, contains this reference.

268. An explanation that probably came from Bashō's hosts. Other texts include the following sentence here: "The gazetteer says something like, 'The name Dewa comes from the fact that the province presented bird feathers as tribute.'" See Imoto 1972, 370.

Gassan, and Yudono are together known as the Mountains of Dewa.[269] This temple is a subsidiary of the Tōei Temple in the Shogun's City and is a place where the moon of Tendai concentration and insight shines brightly, where the lamp of the Law of perfect understanding and unified vision sheds forth its light.[270] Monks' halls stand roof against roof; ascetics encourage each other in their rigors, showing forth the virtues of a land and mountain of holiness that people honor yet also hold in awe. One can only deem it a mountain of splendor that will flourish on into the future.[271]

On the 8th we climbed Mount Gassan.[272] Ritual cords dangling from our necks and white turbans wrapped around our heads,[273] we set off on our climb, guided by someone called a strong man,[274] feeling as if we were surrounded by a mountain of cloud and mist as we tramped along on ice and snow. After climbing eight *li*, I had a strange feeling, as if we had ventured beyond the cloud-barrier[275] into the orbits of the sun and the moon. Short of breath and numb of body, we finally reached the summit, as the sun went down—and there was the moon.[276] With bamboo grasses for pallet and pillow,[277]

---

269. Dewa Sanzan.

270. Tendai was an aristocratic sect of classical times that was associated with "concentration and insight" (*shikan* 止観), a doctrinal concept of great influence in medieval Buddhism and still well known in Bashō's day. Kan'eiji was a Tendai center in Edo that was the family temple of the Tokugawa house. During his journey Bashō visited a number of temples and shrines associated with Kan'eiji (Tōshōgu in Nikkō, Chūsonji in Hiraizumi, Ryūshakuji, and Kōyōin Shionji in Haguro), indicating a close relationship. Fukasawa and Kusumoto (2009, 229) note that Kondō Yōzō suggests that Bashō's journey may have been sponsored in some way by the temples.

271. No doubt this statement is also praise for their host, Egaku, and by extension, Tōeizan, his temple in Edo.

272. Sora's account says they climbed Gassan on the 6th. Some scholars argue that Bashō simply made a mistake in recording, others that he pushed the date forward in order to be closer to the full moon over the mountain—Gassan, which means "Moon Mountain." See Fukasawa and Kusumoto 2009, 231.

273. Ritual clothing worn by worshippers. The *yūshime* 木綿 was a cord necklace made up of rings of woven cloth.

274. *Gōriki* 強力, a bearer and guide.

275. *Unkan* 雲関, "cloud barrier," resonates with the many earthly barriers the travelers have been through on the road.

276. Rather than the moon "coming up" at this time, the phrasing (*hi bosshite tsuki arawaru*) suggests that it had already been visible for some time but looked much brighter in the darkness after sundown. See Fukasawa and Kusumoto 2009, 232.

277. Sora's account indicates that the men did not bed down in the open but slept in a hut near the summit, although it is possible that bamboo grasses were used on their pallets. See Fukasawa and Kusumoto 2009, 232–33.

we lay down, waiting for break of day. When the sun came up and the clouds cleared, we descended to Yudono.

On the valley's edge stood a swordsmith's hut. Electing to use the sacred waters here, the swordsmiths of this province would purify themselves before forging a blade and when it was done mark it with the signature, Gassan, a name that gained worldly renown. I was reminded of blades forged at Longquan, and as I imagined ancient blades tempered here I gained new appreciation for the dedication of adepts who followed the ways of Gan Jiang and Mo Ye.[278] I sat down on a rock to rest and noticed some buds about half-way out on a cherry tree just three feet high. How unexpected that the heart of the late cherry, beneath accumulating snow, should not forget about spring! It was like catching the scent of those plum blossoms that "flower in blazing heat,"[279] and I remembered more poignantly the poem by Archbishop Gyōson.[280] But I must put down my brush here and write no more, for it is strictly forbidden among ascetics doing devotions there to tell others the details of what they do.[281]

After we returned to the residence we were summoned by the Ajari, and I wrote down the poems I had written about our circuit round the Three Peaks on poem strips for him.[282]

---

278. A husband and wife in the ancient kingdom of Wu who were renowned as swordsmiths. The work of swordsmiths was considered sacred in many ways, and their profession was often associated with sacred mountains as symbols of strength, timelessness, and remoteness from the everyday world.

279. See lines from *Zenrin kushū* 禅林句集, a collection of Zen writings from the Muromachi era: "The plantain plant beneath the snow—a Mo Jie painting; the plum blooming beneath the blazing sun—a Jian Zhai poem" (雲裏芭蕉摩詰画 /炎天梅藥簡斎詩). "A flower blooming beneath the blazing sun" is a metaphor from Zen discourse referring to anything unusual. See Fukasawa and Kusumoto 2009, 235.

280. *KYS* 521. "Written when he was at Ōmine and was surprised to see a cherry tree in bloom. 'Let us enjoy / this moving scene, together, / mountain cherry tree. / No one else even knows / that you have blossomed'" (*morotomo ni / aware to omoe / yamazakura / hana yori hoka ni / shiru hito mo nashi*). Gyōson was a Tendai monk.

281. This refers to the rites done at Yudono. All mountain practices, many traceable to early Buddhist esoteric teachings or Shinto pantheistic tenets, were considered sacred. Scholars assume that Sora was more devout in this regard than Bashō, but there is no indication that he too did not participate.

282. Bashō carried *tanjaku* for such occasions, as had *renga* masters in ages past. Since medieval times poets had offered their poems on strips (*tanjaku*) as gifts or, as in this case, gratuities. Bashō's three *tanjaku* have been preserved in the collection of the Yamagata Museum of Art. See Okada 1972, 76; Uozumi 2011, 91.

Such coolness!	*suzushisa ya*
Just a sliver of moon glimpsed	*hono mikazuki no*
at Mount Haguro.[283]	*haguroyama*

How many times	*kumo no mine*
did cloud peaks crumble to show	*ikutsu kuzurete*
Moon Mountain?[284]	*tsuki no yama*

Of Yudono	*katararenu*
I cannot speak, but *see* here—	*yudono ni nurasu*
drenched sleeves.[285]	*tamato kana*

At Mount Yudono	*yudonoyama*
I tread a path strewn with coins	*zeni fumu michi no*
and my tears.[286]	*namida kana*
Sora	

We left Haguro behind for the castle town of Tsurugaoka, where we were welcomed into the house of a warrior named Nagayama Shigeyuki.[287] While there we composed a *haikai* sequence together, with Sakichi, too, who had come this far to see us off.[288]

---

283. *Bashō kushū* no. 237. A note of thanks to the poets' hosts and the shrine itself.

284. *Bashō kushū* no. 226. Scholars put forward various interpretations of this poem, arguing either that "peaks of cloud" dissipate to reveal Mount Gassan, that throughout the day clouds constantly roil about the peak, or that the gods created the mountain by piling clouds one on top of another. Fukasawa and Kusumoto 2009, 237. The vantage point of the poem—whether from down below, on the slope, or on the peak—is unclear.

285. *Bashō kushū* no. 294. Yudonoyama means "hot spring mountain," indicating that there was a hot spring there. It is also called Koinoyama, "the mountain of love." One interpretation links it back to the prohibitions about speaking of rites undertaken there, while another takes the meaning to be that feelings of love can be better expressed by tears than by words. See Fukasawa and Kusumoto 2009, 238.

286. An earlier version of this poem read, "Treading on coins, / I forget about the world / at Yudono" (*zeni fumite / yo o wasurekeri / yudonoyama*). Bashō probably revised it himself when he wrote up *The Narrow Road through the Hinterlands*. A regulation of the place against picking anything up from the ground explains the phrase "a path strewn with coins" (Fukasawa and Kusumoto 2009, 238–39).

287. Bashō refers to Shigeyuki with the ancient word for samurai, *mononofu*. Sora's diary tells us that Bashō had a flare-up of his chronic ailment in Tsurugaoka. See Kanamori 2000, 257.

288. Sakichi had no doubt acted as a guide along the way and introduced Bashō as a representative of Egaku Ajari. The sequence was composed at Shigeyuki's house, where the travelers stayed, by Bashō, Sora, Sakichi, and Jūkō. It was sometime during these days that Sakichi asked the

We boarded a boat and went to Sakata, where we stayed at the home of a physician named En'an Fugyoku.[289]

After Atsumi's heat	*atsumiyama ya*
I look toward Fuku Bay	*fukuura kakete*
in evening cool.[290]	*yūsuzumi*

It takes the hot sun	*atsuki hi o*
and pushes it into the sea—	*umi ni iretaru*
Mogami River.[291]	*mogamigawa*

Already I had seen countless fine sights—rivers and mountains, water and land—but still I pushed on to Kisagata. We set out from Sakata harbor, heading northeast, over mountains and ocean strands, treading on sand, going ten *li* by the end. Just as the sun was about to go down, a shore wind kicked up, tossing sand into the air, and a misty rain began to fall, obscuring Mount Chōkai. As we "felt our way in darkness," we recalled that "rain is fine too—something different" and that "clear skies after rain are a true delight."[292] We ducked into a fisherman's shack and pulled

---

questions that would become the basis for the poetic dialogue presented in *Kikigaki nanukagusa* 聞書七日草.

289. Sora notes that Fugyoku was actually not at home when they first arrived, which meant they spent their first night at an inn (Kanamori 2013, 110). Their guide was Kon no Kahei (mistakenly identified as Imano Kahei in Sora's record), who provided food, etc. (Kanamori 2013, 120). Also there, having come in from Mino, was Bashō's disciple Teiji, who accompanied them in Kisagata.

290. *Bashō kushū* no. 280. This was the first verse of a sequence composed by Bashō, Sora, and Fugyoku over a period of three days.

291. *Bashō kushū* no. 209. Scholars argue about the meaning of *atsuki hi* 暑き日, many insisting it means "a hot day," others "the hot sun," and a few, both. The use of the verb *iru* in transitive form would seem to argue for "the hot sun." See Fukasawa and Kusumoto 2009, 243–44. This verse was the *hokku* for a sequence composed with local poets, including Fugyoku and Terashima Hikosuke. The first line of the *hokku* first read, *suzushisa ya*, "Such coolness."

292. The phrases in quotations are from a Chinese poem by the Japanese monk Sakugen, who recalls a poem by Su Shi about West Lake when Sakugen passes that same lake at night: "I recall lines committed to memory, 'fine in rain, pleasant under clear skies,' / and as I grope in the dark, I sense West Lake" (参得雨奇晴好句 / 暗中模索識西湖). See Imoto 1972, 373, n. 16; Yokosawa 1995, 262–63. Hisatomi argues for "with nothing to do" rather than "as I grope" (see Fukasawa and Kusumoto 2009, 245–46).

our knees up to wait for the rain to let up.[293] That next morning, the skies had cleared and the morning sun shone so radiantly that we set out by boat into Kisagata Bay. First we took the boat in at Nōin's Isle and visited the place where he was in seclusion three years; then we got out on the opposite shore and saw the memento of the monk Saigyō, an old cherry tree that recalls his poem with the line, "boats rowing over flowers."[294] Up on shore was a tomb that was said to be the grave of Empress Jingū; and there was a temple, the Kanmanjuji.[295] I had never heard of an imperial visit to this area, though. I wonder what there is to the story. Seated in the chief monk's quarters of the temple, we rolled the blinds up to see the view,[296] and there it was, a panorama: Mount Chōkai propping the heavens up to the south, its silhouette reflected in the bay; Muyamuya Barrier far off to the west; the road toward Akita running along an embankment into the east; and the sea commanding all to the north, its waves breaking at a place called Shiogoshi.[297] The bay is about a *li* wide and a *li* long and resembles Matsushima yet is not the same. Matsushima seems to smile, Kisagata seems to frown. There is loneliness there, and along with that, sadness: a land that appears troubled at heart.

---

293. Fukasawa and Kusumoto 2009, 246, point out that as Fugyoku was hosting the travelers on this excursion, it is unlikely that they actually rested in any fisherman's hut. See *GSIS* (no. 519) by Nōin: "Written at a place called Kisagata, when he visited Idewa Province. 'In this world / one can live even like this: / for my home— / a rude fisherman's hut / on Kisagata Shore'" (*yo no naka wa / kakute mo henikeri / kisagata no / ama no tomaya o / waga yado ni shite*).

294. When, or if, Nōin lived on the island in question is unknown. The poem appears in *Tsugioshū* 継尾集, a poetry collection compiled by Fugyoku in the early 1700s. Although attributed to Saigyō, it is of uncertain provenance: "At Kisagata / cherry blossoms are overcome / by breaking waves: / fishermen in their boats / rowing over flowers" (*kisagata no / sakura wa nami ni / uzumorete / hana no ue kogu / ama no tsuribune*). See Fukasawa and Kusumoto 2009, 246.

295. No record connects Empress Jingū with this place or its gravesite. Her official tomb is in Nara. The name Kanmanjuji, "temple of tide-controlling jewels," refers to a story about the empress finding jewels on the beach at Kisagata.

296. A reference to a poem by Bai Juyi about raising the blinds to see the snow on Mount Xianglu. Bashō may have known it from section 280 of *The Pillow Book of Sei Shōnagon*. See *Makura no sōshi*, 321.

297. Fukasawa and Kusumoto 2009, 247, point out that here Bashō is reconstructing a view in his mind at the time of writing. Not all four of the four directions could have been visible from the temple window.

At Kisagata: *kisagata ya*
mimosa flowers in the rain,   *ame ni seishi ga*
like Xi Shi.[298]   *nebu no hana*

At Shiogoshi: *shiogoshi ya*
high tide high on crane's legs   *tsuruhagi nurete*
and cool seas.[299]   *umi suzushi*

Festival:

At Kisagata: *kisagata ya*
what sorts of food do they eat   *ryōri nani kuu*
on shrine day?[300]   *kamimatsuri*
      Sora

At fishers' houses   *ama no ya ya*
they lay down door planks   *toita o shikite*
in evening cool.[301]   *yūsuzumi*
      Teiji, merchant of Mino Province[302]

---

298. *Bashō kushū* no. 379. The metaphor of mimosa "in the rain" is appropriate for the sad ending of Xi Shi (see n. 199 above) and the lonely sadness Bashō earlier attributed to Kisagata. Scholars often mention this *hokku* as Bashō's way of working the poetic category of love—a staple in linked verse—into his text. It is one of four poems that appears in a *kaishi* given to Teiji, probably in gratitude for his labors, that has been preserved in the Kakimori Bunko in Itami.

299. *Bashō kushū* no. 239. A headnote in a *hokku* collection indicates that this poem was an actual observation of a crane foraging in the tidelands. See Fukasawa and Kusumoto 2009, 249.

300. The festival at Kumano Gongen Shrine, held on the 17th, involved food offerings. See an *uta* by Nōin: "I have a question / for the Heaven Dwelling Maiden / of Toyooka: / How many ages have passed / for the God of Kisagata?" (*ame ni masu / toyookahime ni / koto towamu / iku yo ni narinu / kisagata no kami*). See Fukasawa and Kusumoto 2009, 250.

301. Bashō edited this poem, the first line of which originally read simply, "Kisagata." Peasants living near the sea would take planks from sliding doors down to the beach to sit on and enjoy the cool of night.

302. Teiji was evidently a traveling merchant who came to Sakata to assist the poets in the next part of their trip, writing letters of introduction for stops along the way. He arrived on the 16th. He wrote recommendation letters for Bashō that helped him get lodging down the road (Kanamori 2000, 277).

Seeing an osprey nest on a rock:

Promised, perhaps,	*nami koenu*
that waves won't come so high?	*chigiri arite ya*
Osprey nest.[303]	*misago no su*
Sora	

Not ready to say farewell to Sakata, we stayed several days, but then headed off toward the clouds over the Hokuroku Road. Thoughts of how far we had yet to go[304] weighed on my spirits as I learned that it was another 130 *li* to the Kaga provincial seat. We passed through the Nezu Barrier[305] and turned our steps into Echigo and on into Etchū, finally arriving at Ichiburi Barrier. During the nine days[306] that sojourn took, I suffered in the muggy heat and felt very low; then my ailment flared up and I stopped writing things down.[307]

In the Seventh Month	*fumizuki ya*
even the night of the 6th day	*muika mo tsune no*
is not the same.[308]	*yo ni wa nizu*

---

303. The word *chigiri* 契, "vow" or "pledge," suggests love as a category, which foreshadows what is to come at Ichiburi. Fukasawa and Kusumoto 2009, 251, posit an allusion to a *hokku* by the *renga* master Sōgi (*Shitakusa* 下草 no. 1378): "For how many ages / was the promise of no high waves? / River of Heaven" (*nami kosanu /chigiri ya iku yo / ama no kawa*).

304. Kanamori 2013, 138–39, notes that Bashō must have been somewhat heartened by the send-off he received by Fugyoku and seven others, who accompanied Bashō and Sora by boat as far as Sode Bay. A poem by Tao Qian contains the line "Far, far ahead, I face white clouds" (遥々望白雲). See Fukasawa and Kusumoto 2009, 253.

305. Kanamori 2000, 278–79, notes that Bashō and Sora actually separated briefly at the beginning of this leg of their journey, probably because Sora did not have proper documents for passing through Nezu Barrier. Bashō went on horseback down the coastal road and Sora by way of the mountain road through Yumoto, perhaps taking advantage of the hot springs there. They met up again around Nakamura on the mountain road (Kanamori 2013, 284).

306. It appears that the period was sixteen rather than nine days. One explanation is that "nine days" refers just to the time he was ill; another is that "nine days" referred only to his time in Izumozaki and Ichiburi. See Fukasawa and Kusumoto 2009, 254.

307. Sora records nothing about this flare-up, but he does frequently note the dreadful heat, which doubtless contributed to his own illness and Bashō's.

308. *Bashō kushū* no. 307. The headnote to this poem in a record left by Sora says that it was composed for a sequence (just twelve verses) composed at Naoetsu in Echigo Province (Fukasawa and Kusumoto 2009, 255). The 7th day of the Seventh Month was the Tanabata Festival (Star Festival) celebrating the ancient story of the Weaver Girl and the Herd Boy (Vega and

Over rough seas   *araumi ya*

it stretches off to Sado—   *sado ni yokotau*

the River of Heaven.[309]   *amanogawa*

This day we passed through the hardest patches of the North Country, places named Oyashirazu, Koshirazu, Inumodori, Komagaeshi,[310] and so on; and I was worn out. But no sooner did I put my head down on my pillow of grass than I heard the voices of two young women talking, and the voice of an old man, too, all coming from the room next to us, toward the front of the inn.[311] It turned out that the women were pleasure women from Niigata in Echigo, going on pilgrimage to Ise. The man, however, was only taking them this far, and what I had overheard was their dictating letters for home and little messages for him to take back. I fell asleep listening to them, touched by their complaints of life "amidst white waves / breaking against the shore,"[312] so many fishermen's daughters floating idly through the world, selling themselves day after day, caught in the cycles of karma.[313] The next morning, as we were departing, they approached us: "The road is a daunting place and we are feeling anxious and discouraged, not knowing the way," they said. "Even if only unseen, in behind, could we follow along with you? Wearing those robes, you must have compassion, so won't you show us Buddha's mercy, and let us join you—for just a brief while?"[314] They were in tears, and I felt sorry for them, but I quickly said this and brushed them off, "We stop at too many places along the way. You should just go along and stay near other

---

Altair) meeting over the Milky Way on that night. Although Chinese in origin, the festival was a fixture in Japan from the eighth century onward.

309. *Bashō kushū* no. 430. Most scholars maintain that by placing this *hokku* after the previous one, Bashō meant to connect it to the Tanabata Festival, emphasizing the way the River of Heaven connects the mainland to the island. Opinions differ over whether the poem was composed at Izumozaki or Naoetsu.

310. The names of all four of these obscure places express the rugged nature of the terrain: "Children Disavow Parents," "Parents Disavow Children," "Dogs Turn Back," and "Ponies Sent Back." The names are not listed in accurate order. See Fukasawa and Kusumoto 2009, 262.

311. For an explanation, see Fukasawa and Kusumoto 2009, 262.

312. See *Wakan rōeishū* no. 722 (also SKKS 1703), an anonymous poem in the section "Ladies of Pleasure": "Amidst white waves / breaking against the shore / I live my life— / a fisherman's child, / with no place for home" (*shiranami no / yosuru nagisa ni / yo o sugusu / ama no ko nareba / yado mo tomezu*).

313. Gōin 業因. The effects of prior sinful acts.

314. Because of his robes, the women mistake Bashō for an ordained priest.

people on the road. The gods are sure to protect you and keep you safe." For a while I could not stop thinking about their plight.

In the same house,	*hitotsuie ni*
pleasure women sleeping, too.	*yūjo mo netari*
Bush clover and the moon.[315]	*hagi to tsuki*

I told this to Sora, for him to write it down.[316]

We crossed over the many streams that make up Kurobe Shijūhachigase, "the Forty-Eight Streams of the Kurobe River," and came out at a bay called Nago. Though it wasn't spring, I thought of the waves of wisteria at Tako Bay[317] and wondered if even

---

315. *Bashō kushū* no. 563. *Jiamari* in the first line. Fukasawa (along with many others) argues that it was in order to include this *hokku*, written when Bashō was writing up his account years later, that Bashō created this whole episode (Fukasawa 2009, 383). Many readings take bush clover as a metaphor for the women and the moon as a metaphor for Bashō, although some doubt that Bashō would use a metaphor that implies such distance between beings who are after all both living in the world. See Fukasawa and Kusumoto 2009, 264–65. Others see that reading as naïve. Fukasawa's approach, which draws partly on what he sees as a clear allusion to Saigyō's chance meeting with a prostitute as described in the Noh play *Eguchi*, sees Bashō's *hokku* as a sober reflection on how he had mistaken the worldly form of the women (bush clover) just as they had mistaken him for a priest, and that only now does he see that the moonlight shining on their beautiful form revealed them as a manifestation of the bodhisattva Fugen (Fukasawa 2009, 382–85)—thus revealing a false distinction. At the heart of the poem is the old trope of moonlight shining on dew—a metaphor for ephemerality.

316. Most modern Japanese scholars believe this whole episode was concocted by Bashō, among other reasons, because he wanted to work the poetic category of love into his account. Their first evidence is that Sora makes no mention of it in his account, despite the fact that Bashō says he instructed Sora to write it down. Others are not convinced that the incident did not happen. See Eguchi 1998, 137–38; Fukasawa and Kusumoto 2009, 265–68; Satō Katsuaki 2014, 90; Yamamoto Kenkichi 2012, 424. After researching travel habits at the time, Kanamori 2013, 206–9, concludes that there are other reasons to consider the episode a fiction—because prostitutes would hardly have been allowed to go on a monthlong vacation and because travelers from Niigata to Ise would have taken a different road. Fukasawa 2009, 384, suggests that Bashō added the note about having Sora write the incident down as a sly way to lend ironic credence to his story.

317. The area was associated with Man'yō-era visitors, the poets Kakinomoto no Hitomaro and Ōtomo no Yakamochi. See *SIS* 88 by Kakinomoto no Hitomaro: "At Tako Bay / waves of wisteria glow / even beneath the waves. / Let's put sprigs in our caps— / for those who haven't seen" (*tako no ura no / soko sae niou / fujinami o / kazashite yukan / minu hito no tame*). The association between the place and wisteria accounts for the name of the nearby shrine, Fujinami, "Wisteria Waves."

in early autumn . . . and asked someone for directions. "It's five *li* from here—you just follow the shoreline and go on into the area up against the mountainside facing you; but there'll be reed-roofed fishers' huts, scruffy places, and that's all, so it's unlikely anyone will put you up for the night." This warned us off, so we traveled on into Kaga Province.[318]

> The scent of early rice . . .   *wase no ka ya*
>
> and on my right as I cut through,   *wakeiru migi wa*
>
> waves on a rocky shore.[319]   *arisoumi*

We passed by Mount Unohana and Kurikara Gorge, and arrived in Kanazawa, on the 15th of the Seventh Month. Here there was a merchant named Kashō, who had traveled up from Osaka.[320] We stayed in the same lodging.

Isshō was a man known among followers of the Way of *haikai*, who had a certain reputation, but it turned out that the winter before he had died, still a young man.[321] His older brother[322] held a memorial sequence in his honor:

> Shake, burial mound—   *tsuka mo ugoke*
>
> as I join my weeping voice   *waga naku koe wa*
>
> to the autumn wind.[323]   *aki no kaze*

---

318. No doubt the author intentionally includes this rebuff immediately after Bashō's own rejection of the prostitutes in the previous episode.

319. *Bashō kushū* no. 638. Scholars point out that on the road into Kaga Province the sea would not be visible on the right. Hori and Imoto 1972, 178, argue that the poem was written from the top of Kurikara Pass.

320. Another Osaka merchant whose travels took him into the provinces.

321. He died in the Twelfth Month of 1688 at just thirty-six. Yamane 2017, 71, argues that Bashō must have received word on the road that Isshō had died, motivating him to arrive for the Bon festival on the 15th of the Seventh Month, but Sora's diary seems to indicate that they learned of his death only upon arrival.

322. A man named Besshō.

323. *Bashō kushū* no. 444. *Jiamari* in the first line. According to the lunar calendar, autumn began with the Seventh Month. The memorial sequence was composed on the 22nd day of the month, a full week after Bashō arrived in Kanazawa. Although Kanazawa was a major center of *haikai*, and during his nine days there Bashō had meetings with many poets and participated in at least three *kasen*, he mentions only this event, probably because he wanted to focus on the loss of his student. Twenty-eight poets offered *hokku* for the memorial event, which was held at Gannenji. Bashō had never met Isshō face-to-face, and his poem expresses his disappointment and sense of personal loss.

When invited to the hut of a certain man:

Autumn's cool.	*aki suzushi*
Let's each of us peel his own—	*tegoto ni muke ya*
melon, eggplant.[324]	*uri nasubi*

Composed along the way:

Bright and blazing,	*aka aka to*
the aloof sun beats down—	*hi wa tsurenaku mo*
despite autumn wind.[325]	*aki no kaze*

At a place called Komatsu:

A sweet name, Young Pine—	*shiorashiki*
where winds are buffeting	*na ya komatsu fuku*
bush clover, miscanthus.[326]	*hagi susuki*

At this place we paid our respects at Tada Shrine, which has in its holdings the helmet and a scrap of brocade owned by the Steward Saitō Sanemori.[327] The story goes that in ancient times Lord Yoshitomo awarded the helmet to Sanemori when the latter

---

324. *Bashō kushū* no. 652. The "certain man" was Saitō Issen. This *hokku* was composed for a sequence involving thirteen poets on the 20th after a banquet where scholars assume melon and eggplant were served (see Kanamori 2013, 228).

325. *Bashō kushū* no. 445. It is not clear whether this *hokku* was written on the way *to* Kanazawa or on the way *from* Kanazawa to Komatsu (see Fukasawa and Kusumoto 2009, 274) or at Gen'ian, the home of Hokushi at the foot of Utatsuyama, where the verse was used as the *hokku* for a sequence (Kanamori 2013, 224–25). Scholars argue about whether *aka aka*, in *kana* in the original, indicates the characters for "red" (赤々) or "bright" (明々).

326. *Bashō kushū* no. 569. The place name Komatsu means "young pine." The *hokku* was composed for a forty-four-verse sequence (*yoyoshi*) composed by ten people on the 25th at the home of Fujimura Izu (*haikai* name, Kosen), head priest at Hiyoshi Shrine. Kanamori 2013, 236–38, notes that the group assembled were associated with another participant, Kansei, the most prominent *haikai* master in Komatsu at the time. The next day Kansei hosted a fifty-verse sequence at his house.

327. The following story is based on an episode in *The Tales of the Heike* (*Heike monogatari*, 64–67), which relates how at the Battle of Shinohara, Sanemori, in his seventies, was granted the privilege of wearing a captain's clothing so as not to be dismissed as an old man. Higuchi no Jiro, who knew him, identified Sanemori's head and acted as messenger to the defeated Heike concerning Sanemori's fate. See McCullough 1988, 233–35. According to legend, the brocade was

fought for the Genji; and surely it could not have been owned by an ordinary samurai. Sweeping back from the visor to the flaps was a decoration in the form of chrysanthemum tendrils, inlaid with gold, topped off by a pair of horns on a dragon head. Shrine records tell how after Sanemori died in battle, Kiso Yoshinaka presented the helmet, along with a petition, to this shrine, where it has been preserved, as well as the story of how Higuchi no Jirō brought the things as an official messenger. There was the whole story, right before my eyes in the shrine's legends.[328]

So cruel a fate!	*muzan ya na*
From beneath the helmet,	*kabuto no shita no*
a cricket's sound.[329]	*kirigirisu*

As we approached Yamanaka Hot Springs, we walked along glancing back at Shirane Peak behind us. At the edge of a mountain was a Kannon Hall. The Tonsured Emperor Kazan placed a statue of the Great Teacher Jikaku there after completing his pilgrimage circuit of the Thirty-Three Sites, and granted the place the name Nata—combining the character *na* 那 from Nachi with *ta* from Tanigumi 谷汲.[330] There are many remarkable stones, old pines planted in rows, and a small hall thatched with reeds built on top of a rock: altogether, a marvelous place.

Whiter still	*ishiyama no*
than Ishiyama's stones:	*ishi yori shiroshi*
the autumn wind.[331]	*aki no kaze*

---

given to Sanemori as a gift from Taira no Munemori. It is unlikely that these relics are authentic, but Bashō seems to have thought them to be.

328. Actually, not the shrine legends (*engi* 縁起) but another document. See Fukasawa and Kusumoto 2009, 277.

329. *Bashō kushū* no. 552. The exclamation *muzan ya* is a quotation from Higuchi no Jirō as he identifies Sanemori's head in the Noh play *Sanemori* 実盛, 194. On the 27th, Bashō presented this *hokku*, along with a *kasen* involving Kosen and Kansei, as an offering at Tada Shrine.

330. After taking the tonsure, Kazan made the circuit of thirty-three Kannon temples, beginning with Nachi in Kii Province and ending with Tanigumi in Mino.

331. *Bashō kushū* no. 446. Scholars are divided as to whether Ishiyama refers to Ishiyama in Ōmi or the stones at Nata. The whitish rocks around the temple at Nata were probably what Bashō had most immediately in mind. See Hori and Imoto 1972, 183. The adjective "white" used in reference to the wind probably is meant to be subjective, indicating the "feel" of the crisp breezes of autumn. Ogata 2001, 379–80, and Fukasawa and Kusumoto 2009, 279–280, offer examples from Chinese and Japanese texts that describe the autumn wind as "white" or "colorless."

We bathed at the hot spring. Its virtues are second only to those of Arima,[332] we were told.

At Yamanaka Springs—	*yamanaka ya*
no need for chrysanthemums	*kiku wa taoranu*
to create a scent.[333]	*yu no nioi*

The man who served as our host was named Kumenosuke and he was still a youth. His father enjoyed *haikai* and had in the past put Teishitsu of Kyoto to shame[334] on a visit, so much so that after Teishitsu returned to Kyoto he became a disciple of Teitoku and gained worldly renown. It is said that after achieving fame, Teishitsu would never accept fees for commenting on poetry[335] by people from this village. By now the story is old.

Sora had come down with a stomach ache, and set off for Nagashima in Ise, where he had relations.[336] He wrote this down before he left:

---

332. Arima in Settsu Province was one of the most prominent of all hot springs.

333. *Bashō kushū* no. 577. This *hokku* is obviously intended as a statement of gratitude to Bashō's host. Chrysanthemums were often used to scent spring waters, but the poem contends that the waters are already so beneficial that there is no need to add scent. Kumenosuke, just fourteen at the time of Bashō's visit, was given the name Tōyō during this visit. Chrysanthemums were believed to have medicinal effects. Bashō may have had in mind the Noh play *Kiku jidō* 菊慈童, about an exiled servant to a noble clan who becomes an immortal (*sennin* 仙人) after drinking dew from a chrysanthemum leaf. See Hori and Imoto 1972, 182.

334. *Fūga ni hazukashimerarete* 風雅に辱閉められて, "to be embarrassed in poetic [competition]."

335. Bashō uses the word *hanji* 判詞, a term for judgments on poems since classical times.

336. Sora had been taken in by his uncle at the Taichiin in Ise Nagashima as a young man and probably thought of the place as his home. In his record, Sora writes that he was ill in Kanazawa on the 17th and does not accompany Bashō on a local visit. On the 21st he sought medicine. Finally, on the 5th of the Eighth Month, at Yamanaka, where the travelers had probably gone so that Sora could avail himself of the famed hot springs there (see Kanamori 2013, 243), he parted from Bashō and headed toward the home of relatives in Ise. Scholars are dubious about Sora's reasons for leaving (see Sakurai 2006, 164), some arguing that the men had had a falling out, or that Sora had to raise money, to arrange for disciples in Ōgaki to go meet him in Tsuruga for the last leg of the trip, or to prepare for the upcoming trip the men would take to the Grand Shrines at Ise (Horikiri 2003, 195). Takatō 1966, 428, argues that he did not want to be a burden to the master or in any way alter his travel plans. In any case, on the 3rd day of the Ninth Month, he rejoined Bashō in Ōgaki. Bashō's Kanazawa disciple Hokushi accompanied Bashō for some time, and another disciple, Rotsū, met him in Tsuruga.

On ahead I go—   *yukiyukite*
and if I collapse, it will be   *taurefusu tomo*
in fields of bush clover.[337]   *hagi no hara*

Sad was the one leaving, unhappy the one who stayed on, like lapwings parting from their mates and wandering alone through the clouds.[338] I wrote something too:

From today   *kyō yori ya*
I will erase the vow I wrote.   *kakitsuke kesan*
Dew on my rain hat.[339]   *kasa no tsuyu*

I stayed at Zenshōji, a temple on the outskirts of the castle town at Daishōji. Still in Kaga Province.[340] The night before, Sora had stayed at the same temple and left me this:

All night long   *yomosugara*
I hear autumn wind blowing   *akikaze kiku ya*
on the mountain behind.   *ura no yama*

One night of separation was the same as a thousand.[341] I too heard the autumn wind as I lay down in the guest dormitory. As dawn began to light the sky, I heard

---

337. The first line of this poem originally read, *izuku ni ka*, which would make the poem mean, "No matter where, / if I collapse it will be / in fields of bush clover," alluding to a poem by Saigyō (*Sankashū* 916): "From among his many poems on transience: 'Where will it be / that I get so sleepy / that I collapse? / A sad thought to ponder / amidst dew on the roadside'" (*izuku ni ka / neburineburite / taurefusan to / omou kanashiki / michishiba no tsuyu*). Kanamori 2013, 256–57, argues that Sora wrote the poem after leaving for Nagashima and that Bashō did not see it until the summer of 1691, at Rakushisha. Bashō changed the first line from *izuku ni ka* to *yukiyukite* when editing it for *Sarumino* 猿蓑 (no. 1830).

338. *Mengqiuji* 蒙求集, a Tang dynasty work by Li Han, quotes a poem on parting containing the lines "Two lapwings fly off to the north; one returns south alone" (隻鳧俱北飛 / 一鳧独南翔). Fukasawa and Kusumoto 2009, 284.

339. *Bashō kushū* no. 518. Dew is conventionally linked to the "bush clover" of Sora's *hokku*, while also serving as a metaphor of dew as tears, with which the poet will erase the vow the two men wrote to travel together. See pp. 59–60 in *Knapsack Notes*. Kanamori 2013, 257, argues that Bashō wrote this verse much later.

340. The name Daishōji 大聖寺 came from a temple, but in Bashō's time it indicated the castle town that had grown up around it. Eguchi 1998, 171, notes that Zenshōji was the family temple of Kumenosuke, the innkeeper who had hosted him in Yamanaka, which probably explains why Sora and Bashō both stayed there.

341. Fukasawa and Kusumoto 2009, 286, note a number of sources, Chinese and Japanese, that express this same idea.

sutra-chanting and the sound of a gong and went into the dining hall. Hoping to make it to Echizen that day, I was anxious to get away as I walked down the temple hill. But a few young monks, paper in hand, came as far as the foot of the steps to see me off. As it happened, the leaves were falling from a willow in the courtyard:

Wishing I could stay   *niwa hakite*
to sweep them from your temple courts—   *idebaya tera ni*
fallen willow leaves.[342]   *chiru yanagi*

This I wrote in a hurry, not even taking off my sandals.

We passed across the border into Echizen, going by boat on Yoshizaki Inlet, and visited the Shiogoshi Pines.

All through the night   *yomosugara*
storm winds transport waves   *arashi ni nami o*
onto the shore—   *hakobasete*
where moonlight drips from branches   *tsuki o taretaru*
on the Shiogoshi Pines.[343]   *shiogoshinomatsu*
          Saigyō

This one poem encompasses all the scenery of the place. To say more would be like "adding a useless extra finger to one's hand."[344]

The chief priest at Tenryūji in Maruoka[345] was an old acquaintance,[346] so I went to visit. Also, Hokushi of Kanazawa,[347] intending to see me off, had ended up continuing

---

342. *Bashō kushū* no. 558. It was customary for visitors to help with chores. The willow leaves in the courtyard link back to the autumn wind of the poem from the night before. The consensus is that this poem was written later, when Bashō was writing up his account, and that the whole incident may be at least partially fanciful. See Hori and Imoto 1972, 183; Sakurai 2006, 171.
343. Source unknown. Some scholars argue that it is a poem by Rennyō Shōnin. In Bashō's time, it was probably believed to be by Saigyō. See Fukasawa and Kusumoto 2009, 289–90.
344. Probably a reference to the "Webbed Toes" chapter of *Zhuangzi* (see Fukasawa and Kusumoto 2009, 290). See Mair 1994, 75.
345. Actually Matsuoka.
346. Taimu. He had been at Tenryūji in Shinagawa and knew Bashō from that time.
347. Resident of Kaga. Sword sharpener. He had been with Bashō since the 24th of the Seventh Month, for more than three weeks (Sakurai 2006, 156; Yamane 2017, 220), taking charge of passport documents, etc. (Yamane 2017, 183–84). Chikui, who also came along from Kanazawa,

on. He couldn't pass any scenery by without working on a poem, coming up with some moving compositions along the way. But the time had come to part:

To rend in two   *mono kakite*
a fan scribbled with poems—   *ōgi hikisaku*
a true regret.[348]   *nagori kana*

I went fifty *chō* into the mountains to do obeisance at Eiheiji, temple of Zen Master Dōgen.[349] It is said that he had praiseworthy reasons for going into the mountains, avoiding the broad expanse of the imperial city,[350] to establish his legacy.

Fukui was just three *li* away, but I had my evening meal before departing and ended up making my way in the dusky light.[351] An old recluse named Tōsai lived there.[352] Some years back he had come up to Edo and called on me; more than ten years before, it must have been. "How much has he aged?" I wondered. "Or might he be dead?" I asked around and was told he was still among the living, in such and such a place. His home was set back from the shopping streets, a non-descript little house engulfed by evening glory and snake-gourd vines, its door concealed behind cockscomb and goose-foot.[353] "This must be it," I thought. When I knocked on the door, a shabby-looking

---

had probably returned to Kanazawa on the 25th day of the Seventh Month. See Yamane 2017, 129.

348. *Bashō kushū* no. 533. A poem on parting in which a summer fan is disposed of as autumn begins. Here the poet uses the fan as scratch paper and then rips it in two. Rending it in two refers to Bashō and Hokushi taking different roads.

349. Eiheiji was established in 1244 by Dōgen, founder of the Sōtō sect of Zen. He purposely chose a remote site in order to avoid the political entanglements of Kamakura or Kyoto.

350. A reference to a poem in the *Book of Songs* that describes the ruler's domain as a thousand *li* square. See Imoto 1972, 382, n. 7.

351. Scholars often assume that Bashō was alone traveling from Matsuoka to Fukui, the only time he traveled alone on his journey to the hinterlands. However, Sakurai and others argue that surely Hokushi would have made arrangements with his hosts at Tenryūji to send a guide along to Fukui (Sakurai 2006, 175; Kanamori 2013, 279), where Tōsai would certainly have known that Bashō was coming.

352. Recent scholarship argues that much of this episode is basically fiction, written to work a little "old romance" into his narrative, although that Bashō visited a man he calls Tōsai seems certain. Again, he plays with the characters of the name, rendering it as 等裁 rather than 洞哉. See n. 101 above. See Fukasawa and Kusumoto 2009, 296; Kanamori 2013, 280–81.

353. *Yūgao*, *hechima*, *keitō*, and *hahakigi* are all spreading plants associated with run-down, abandoned places.

woman came out and said, "And where might you be from, reverend sir?"[354] The master is off at the house of a certain man who lives nearby. If you need to see him, please go there." I realized that she must be his woman. "How charming," I thought, "just like something from an old romance."[355] I set off right away to call on him and stayed in his house for two days. When I set out again, hoping to see the full moon at the port of Tsuruga,[356] Tōsai said he wanted to go along and see me off, so he tucked up his skirts and cantered off in high spirits, saying, "I shall be your guide."[357] Before long, Shirane Peak disappeared, and Hina Peak loomed ahead. As we crossed Asamuzu Bridge, the ears were out on the reeds. After Uguisu Barrier, we climbed over Yuno'o Pass and came to Hiuchi Castle. At Kaeruyama, "Mount Return," we heard the first calls of wild geese,[358] and at dusk on the 14th sought lodging at the Bay of Tsuruga.[359]

That night the moon shone unobscured. "Will tomorrow night be so clear?" I asked. As my host offered me saké, he said, "Along the Koshi Road,[360] one can't know whether the night will be clear or cloudy."[361] That night I paid my respects at Kei Myōjin, the funeral shrine of Emperor Chūai.[362] There was a rustic look to the precincts.

---

354. The word used by the woman is *dōshin* 道心, a term used rather broadly for monks.

355. Most likely Bashō has in mind a passage in the *The Tale of Genji* where Genji happens upon an unknown young woman in a rustic little house while on his way to visit another of his women. See *Genji monogatari*, vol. 1, 209–11; Cf. Tyler 2001, 55–56.

356. The moon is the autumn image and here follows on a whole catalog of autumn images: autumn wind, bush clover, miscanthus, dew, falling leaves. The men arrived in Tsuruga on the 14th. A poem journal passed down in the lineage of Bashō's student Keikō records fourteen moon poems (one went missing) composed by Bashō on the trip, which probably lasted until the 18th (Sakurai 2006, 187).

357. This continues a pattern in which hosts not only provide lodging and food but also serve as guides to the local sights.

358. "First calls of wild geese" refers to geese returning from the north to winter in central Japan. The name Mount Kaeru is mentioned only because it resonates with the returning geese, the verb *kaeru* meaning "to return."

359. Here Bashō gives a catalog of *utamakura* and historical places without elaborating, perhaps signaling that he is approaching the end of his narrative—the rapid presto (*kyū*) section, in the terminology of linked verse.

360. Generally, the road between Fukui and Niigata, through the provinces of Echizen 越前, Etchū 越中, and Echigo 越後, all of which contain the character *koshi* 越; a synonym for the Hokuroku Road. Tsuruga was in Echizen.

361. The recluse here takes a well-known phrase (*meiya no insei hakarigatashi* 明夜の陰晴は かりがたし) recorded in *Nihon saijiki* 日本歳時記 (1688), deriving from a Chinese poem by Sun Mingfu. Imoto 1972, 384.

362. Kei no Myōjin; more correctly, Kei Jingū. One of the chief shrines of the entire region, whose origins go back to prehistoric times.

Moonlight spilled down between the pines, making the white sand in the forecourt look as if strewn with frost. The chief priest of the shrine told us its story: "Anciently, Yugyō the Second,[363] when offering up a petition, cut reeds with his own hands, and hauled sand, and drained the marshy areas—making it easier for pilgrims coming to worship. The ancient rite continues today: the generations of Yugyō haul sand to the forecourt,[364] and call what they do, 'Carrying Yugyō's Sand.'"[365]

> Pure moonlight—   *tsuki kiyoshi*
> shining down on the sand   *yugyō no moteru*
> hauled by Yugyō.[366]   *suna no ue*

On the 15th it was just as my host had said—it rained.

> Full moon time—   *meigetsu ya*
> in the changeable weather   *hokukokubiyori*
> of the north country.[367]   *sadame naki*

The skies cleared on the 16th, so we went out to gather little *masuho* shells,[368] gliding along by boat off Ironohama—seven *li* on the ocean.[369] A man named Ten'ya so-and-so[370] kindly provided us with food in compartment boxes and wine flasks of bamboo

---

363. Also known as Taa Shōnin. Heir of Ippen Shōnin, founder of the Time (*jishū* 時宗) sect of Buddhism.

364. There is disagreement about whether at the time of Bashō's visit it was Yugyō the 42nd, 43rd, or 44th that held the position of chief priest.

365. While on pilgrimage, Taa visited Kei Shrine and assisted in repairing the pathway to the structure (Fukasawa and Kusumoto 2009, 298–99).

366. *Bashō kushū* no. 501. This is one of the fifteen poems mentioned in n. 356.

367. *Bashō kushū* no. 462. The 15th was the night of the full moon. This too is one of the fifteen poems mentioned in n. 356.

368. See a poem by Saigyō (*Sankashū* 1282): "Here people gather / *masuho* shells that give a red tinge / to the surf— / which must be why they call it / the Beach of Colors" (*shio somuru / masuho no kogai / hirou tote / iro no hama to ha / iu ni ya aran*). *Masuho* shells were small shells of a pinkish hue.

369. Ironohama. Scholars argue about whether the place was a legitimate *utamakura* or not. See Fukasawa and Kusumoto 2009, 304–5. Scholars agree that in fact the distance was only a little over two *li*. Ogata (Fukasawa and Kusumoto 2009, 305) suggests that Bashō may have in mind a place in called "Seven-*Li* Rapids" (七里瀬) in Zhejiang Province in China, where Yan Guang went to leave the world behind.

370. Sora's account notes that he left a letter with Ten'ya to give to Bashō, indicating the network the travelers depended upon. Ten'ya was a wealthy merchant and hosted his guests lavishly.

and sent a bunch of servants with us in the boat, and with a following wind we made the trip in no time at all.[371] On the beach were just a few small fishermen's houses and a forlorn-looking temple of the Hokke sect.[372] Here we drank our tea, warmed our saké, and bore up against the loneliness of falling dusk.

In forlorn feeling
it surpasses even Suma:
this autumn shore.[373]

sabishisa ya
suma ni kachitaru
hama no aki

Between breaking waves:
small shells mixed with scraps
of bush clover blossom.[374]

nami no ma ya
kogai ni majiru
hagi no chiri

I had Tōsai take up the brush to write a note about our day and left it with the temple.[375]

Rotsū came all the way to the harbor to meet me and accompanied me to Mino.[376] On horseback we made good time, and when we arrived at the Ōgaki Domain, Sora had come from Ise to join me again, and Etsujin came, too, hurrying in on horse himself—all of us gathering at the house of Jokō. Zensenshi, Keikō and his son,[377] and other friends came calling day and night, showing me happiness and kind concern,

---

371. Ogata (referenced in Fukasawa and Kusumoto 2009, 304) notes a passage in the Suma chapter of *The Tale of Genji* where a tailwind helps the boat taking Genji into exile get to his destination in no time at all (*Genji monogatari*, vol. 2, 178; Cf. Tyler 2001, 238–39). Ogata argues that it is the presence of this scene in Bashō's mind that explains the reference to Suma in the following poem, and its dark tone.

372. Honryūji.

373. *Bashō kushū* no. 462. Bashō had of course visited Suma a few years before, as noted in *Knapsack Notes*. See pp. 68–69.

374. *Bashō kushū* no. 565.

375. A text survives in Honryūji, signed by "Tōsai of Fukui." Bashō's *hokku* there is different: "Bush clover, scatter! / Small flowers, small shells / small saké cups" (*kohagi chire / masuho no kogai / kosakazuki*). See Kon 2005a, 202.

376. The men probably left somewhere between the 18th and the 20th and arrived in Ōgaki the next day, on horseback. See Sakurai 2006, 187–89; Kanamori 2013, 314–16.

377. Keikō had three sons, all disciples of Bashō. Their *haikai* names were Shikin, Sensen, and Bunchō.

as if I were one come back from the dead.[378] Although still feeling weary from my journey, when the 6th day of the Long Month[379] came I set out once more, getting on a boat once again,[380] determined to witness the transfer of shrine sites at Ise:

> Off to Futami: *hamaguri no*
> a clam parting from its shell   *futami ni wakare*
> as autumn moves on.[381]   *yuku aki zo*

---

378. A nod toward his statement at the beginning of *The Narrow Road through the Hinterlands* about hoping he would complete his journey alive.

379. Nagatsuki, the ninth lunar month.

380. Another connection back to the beginning of his text. His journey began with a boat and now ends with one. As Ueno 1989, 164–65, argues, it is also significant that Bashō here presents himself as if alone, not mentioning that the boat was provided by Bokuin, who accompanied him part of the way, along with Sora, Jokō, and Rotsū.

381. *Bashō kushū* no. 426. Futamigaura is the port where he will disembark to trek on to Ise, with Sora and Rotsū as companions. The shrines at Ise are dismantled and rebuilt every twenty-one years. The rite would take place in the Ninth Month of 1689. Bashō was there from the 9th for ten days or so and then departed for Iga Ueno.

THE SAGA DIARY

INTRODUCTION

Matsuo Bashō's 1689 trek through the northern provinces ended in autumn at Ōgaki. Rather than returning to Edo, however, he traveled to Ise and then stayed in the Kyoto area for more than two years, visiting his hometown of Iga Ueno on at least three occasions, and also going to Nara, to several places in Ōmi Province, and into Kyoto proper. Several important works came out of this experience, including the most prominent anthology of his now flourishing school (*Sarumino*), his first and most well known example of *haikai* prose, and what would turn out to be the last of his travel accounts, *The Saga Diary*.

But is *The Saga Diary* a travel journal at all? The text covers little more than two weeks in the author's life, from the 18th day of the Fourth Month to the 4th day of the Fifth Month of 1691, when he was staying with a disciple in the Kyoto area. Inasmuch as he was away from his home in Edo and did some sightseeing during the days in question, it seems justifiable to place the work in the travel journal category, but only just. One can of course argue that in many ways the piece is essayistic, a memoir not just of travel but of poetic practice. Nonetheless, since the Pacific War, Japanese collections of Bashō's travel writings have tended to include it, and I do so here.

It was not in Kyoto proper but in a suburb called Saga to the west of the city that Bashō stayed during his visit, close to the Ōi River and Arashiyama and in the shadow of majestic Mounts Atago and Takao that stand at the northwest edge of the Kyoto basin. Today the area is celebrated for its bamboo groves and temples such as Tenryūji and Hōrinji, and for shrines such as Nonomiya, the setting for a scene in *The Tale of Genji*.[1] Already in Kyorai's time there were hundreds of houses in the area, and already its historic sites and bamboo groves attracted sightseers and pilgrims, although not so many as today.

---

1. See the Sakaki chapter (The Green Branch) of *The Tale of Genji* (*Genji monogatari*, vol. 1, 76–80; Cf. Tyler 2001, 193–96). A Noh play—*Nonomiya*, "The Wildwood Shrine"—recounts the story (see Tyler 1992, 205–214).

In Saga, Bashō stayed in a villa[2] owned by one of his chief disciples, Kyorai, whose own main residence seems to have been in a house just east of the imperial palace in the city, six or so miles to the east.[3] The younger brother of a prominent Kyoto physician, Kyorai was of samurai birth and was still involved in assisting his brother in his medical practice and serving as an expert consultant on calendrical matters to royalty and court nobles, which made him wealthy enough to act as one of Bashō's benefactors. Kyorai had bought the Saga villa, previously owned by a rich merchant, as a place to get away from the noise of the city when his schedule allowed and was no doubt happy to be able to offer lodging in pleasant surroundings to his master. Kyorai called his place in Saga "The Cottage of Fallen Persimmons" (Rakushisha), a witty name that he explains in a short prose piece dating from 1689.

In Saga there is an old house, and around it are forty persimmon trees. Four and then five years went by, and the man I had looking after the place[4] never brought me any fruit, nor had I heard that he was selling it. So I was always berating him, saying, "If the fruit falls in a storm, I will be shamed before Wang Xiang, and if kites and crows take it I will be deprived of the blessings of Heaven."

This year, around the end of the Eighth Month, when I was at my Saga house, a merchant from the city happened by and offered to buy my whole crop, before the fruit was even picked, and for a thousand coins he went off in high spirits.

That night I stayed over, and I heard thumping on my roof and the sound of wind thrashing the trees in the garden, which kept the fruit falling all night long. The next morning the merchant came and looked at the trees. "I'm white-haired now, and from my youth I have been dealing in persimmons, but I've never seen them all fall like this. Would you consider returning me the money I gave you?"

I felt so sorry for him that I gave the money back.

---

2. In a letter, Bashō calls it a *shimoyashiki*, or second home (see Tanaka 2005, 386), and in a *haibun* he calls it a *bessho* (別墅), country house (*Rakushisha no ki* 落柿舎記, 520); certainly it was not an *iori* 庵, or hut, in a literal sense. The house was over 3,500 square feet (100 *tsubo*) and the lot about 1.6 acres (2,000 *tsubo*), with forty persimmon trees (see Satō Nobi 2014, 96).

3. We know that he had another home across the Kamo River in the area of the imperial cloister Shōgoin.

4. A man named Yohei, who also seems to have served as caretaker and cook.

It was after he had left, when I was writing a letter to a friend that for the first time I signed myself, "Kyorai of the House of Fallen Persimmons."

You, Lord of Persimmons—	*kakinushi ya*
your limbs are too close	*kozue wa chikaki*
to Storm Mountain![5]	*arashiyama*

Wang Xiang was a man counted among the Twenty-Four Filial Exemplars in Chinese folklore who was honored for a number of filial acts, one of which was protecting a pear tree in a storm when asked to do so by his mother. The reference shows Kyorai's knowledge of the Chinese classics while also confirming his commitment to the literati life, following the example of his master.

Bashō already knew the cottage, having spent time with Kyorai there in the Twelfth Month of 1689.[6] It was a substantial but rustic place, according to Bashō's own testimony.[7] But his diary tells us that it was the out-of-the-way location and run-down state of the place that appealed to the *haikai* master. Indeed, Bashō seems to have thought about staying in the city with another disciple,[8] but chose Rakushisha for its tranquil atmosphere and the possibility of a few solitary days. ("There is nothing more interesting than living alone," he notes, a few days into his stay.)[9] Indeed, one reason he went was doubtless for his health, which had been taxed on his recent journey through the hinterlands. He wanted a place to hole up for a while during the rainy season, and Kyorai's villa seemed a ready candidate.[10]

---

5. *Rakushisha no ki*, 500–501. Today's Rakushisha was erected much later. The original villa consisted of more than one building and was on a larger lot that was almost certainly on a different spot, closer to Nonomiya, or in a bamboo grove near the Rinsenji in Kawabata Village, Lower Saga (see Horikiri 1991, 22; Ōuchi and Wakaki 1986, 61–62).

6. Kyorai left a short prose account of Bashō's visit in his *Hachitaki no ji* 鉢扣の辞. Rakushisha is not mentioned in the piece, but modern scholars conclude that the events described took place there. See Kuriyama et al. 1972, 498–99; Abe Kimio and Asō 1964, 474, n. 18. Kon 2005a, 217, makes the location either Rakushisha or Kyorai's house in the city, but the content of the piece, which describes the two men waiting until nearly dawn for pilgrims to pass by beating gourds as participants in a Buddhist celebration, would seem to indicate that they were somewhere on the outskirts of the city rather than at its heart. In either case, it seems certain that Bashō had at least visited the place before.

7. See p. 159.

8. See a letter, probably to Kyorai, in Tanaka 2005, 375.

9. From early on Bashō imagined Rakushisha as a retreat of sorts. In a letter sent to Kyorai in the spring of 1686, when Bashō's planned summer trip to Kyoto did not materialize, he was so anxious to have some quiet time that he asked Kyorai not to let people in the area know that he would be staying there. See Tanaka 2005, 88.

10. Bashō mentions rainfall on six of the days he spent at Rakushisha, and it is likely that it rained other days as well.

That he enjoyed the place is clear from a *haibun* piece dating to that same summer titled simply, "A Record of Rakushisha" (*Rakushisha no ki*, 1691):

> The country villa of a certain Kyorai of Kyoto stands in a grove of bamboos in Lower Saga, at the foot of Arashiyama and close by the waters of the Ōi River. The area is tranquil and isolated, good for clearing one's mind. Kyorai is a lazy sort, and the grasses grow tall outside his windows, while scores of persimmon trees nearly take over the yard. The water leaks through during summer rains, mold grows on the bamboo mats and sliding doors, and it's not a great place to sleep the night. I felt Kyorai's hospitality more when I was in the shade beneath the trees.[11]

The truth is, however, Bashō had few moments of solitude in Saga, as the diary reveals. While disciples were often unable to come during the day, someone was usually there at night. And after leaving Kyorai's cottage, Bashō would stay on in Kyoto until the summer, hosted by several disciples, mostly Bonchō but also perhaps Kyorai, whose house near Shōgoin seems to have acted a base for sightseeing at nearby places—Ichijōji, Shisendō, and Kamo Shrine.[12] Moreover, while in the city he also took in some plays and enjoyed the Kyoto nightlife, belying his reclusive persona. As noted before, although he wore monkish robes, as did many artists, he was not an ordained priest and did not abide by religious vows.

It was not until the end of the Tenth Month of 1691 that Bashō headed back up the Tōkai Road toward Edo, where he moved into a rental house in Nihonbashi, bringing a long season of travel to an end. When disciples began showing up at his door, asking how he had fared, he responded with this:

> Unsure of my place in the world, I spent many nights on the road these past six or seven years. But bearing up against my many ailments, I made my way back to the Musashi Moors, never forgetting the sympathy of my old friends and students over all that time. This is a poem I wrote when day after day people came to my door, asking after me:

> Somehow, I survived: *to mo kaku mo*
> a snow-topped, withered clump   *narade ya yuki no*
> of miscanthus.[13]   *kareobana*

---

11. See Bashō's *Rakushisha no ki* 落柿舎記, 520.
12. Kon 2005a, 297.
13. *Yuki no kareobana* 雪の枯尾花 (1691), 529.

Writing "six or seven years" can only mean that he was thinking back to his first journey, in 1684, perhaps suggesting that he felt he had reached an end to his trekking. In the Fifth Month of 1692, he moved into a new Bashōan, built near the site of the old one by disciples. And for his many supporters in Edo, it must have seemed that he was back to stay. But a sentence in a *haibun* piece he wrote at the time he moved into his new home may have given them pause. For after praising the rustic look of his dwelling he wrote, "The site faces Mount Fuji, and the gate is placed sideways so as not to obstruct the view."[14]

Fuji was of course on the road west, and in the summer of 1694, Bashō got a closer view of it again, then going on to visit people and practice his profession in Nagoya, Iga Ueno, Ōtsu, Zeze, Kyoto, Nara, and finally in Osaka. Various comments make it clear that for some years he had wanted to visit Shikoku and Kyushu, but his health would not allow it.[15] As noted before, he fell ill and died in Osaka, on the 12th day of the Tenth Month of that same year. Thus *The Saga Diary* became the last of his travel writings.

***

One can argue that *The Saga Diary* is both a work of literature—that is, a product of aesthetic fashioning—and a diary of poetic practice with a few intimate details thrown in for good measure. Such a distinction, however, may not be useful in examining Bashō's writing, for it seems clear from an examination of his entire oeuvre that he would have thought of all he wrote in *The Saga Diary* as "literary" in the sense that it documented his life as a poet and was a product of his design.[16] He includes allusions to quotidian experiences, of course—descriptions of his room, chats with disciples, sightseeing, and so on—but even those details are designed to emphasize the author's identity as a *haikai* poet and the varieties and vagaries of poetic discourse. Thus, while he uses a diurnal or journalistic format, what Bashō writes about connects him back very explicitly to Chinese and Japanese reclusive figures such as the Tang dynasty poet Bai Juyi, the medieval Japanese poet-recluse Kamo no Chōmei, and a more recent literatus, Kinoshita Chōshōshi. Moreover, he includes lots of poems in various genres, by himself and colleagues, written under various circumstances, and

---

14. *Bashō o utsusu kotoba* 芭蕉を移す詞 (1692), 534.
15. Tanaka 2005, 225, 236, 247, 409.
16. Nakamura 1971, 170.

refers to a host of literary works in both Chinese and Japanese, as well as a few descriptive pieces on the state of the Rakushisha, a short meditation on loneliness, and a brief but moving personal and poetic essay about dreams, inspired by the appearance in his own dream on the night of the 28th of his disciple Tokoku, who had died just a year before.

Nakamura Shunjō posits that Bashō wrote his diary up as a keepsake for his host, Kyorai—an entirely reasonable proposition.[17] But *The Saga Diary* is also an artifact of practice that reveals much about the many dimensions of Bashō's profession. Indeed, it perhaps gives us our most concrete picture of what life was like for him during his longish stops at places (Ōgaki, Ise, Kurobane, Kanazawa, and so on—the list is a long one) on other journeys. As always, he is constantly involved in correspondence, about some private matters but also about poetic matters. He sends poems to disciples and they send poems to him. Such communication was an integral part of his poetic practice. He also alludes to other literary chores. One rainy day, for instance, when he is alone at Rakushisha, he tells us that he is writing up a draft of an essay about his life at another hut, the Genjūan, located just west of Ishiyamadera on the shores of Lake Biwa, where he had stayed the previous summer. Titled *Genjūan no ki*, or "Record of a Phantom Cottage," this would become one of Bashō's most highly praised works, initiating a new kind of poetic prose referred to by an already-existing term, *haibun*.[18] Somewhat surprisingly, perhaps, we know that he asked not only disciples but also Kyorai's brother, Gentan, a physician well-schooled in Chinese classics, to read and make comments on his piece. Rather than a disciple, Gentan might better be designated as patron, benefactor, and prime member of Bashō's Kyoto poetic network. Evidently some of his comments inspired Bashō to revise his text.

Other documents show that another of his projects at the time was a new anthology of *haikai* that he, Kyorai, and Bonchō were working on, with Bashō acting as supervisor.[19] Called "The Monkey's Straw Raincoat," or *Sarumino*, that collection would become even more prominent than *Genjūan no ki*. At the time, the publishing of such anthologies, including both *hokku* and *haikai renga*, or linked-verse sequences, was

---

17. Nakamura 1971, 170.

18. It is also possible that he was working not on *Genjūan no ki* but on a final draft of *Knapsack Notes*—or on both.

19. Itō Yoshitaka 2011, 50. Ōuchi and Wakaki 1986, 98, note that Bashō, Kyorai, and Bonchō spent four full days together at Rakushisha and probably were discussing the anthology during that time. *Genjūan no ki* was included in *Sarumino*.

the way masters publicized the works of their schools.[20] There seems little doubt that selections for the anthology figured prominently in conversations between the master and his two collaborators when they attended upon him at Rakushisha, or that other disciples coming to visit—and there were many—were interested parties. *Sarumino* was a public statement and much more significant in *haikai* discourse than *The Saga Diary*, which circulated in manuscript only among disciples and was not published in a woodblock edition for more than fifty years. Interestingly, Bashō describes none of these things in his diary, but knowing that he was engaged in this way reinforces the image of him as not on vacation at all but constantly involved in literary affairs.

In the end, forty of Bashō's *hokku* were included in *Sarumino*, and twenty-five of Kyorai's. But it was another poet, Bonchō, also known as Kashō (also read Kasei), who was most richly represented, with forty-one poems.[21] Although not so prominent as Gentan, Bonchō was another physician working in Kyoto. Both he and his wife, known by her *haikai* nom de plume Ukō, had become disciples of Bashō only recently, but they obviously thought of themselves, along with Kyorai,[22] as hosts of the master in Kyoto, providing food and staying overnight at times.[23]

Of course, *The Saga Diary* does offer information about things he did during his stay that we might not identify as "literary" at all. For example, while recording part of a linked-verse sequence composed by himself and four disciples, he also tells us how all five people sleeping in the cottage one night could not sleep and spent the night eating sweets, drinking saké, and chatting. And he tells us he was a tourist, duly noting sight-seeing ventures to temples and places of historical interest, as well as a boat trip on the Ōi River toward the end of his stay, accompanied by his disciple Sora, who had been his companion for *The Narrow Road through the Hinterlands*. However, it goes without saying that such experiences were material for refashioning, and we can be sure that as a *haikai* master Bashō stayed in character upon his stage. A literati pose was always

20. The final draft of *Sarumino* was finished in the Fifth Month and was published in wood-block format by Izutsuya in Kyoto in the Seventh Month of 1691, while Bashō was still in the Kyoto area. Ten days after its publication, Bashō sent a letter to Kyorai asking how well it was selling (Tanaka 2005, 391). Recent scholarship emphasizes Bashō's direct involvement in the compilation process. See Itō 2011, 50.
21. Bonchō, along with Kyorai and Bashō, was also a participant in the four linked-verse sequences published in the anthology.
22. Bonchō was likely introduced to Bashō by Kyorai, who became acquainted with him through his physician brother; another possibility is another Bashō disciple who was a physician to noble houses, Nakamura Fumikuni (precise dates unknown).
23. Ōuchi and Wakaki 1986, 94, say that both Kyorai and Bonchō guided Bashō from the city out to Rakushisha.

expected, and that is what we see in *The Saga Diary*. It is not without significance that of the many people, especially from his home in Iga, who must have corresponded with or perhaps even visited him at Rakushisha, the only ones he mentions explicitly are fellow poets.

Indeed, his careful inclusion of poets, along with their poems in most cases, is a key to understanding an important aspect of Bashō's life as a *haikai* master and the head of a poetic network. For however much he may have presented himself as a solitary figure, *The Saga Diary* shows that escaping professional obligations in a place like Kyoto was not possible for a man in his position. A half-dozen disciples visited during his stay, and a few of them were acting as couriers for others who could not make the trip. On his travels through the hinterlands, he no doubt had experienced real solitude—when he was not being feted by rural poets, that is; not so in Kyoto.

As noted above, documents show that when he left Kyorai's villa, Bashō moved into Kyoto for the summer, staying at Bonchō's house in Ogawa Sawaragichō and at Kyorai's house near Shōgoin, both places where solitude would be in even shorter supply.[24] Unfortunately, he left no descriptions of these days. Nor did he write about his stay at a newly restored Rakushisha in the summer of 1694, for a full three weeks.[25] All that we have about his life in Kyorai's retreat, therefore, is *The Saga Diary*.

This leads to a final point related to Bashō's evolving concept of *karumi*, or "lightness," a dedication to the primacy of the ordinary that was emerging in his discourse around the time of his stay in Kyoto.[26] For surely the light rhetorical touch the poet so often presents in *The Saga Diary* is an expression of that ideal—as articulated in his spare and matter-of-fact style, his resort to primarily mainstream allusions, and his presentation of himself as a carefree wanderer.

---

24. It may be that he also rented a house.
25. He was there from the 22nd day of the intercalary Fifth Month to the 15th day of the Sixth Month. In the autumn of 1693, Kyorai did a thorough remodeling, tearing down the old building and replacing it with one somewhat smaller (Ōuchi and Wakaki 1986, 130–31), but still much larger than Bashō's huts in Edo, Zeze, and Ōtsu. Subsequent statements in various documents do not make the later fate of Rakushisha clear. Some hint that he sold it not long after Bashō's death, others that it was still his for some years (see Shibata 1986, 169–71).
26. On this topic, see Ueda 1967, 165–70.

THE SAGA DIARY

The year 1691, Fourth Month, 18th day: I arrive at Kyorai's Rakushisha after enjoying a stroll through Saga. Bonchō comes along but at dusk returns to Kyoto. As I am to stay a while, Kyorai has prepared a pallet in a small corner room, mending the sliding doors and having the weeds outside dug up. He has provided a low desk, an inkstone, and a box for paper and writing things, along with books—the writings of Bai Juyi, *One Hundred Poems by One Hundred Poets of Japan*, *The Tale of Yotsugi*, *The Tale of Genji*, *The Tosa Diary*, and *The Pine Needle Anthology*.[27] Also a stack of five lacquer-ware boxes decorated with Chinese-style scenes, piled with sundry sweets and a bottle of the finest rice wine and cups. What with bed things and dainties brought in from Kyoto, I lack for nothing. All thoughts of poverty leave my mind and I settle down to enjoy the tranquility.[28]

4.19: Off after noon to visit Rinsenji.[29] In front of it flows the Ōi River, with Arashiyama rising on the right, its peaks extending down to Matsuno'o Village. Lots of pilgrims going to and from Kokuzō.[30] The site of the house of Lady Kogō is said to be in the bamboo groves of Matsuno'o, but there are three such sites in Upper and Lower Saga.[31] One wonders which is correct. Nearby is the site of Komadome Bridge, the bridge

---

27. A list tailor-made to suit Bashō, who claimed the entire canon of classical literature as his own: the works of the venerable Chinese poet Bai Juyi; *Honchō ichinin isshū* 本朝一人一首 (early Edo period), a collection of Chinese poetry written over the centuries by Japanese courtiers, monks, and scholars; *Yotsugi monogatari* 世継物語, a narrative history of the Japanese court in Heian times (probably referring to either *Ōkagami* 大鏡, c. 1123; or *Eiga monogatari* 栄花物語, c. 1037–92); *Genji monogatari* (early tenth century), the greatest tale of classical times; *Tosa nikki* the most well known of all classical travel records; and *Shōyōshū* 松葉集 (precise dates unknown), a collection of *waka* poems about famous places to stir the imagination of a traveler. One cannot rule out the possibility that Bashō chose titles from a larger list to emphasize.
28. This whole passage echoes Kamo no Chōmei's description of his hut in *Hōjōki*. See *Hōjōki*, 20–21; McCullough 1990b, 388–89.
29. Okada 1972, 116, argues that the way Kyorai begins showing Bashō the sights at Rinsenji suggests that the Rakushisha was close to that temple.
30. The popular name for Hōrinji.
31. The area of Daikakuji and Seiryōji was referred to as Upper Saga, while the area around Hōrinji and Tenryūji was called Lower Saga. Lady Kogō was an imperial concubine forced into retirement in Saga for a time.

where Nakakuni is said to have stopped his horse,[32] so we decide to take a little time and see it. Her grave marker is next to Sangen Teahouse, in a thicket, where a cherry tree is planted to mark the spot. Serving the emperor, she spent her time amidst the finest silks and brocades, yet at the end here she is, so much dust in the bushes. The willows of Zhaojun Village and the flowers of the hall on Mount Wu come to mind.[33]

A string of trials—	*ukifushi ya*
and now just bamboo shoots	*take no ko to naru*
to mark her end.[34]	*hito no hate*
Storm Mountain.	*arashiyama*
Through the thickest thickets	*yabu no shigeri ya*
winds make their way.[35]	*kaze no suji*

Back to Rakushisha as the sun goes down. Bonchō in from Kyoto, Kyorai back to Kyoto. Early to bed.

4.20: Ukō comes to see the North Saga Festival.[36]

Kyorai in from Kyoto. We chat about a *hokku* he composed on the way.

---

32. *Tales of the Heike* (*Heike monogatari*, 433–42; see also McCullough 1988, 201–6) tells how Minamoto no Nakakuni was dispatched from Emperor Takakura to visit Kogō. The bridge, literally the Bridge Where He Stopped His Horse, may refer to a small bridge associated with Togetsu Bridge. Lady Kogō returned to the palace for a time but was driven away again, becoming a nun.

33. Stories of these two pathetic beauties of ancient China, both well known in Edo Japan, appear in various sources, from folktale collections to Noh plays. The first is about the famed beauty Wang Zhaojun, who after suffering neglect at the Chinese imperial court was sent as a wife to the northern border state of Xiongnu, to suffer even more. The second is about a Chinese king napping at noon near Mount Wu who receives a visit from a heavenly maiden in a dream. The backstories both involve beautiful women who are powerless and suffering. Bashō probably has in mind a couplet by Bai Juyi in *Wakan rōeishū* (no. 104): "The flowers at shrine to Princess Wu are red—like her lipstick; the willows at Zhaojun's village are deeper green than her eye shadow" (巫女廟花紅似紅 / 昭君村柳翠於眉). See Imoto 1972, 390, nn. 4, 5.

34. *Bashō kushū* no. 349.

35. *Bashō kushū* no. 353.

36. A yearly festival, held on the day of the boar midway through the Fourth Month. Ukō doubtless wants to see the grand parade honoring the portable shrines (*mikoshi*) of Atago Gongen Shrine and Nonomiya as they travel from their temporary resting place (*otabisho*) in front of Seiryōji off to Daikakuji.

Grappling children	*tsukamiau*
of different heights—	*kodomo no take ya*
in a barley field.[37]	*mugibatake*

About Rakushisha: it is just as it was when built by its first owner,[38] and is falling down here and there. My own heart is moved more by its current lamentable state than what it must have looked like when it was just built, long ago. The engraved beams, the decorated walls—all have been battered by winds and drenched by rain, and the unusual stones and crafted pines are half buried under weeds. In front of the bamboo veranda is a single yuzu tree[39] that gives off a nice scent:

Yuzu flowers	*yu no hana ya*
bring the past to mind.	*mukashi shinoban*
Tray room.[40]	*ryōri no ma*

A cuckoo.	*hototogisu*
And spilling through tall bamboos,	*ōtakeyabu o*
moonlit night.[41]	*moru tsukiyo*

Ukō's poem:

I shall come again,	*mata ya kon*
so redden up, strawberries!	*ichigo akarame*
Saga Mountains.	*saga no yama*

From the wife of Kyorai's brother come sweets and condiments.[42]

---

37. In *Sarumino*, this poem (no. 1761) is credited to a man from Zeze named Yūtō. Ōuchi and Wakaki 1986, 95, argue that Kyorai allowed Yūtō the credit because no other poem of his was included in the anthology.

38. A source that most take as spurious says the place was constructed by Mitsui Shūfū, a rich merchant, who was definitely an acquaintance of Bashō and some of his disciples. See Imoto and Yayoshi 1968, 142, n. 10.

39. A dwarf citrus. Fruit of the tree was used in cooking.

40. *Bashō kushū* no. 375. *Ryōri no ma* refers to a room off the kitchen where food was prepared and put on trays before serving (Ueno 1985a, 280).

41. *Bashō kushū* no. 313.

42. Gentan's wife was named Taga.

On this night, I have Bonchō and Ukō stay over, so the five of us, heads in the middle, sleep beneath one mosquito net, all crowded together.[43] Around midnight, we're all up and unable to get to sleep, so out come the treats sent earlier and saké cups, and we chat the night away till it's almost dawn. Summer the year before, when I was sleeping at Bonchō's house, four people, all from different provinces, slept together in a two-mat room under one mosquito net.[44] I had scribbled down something like, "each with their own thoughts, and dreams of four kinds,"[45] and when I mention it we break out laughing.[46] With the new day, Ukō and Bonchō return to Kyoto. Kyorai stays on.

4.21:

Feeling a little dull from lack of sleep. On top of that the sky is not as it was yesterday, with clouds forming from morning onward and the sound of raindrops falling off and on, so I stay the whole day on my bed. As evening falls, Kyorai returns to Kyoto. No one is with me after that, and since I can't get to sleep after lying down all day, I take up the scribblings I had dashed off at Genjūan and make a fair copy.[47]

---

43. Here I am following Toyama, who takes the word *kamishimo* (or *jōge*) to refer to the top and bottom of the single mosquito net. Another possibility is that the term refers to "high and low" in the sense of social ranks, Kyorai and Bonchō on top as samurai, then Bashō and Ukō—a tonsured woman (see Ueno 1985a, 280). Still another is that Bashō and Kyorai are at the top of the net and Bonchō and his wife at the bottom, with their heads close together in the middle (Sugiura and Miyamoto 1959, 126, n. 3). Imoto and Yayoshi 1968, 143, no. 16, wonder if the phrase *kamishimo* might mean *jōzu* and *heta*, the skilled and the unskilled. There is also debate about who the fifth person is. Toyama 1978, 186, n. 9; Ueno 1985a, 280; and Sugiura and Miyamoto 1959, 126, n. 3, argue that it is a servant accompanying Bonchō, which makes the most sense. Others say it refers to Yohei, although we know that he lived on the lot (see Imoto 1972, 391, n. 18; Satō Nobi 2014, 121) and would have no need to stay over in such cramped conditions. In a supplementary note, Imoto and Yayoshi 1968, 200–201, n. 3, hazard that perhaps a sleep-deprived Bashō simply made a mistake.

44. In his eulogy for Jōsō, *Jōsō ga rui* 丈草誄 (1705), 334, Kyorai recalls this incident. Bashō was from Iga; Kyorai from Hizen; Bonchō from Kaga; and Jōsō from Owari. The conception relates to their birthplace provinces, rather than where they were living at the time of writing.

45. The idea of "dreams of four kinds" ultimately alludes to the Chinese work *Zhujing yaoji* 諸経要集 (late seventh century), a compendium of wisdom from various sutras collected by Daoshi. From it came common sayings such as "Same bed, different dreams" (*dōsho imu* 同床異夢). See Imoto 1972, 392, n. 5.

46. The humor comes from applying a comment in a sutra to so quotidian a situation.

47. "Fair copy" translates *seisho* 清書, something written with care and often incorporating corrections and emendations. Most likely the text in question was *Genjūan no ki*, although Ueno notes that some scholars think it was *Knapsack Notes*, and of course it may refer to a number of pieces as well, since the Japanese does not indicate singular or plural. Bashō had spent the autumn of the year before in the Genjūan in an area near Ishiyama supervised by Kyokusui's uncle.

4.22: Rain falls through the morning. I'm by myself and feeling a bit lonely, so I amuse myself writing this:

Sadness governs those who mourn, while pleasure governs those drinking saké.[48] "If not for solitude, how dismal life would be," Saigyō wrote,[49] so it would be solitude that governed him. He also wrote,

Who are you calling	*yamazato ni*
in this mountain village,	*ko wa mata tare wo*
you calling bird?	*yobukodori*
And here I had imagined	*hitori sumamu to*
I would be living alone.[50]	*omoishi mono o*

Nothing is so enjoyable as living alone. The recluse Chōshō said, "When a visitor gains a half-day of tranquility, his host loses the same."[51] Sodō was always moved by those words. As for me, I write in the same vein:

I am so gloomy	*uki ware o*
I could use more solitude,	*sabishigaraseyo*
lonesome bird.[52]	*kankodori*

This poem was composed when I was staying alone in a certain temple.[53]

In the evening I get a letter from Kyorai.

---

48. An allusion to lines from the "Old Fisherman" chapter of *Zhuangzi*. Mair 1994, 320, translates the lines this way: "In wine drinking, joy is primary; in situations of mourning, sorrow is primary." The phrases come up in a conversation about government between Confucius and an old fisherman.
49. The final two lines of poem 1019 in his personal collection, *Sankashū* (late Heian period). The first three lines read, "I have given up / all hope of having visitors / in my mountain home" (*tou hito mo / omoitaetaru / yamazato no*).
50. *Sankashū* 59. The original text reads slightly differently: *yamazoto ni / tare o mata ko wa / yobukodori / hitori nomi koso / sumamu to omou ni*. The meaning is virtually identical. The "calling bird" is usually identified as the cuckoo (*hototogisu*).
51. An allusion to *Sanka no ki*, 232, by Kinoshita Chōshōshi. The full quote is less inhospitable: "It would appear that if a guest gains half a day of quiet, then his host loses half a day of quiet, but how can chatting between like-minded people be a waste of time?"
52. *Bashō kushū* no. 318. Toyama 1978, 189, n. 7, notes that although *kankodori* is usually taken to be a cuckoo, a literal reading of the first two characters—solitude and old—creates more somber connotations.
53. Taichiin in Nagashima, Ise, where Bashō visited midway through the Ninth Month of 1689, after the trek through the hinterlands.

Turns out that Otokuni was passing through on his way back to Bukō,[54] and has delivered a bunch of letters from old friends and disciples. Among these is one from Kyokusui,[55] who had visited the site of my Bashōan, which I let go; and he also said he had visited Sōha.

Who so long ago	mukashi tare
used to wash his pots here?	konabe araishi
Now—violets.[56]	sumiregusa

Kyokusui added: "The place I am living is no bigger than the length of two bows and the only thing green is a single maple."

A young maple	wakakaede
puts out tea-brown leaves:	chairo ni naru mo
a moment's glory.[57]	hitosakari

From Ransetsu's letter:

Fern fronds—	zenmai no
lowly chaff cast off to get at	chiri ni eraruru
less lowly bracken.[58]	warabi kana

A servant's term ends.	dekawari ya
I feel the sadness I felt	osanagokoro ni
as a child.[59]	monoaware

The other letters are full of things that move me and make me wistful.

---

54. Literally, the Shogun's Bay, the name for Edo that Bashō uses throughout the diary.
55. Then on duty in Edo.
56. A *hokku* by Kyokusui. See a poem by Fujiwara no Kinzane from *Horikawain hyakushu* 堀河院百首 (1099–1103), no. 1106: "The fence that stood / round the house of my love / is all a ruin. / Now amongst the grasses / are violets, and that is all" (*mukashi mishi / imo ga kakine wa / arenikeri / tsubana majiri no / sumire nomi shite*). A different version of the *hokku* ended up in *Sarumino* (no. 1963): "Violets growing— / what remains now where once / he washed his pots" (*sumiregusa / konabe araishi / ato ya kore*).
57. The glory of maples comes out in autumn, but in spring the brownish leaves have their own beauty.
58. Bracken and *zenmai* were both edible herbs, the former referred to as royal dust (*murasaki no chiri*). The poem suggests that the ferns surrounding the bracken are "dust among the dust," or even lowlier than the bracken—something yanked out and thrown aside.
59. Servants' terms usually ended in the Third and Ninth Months.

4.23:

Hands clap	*te o uteba*
and dawn comes in the echo.	*kodama ni akuru*
Summer moon.[60]	*natsu no tsuki*

Bamboo shoots.	*take no ko ya*
How I loved to draw them	*osanaki toki no*
when I was young![61]	*e no susami*

Day by day	*hitohi hitohi*
barley tassles show more color	*mugi akaramite*
as larks sing.[62]	*naku hibari*

I'm useless	*nō nashi no*
and I just want to sleep.	*nemutashi ware o*
Uppity warbler![63]	*gyōgyōshi*

On the topic "Rakushisha":

Fields of beans	*mame uuru*
and firewood shacks, both—	*hata mo kibeya mo*
places of note.[64]	*meisho kana*
Bonchō	

At evening, Kyorai in from Kyoto.

---

60. *Bashō kushū* no. 249. It was customary to stay up and wait for the moon to appear on the 23rd, which meant drinking parties. The summer night is so short that the party seems to end before it has begun. Imoto and Yayoshi 1968, 202, n. 9, note that the sound of clapping is from somewhere in the neighborhood.

61. *Bashō kushū* no. 348. Saga was known for its bamboo groves, and Rakushisha was located in one of them. Bamboo was one of the first subjects given to young people learning to sketch.

62. *Bashō kushū* no. 346. Probably a reference to the fields around Kyorai's village, where barley would be ripening. The call of the lark draws one's gaze out into the landscape.

63. *Bashō kushū* no. 320. *Gyōgyōshi* has a double meaning, meaning both "reed warbler" (行行子; modern *yoshikiri* 葭切) and "pompous" (仰々し). At this time of year, the birds would be building nests and raising chicks.

64. *Meisho* 名所, "places of note," refers to famous places in poetry. Bonchō elevates the low surroundings of the villa into high literary status, using one of the primary rhetorical strategies of *haikai*.

Letter from Shōbō in Zeze, letter from Shōhaku in Ōtsu. Bonchō comes. Visit by the priest of Honpukuji in Katada,[65] who stays the night.

Bonchō returns to Kyoto.

4.25:

> Senna returns to Ōtsu.
> Fumikuni and Jōsō visit.

> On the topic "Rakushisha":

> He faces Saga's peaks, birds and fish for companions;
> and this house the master loves—it's like a peasant's, run-down.
> The tips of the persimmon branches still show no red fruit,
> but these green leaves—they offer themselves for writing poems.[66]
> Jōsō

> "Visiting the Grave of Lady Kogō"

> Bearing up under pain, she left the inner palace,
> and when he sought her, in moonlight, in a village in the fields,
> he found her only by her koto's sound, sole remnant of former days.
> Where now is her lonely grave, among these groves of bamboo?[67]
> Same

> Just budding
> and already leaves throng—
> round the persimmons.[68]
> Fumikuni

medashi yori
futaba ni shigeru
kaki no sane

---

65. Senna.

66. A Chinese poem. People sometimes used persimmon leaves as scratch paper for writing poems. The line thus means two things: that the beauty of the green leaves suggests topics for poems and that the leaves offer themselves as paper.

67. Another Chinese poem. See pp. 157–58 and nn. 31–34 above. It seems likely that the poet visited the grave while at the villa, or at least heard about it from Bashō. The poem draws on the story of Nakakuni's visit to the lady's house, which takes place on a moonlit autumn night.

68. A note of praise for Kyorai's villa. The trees are just showing buds, yet already leaves around the buds are coming out.

Composed on the road:

A cuckoo calls—	*hototogisu*
from hackberry that for him	*naku ya enoki mo*
is plum and cherry.[69]	*mume sakura*
Jōsō	

From a poem by Huang Tingjian that moved me:

He shut his door, to concentrate on poems—did Chen Wuyi;
He flourished his brush before guests—did Qin Shaoyou.

Otokuni comes and we chat about things in Bukō. Also, he had a linked sequence composed swiftly as a candle burned down.[70] From which a few verses:

A lay-monk	*hanzoku no*
tucks a poultice away	*kōyakuire wa*
against his breast.	*futokoro ni*
For crossing Usui Pass	*usui no tōge*
it's wise to use a horse.[71]	*uma zo kashikoki*
Kikaku	

Bamboo box at his waist,	*koshi no ajika ni*
he cavorts beneath the moon.	*kuruwasuru tsuki*

---

69. Imoto 1972, 396, interprets the poem as expressing the impression of the passing cuckoo, whereas Toyama 1978, 195, n. 1, takes it as a comment on the scene by the "poet" speaker who looks out after the cuckoo's call. The hackberry is a summer image, while plum and cherry are associated with spring.

70. *Shoku gobu haikai* 燭五分俳諧, a subgenre of linked verse in which poets pushed themselves to finish before the candle about five *sun* long (1.5 centimeters) burned down.

71. This is the first of three two-verse links (*tsukeku*) Bashō quotes from the materials brought by Otokuni. A lay monk, with no belt for a pouch, tucks into the breast of his robe a poultice he is carrying to treat his aching body while traveling. The author of the link warns him that he should take equal care and take a horse over an upcoming mountain pass on the Nakasen Road.

After the storms	*nowaki yori*
it shelters a wandering exile:	*runin ni watasu*
a solitary hut.[72]	*koya hitotsu*
Same	

At Mount Utsu	*utsunoyama*
he borrows from a woman	*onna ni yogi o*
bed things for the night.	*karite neru*

With lies he pleads his case—	*itsuwari semete*
till she loses her resolve.[73]	*yurusu shōjin*
Same	

Beginning about four in the afternoon, we have wind and rain, then sharp claps of thunder, and hail. The hailstones are three *monme* in weight. They fall at the dragon passing hour.[74] The largest are like apricots, the small ones like dwarf chestnuts.[75]

4.26:

Just budding	*medashi yori*
and already lots of leaves—	*futaba ni shigeru*
round the persimmons.[76]	*kaki no sane*
Fumikuni	

---

72. *Ajika* 箕 is a box of bamboo made for carrying grasses or dirt, although Imoto 1972, 396, n. 7, suggests that here it is used as a creel. The link gives the man an identity: he is a banished man who is able to stay in a hut abandoned after the ravages of a storm.

73. Here the first verse presents a traveling man begging bedclothes for a night at Utsuyama. In the link, he has persuaded the woman into his bed. Ueno 2008, 81, presents a different interpretation that focuses on the word *shōjin* 精進, which he takes to mean not the general "pleading" but abstinence on the death date of a parent. On this reading, the woman is the one attacking the visitor for his excuses, to get him to stay for just one night, which he agrees to do. Thus the link would read: "His lies under attack, / he gives in on abstinence."

74. A reference to *Wu zazu* 五雜俎 (c. 1616), a miscellany by Xie Zhaozhe. In Chinese cosmology, the dragon was associated with rain and clouds. See Imoto 1972, 396, n. 12. A *monme* is about 0.13 ounces in weight.

75. *Karamomo* (modern *anzu*) and *shibakuri* 柴栗.

76. An aforementioned *hokku* by Fumikuni (see n. 68 above), used here to begin a sequence composed by Kyorai and his visitors. As a *hokku*, it serves as a compliment to Kyorai and establishes the season as early summer. Persimmons ripen in the autumn. *Futaba* refers to the two leaves that sprout around the fruit.

Dust sprinkled in the fields—	*hatake no chiri ni*
these flowers on the deutzia.[77]	*kakaru unohana*
Bashō	

Look, a snail	*katatsumuri*
uselessly brandishing	*tanomoshige naki*
his tiny horns.[78]	*tsuno furite*
Kyorai	

While one draws water,	*hito no kumu ma o*
another waits for the bucket.[79]	*tsurube matsu nari*
Jōsō	

In dawn moonlight—	*ariake ni*
a Thrice Monthly Courier	*sando bikyaku no*
on his way?[80]	*yuku yaran*
Otokuni	

4:27:

No one comes. Peaceful day.

4.28:

In a dream, I speak of Tokoku,[81] and wake up in tears.

---

77. Deutzia plants flower in the summer. *Hatake* (cultivated fields) links back to the persimmon trees of Fumikuni's *hokku*.

78. Kyorai's speaker looks down into the deutzia and spies a snail, also associated with summer in *haikai*, brandishing its weak horns against the falling flowers.

79. The snail of the previous verse now appears in a new context, near a well where someone looking around while waiting to draw water spots it on the ground. This verse contains no seasonal reference and would be in the miscellaneous category according to the conventions of linked verse.

80. The dawn moon (*ariake* 有明) puts this verse into the autumn category. "Thrice-Monthly Courier" (*sando bikyaku* 三度飛脚) refers to messengers that traveled three times a month on a set schedule between Edo and the Kyoto-Osaka area, starting out on the 2nd, 12th, and 22nd days of each month (see Ueno 1985a, 292). In the link, the person waiting to draw water early in the morning sees the messenger already on his way.

81. Tokoku had accompanied him on parts of the journey—from Ise to Iga, on to Yoshino and then Kyoto, where they parted—as described in *Knapsack Notes*. He had died in the Third Month of 1690 in Mikawa, aged about thirty years.

It is the heart's engagement with things that creates dreams. When your *yin* is spent, you dream of fire; when your *yang* wanes, you dream of water; when a bird flies off with a lock of your hair in its mouth, you dream of flying; and when you undo your sash and lie down to sleep, you dream of a snake—so it is said.[82] That story in *Suichinki*, and also the story of the Huaian Kingdom under the locust tree, and the story of Zhuangzi and the butterfly—each of these teaches principles, and such stories are endlessly fascinating.[83] But my dreams—they are nothing like the dreams of sages and princes. In the daytime my mind is all delusion and confusion, and it's the same with my dreams in the night. My dream of Tokoku is an example of what is called dreaming of what is on your mind.[84] Out of great regard for me, he came all the way to my hometown in Iga, and then we spent days and nights together in the same room and helped each other while on our trek. For a hundred days or so he was with me like my shadow. Sometimes we amused ourselves; other times we sorrowed. And it's because his devotion pierced my very soul that I never forget about him. After awaking, I weep again.

4.29 and 4.30:[85] Among the poems of *One Hundred Poems by One Hundred Poets of Japan*, I read one on Takadachi in the North Country.

> High in the heavens looms Takadachi, like a star-studded helmet;
> Koromogawa stretches off to the sea, like a crescent moon.[86]

This bears no resemblance to the actual scene.[87] Old masters they may be, but one who never traveled to a place will not be up to describing it.

---

82. A rough paraphrase of statements of the Daoist classic *Liezi* 列子 that discusses dreams and their causes and purposes in terms of yin and yang. See Imoto 1972, 397, n. 19; Graham 1960, 66–67.

83. All three of these stories from ancient China were well known among Japanese literati. The first (told in *Zhen zhong ji* 枕中記 [987]; the title *Shui zhen ji*, J. *Suichinki* 睡枕記, being most likely a mistake) is about a despondent scholar invited by a Daoist monk to lay his head on a pillow, where he dreams a whole lifetime of success and wealth, and then failure and ruin—only to wake up and realize that the monk has instructed him about the nature of human existence. The second is a Tang dynasty story about a man who dreams of a "kingdom under a locus tree" (*huaianguo* 槐安国) that turns out to be a kingdom of ants. The third story tells how Zhuangzi fell asleep and dreamed he was a butterfly and then after waking did not know whether he was a man who had dreamed of being a butterfly or a butterfly dreaming he was a man (Imoto 1972, 398, nn. 1–7; Mair 1994, 24).

84. The word Bashō uses here is *nenmu* (念夢), a synonym of *Liezi's shimu* (思夢).

85. The manuscript is confusing here, seeming to put "Among the poems . . ." and the quoted poem on consecutive days. I follow Ueno 2008, 85, n. 1, in treating 4.29 and 4.30 as one entry by Bashō. He also assumes that 4.23 is one entry including both that day and 4.24.

86. *Honchō ichinin isshu* no. 446. Listed as anonymous.

87. Bashō had seen these sights—the Takadachi and the Koromo River—on his trip to Hiraizumi. See p. 121.

5.1:

Riyū, from Menshōji in Hirata, Ōmi Province, pays a visit.

Letters from Shōhaku and Senna.

Bamboo shoots	*take no ko ya*
not taken to eat are left—	*kuinokosareshi*
laden with dew.[88]	*nochi no tsuyu*
Riyū	

Summer underclothes	*kono goro no*
now feel right against the skin.	*hadagi mi ni tsuku*
Fourth Month.[89]	*uzuki kana*
Shōhaku	

It kept us waiting,	*mataretsuru*
but the Fifth Month's near!	*satsuki mo chikashi*
Rice-cakes from the groom.[90]	*mukochimaki*
Same	

5.2:

Sora comes, telling me about going to see the cherry blossoms in Yoshino and his pilgrimage to Kumano. We chat about friends and disciples in Bukō.

I push on	*kumanoji ya*
along Kumano Road and find . . .	*waketsutsu ireba*
the summer sea.[91]	*natsu no umi*
Sora	

---

88. Some bamboo shoots that escaped being dug up for eating now protrude from the ground and are of no use—just another plant laden with dew.

89. The Fourth Month was the first month of summer, according to the lunar calendar. *Hadagi* 肌着 refers to light underclothing.

90. On the 5th day of the Fifth Month (*tango no sekku*) people prayed for the health of male children. On that day a recently married bride would visit her parents, along with her husband, bringing a special kind of rice cake as a gift. Just who is anxiously waiting—the bride, her husband, or her parents—is unclear (Ueno 1985a, 297). This poem is introduced by a headnote that is undecipherable. Ueno hazards that it might be a garbled attempt at *chimaki* ("rice cakes from the groom"), offered as a topic.

91. By Sora. Kumano is located on the eastern edge of the Kinai Peninsula, bordering on the ocean. Sora had traveled from Edo to Kyoto, and from there southeast to Nara, Yoshino, Mount Kōya, and Kumano, and then back across the peninsula to Osaka and Kyoto—a two-month trek, beginning in spring and ending in summer.

Toward Ōmine	ōmine ya
I went, far into Yoshino—	yoshino no oku o
to where blossoms end.[92]	hana no hate

As the sun is heading down, we go out on the Ōi River in a boat, following the skirt of Arashiyama up into the Tonase rapids. Rain begins to fall and we return home around nightfall.[93]

5.3:

Last night's rainstorm continues on, throughout the day and on into the night. We keep on chatting about things in Bukō until the night is gone.

5.4:

I stay down the whole day, worn out from not sleeping the night before. Around noon the rain lets up.[94]

The next day I will be leaving Rakushisha, and I am feeling a little sorry to go, so I go and look at all the rooms, one by one:

Summer rains.	samidare ya
Poem squares peeling away	shikishi hegitaru
leave marks on the walls.[95]	kabe no ato

---

92. Also by Sora. The last line of the poem, *hana no hate*, is vague. Imoto 1972, 399, takes it to mean the last blossoms of the year. Toyama 1978, 199, takes the phrase to mean the far edge of Yoshino's blossoms. A slightly different version of the poem appears in *Sarumino* (no. 1984), with the headnote, "Written when he went deep into Yoshino, having heard that 'blossoms too have depths.'"
93. Of this excursion Sora writes, "Headed out to Saga, met the Old Master. Kyorai was with him. Got on a boat and enjoyed a trip on the Ōi River. Rain started falling, so we returned. Rain got gradually worse." From this it appears that Kyorai went along. See Sugiura and Miyamoto 1959, 126, n. 6.
94. As Ueno 1985a, 301, points out, the diary does not mention that Sora was still with Bashō until the evening of this day.
95. *Bashō kushū* no. 223. *Shikishi* 色帋 are squares of paper inscribed with poems. Evidently the former owner had pasted some on his walls, where now the squares have peeled away, leaving marks. To Bashō this no doubt brought to mind how the *Hyakunin isshu* began as a collection put together by Fujiwara no Teika to be used to paper the walls of the house of his son's father-in-law, which was located in the Saga area. We know from various sources that Bashō was a careful student of Teika. See Muramatsu 1985, 34, 38.

GLOSSARY OF LITERARY TERMS

ageku 挙句. The final verse of a linked-verse sequence.

chōka 長歌 (long poem). Poems of alternating five and seven syllables, of more than five lines in length, concluding with a seven-seven couplet. One of the major genres of the *Man'yōshū*.

dai 題 (conventional poetic topic). Prescribed topics. Composition on *dai* was central to poetic culture from the late medieval period onward. Examples ranged from simple *dai* ("cherry blossoms") to more complex ones ("frost on a mountain path"). In *haikai* practice, *hokku* were sometimes written on *dai*. Later, many *dai* became *kigo*.

fueki ryūkō 不易流行 (the changing and the unchanging). A concept taught by Bashō near the end of his career as a way to understand the dynamic flow of the natural world, human experience, and poetry. The concept is important in approaching the nature of flow in both the composition of linked verse and the practice of travel.

fūga 風雅. In medieval *waka* the term means "courtly elegance." Bashō appropriates the term to mean "poetry" in a general way and, specifically, *haikai*, thus elevating a popular form into the realm of serious art.

fūga no makoto 風雅の誠 (the truth of poetry). A somewhat vague term used by Bashō in his later years to suggest the highest level of artistic accomplishment, transcending popular categories and hierarchies in pursuit of ultimate truth in the everyday.

haibun 俳文 (*haikai* prose). The term predated Bashō, referring to short prose works—often just a few lines long—that served as prefaces or headnotes. Bashō gave it new meaning and life as an elegant, elliptical, and allusive prose poem that was one influence in the development of his narrative approach in travel writing. *Genjūan no ki*, written about the same time as *The Narrow Road through the Hinterlands* and published in *Sarumino*, is seen as inaugurating his version of the genre.

haikai renga 俳諧連歌. *Haikai* linked verse, as opposed to classical linked verse of the medieval and late medieval periods. Before Bashō's time, the primary form of *haikai renga* was the hundred-verse sequence (*hyakuin*), but he more often composed thirty-six-verse *kasen*. The term *haikai renku* 俳諧連句, although of much later derivation, is now often used to refer to the genre of Bashō's time.

hibiki 響 (echo) or *hibikizuke* 響付. Term for the linking verses based on suggestion by overtones in a previous verse. Associated terms are *nioizuke* 匂付 (linking by scent), *utsurizuke* 移付 (linking by transference), and *omokagezuke* 面影付 (linking by reference).

hokku 発句. The first verse of a linked-verse sequence. By convention, each *hokku* had to be an independent grammatical statement, to include a "cutting word," and to include a season word. In gatherings, the *hokku* was supposed to be rhetorically formal and often offered respects to the host (or guest).

hyakuin 百韻. A hundred-verse linked-verse sequence, the standard unit of composition in classical linked verse and still of importance in Bashō's time.

jiamari 字余 (hypermeter). Lines with excess syllables, occurring most often in the first line of a link.

jimon 地文 (design and background). A term used to characterize the texture of a *renga* sequence, involving both outstanding links and scenes and more straightforward links and scenes that form the background of a sequence.

johakyū 序破急. A term used to characterize the dynamic of a linked-verse sequence as involving a three-part progression: a formal, smooth beginning (*jo*); a less restrained, more animated middle section (*ha*); and a rapid, presto section or conclusion (*kyū*). The ideal also appears in writings on Noh drama and is in many ways musical in its essence.

kaishi 懐紙. Literally, "pocket paper." A square sheet of paper on which poems, often with headnotes, were recorded.

kakekotoba 掛詞. A word that offers two meanings. In most cases a homonym that functions as the end of one phrase and the beginning of another.

kanshi 漢詩. Chinese poem, whether written by a Chinese or Japanese poet.

karumi 軽み (lightness). Term for the aesthetic Bashō propounded in his last years, involving a light rhetorical touch in linking, simple and straightforward rhetoric, and everyday vocabulary.

kasen 歌仙. A thirty-six-verse *renga* sequence. The length most favored by Bashō. Rules governing intermission, seriation, and repetition of thematic and lexical categories for the *kasen* were adapted from rules for the hundred-verse *hyakuin* but were less complex and burdensome.

kigo 季語 (season word). All *hokku* were required to include such a word from established lists.

kikō 紀行 (travel record). A word used in reference to travel diaries from the earliest times until Bashō's day.

kireji 切字 (cutting word). Particles and verb suffixes employed in most *hokku* to help make a statement grammatically and conceptually complete.

kobumi 小文. A short piece of writing. Bashō uses the term in the title of *Knapsack Notes* (*Oi no kobumi*). Some modern scholars see it as a better term for his travel writing than *ki* 記, which has connotations of a simple listing or record.

kuchō 句帳. Logbooks of poems kept by poets, especially on the road.

kyōku 狂句 (crazy verse). Highly comic *renga*, moving a step beyond the usual humor of *haikai* toward the zany antics of "freewheeling" and rhetorical play. Related to *kyōka* 狂歌 ("madcap *uta*") and *kyōshi* 狂詩 ("madcap *kanshi*").

maeku 前句. Term for the verse to which a poet is linking, the immediately previous verse in a sequence.

maekuzuke 前句付. A verse-capping game in which masters provide a verse for which students produce links (*tsukeku*) competitively. Another popular form that Bashō rejected for himself and his students.

makoto 誠 (truth, sincerity, honesty). Of importance in classical *uta* discourse but also an important term in the Zhu Xi Confucianism in Bashō's day.

michi no nikki 道の日記 (road diary). The word Bashō uses for travel diaries of the past in *Knapsack Notes*.

mitsumono 三物. Term for the first three verses of a full *renga* sequence or for a three-verse text composed with no intention of going on to complete a full sequence. In Bashō's day, the various *renga* masters arranged for publication of a New Year chapbook (see *saitanchō*) of *mitsumono* at the beginning of each year, usually involving their most prominent disciples.

nijūshisetsu 二十四節. A twenty-four-verse *renga* sequence. Also called *ebira* 箙.

nikki 日記 (diary). A general term for diurnal journals, referring both to everyday and literary diaries.

renga 連歌 (linked verse). A communal form of poetry in which people in a gathering (*za*) would produce alternating 5-7-5 and 7-7 verses in the round. Classical *renga*—which was still being composed in Bashō's day—abided by courtly standards in rhetoric and content, whereas Bashō's genre of *haikai renga* allowed more humor, plebeian vocabulary, and less adherence to strict formal rules.

rensaku 連作. Short writings linked in a series.

saitanchō 歳旦帳. A small chapbook published by *renga* masters each New Year as a sort of declaration for their schools.

shikimoku 式目. The rules of linked verse.

shū 集. A collection of poems. Bashō is famous for seven such anthologies but was represented in many other collections.

shuhitsu 執筆 (scribe). In Bashō's day, masters employed scribes—usually disciples—to record the results of *renga* gatherings and to point out any transgressions of the rules of linked verse. Bashō served as a scribe in his early career in Edo, and later Sora and other disciples served as scribes for Bashō.

soku 疎句 (distant linking). General term for linking verses less by wordplay, convoluted reason, intentional misreading, and/or parody than subtlety and full engagement with the *maeku*. Companion concept to *shinku* 親句, "close linking."

tabi nikki 旅日記 (travel diary). Another word for travel writing, similar in meaning to *michi no nikki*.

tanjaku 短冊. Later, pronounced *tanzaku*. Strips of paper on which poems were written, usually as gifts. Bashō's letters reveal that he often arranged for poem strips—not just his own but those of other masters—to be sent to patrons and carried paper on the road to respond to requests.

tenja 点者. A *haikai* "marker" who made his living by correcting and commenting on the work of his students, which involved recording short or long marks (*ten*) indicating degrees of excellence. Bashō was a marker in his early days in Edo.

tentori haikai 点取俳諧 (competitive *haikai*). A practice involving students competing against each other for points (*ten*) from their masters. A popular form during Bashō's day, which he rejected when he left his practice in Nihonbashi.

tsukeku 付句 (link). The name for any two verses in sequence in linked verse, or the second verse in any sequence of two verses.

uta 歌 or *waka* 和歌. The 5-7-5-7-7- poetic form of classical times that remained the most prestigious form even in Bashō's day.

utamakura 歌枕 (pillows for poems). The names of places made famous by poems written about them since ancient times.

waka see *uta*

yojō 余情 (overtones). An aesthetic ideal based in understatement and the evocation of feelings beyond the surface. In Bashō's poetics, related to linking verses by suggestion rather than wordplay.

yoyoshi 四十四, 世吉. A forty-four-verse linked-verse sequence.

za 座. The name for a place where a poetic gathering was held, whether in formal or informal terms. Particularly important in the world of *renga* and *haikai*.

zōka 造化 (the "creative" or "transformative"). A term used by Bashō in reference to the dynamic spirit that informs the natural world and the inner workings of the cosmos, which he encourages poets to embrace in their own artistic creations.

APPENDICES

Travel in Bashō's Day

From the early 1600s on, the Tokugawa dynasty worked hard to ensure peace and stability. Among many other things, this required improving roads—mostly medieval in origin—for the use of government officials and travelers generally. During the Kan'ei era (1624–1644) the government standardized widths (more than six meters wide for great arteries, four or five for lesser conduits), provided surfacing, and also put in place along the roads a network of way stations (*shukuba*) that offered lodging and transport services.[1] Its first concern was to facilitate alternate daimyo attendance in Edo (*sankin kōtai* 参勤交代), which from the mid-1600s on was compulsory, but the system served private travelers as well.[2] The distance between stations varied from place to place but was generally not more than 2.5 *li* 里.[3] Stations included separate lodging (*honjin* 本陣, "encampments") for official samurai assemblies as well as inns. Provisions for couriers (*hikyaku* 飛脚) carrying official mail for the government and daimyo, as well as for private correspondence, were also found at stations.[4]

The government system of Five Roads (*gokaidō*; listed below) was established in the most well-traveled areas of the country only, omitting the far northern provinces and Ezo (which came to be called Hokkaidō only in 1869) and the far south. All five of the roads began at Nihonbashi in Edo.

---

1. Kanamori 2000, 18–24. Technically, *shukuba* refered to a main street of inns, but towns grew up around them.
2. Daimyo were required to maintain residential estates in Edo and to spend at least half of their time there. Going back and forth, they traveled with large retinues, sometimes in the thousands, and had their own lodging areas called anachronistically *honjin*, or "encampments."
3. See Inagaki 1993, 8–19; Watanabe 1989, 120–23. A *li* was about 3.9 kilometers or just under 2.5 miles. A *li* was divided into thirty-six *chō* 町, a unit of measure equal to approximately 110 yards.
4. Bashō was occasionally able to use daimyo couriers in places where he had such connections. His letters and statements in his writings also make it clear that he used local courier services (*hikyaku toiya* 飛脚問屋) running between places like Edo and Osaka, or Kyoto and Iga or Ise, and that visitors often brought correspondence with them. See Kanamori 2013, 133–36.

The Tōkaidō 東海道 (Tōkai Road), running mostly along the coast between
  Edo and Kyoto.

The Nakasendō 中山道 (Nakasen Road), running through the mountains of
  central Honshū between Edo and Kyoto.

The Kōshūkaidō 甲州街道 (Kōshū Road), running between Edo and Shimo
  Suwa, a stop on the Nakasendō in Shinano Province.

The Nikkōkaidō 日光道 (Nikkō Road), running between Edo and Nikkō, site
  of a great shrine and temple complex associated with the Tokugawa clan.

The Ōshūkaidō 奥州街道 (Ōshū Road), running between Edo and Shirakawa,
  the gateway to the hinterlands.

The Tōkaidō (Eastern Seaboard Road) was the most traveled of all the roads. It was
paved with gravel in many places and with stone in many snowy areas, and all along
its three-hundred-plus miles there were signposts and towns with lodgings, stables,
and transport services, relay services, and bridges. Users of the road included first of all
daimyo with their large retinues, followed by official couriers. But using the same roads
were private couriers, merchants, pilgrims, farmers transporting goods, and, increasingly, tourists out to see the sights and spend their money at inns, teahouses, and
provisioners that offered everything from sandals to tea and dried rice-balls. Bashō and
his traveling companions stayed at inns less frequently than is commonly thought,[5]
instead being lodged in finer rooms provided by patrons or temples, where they could
anticipate better food and hygiene.

Along all roads there were checkpoints, so-called barriers (*sekisho*) manned by
officials of the Tokugawa government as a way to monitor movements and provide
for policing and surveillance, while domain governments set up *bansho* on their
borders that served similar purposes. These were often imposing installations, with
administrative buildings and garrisons in fenced compounds, positioned in places
that made bypassing them difficult. That there were nearly thirty checkpoints on
the roads in and out of the Sendai Domain is proof enough that governments were
not lax in their attempts to remind travelers of daimyo authority.[6] Some checkpoints
were more imposing than others: whereas there was a complement of sixty samurai on duty at the Sakai Sekisho on the road into Kanazawa in the early 1600s,[7]

---

5. Kanamori 2013, 50–51, calculates that during the five-month journey of 1689, he stayed in
inns only about 25 percent of the time.
6. Kanamori 2013, 21.
7. Yamane 2017, 44.

a remote domain border station in the far north might be staffed by only a handful of guards, none of them true samurai. A midsize place such as Daishōji Sekisho between Komatsu and Fukui had a complement of twenty-eight *ashigaru*, or common soldiers.[8]

There were of course many other roads, all over the country, some of them maintained by local governments or merchants. Of particular importance to Bashō in his earliest journeys were the various roads that connected his hometown in Iga Ueno with Kyoto, Ise, and the areas around Lake Biwa and the Nagoya area; and later he made use of local roads that ran between Sendai and Sakata on the other side of Honshū and the Hokurokudō 北陸道, which ran between Echigo and Wakasa on the rugged coast of the Japan Sea. *The Narrow Road through the Hinterlands* makes it clear that that road and the many tributaries that ran into it were a little rougher than the Five Roads, although nothing like frontier territory except perhaps over the mountain pass on the way into Obanezawa.

Ironically, government presence may have been most keenly felt on less-traveled roads, especially when travelers were not locals known by guards. On the Tōkaidō male travelers were generally able to pass though checkpoints with just a brief interview,[9] but the law stipulated that they be ready to show documents called *tegata*, which might include identification papers containing their birthplace, address, formal name, and destination; the number in their traveling party; and sometimes evidence of funds and the purposes behind their travel. Many travelers also carried invitation letters from friends, family, and patrons, all bearing the proper seals. And in the north the formal presentation of those documents was usually required. The normal process involved showing entry documents (*irihan* 入判) upon arriving in a new domain and then showing exit documents (*dehan* 出判) upon leaving, all being obtained for a fee by a visit to the appropriate magistrate (*bugyō* 奉行). Samurai, who carried weapons and usually had political affiliations, were restricted in their movements and usually had to endure more interrogation; likewise, merchants and tradesmen, who often carried goods for trade, were closely monitored and sometimes subject to tariffs. Farmers seem seldom to have gone far from their homes, partly because of the expense involved; and women faced special obstacles, being more subject to detention and searches than men. For men wearing monkish robes, however, travel was easier, as they did not carry weapons and were not involved in trade. Many scholars believe that it was partly for this reason

8. Yamane 2017, 183.
9. Kanamori 2013, 28.

that Bashō and his traveling companions chose to wear dark robes.[10] Most itinerant *renga* masters and artists in the late medieval period had done the same.

Checkpoint guards (*sekimori* 関守 or *banmori* 番守)—samurai at major places, local farmers at lesser ones—were employed to be suspicious of strangers. Thus, having local contacts, as Bashō and his companions usually did, could make a difference in gaining swift passage. In addition to fees paid to magistrates, however, the payment of gratuities if not bribery was probably common, and often officials served unofficially as middlemen for inns, stables, and palanquin bearers. Opportunities for graft were abundant as the roads to and from checkpoints were lined with shops and inns.[11]

It should be mentioned that Bashō also traveled by boat, on rivers and in bays. Water transport of people and goods was an important part of the economy, and ferrying services were widely available in major population areas—between Atsuta and Kuwana on Ise Bay, for instance. In order to discourage travelers from trying to bypass checkpoints, in the hinterlands only certain waterways were approved for travel—such as sections of the Mogami River in Yamagata—and they had their own checkpoints.[12] Bashō routinely used boats on the waterways of Edo, while also making use of ferry boats that transported travelers across rivers and bays and sometimes along ocean coastlines.

Haikai Poetry in Bashō's Day

In Bashō's day, the word *haikai*—sometimes translated as "comic poetry" or "unconventional poetry"—most commonly referred to the composition of *haikai no renga*, or linked verse, a communal form in which poems worked in the round to create sequences of alternating 5-7-5 and 7-7 syllable verses, composed according to strict rules concerning seriation, repetition, and intermission of themes and words. The thirty-six-verse *kasen* was the most common form for Bashō, although sequences of forty-four, fifty, and one hundred verses were also composed. The first verse of those sequences, called the *hokku*—what would later become haiku—had by his day gained an independent status. Bashō actively participated in *kasen* and composed many independent *hokku* but was perhaps more given to revision than many other masters. The total

---

10. Kanamori 2013, 51, points out that another reason for wearing monkish robes was to make it easier to lodge in temples, where accommodations were usually a cut above those at roadside inns.
11. Kanamori 2000, 34–36; Inagaki 1993, 13–19.
12. Kanamori 2013, 83.

number of his known *hokku* is just over one thousand, not a large number for a career that spanned more than three decades.

In his youth, Bashō was affiliated with the *haikai* master Kitamura Kigin of Kyoto, mentor of his samurai patron in Iga Ueno and a poet of the old Teimon school. When he went up to Edo, however, he became more associated with the dominant school there, the so-called Danrin school of Nishiyama Sōin, a master of classical linked verse (*renga*) who took up the more plebeian genre of *haikai* as a diversion. The Danrin school stressed ideals that, in the beginning, at least, Bashō could embrace—novelty and wit, as well as allusive linking based on classical learning less than on superficial wordplay. But he was soon disenchanted with the professional obsessions of the *haikai* masters around him: the subgenres of *tentori haikai*, or linked-verse competitions, and *maekuzuke*, a kind of verse-capping game in which a teacher gave his students a verse and required back "links." Marking—meaning the granting of points, appraising, correcting, and commenting on such assignments—was inevitably the preoccupation of a poet's waking hours, constituting a recipe for boredom for anyone of true artistic commitment. Nevertheless, it was as a marker (*tenja*) that Bashō supported himself from his arrival in Edo in 1672 until he opted out of the marker lifestyle and removed to Fukagawa in 1680.

After his move from the heart of the city, Bashō primarily relied on the support of patrons for his livelihood and gave up *tentori haikai* and *maekuzuke*.[13] Instead, he committed himself to practicing linked verse, in the *kasen* and *hokku* forms. In this sense he was still a teacher, but one with a different agenda that was little invested in facile competition for points or prizes. What he produced was still very much in the tradition of *haikai* in terms of vocabulary and rhetoric, but also sought to connect back to the ideals of earlier genres, court poetry (called *uta* or *waka*) and classical linked verse. The rules for the *haikai kasen* were less elaborate than those of the *renga hyakuin*, but the basic thematic and lexical categories involved were the same.[14] And he also embraced modes of linking and aesthetic ideals that resonated with those of great poets of the past. In

---

13. Bashō's letters show that he continued to offer some critique and feedback in correspondence with disciples. In a sense he had given up retail and become a consultant.

14. The most important thematic categories were the four seasons, love, and miscellaneous (Buddhism, Shinto, lamentation, travel), while the list of lexical categories was long, including mountain imagery, water imagery, plants, dwellings, etc. On the surface the rules may seem numerous and complicated, but their purpose is easily stated: to ensure constant change and variety within the progress of a sequence—an ideal related to what Bashō called *fueki ryūkō*, "the changing and the unchanging." For a summary, see Ueno 1992, 3–17. In English, see Shirane 2002, 180–206; Miner 1979, 132–39.

this sense he chose to rely on so-called *soku*, or "distant linking" through suggestion and "echo" (*hibiki*) rather than verbal antics and pursued not novelty but old aesthetic ideals such as *aware*, the sadly beautiful, or *sabi*, the lonely or forlorn—although always with new inflections. This did not mean that he forsook the philosophical ideals of *haikai* for older genres, however, as witnessed by his later ideal of *karumi*, or "lightness," which was innately related to the *haikai* emphasis on everyday subject matter and imagery. If his project was revolutionary in any sense, it is in this commitment to creative and not slovenly engagement with the past, within the present.

Bashō and Religion

Knowledge of classical Japanese literature, including poetry in the *uta* and *renga* forms, prose classics such as *The Tale of Genji*, and Noh plays was virtually required of Bashō as a *haikai* master, and it is apparent that he was a serious student of the classical Japanese canon, as well as Chinese poetry. It is also easy to document Bashō's engagement with philosophical and religious texts and traditions via allusions and direct references to Daoist, Buddhist, and Confucian texts, as well as nativist traditions, specifically National Learning (*kokugaku*) and Shinto—all of which had not just spiritual but also social and political dimensions that were inevitably a powerful force in artistic and intellectual affairs. We also know that he had close relationships with a number of priests, including most prominently Butchō, a Zen priest who lived near Bashō's Fukagawa cottage, whom he briefly visited at the former's hometown Kashima in 1687 and alludes to in *The Narrow Road through the Hinterlands*.

However, as noted in the Introduction, scholars are not in full agreement about the extent of Bashō's affiliation with the Zen sect. His recent biographers—Kon Eizō, Ogata Tsutomu, Satō Katsuaki, Kusumoto Mutsuo, Takahashi Shōji, and Tanaka Yoshinobu, to name a few of the more prominent ones—all allow that the influence of Butchō and Zen was substantial. Tanaka represents the mainstream of historical and philological scholarship in arguing that what Bashō studied with Butchō was not just Zen but Daoist texts (preeminently *Zhuangzi*) and the Chinese poets and, further, that when he put on the dark robes worn by monks and nuns it was an announcement of his devotion to *haikai* as a Way rather than a formal tonsure.[15] Takahashi dissents,

---

15. Tanaka 2008, 92–117; 2009, 31–33. In his commentary on Bashō's letters, Tanaka does note that Bashō's signing himself Bashō Tōsei calls to mind the names of medieval Zen monks such as Ikkyū Sōjun (see Tanaka 2005, 82, 150).

insisting that when Bashō moved to Fukagawa in 1680, he was truly renouncing the world and becoming a monk formally, under Butchō's direction, and that he continued to practice as a monk the rest of his life.[16]

Bashō says explicitly in 1685 that he is "neither monk nor layman" but something in between; he is obviously referring to his decision not to take formal vows, and in a 1690 text he also reveals that he once considered entering the priesthood but did not.[17] For these reasons alone, it would seem that Takahashi's contentions are somewhat extravagant. The one thing a study of Bashō's life makes clear is that he was involved until the end of his life in literary commerce, not just writing his own *haikai* but also putting together collections, arranging for them to be published, and serving as a master for linked-verse sessions and providing critiques for students. Such a level of professional engagement would seem unlikely for anyone who thought of himself first and foremost as a Zen monk—although to be fair one must admit that Zen beliefs and practices were notably elastic.

What complicates all of this is that the literary and religious discourses were so intertwined in Bashō's time, and that religious institutions were so involved with social and political discourses. Even his reading of so-called secular classics such as *The Tale of Genji* must have owed much to Buddhist ideas and ideals. And the two poets that he looked to most obviously as models—Saigyō and Sōgi—were themselves monks in whose work the centrality of Buddhist thought is beyond dispute. Moreover, many of the people he visited on his travels, and with whom he composed poetry, were either ordained priests or lay monks. In this sense, it can fairly be claimed that Bashō's worldview was Buddhist in its fundamental assumptions about life, death, and everything in between, and that those assumptions informed his spiritual life and partially informed his poetics. His concepts of "the changing and the unchanging" (*fueki ryūkō*) and "lightness" *(karumi)* derive from Buddhist/Daoist ideas about nature and temporality that are ever-present in his linked verse and in his critical statements about his art.[18] Nor need one hesitate to recognize the influence of Zen in his dedication to the quotidian and the here and now of everyday human experience as the foundation of his poetics, or in his insistence on "putting oneself aside" and "learning of the pine from

---

16. See Takahashi 2002.
17. The references are to *Kashima mōde* (see below), and his most famous *haibun, Genjūan no ki* (Muramatsu 1972, 500). Hisatomi 2002, 9, n. 4, also notes that Bashō describes himself and his traveling companion as "like beggar priests on pilgrimage" because he is not truly tonsured.
18. See Qiu 2005, 136–40.

the pine, of the bamboo from the bamboo."[19] Insisting that he was not a Zen priest in formal terms does not mean rejecting claims of Zen influence—and Daoist influence, which for him was probably filtered through a Zen lens—in his work.

Thus Buddhism in general and Zen in particular figure greatly in Bashō's world—meaning institutions, practices, and ideas. Indeed, even his understanding of so-called secular texts must have been grounded in Buddhist themes and assumptions. No summary of Bashō's religious affiliations would be complete, however, without mentioning the Way of the Gods (*kami no michi* 神の道). Shrines were as much a part of the landscape in his day as Buddhist temples; indeed, the syncretist movements of the late medieval age had led to a situation in which the boundaries between those two discourses were largely blurred by various methods of cooperation that ended with Buddhist temples being part of the Shinto landscape and sharing deities. It is not surprising, then, that he visited as many shrines as temples on his travels. A measure of his devotion to native religion is that he visited the Grand Shrines at Ise six times that we know of—more than any other site, this despite being barred from entry into the inner precincts that were off-limits to those wearing Buddhist robes.

The question of whether this devotion to central Shinto institutions amounted to endorsement of the Tokugawa regime that was their guarantor is a thorny one. Bashō's famous declaration of how the light from Nikkō "shines throughout the heavens, its beneficence overflowing in all eight directions, where peace prevails in the homes of all four classes of people" certainly seems like praise for the regime. But scholars equivocate. Suzuki Hidekazu speaks for many (Satō Katsuaki and Hagiwara Yasuo among them) in stating that Bashō is expressing gratitude toward the Tokugawa for establishing peace.[20] However, Yokosawa contends that the praise is conventional and represents no more than vague gratitude for peace after a long period of warfare and disruption during the period of Warring States (1467–1603).[21] Likewise, Ogata Tsutomu believes that Bashō purposely focuses on the natural world rather than on religious or political imagery,[22] while Ueno Yōzō notes how Bashō avoids any specific reference to Tōshōgu, the name of the Tokugawa shrine, and Miyawaki Masahiko says the most important thing for Bashō is the traditional *waka* term *hi no hikari* 日の光, "the light of the sun," which

---

19. *Sanzōshi*, 547–48.
20. See Horikiri 2003, 45–46. Tanaka 2009, 59, argues that Bashō's reverence for the site was so profound that he created a neologism—*keihai su* 詣拝す—in order to express it, although he does not commit himself to a political interpretation.
21. Yokosawa 1995, 185.
22. Fukasawa and Kusumoto 2009, 77.

are constituent characters of the shrine's name.[23] Aligning Bashō's political leanings with his religious commitments is, then, a difficult task. There can be no doubt that his ethics were influenced by mainstream discourse of the time, which was a mixture of Buddhist, Confucian, and Shinto tenets; beyond that one must analyze each relevant statement on its own terms and in its own context.[24]

Finally, we should also keep in mind that Bashō's hometown of Iga Ueno was in a mountainous area where esoteric mountain asceticism—a religious movement that was a hodgepodge of Shinto, early Buddhist, Daoist, and native folk beliefs and practices— was widely practiced and that Bashō participated in rituals at the Three Mountains of Dewa.[25] Like most people of his day, he probably accepted animist beliefs at some level, feeling spiritual power in sacred places and landscapes.

Bashō's Family and Other Relationships

Bashō's letters and other documents, including his travel writings, show that all of his life he maintained close ties with his family in Iga, which included his older brother, head of the household, and four sisters (one older, three younger). In his early years in Edo, he relied on the Iga network for support and later often organized journeys around visits to Iga, where he also had friends and disciples. He recognized his brother as head of the Matsuo house and not only wrote him often but sometimes sent money[26] and accepted family obligations. One of his nephews, Ihei, born in Kamo, Yamato Province, came to live in Edo, while another named Kahei came to Edo and eventually became a *haikai* master under the name Tōrin. Still another, known as Tōin, definitely accompanied Bashō back to Edo when the latter returned from a visit to Iga in 1676 and was in some sense under Bashō's sponsorship—the term used being *yūshi* 猶子, which usually is used to mean a nephew adopted as heir.[27] Recent scholarship

---

23. Ibid., 77–78. *Waka* can be used to refer to all genres of Japanese poetry, but Miyawaki refers specifically to the *uta*, the 5-7-5-7-7 form associated with the traditions of the imperial court.
24. For more on this issue, see Carter 1997.
25. A complicating factor here is that a visit to the Three Mountains was evidently not on his itinerary from the beginning (see Uozumi 2011, 78–79 and a letter to Sanpū in Tanaka 2005, 201). On the other hand, his account leaves no doubt that he was moved by the ritual. For an analysis of Bashō's relationship with Shinto beliefs and institutions, see Fukasawa Tadataka 1997, 175–80.
26. See Yamamoto Yuiitsu 1994, 146–49.
27. Takahashi 1993, 47, argues that *yūshi* means "nephew" in this context and that he was more like a ward (*yōshi* 養子).

establishes that Tōin worked in Edo for a man named Ishimaru Kentō.[28] Unfortunately, Tōin was plagued by a lung ailment and died sometime in the spring of 1693, after Bashō had personally nursed him for some time.

Some documents say that Bashō had a mistress or common-law wife in his early years, in Iga Ueno and perhaps for a time in Edo, a completely plausible theory given the mores of the time. It appears that later she ended up living with or near him, after taking the tonsure with the Buddhist name Jutei. (Other theories are that she was Tōin's wife or that she and Tōin had an affair, which was the immediate reason for Bashō moving out of Nihonbashi and into Fukagawa—to avoid notice.)[29] Her son, Jirōbei, was in his late teens and living at the Bashōan in 1693 and accompanied Bashō on what would be the master's last journey. Jirōbei returned to Edo upon news of his mother's death but quickly returned west and was at Bashō's bedside when the master died.

In recent years, questions about Bashō's sexual relationships with men have also arisen, especially his relationship with a man named Tokoku, whom he first met in Nagoya in 1684. When Tokoku fell afoul of the law a few years later, Bashō visited him in his place of exile, and later the two men journeyed together through the mountains of the Kii Peninsula when the cherry blossoms were in full bloom, continuing on to the coast at Suma. The precise nature of the relationship is impossible to determine, but scholars are unanimous in concluding that there was something special between them. Imoto Nōichi, for instance, says, "He was someone Bashō had special love for,"[30] while Muramatsu says explicitly that the relationship was homosexual.[31] Hori Mizuho, an employee of *The Asahi Shimbun*, allows the possibility of a sexual relationship but ultimately argues that Bashō suppressed such instincts for the sake of his art.[32] Novelist Shimizu Motoyoshi and travel writer Arashiyama Kōsaburō show no such hesitations.[33] There is no doubt that Bashō was devastated when Tokoku died a few years later, as recorded in *Saga nikki* (see pp. 167–68). Mangikumaru, the name Tokoku adopts for his journey with Bashō, seems to gesture toward the world of *shudō* 衆道, male-male sexuality involving a mature man and a youth. Yet Tanaka notes

---

28. Kon 2004, 399–404. Kon argues that it was from his employer that the young man received the character *tō* in his name and not from Bashō Tōsei.

29. For the many theories involved in this question, see Kon 1989, 206–13; Takahashi 1993, 49–56; Tanaka 1998; Itō 2011, 52–53.

30. Imoto 1972, 298, n. 6. See also Yokosawa 1995, 140–41.

31. Muramatsu 1985, 41. Takahashi 1993, 37, alludes to Bashō's note in a commentary as a revelation of his *danshoku* 男色, which is usually translated as "homosexuality."

32. Hori Mizuho 1993, 220–33.

33. Shimizu 1999, 38–52; Arashiyama 2000, 162–88.

that a character named Gangikumaru 岩菊丸 appears in an early seventeenth-century commentary on *Taiheiki* titled *Taiheiki hiden rijinshō* (太平記秘伝理尽鈔) and suggests Tokoku may have that in mind rather than anything else when he concocted his name.[34] In the absence of more evidence, the issue will doubtless remain unresolved, although it must be said that there is nothing in our knowledge of Edo culture that would rule out a male-male sexual relationship for a person in Bashō's situation.

Bashō's relationship with disciples involved varying degrees of dependence. Some, like Sanpū, were not just students but patrons who supplied him with material needs, along with assisting him in his poetic affairs. Traditionally, Kikaku, Sanpū, Ransetsu, Kyorai, Kyoriku, Shikō, and Jōsō have been singled out for special attention by scholars as stalwart figures in his school. Inevitably, however, relationships changed over time; students might disagree with the master or just lose interest. For instance, Bonchō, his Kyoto disciple in the late 1680s, fades from the record after 1691. Management, via letters or face-to-face meetings, was always necessary, and despite all his efforts, it seems that politics was often local. Furthermore, Bashō's networks were regional, centered in Edo, the Nagoya area, Iga Ueno, the Kanazawa area, and the Kyoto area, where prominent disciples acted as *haikai* masters themselves, with their own students and allegiances. Thus, however paternalistic they may look on the surface, master-disciple relationships were not like family relationships that persisted despite distance and conflicts.

THE QUESTIONS OF GENRE AND TITLES

Scholars often debate the question of what titles Bashō intended for the writings translated in this book. The only thing we can say with relative certainty is that the poet himself chose the title *The Narrow Road through the Hinterlands*, which we know from actual manuscript evidence. If there is one other note of certainty in the discourse, however, it is that, as I note in my introductions, he seems to have resisted using the term *kikō*, or "travel record."[35] For this reason, Takahashi, for instance, eschews that word and calls the works *kobumi* 小文 ("short writings"), while Ueno opts for the word *bunsho* 文章 ("prose writing").[36] Other scholars do not go so far but always admit the problem.

---

34. Tanaka 2005, 232.
35. "Resisted" translates the Japanese word *teikō* 抵抗. Ueno 1989, 149–52.
36. See Takahashi 1993, 174–75; Ueno 1989, 149–52.

Obviously, one explanation for this is that Bashō did not arrange for publication of these writings himself and therefore was never obliged to firmly decide on titles. (The titles that include *kikō*—*Nozarashi kikō*, *Sarashina kikō*, and *Kashima kikō*—as used by scholars in modern editions were all attached to the relevant texts after his death.) Yet this fact alone is not enough to conclude that he wanted his writings to be read as something unrelated to the travel writing of his own tradition. On the contrary, it is impossible, after looking at passages in the works themselves and early comments by prominent disciples, to argue that the writings translated in this book were not from the beginning thought of as within the discourse of travel writing in some sense. The way at the beginning of *Knapsack Notes* he situates himself in the same discursive world as "road journals" (*michi no nikki*) by Ki no Tsurayuki and the Nun Abutsu is enough to justify placing him in that company.

It seems prudent, therefore, to follow the master's lead and treat the texts translated in this book as travel writings, *but with a difference*. Ueno Yōzō summarizes the point well as he concludes a thorough analysis of the question:

> So, what should we make of the prose writings in which Bashō relates his travels? However hazy, a contour does seem to emerge. His "travel journals" are not meant merely to narrate his travels. Rather, he makes use of travel as a device to narrate the meanings of natural and human encounters as they appear before him. Using concrete forms as they occur in time and space, he writes to record his experiences.[37]

Ueno's choice of the word *tsuzuru* (綴 る, which I have translated as "narrate" but might also be rendered as "relate," "detail," "document," or "delineate") is crucial, as it has connotations of not just telling but of sealing or sewing things together. That is something Bashō's travel writings undeniably do, making them in that sense narratives, regardless of what name one chooses to attach to them.

Fact and/or Fiction: The Challenge of Sora's Diary

The appearance in 1943 of a short work titled *Sora nikki*, or "Sora's Diary," covering the same time period as *The Narrow Road through the Hinterlands*, sent shockwaves

---

37. Ueno 1989, 151.

through the world of Bashō studies.[38] It turned out that Sora had left a fairly detailed daily record of places visited, distances traveled, people met, sometimes even money spent, and so on, refraining from any personal comments or literary flourishes and even omitting most poems. But comparison of the accounts did reveal discrepancies, and the assumption from the beginning was that Sora's account must be the more factual of the two—which was another way of saying that the Master had occasionally played fast and loose with the facts. Before long scholars were questioning the veracity of episodes in the other works as well: his encounter with an abandoned child in *Bones Bleaching in the Fields*, his fall from a horse in *Knapsack Notes*, and so on.

However, it was *The Narrow Road through the Hinterlands* that came under greatest scrutiny. The two works follow the same basic timeline and the same itinerary. But even a brief comparison of the two leads one to the conclusion that Bashō's work needs to be seen as more than a series of journal entries, to be seen as "a consciously crafted work of literature," to quote what Francine Prose says about the diary of Anne Frank.[39] Scholars should have known, of course; many probably did. Among other things, it was well known that the master had not finished work on his record until just before his death, fully four years after the journey, dilly-dallying in ways a straightforward chronicler would surely not.[40] Now it became clear that when he says near the beginning of *Knapsack Notes*, "Don't hear what I say too seriously," he also means "don't take me too literally."

The discrepancies between the works are not great but they are numerous, and they reveal a pattern, as is obvious when one compares entries like these on the visit of the travelers to one of their first destinations, Nikkō, a complex of temples and shrines under the direct patronage of the Tokugawa family and a major tourist attraction of the day:

Bashō: On the 30th we lodged at the foot of Mount Nikkō. The proprietor of the place said this: "I'm called Buddha Gozaemon—because my aim is to be forthright in all things. So relax, be my guest: lie down on

---

38. A number of texts were discovered, including lists of shrines visited and *utamakura*. The journal is titled *Genroku ninen nikki* 元禄二年日記, *A Journal of the Second Year of the Genroku Era*. Since the Edo period references to a Sora journal had circulated, but it was only on publication of the journal in 1943 that the contrasts became apparent, and only in the postwar era that scholars began to seriously think about their implications.

39. Francine Prose 2010. *Anne Frank: The Book, the Life, the Afterlife*. New York: HarperCollins e-books. 3 of 383, digital.

40. As noted above (p. xxix), Eguchi 1998, 23, says, any person whose purpose was to keep a journal would have written a good deal on the road, and polished it up soon after returning "before his memories began to fade."

your pillows of grass and spend the night at your ease." What Buddha might it be, I wondered, who reveals himself thus in our world of dust, assisting men who are like beggar priests on pilgrimage? Observing him, I saw that he was without guile, straightforward to a fault. Indeed, he was "close to benevolence—strong, unyielding, simple, discreet," a man one could praise for his purity of disposition. On the 1st day of the Fourth Month, we offered obeisance at Oyama.

Sora: Fourth Month, 1st: Light rain falling since night before. Left inn 7 a.m. Rain let up for a while but continued off and on. Cloudy all day. Arrived at Nikkō around noon. Rain let up. Delivered letter from Shimizudera to Yōgen'in. A monk accompanied us as messenger to Dairakuin. As guests happened to be at Dairakuin, we waited until about 3 p.m., then toured Shrine. Day ended and we stayed at inn of man called Gozaemon in Kamihatsuishi-machi, Nikkō. 1 *kan* 240 *mon*.[41]

The contrasts here are obvious and instructive. First is that the passages don't agree on dates. Sora is correct: in fact, there were only 29 days in the Third Month of 1689. So Bashō is, at the least, taking liberties. Rather than admitting that their visit to Oyama was a rather hurried affair at the end of the day, he takes the liberty of moving the date of arrival to the night before—thus making the visit not in the afternoon but the next morning, when the men would notice new green growth in the fresh light of a new day. He also says nothing about the letter of introduction the travelers brought from a patron at a temple back in Edo, the various offices they had to work through to be allowed to make a proper visit, and money expended—all things that would have created a different mood altogether. Finally, whereas Bashō gives a lively description of their innkeeper, Gozaemon, Sora gives only a name and an address, and this despite the fact that one might expect Sora, as a student of Shinto, to be impressed with the man's forthright-ness—a fundamental ideal in Shinto ethics. This is the pattern a careful reader identifies immediately: Sora is creating a factual account that might be of use to another traveler or as a prompt to his own memory, in contrast to his master's more artistic and affective tableaux. Needless to say, Bashō's writing shows more fashioning and a higher level of aesthetic and emotional engagement.

Bashō's record thus reveals fashioning, usually involving amplification and elision more than anything else. It should be noted, however, that there are sections of the

---

41. See p. 100 and Ogata 1995, 313.

work that scholars examining Sora's accounts almost universally conclude that Bashō has made up. The most famous example is an episode set in Ichiburi, the site of a barrier on the border between Echigo and Etchū, on the Japan Sea coast on the way to Kanazawa. By all accounts Ichiburi, administered by the Takada Domain, was a small and insignificant checkpoint. And Sora only mentions it in passing, writing on the 12th day of the Seventh Month, "Arrived at Ichiburi just before 5," and on the 13th, "Left Ichiburi." Bashō, however, describes a rather noisy inn and tells an amusing and touching story. As he was trying to go to sleep, he relates, he overheard a conversation involving two young prostitutes and a man who has been accompanying them; then he goes on to describe how the next morning the women approach him to ask if they might perhaps accompany the men for safety's sake—a request that Bashō feels he must turn down, perhaps thinking that men with shaved heads should not be seen in such company. Scholars, who on the basis of textual analysis conclude that this scene was almost certainly added into the text late in the composition process,[42] explain Bashō's motives in various ways. The first and most prominent is that Bashō, ever the linked-verse poet, wanted to include in his record a few examples of the love category, which according to the rules had to be represented in all proper sequences.[43] Another is that he wanted to offer a variation on a famous story about his mentor Saigyō's encounter with a prostitute on his travels.[44] Of course, one can argue that Sora did not record the incident because of its sensitive nature, or even that Bashō is conflating experiences somehow, but scholars generally conclude otherwise: exercising poetic license, they argue, he made the story up—and that means all of it, even the last sentence in which Bashō asks Sora to write down what happened.[45] Some scholars continue to insist that the episode cannot be dismissed as entirely fictional, given Bashō's penchant for focusing on such chance encounters; others agree that the episode is probably fictional but equivocate, suggesting, for instance, that Bashō inserted a factual episode from an experience elsewhere.

---

42. Uozumi 2011, 231–33; Fukasawa and Kusumoto 2009, 383–85; Sakurai 2006, 145–46.

43. Other passages of the text that might be seen in the love category, at least in terms of vocabulary, are those involving the little girl Kasane and the wife of Tōsai in Fukui. As Eguchi 1998, 132–42, argues, Bashō shies away from any hint of sexuality in his descriptions, but just the mention of a woman was enough to satisfy the conventions.

44. See Fukasawa Shinji 2009, 373–79. Another obvious reason to question the story is that it is just too perfect: too complete a variation on Saigyō's story and too well-precedented a portrait of the plight of prostitutes.

45. See Fukasawa Shinji 2009, 384; Ogata 2001, 348–49; Horikiri 2003, 173. There is no evidence that Sora did as requested (see Fukasawa Shinji 2009, 384).

Sora's diary is now widely available, making it possible for readers to compare accounts. In my translation of *The Narrow Road through the Hinterlands* I have noted a few of the most obvious discrepancies. In all, I agree with Tanaka Yoshinobu when he says that the chief characteristic of *The Narrow Road through the Hinterlands* is that it takes real experiences and refashions them.[46] Just as Bashō routinely revised poems for artistic (or religious or philosophical) effect, he did so when he wrote up his travel records. Fortunately, his modest hopes are nicely voiced in *Knapsack Notes*: "The scenes one saw at this place or that do stay in one's mind, and the pains one suffered spending the night at lodgings in the mountains and fields—well, they may provide things to chat about later on. So, then, as a gesture toward the world of wind and clouds, here I have assembled, not always in strict order, jottings about places that have remained in my memory."

Scholars argue that there are sections in Bashō's other travel records that may be fictional, such as the scene where he and his traveling companion come upon an abandoned child near the Fuji River on the Tōkaidō in *Bones Bleaching in the Fields*. Here we do not have anything like Sora's diary to allow for comparison, but the issue remains the same. It seems certain that Bashō actually passed by the Fuji River on his journey, but is the incident he describes factual or fictional—or perhaps a combination of both? The answer has to be that we cannot know. Since the discovery of Sora's diary, however, we have to conclude that fashioning was part of Bashō's method, as much a part of his writing in prose, perhaps, as in his poetry. Imoto Nōichi, writing about *The Narrow Road through the Hinterlands*, sums mainstream opinion on the matter up succinctly:

> Bashō did not write the work immediately after his journey, but a few years later, in 1692–93, which means that it was not a literal account of a journey but a highly creative work of travel writing. It was his ideas about art and of life that were his foundation, not the facts of travel, which for him were of little interest. It was only when it became a literary work that its meaning emerged; a travel record that did not have literary qualities was to him not a travel record at all. That is why he made bold to omit things, to alter facts and to include things that never happened—at least, that is how I think about it.[47]

---

46. Tanaka 2009, 57. "Refashions" translates *saikōsei* 再構成, which might also be rendered as "restructure" or "reconstitute."

47. Imoto 1970, 385.

EXCERPTS FROM LINKED-VERSE SEQUENCES

Bashō is now known for his *hokku,* but his first priority as a professional was composing linked-verse sequences with his disciples. Below I have translated excerpts of five sequences from the era of his travel writings. All but one of them was composed while he was on the road. They involve poets of varying ages, occupations, and literary experience. My short commentaries give the thematic category of each verse as dictated by the rules of the genre (*shikimoku*), a few words about links between verses (guidebook—travel hat), and other explanation as needed. Each link constitutes a complete statement (verse 2 linking back to verse 1, then verse 3 linking back to verse 2, and so on), but meanings and perspectives often change as the sequence moves forward.

The conventions of *haikai* linked verse are designed to create variety and change by enforcing standards of seriation, intermission, and repetition—in a broad sense, to create a textual representation of the Buddhist concept of *mujō* (constant change, ephemerality). The relevant thematic categories—the four seasons, love, and a miscellaneous rubric that includes travel, Buddhism, Shinto, etc.—hark back to the courtly tradition; but also important are categories taken from medieval lexicography (plants, mountains, waters, rising things, etc.). In *haikai,* however, the rules were less stringent, and the range of allowed imagery was much broader. While not a truly subversive form, *haikai* was after all based on the idea of expanding the borders of poetic expression. That the theme of travel pops up rather frequently in the examples that follow may first of all be a result of my choice of links to translate, then. But it is also true that scenes of travel appear more often in sequences composed on the road—a natural state of affairs.

For the texts of the translated sequences and commentary, see Abe Masami 1965–89, vol. 4, 362–65 (for the sequence from 1685), vol. 5, 127–30 and 424–25 (for the sequences from 1686 and 1687), and vol. 7, 240–43, 440–46 (for the two sequences from 1689).

Narumi, Summer 1685

On 4.4 of 1685, Bashō was staying at the house of his disciple Chisoku in Narumi. That evening he, his host, and a group of local poets produced a twenty-four-verse *haikai* sequence (*nijūshisetsu*). It was the third sequence he had directed in the previous ten days, involving twelve poets altogether, many of whom became official disciples at the time. In his *hokku,* Bashō speaks as a *haikai* master, declaring half in jest that his thoughts were constantly on poetry. What he had in mind was probably section nine of *Tales of Ise*, involving irises in a place called Yatsuhashi, not far from Narumi. His verse obeys all the conventions for a *hokku*, presenting a complete statement, including a *kigo* (season word), and focusing on the surroundings at the time of composition.

1	Ah, irises:	*kakitsubata*
	they get me to thinking	*ware ni hokku no*
	of first verses.	*omoi ari*
	Bashō	
2	Waves crest in the barley—	*mugiho nami yoru*
	end result of moisture's gift.	*uruoi no sue*
	Chisoku	
3	Crows, two of them,	*futatsu shite*
	brush low over a travel hat	*kasa suru karasu*
	in dusky light.	*yūgurete*
	Tōyō	
4	On the path back, a guidebook	*kaesa ni sode o*
	somehow drops from a sleeve.	*moreshi meishoki*
	Kōtan	

1 *Summer*. *Kakitsubata* (iris) is a summer *kigo*, or season word. There were probably irises in bloom at Chisoku's house. 2 *Summer*. Moisture—irises. Chisoku thanks Bashō for his generosity. 3 *Miscellaneous* (*travel*). Dusky light—after. Crows swoop by as a traveler walks by barley fields, drawing our eyes from earth to sky. 4 *Miscellaneous* (*travel*). Guidebook—travel hat. Bothersome crows lead to a mishap for a traveler.

Edo, Winter 1686

Travelers to Edo visited Bashō frequently, keeping him in touch with students. Jokushi, an Ōgaki disciple, called at the master's Fukagawa cottage at the end of 1686. A samurai, Jokushi was often on assignment in Edo and had known Bashō for some time. Together they composed a *kasen* (two verses of which are missing). Also participating were Bashō's chief disciple, Kikaku, and a number of other disciples close to Kikaku— Senka, Kosai, and Rika, all Edo men. The following sequence of six linked verses alludes to places and scenes outside the city, specifically naming Ise and Mino.

25

26 Planning a trip to Ise—   *ise omoitachi*
    straw sandals, sedge hat.   *waraji sugegasa*
        Kosai

27 Off for Mino.   *mino naru ya*
    With shouts a clam boat leaves   *hamaguribune no*
    in early morning.   *asayobai*
        Senka

28 Breaking up in the current: *nagare ni yaburu*
    paper lanterns at Obon time.   *kirikake orikake*
        Rika

29 Down goes the moon—   *tsuki irite*
    fearsome lightning remaining   *inazuma nokoru*
    in the cattails.   *gama sugoku*
        Jokushi

30 All the labor of the year—   *kotoshi no rō o*
    in a load of parched rice.   *ninau yakigome*
        Bashō

31 Down in her grave   *tsuka no shita*
    Mother is sure to be cold   *haha samukaramu*
    in autumn wind.   *aki no kaze*
        Kikaku

26 *Miscellaneous (travel)*. Someone plans a trip to the Grand Shines at Ise, a major attraction for pilgrims. 27 *Miscellaneous (travel)*. Mino—Ise; clam boat—Ise. Mino was Jokushi's home province. The shore is a congregating place, for people of various motivations. 28 *Autumn*. Current—boats. At the time of Obon (the Festival of Spirits) lanterns were floated in rivers, a rite that was particularly associated with the Nagoya area. 29 *Autumn*. Lightning—lantern; cattails—current. The night wears on, the Obon festival just about over. 30 *Autumn*. The time has come to offer parched rice from the harvest to temples, shrines, and neighbors. Lightning makes for precarious travel. 31 *Autumn*. Rice was also offered at graves. The verse contains a clear allusion to *SKKS* 796, in which Fujiwara no Shunzei thinks of his deceased wife hearing the wind in the pines down in her grave.

Nagoya, Winter 1687

In a letter to Sanpū in Edo dated 12.13 of 1687, Bashō described his recent days among disciples in the Mino-Owari area, whom he was visiting for the second time. Despite his complaints, he cannot have been unhappy with his reception:

> By 11.5, I made it to Narumi and thought I would go on to Iga in a few days, but word came by messengers from Ise and Nagoya, and I was pressed to go to Nagoya, so I agreed to stay until the 13th. . . . I have been treated well, and *haikai* masters from Gifu and Ōgaki have also come to visit. People in neighboring provinces say they are waiting for me, so I have told them I will come in the spring.

It was in Nagoya on 12.4 that Bashō and five disciples from Nagoya had met at the cottage of a man named Chōsetsu to compose a thirty-six-verse sequence. The last verses of the sequence provide portraits of a number of freewheeling spirits. Bashō makes a very specific reference to his friend and fellow traveler Etsujin, poking fun in a gentle way. The final verse (*ageku*, or "offering verse") shows a world at peace, as the conventions of the genre required.

33 Those traveling robes—   *tabigoromo*
   might that be Jūzō   *owari no kuni no*
   of Owari?   *jūzō ka*
       Bashō

34 Failing to render Fuji—   *fuji kakikanete*
   he gets back on his horse.   *mata uma ni noru*
       Yasui

35 A saké cup   *futokoro ni*
   in the breast of his robe—   *sakazuki iruru*
   at blossom time.   *hana narishi*
       Jokō

36 The gentle ruffling of willows   *kage yawaraka ni*
   reflected in the water.   *yanagi nagaruru*
       Etsujin

33 *Miscellaneous* (*travel*). Travel robes—sleepy. Bashō takes a liberty: "That shape on the floor, might it be that lazy Etsujin?" 34 *Miscellaneous* (*travel*). Fuji—traveling robes. Now the man in the traveling robes stops to sketch Fuji but is not happy with the results. 35 *Spring*. Blossom time—Fuji. Unable to produce a proper sketch of Fuji, he resorts to another way to enjoy the blossoms. 36 *Spring*. Willows—blossom time. On a riverbank, a man enjoying saké sees the reflection of the willows in the water.

Haguro, Summer 1689

Bashō's account of his stay in Haguro focuses on climbing the sacred mountain, but Sora writes about the kind treatment the men received over the nine days they spent in the area. As usual, they were shown nearby temples and shrines, and were treated to fine meals, including the tea and noodles that were considered invigorating for climbing pilgrims. They also participated in a linked-verse sequence, which was composed in stages: the first six verses on the 4th day of the Sixth Month; verses seven to eighteen the next day; and the rest on the 9th, at a banquet held by Egaku Ajari, their patron. Several priests participated, one of them a man from Kyoto named Chōsetsu whom they seem to have known. On the 7th and 8th—between poetry gatherings—they made the devotional climb up the slopes.

Four of the poets were clearly amateurs and we assume that Bashō may have helped them along. The theme of travel (a subcategory in the category of Miscellaneous) dominates the part of the sequence quoted here, perhaps more than it should according to the conventions—and despite the attempt of Sora in verse ten to move things in a new direction. In this case social circumstance and the mood of the *za* clearly prevailed over any aesthetic purposes.

7   Getting sleepy—
    at noon, beneath clouds,
    travel hat off.
       Chōsetsu

                                    inemurite
                                    hiru no kageri ni
                                    kasa nugite

8   A hundred *li* on his way—
    a Kiso oxherd and his stock.
       Bashō

                                    hyakuri no tabi o
                                    kiso no ushioi

9   Full of mountains,
    he sets himself to writing
    a castle record.
       Rogan

                                    yama tsukusu
                                    kokoro ni jō no
                                    ki o kakan

10 He stops cold, ax in hand—
   in a grove 'round a shrine.
   Sora

ono mochisukumu
shinboku no mori

11 On he goes,
   seeking traces left by poets.
   No inn in sight.
   Chōsetsu

utayomi no
ato shitaiyuku
yado nakute

7 *Miscellaneous* (*travel*). A traveler rests at midday, beneath a passing cloud. 8 *Miscellaneous* (*travel*). On his way, Kiso—travel hat. Bashō had walked the Kiso Road on an earlier journey and no doubt the peaks around Haguro had a similar feel. 9 *Miscellaneous* (*travel*). Mountains—Kiso. Might Rogan be thinking that his master would write an account of his current journey? He may also be alluding to the fate of Kiso Yoshinaka after defeat at Hiuchi Castle in Echizen, as related in *Tales of the Heike* and popular legend. A castle record would tell the origins and history of a castle, much like a shrine or temple record. 10 *Shinto*. Shrine—mountains, castle. The first thing any account should say is that the grove is sacred, as a man out cutting wood realizes. 11 *Miscellaneous* (*travel*). Two of the many interpretations: a man visiting famous poetic sites comes upon a grove, where a ruffian honors the sacred space and lets him be; or that same man is impressed by an atmosphere so sacred that woodcutters do not cut the trees there.

Yamanaka, Autumn 1689

After nearly a month trekking down the coast of the Japan Sea, Bashō and Sora arrived in Kanazawa, castle town of the mighty Kaga Domain, where they expected a fine welcome from *haikai* poets in the area, especially one Isshō, a tea merchant and *haikai* enthusiast whom he knew by reputation. They soon learned, however, that he had died at the end of the previous year.

The next day another follower, Chikujaku, sent palanquins to take the travelers to better quarters in his own inn, run by his son. Over the next week the travelers were feted in grand style and participated in lots of poetry gatherings, including one held in memory of Isshō held at a temple by the deceased's brother, Besshō. Bashō made more than a dozen new disciples, several of whom would become prominent—Otokuni, from Ōtsu; and Hokushi and his brother Bokudō, who had a sword-sharpening business in Kanazawa.

Kanazawa was less than a hundred miles from Ōgaki, their final destination. But in Kanazawa stomach pains kept Sora from attending a number of events. He persevered as they pushed on to Komatsu and Yamanaka Hot Springs, but when his health did not improve—despite assistance from physicians and medications—he decided to set out for his family home in Ise. His journal records the details.

7.27: Arrived at Yamanaka around 5 in afternoon. Stayed in house of Izumiya Kumenosuke. Thunder showers passed by, from the mountains and from the south, moving north.

7.28: Fair skies. Rainfall at night. In the evening, took a look at Yakushidō and other places in town.

7.29: Fair skies. Visit to Dōmyō Pool, but I didn't go. (Located in the Kakusen Gorges.)

7.30: Fair skies. At Dōmyō Pool.

8.1: Fair skies. To Kurotani Bridge.

8.2: Fair skies.

8.3: Rainfall off and on. Clearing in the evening. Couldn't see the moon, so deep in the mountains. Rain through the night.

8.4: Rain stopped in the morning. Fell again at about half past nine, then stopped. Fell again in the night.

8.5: Morning cloudy. Around noon, the Old Man and Hokushi headed for Nata. So they could meet up with Ikoman Manshi. I returned and departed immediately. Headed for Daishōji. Arrived at Zenshōji around five, stayed there. Rainfall through the night.

Sora tells only the bare bones of the story. For instance, we know that Manshi introduced Bashō to the *renga* master Nōjun and also that it was at this time that Bashō introduced to Hokushi his concept of *fueki ryūkō*, or "the unchanging and the changing." And sometime during all these goings on, before Sora set off for Ise, he and Bashō and Hokushi composed a linked-verse sequence, which was not finished when Sora left. The first verse contains the obligatory season word (swallows going south) and reflects the situation of the moment, but in subsequent verses there are images that must have resonated in personal ways: wildflowers blooming along a mountain path, a blue pool like Dōmyō Pool, and being caught in hail on the road.

1	On a borrowed horse,	*uma karite*
	with swallows seeing you off—	*tsubame oiyuku*
	we part ways.	*wakare kana*
	Hokushi	

2	A riot of wildflowers	*hanano midaruru*
	lines a curving mountain path.	*yama no magarime*
	Sora	

3	So fine a moon!	*tsuki yoshi to*
	Off go the trousers	*sumo ni hakama*
	for a sumo bout.	*fuminugite*
	Bashō	

4	A blade darts from its sheath—	*sayabashirishi o*
	then quickly goes back again.	*yagate tomekeri*
	Hokushi	

5	At a blue pool	*aobuchi ni*
	an otter takes a plunge.	*uso no tobikomu*
	The sound of water.	*mizu no oto*
	Sora	

6	Felling scrub wood he goes,	*shibakari kokasu*
	through bamboo grass on the peak.	*mine no sasamichi*
	Bashō	

1 *Autumn Travel.* Swallows heading south—an autumn season word—seem to be seeing Sora on his way. 2 *Autumn Travel.* Mountain path—horse, ways. The beauty of the wildflowers seems like a parting gift. 3 *Autumn.* Moon—mountain. At a village down a mountain path, men are enjoying sumo beneath a full moon. 4 *Miscellaneous.* Violence avoided? Contrasting conflicts: sumo and swordplay. 5 *Miscellaneous.* Sound—blade darting. A link partially based on motion: "darting" and "plunging." He must have had in mind Bashō's already famous *hokku* about a frog jumping into the waters of a pond (*furuike ya*, dating to spring 1683). 6 *Miscellaneous.* Path, bamboo grass—pool. Another forest scene: a recluse gathering wood, perhaps on his way to his hut on the peak.

Figures of Importance in the Texts

In general, *haikai* poets of any consequence appear under their *haikai* names, followed by formal names and common names (*tsūshō* 通称) and brief comments about their status, occupations, place of residence, and so forth. I have consulted numerous sources, including standard reference works, such as *Bashō zenkushū*, *Haikai daijiten*, *Haibungaku daijiten*, *Nihon koten bungaku daijiten*, *Sōgō Bashō Jiten*, *Rekishi daijiten*; the notes of the editions I have used in translating the travel records; and various studies by Abe Masami, Fukasawa Shinji, Horikiri Minoru, Kon Eizō, Kusumoto Mutsuo, Muramatsu Tomotsugu, Ogata Tsutomu, Satō Katsuaki, Shimasue Kiyoshi, Takahashi Shōji, Taketō Takema, Tanaka Yoshinobu, and Ueno Yōzō.

Buddhist Honorary Titles: Daishi 大師 ("great teacher"), Hijiri 聖 ("holy one"), Shōnin 上人 ("saint"), and Ajari 阿闍梨 ("holy teacher") are all high honorifics, usually used in reference to the most exalted Buddhist figures, although not always people with high office. Oshō 和尚 ("reverend") is an honorific that was typically used for head priests of temples. Zenji 禅師 is used for Zen masters.

***

Abutsu *see* Nun Abutsu

Ajiro Minbu 足代民部 (Nakatsu Hirokazu 中津弘員; 1659–1717); Sukenoshin 助之進 and Gondayū 権太夫. *Haikai* names: Setsudō 雪堂 and Korai 胡来. A tour guide (*oshi* 御師) at Ise shrine and *haikai* poet.

Amida (阿弥陀). The most prominent of Buddhist bodhisattva, especially in Pure Land Buddhism.

Archbishop Gyōson *see* Gyōson

Ariwara no Yukihira 在原行平 (818–93). Japanese courtier-poet of the early Heian era. Banished after failed coup.

Ashino Suketoshi 蘆野資俊 (also read Mototoshi; 1637–92); also referred to as Kohō 戸部. Lord of the Ashino Domain. Direct retainer (*hatamoto*) of the Tokugawa house with a stipend of about 3,000 *koku*. *Haikai* name: Tōsui 桃酔.

Asukai Masaaki 飛鳥井雅章 (1611–79). Heir of the Asukai poetic house, specialists in the sport of kickball and court poetry (*waka*).

Asukai Masatsune 飛鳥井雅経 (1170–1221). Founder of the Asukai branch of the Fujiwara house, which specialized in kickball and court poetry (*waka*).

Baba Kinkō 馬場錦江 (1801–60). Minamoto Masatō 源正統; Shōtarō 小太郎. Samurai poet and scholar.

Bai Juyi 白居易 (772–846). Chinese poet of the Tang dynasty.

Bashō (Matsuo Bashō 松尾芭蕉; 1644–94). Born in Iga Ueno, Akasakachō 赤坂町, to Matsuo Yozaemon 与左衛門. In childhood known as Kinsaku 近作 and later as Tadaemon Munefusa 忠右衛門宗房, the latter perhaps a name given by his samurai benefactors in the Tōdō house. After the death of his patron, Sengin, he also went by Jinshichirō 甚七郎 and Jinshirō 甚四郎. Decided to make a career as a *haikai* master and went to Edo, eventually becoming one of the chief poets of his day. *Haikai* names: first, Sōbō 宗房 (the Chinese reading of Munefusa); then Tōsei 桃青 or Bashō Tōsei 芭蕉桃青. He also occasionally used the pen name Fūrabō 風羅坊.

Benkei (Musashibō Benkei 武蔵坊弁慶; d. 1189?). Warrior monk in service to Minamoto no Yoshitsune.

Besshō 丿松 (d. 1716). Merchant in Kanazawa and *haikai* poet. Older brother of Bashō's disciple Isshō.

Biji (Takayama Biji 高山麋塒; 1649–1718); Den'emon Shigefumi 伝右衛門繁文. House elder in service to daimyo Akimoto Tajima Takatomo 秋元但馬喬朝 of Kai Province, who had important positions in the Tokugawa government. Biji served on assignment in Yamura, Edo, Kawagoe, and Yamagata. Met and became a disciple of Bashō in Edo when Akimoto was living in Fukagawa. When Bashō was burned out of his house in 1682, Biji hosted him in Yamura, Kai Province.

Bokudō (Tachibana Bokudō 立花牧童; d. after 1716); Togiya Kisaburō 研屋喜三郎. Older brother of Hokushi. Kanazawa disciple of Bashō.

Bokugen (Terashima Bokugen 寺島羨言; 1646–1736); Izaemon 伊右衛門. Friend of Chisoku in Narumi; father of Yasunobu. Proprietor of daimyo lodgings (*honjinshoku* 本陣職) for the Narumi post station.

Bokuhaku 木白 (later, Taiso 苔蘇; d. 1710); Okamoto Jiemon Masatsugu 岡本治右衛門正次. Samurai in service to Tōdō house in Iga Ueno.

Bokuin (Tani Bokuin 谷木因; 1646–1725); Kudayū 九太夫. Owner of shipping agency in Ōgaki with close ties to the Toda house, which provided him with a mansion near the Kuize River. *Haikai* master who studied *haikai* and classics under Kitamura Kigin; also active in Danrin circles and friend of the Danrin poet Ihara Saikaku. Met Bashō in 1681, when on assignment in Edo. Introduced Bashō to Tōyō and others. Retired from business in 1686, dedicating himself to poetry and scholarship.

Bokuseki (Ozawa Bokuseki 小沢朴尺; d. 1695); Tarōbei 太郎兵衛. Petty official in Ofunamachi, a district in Nihonbashi. One of Bashō's early supporters in Edo.

Bokutaku (Hinata Bokutaku 日向朴宅; 1647–58). A samurai of the Hisai Domain in Ise. Accompanied Bashō to Edo in 1672, introducing him to Sanpū.

Bonchō 凡兆 (d. 1714; early on known as Kashō or Kasei 加生). Known as Bonchō from around 1491. Physician under the name of Inshō 允昌. Wife was Ukō, also a *haikai* poet and disciple of Bashō. Involved in the compilation of *Sarumino*. Bashō often stayed with him when in Kyoto. Jailed for unknown reason in 1693–94.

Bōsui 望翠 (Katano Yoshihisa 片野良久; 1657–1705); Shinzō 新蔵. Merchant in Iga Ueno.

Boyi 伯夷 (precise dates unknown). Chinese hermit of the Zhou dynasty (c. 1122–249 BCE).

Buddha Gozaemon (Hotoke Gozaemon 仏五左衛門; precise dates unknown). Proprietor of inn at Nikkō. Sora identifies him as Gozaemon of Kamihatsuishi 上鉢石.

Bunchō (Akiyama Bunchō 秋山文鳥; d. 1743); Kage'emon Masaitsu 景右衛門昌逸. Third son of Keikō. Samurai of Ōgaki-han.

Butchō (Hirayama Butchō 平山仏頂; 1642–1715). Full Zen name, Butchō Kanan 仏頂河南. Zen priest, referred to by Bashō as Reverend (*oshō* 和尚). Born in Kashima; studied from age fifteen at Yōgakuji 養岳寺 (or 陽岳寺) in Fukagawa. Made abbot of the temple Konponji in Kashima in 1674. Lived at Kaizenji in Asakusa and then at Rinsen'an, a cottage in Fukagawa built for Konponji priests, from around 1674 to 1682; then he returned to Konponji, retired, and lived in Chōkōan, a cottage in Konponji's precincts. Also lived at Unganji, Shimotsuke Province. Bashō's Zen teacher and mentor.

Chen Wuyi 陳無已 (1053–1101); also Chen Shidao 陳師道. Chinese poet.

Chigetsu 智月 (precise dates unknown). Raised in Kyoto and did palace service in youth. Married warehouseman Kawai Saemon and lived in Ōtsu until her death in 1686, when she took tonsure. She became acquainted with Bashō about that time and was active as a *haikai* poet and patron.

Chikui 竹意 (precise dates unknown). *Haikai* poet in Kanazawa.

Chikujaku 竹雀 (precise dates unknown); Kameda Taketomi 亀田武富, Miyatakeya Kazaemon 宮竹屋嘉左衛門. Kanazawa innkeeper. Older brother of Shōshun.

Chinseki (Hamada Chinseki 浜田珍碩 or 珍夕; d. 1737?). Also known as Sharakudō 洒落堂 or simply Shadō. Personal physician to the Honda clan in Zeze Domain. Disciple of Shōhaku and later Bashō.

Chiri 千里 (1648–1716); Kasuya Jinshirō 粕屋甚四郎. Reference works often refer to his surname as Naemura, but that name is not mentioned in Edo period documents. From Takenouchi Village in the Nara area. Lived in the Asakusa district of Edo; accompanied Bashō on his trip of 1684–85 to Kansai (chronicled in *Bones Bleaching in the Fields*). Had a cottage in Takenouchi in later years.

Chisoku 知足 (1640–1704); Shimozato Yoshichika 下里吉親, Kanbei 勘兵衛, later Kin'emon 金右衛門; also Jinbei 甚兵衛. Metals merchant and later saké brewer and village headman (*shōya* 庄屋) in Narumi, Owari Province. Active in the Danrin school, later a disciple of Bashō. Tonsured 1683 with the name Jakushō 寂照.

Introduced to Bashō by Tōyō. Shop name: Chiyokura 千代倉. Wealthy connoisseur of the arts. His heir, Chōu 蝶羽 (1677–1741), also became a disciple of Bashō.

Chōsetsu 聴雪 (precise dates unknown). Nagoya merchant and proprietor of a shop named Minoya 美濃屋.

Chōsetsu 釣雪 (also known as Karaku 花洛; precise dates unknown); Ōhashi Ichizaemon 大橋市左衛門. A monk from Kyoto, associated with the Kanjūbō 観修坊. Evidently in Haguro at the time of Bashō's visit.

Chōshō *see* Kinoshita Chōshōshi

Chōtarō *see* Yoshiyuki

Dainichi Nyorai 大日如来 (Sanskrit Mahavairocana Tathagata). Literally, "Great Sun." The Supreme Cosmic Buddha.

Daisen (Suzuki Daisen 鈴木大舟; dates unknown); Yasōemon 弥惣右衛門. House elder in Toda clan with income of 1,000 *koku*.

Daiten 大顛 (1629–85). Head monk at Engakuji temple in Kamakura; later moved into seclusion at Jōinji in Hirugakojima on the Izu Peninsula. *Haikai* name: Genku 幻吁.

Daoshi 道世 (d. 683). A Chinese Buddhist scholar-monk.

Date Masamune 伊達政宗 (1567–1636). First daimyo of Sendai Domain.

Dōetsu (Honma Dōetsu 本間道悦; 1622–97); Yasaburō 弥三郎. *Haikai* names: Jijun 自準 and Shōkō 松江. Samurai of Ōgaki-han. Wounded in battle during the Shimabara rebellion, became a physician in Edo. Originally from Ōgaki but retired to Itako, Hitachi Province, in the 1680s.

Dōgen Zenji 道元禅師 (1200–1253). Founder of the Sōtō Zen sect and of Eiheiji temple in Fukui.

Dohō (Hattori Dohō 服部土芳; 1657–1730); Hanzaemon Yasuhide 半左衛門保英. Adopted into the Hattori house; served as a lancer in service to Tōdō-han. Childhood friend of Bashō. Spent many years away from home on assignment. Withdrew from worldly affairs in 1688 and dedicated himself to the literary life, becoming one of Bashō's staunchest followers. Never married. Owner of Minomushi Cottage 蓑虫庵 in Iga Ueno, where Bashō occasionally stayed. Author of *Sanzōshi* 三冊子 (1702), an important source for details of Bashō's life and poetics.

Dōsojin 道祖神. Name of a folk god believed to ward off disease and evil spirits on the road. Small shrines to the god, whose origins go back to ancient times in China and Japan, were found at various roadsides.

Du Fu 杜甫 (712–70). Chinese poet of the Tang dynasty.

Du Mu 杜牧 (804–52). Chinese poet of the Tang dynasty.

Egaku Ajari 会覚阿闍梨 (d. 1707); also known as Shōjaku 照寂. From Kyoto. Served as *bettō* (chief abbot) at the temple at Mount Haguro, representing the Tendai temple Tōeizan (also known as Kan'eiji) in Edo.

Emino Asakari 恵美朝獦. Government official of the Nara period. Third son of Fujiwara Nakamaro 藤原仲麻呂.

Emperor Antoku 安徳天皇 (1178–85). Child emperor who died in a sea battle at Dan no Ura, ending the Genpei Wars.

Emperor Chūai 仲哀天皇. Semi-legendary fourteenth emperor of Japan.

Emperor Go-Daigo 後醍醐天皇 (1288–1339). Sovereign who rebelled against the Ashikaga dynasty and set up a rival court, called the Southern Court (*nanchō*), fleeing into the mountains of Yoshino.

Emperor Junnin 淳仁天皇 (733–65).

Emperor Kameyama 亀山天皇 (1249–1305).

Emperor Kazan 花山天皇 (968–1008).

Emperor Keikō 景行天皇 (first century AD).

Emperor Shōmu 聖武天皇 (701–56).

Emperor Takakura 高倉天皇 (1161–81).

Emperor Toba 鳥羽天皇 (1103–56).

Emperor Xuanzong 玄宗 (685–762). Chinese emperor of the Tang dynasty.

Emperor Yao 堯 (c. 2333–2234 BCE). A leader associated with an idealized golden age of Chinese culture.

Empress Jingū 神功皇后 (d. 269?). Semi-legendary empress, consort of Emperor Chūai.

En no Ozuno 役小角. The eighth-century pioneer of Shūgendō. Also known as En no Gyōja 役行者.

En'an Fugyoku 淵庵不玉 (Itō Genjun 伊東玄順; d. 1697). Samurai of Shōnai Domain who became a physician in Sakata, with name En'an (also 潜庵), after studying in Kyoto. Disciple of Ōyodo Michikaze, later of Bashō; *haikai* master in his own right in Sakata.

Ennin 円仁 (794–864). Also known as Jikaku Daishi 慈覚大師. Archbishop of Enryakuji and head of the Tendai sect.

Ensui (Kubota Ensui 窪田猿雖; 1640–1704); Sōshichirō 惣七郎. Proprietor of Uchinokamiya 内神屋, a shop in Iga Ueno, and longtime friend of Bashō. It was in 1687 that a strong Bashō contingent formed in Iga Ueno, including Ensui, Dohō, and others. Took tonsure in 1689 at Honganji in Kyoto, with the name Isen 意専.

Etsujin (Ochi Etsujin 越智越人; 1656–1736); Jūzō 十蔵. Born in Hokuetsu; moved to Nagoya and worked for Yasui as a dyer, also an odd-job man. When Bashō's disciples in Owari took a different direction after his death, Etsujin didn't follow along. Evidently died in poverty.

Fayun Yuantong 法雲圓通 (1027–90). Chinese Chan (J. Zen) monk who constructed a hut on a rock and held daylong sermons there.

Fūbaku (Ogawa Fūbaku 小川風麦; d. 1700); Ogawa Jirōbei Masatō 小川次郎兵衛 政任. Samurai of Iga Ueno with a stipend of 200 *koku*. Became a disciple of Bashō in the late 1680s. *See also* Matsubaya Fūbaku.

Fuchin 斧鎮. A *haikai* poet in Nagoya.

Fudō Myō'ō 不動明王 (Skt. Acala). A protector deity associated with Uraminotaki.

Fugen Bosatsu 普賢菩薩 (Skt. Samantabhadra). One of the chief bodhisattva of the Mahayana Buddhist tradition, associated with devotion and proper actions.

Fujimura Izu 藤村伊豆 (precise dates unknown); Akishige 章重. *Haikai* name: Kosen 鼓蟾. Head priest of Motoori Hiyoshi Shrine in Komatsu.

Fujiwara Hidehira 藤原秀衡 (d. 1187). Head of the Northern Fujiwara house, a noble lineage that ruled northeast Honshū during the twelfth century from their capital at Hiraizumi. He gave shelter to Minamoto no Yoshitsune when the latter was being pursued by his brother, Minamoto no Yoritomo, first shogun of the Minamoto dynasty.

Fujiwara Kiyohira 藤原清衡 (1056–1128). Founder of branch of the Fujiwara clan and Chūsonji temple.

Fujiwara Middle Captain Sanekata 藤中将実方 (d. 998). Appointed provincial governor for Ōshū (the northern provinces of Rikuoku and Dewa) in 995. Legend is that he fell from his horse and died after passing Kasashima Dōsōjin because he failed to dismount and show respect.

Fujiwara Motohira 藤原基衡 (1105–57). Second leader of the Northern Fujiwara, father of Hidehira.

Fujiwara no Ietaka 藤原家隆 (1158–1237). Medieval Japanese courtier-poet.

Fujiwara no Kinzane 藤原公実 (1053–1107). Japanese courtier-poet.

Fujiwara no Kiyosuke 藤原清輔 (1104–77). Japanese poet; author of *Fukuro zōshi* (before 1159), a poetic treatise.

Fujiwara no Masatsune *see* Asukai Masatsune

Fujiwara no Shunzei 藤原俊成 (1114–1204). Medieval Japanese courtier-poet.

Fujiwara no Takayoshi 藤原孝義. Served as governor of Mutsu Province in ancient times.

Fujiwara no Teika 藤原定家 (1164–1241). Medieval Japanese courtier-poet.

Fujiwara no Yoshitsune 藤原良経 (1169–1206). Appointed regent in 1202 and held the office until his death in 1206. Major poet.

Fujiwara Tadahira 藤原忠衡 (1167–89). Third son of Fujiwara Hidehira. Also known as Izumi Saburō 和泉三郎. Stayed loyal to Minamoto no Yoshitsune and died with him.

Fujiwara Takako 藤原隆子 (precise dates unknown). Wife of Minamoto no Akifusa 源顕房.

Fujiwara Yasuhira 藤原泰衡 (1155–89). Heir of Hidehira and leader of Northern Fujiwara at Hiraizumi. He betrayed his promise to his father and at the command of Minamoto no Yoritomo attacked Minamoto no Yoshitsune, who killed himself. Yasuhira was later attacked by the forces of Yoritomo and killed.

Fumikuni (Nakamura Fumikuni 中村史邦; precise dates unknown); Araemon 荒右衛門. Later called Shun'an 春庵. Samurai physician to Terao Naokatsu at Inuyama in Owari Province. Served at the palace of the retired emperor in Kyoto as one of two administrators (*sentōtsuki yoriki* 仙洞付与力), with a stipend of 60 *koku*. Became a disciple of Bashō upon introduction by Kyorai in 1690. In 1692 retired and moved to Edo.

Fūrabō 風羅坊 ("Master Gauze in the Wind"). One of the literary names Bashō adopted in the last decade of his life. *See* Bashō

Fūryū 風流 (precise dates unknown); Shibuya Jinbei 渋谷甚兵. Rich merchant in Shinjō.

Gan Jiang 干将. Ancient Chinese swordsmith. Husband of Mo Ye.

Ganjin 鑑真 (C. Jianzhen; 688–763). Chinese monk who established Tōshōdaiji Temple in Nara.

Gaofeng Yuanmiao 高峰原妙 (1238–95). Chinese Chan (J. Zen) monk who for years retreated into a cave on Mount Tianmu in Zhejiang Province, naming his hut Death Gate.

Gensei 元政 (1623–68). A samurai of Hikone Domain near Kyoto; *waka* poet and Nichiren priest. Author of *Fusō in'itsuden* 扶桑隠逸伝 (1664), a collection of biographical sketches of famous Japanese recluses.

Gentan (Mukai Gentan 向井元端; 1649–1712). Older brother of Kyorai. A prominent specialist in Chinese medicine (practicing under the name Shinken 震軒), on retainer to the noble Ichijō house. Honored with the rank of *hōin*, "Seal of the Law." Sinologue respected by Bashō.

Gokyōgoku Yoshitsune *see* Fujiwara no Yoshitsune

Gōsai 迎西. Monk mentioned in the folktale collection *Senjūshō*.

Great Teacher Nōjo *see* Nōjo Daishi

Guangwen 広聞 (d. 1263). Chinese Zen monk.

Gyōki Bosatsu 行基菩薩 (668–749). Buddhist priest associated with Asukadera in Nara; legendary traveler, cartographer, humanitarian. Bosatsu is a term of praise, literally meaning "bodhisattva."

Gyōson 行尊 (1055–1135). Daisōjō 大僧正, or archbishop. Grandson of an imperial prince who became head priest of the Tendai sect, or Tendai Zasu. Known for doing mountain rigors in his youth.

Haga Isshō 芳賀一晶 (1643–1707). Kyoto *haikai* poet who moved to Edo in 1683 and became a disciple of Bashō.

Han Yu 韓愈 (768–824). Chinese scholar-poet.

Han'en Shōnin 範円上人. Priest. Son of Minamoto no Noriyori 範頼 (d. 1193?).

Hanzaemon 半左衛門 (Matsuo Norikiyo 松尾命清; d. 1701). Older brother of Bashō. Succeeded to head of house upon the death of his father in 1656. Owner of a house near the castle in Iga Ueno.

Hanzan (半残; 1654–1726); Yamagishi Jūzaemon 山岸重左衛門. Retainer of Tōdō house with stipend of 300 *koku*. Probably became a formal disciple of Bashō in 1689. His father and his son also became disciples. Along with Dohō, a leading figure in the Bashō school in Iga Ueno.

Hara Anteki 原安適 (precise dates unknown). Edo physician and *waka* poet; student of Yamamoto Shunshō 山本春正 and friend of Bashō.

Hashimoto Zen'emon 橋本善衛門 was a high-ranking samurai in service to the Sendai Domain.

Heian 平庵 (dates unkown). Retired samurai in Ise Yamada.

Hidehira *see* Fujiwara Hidehira

Higuchi no Jirō 樋口の次郎 (Higuchi Kanemitsu 樋口兼光; d. 1184). Samurai at the time of the Genpei Wars in service to Kiso Yoshinaka.

Hitachinobō Kaison 常陸坊海尊 (precise dates unknown). Samurai attendant of Minamoto no Yoshitsune.

Hōgetsu 抱月 (precise dates unknown). *Haikai* poet in Nagoya.

Hōjō Tokiyori 北条時頼 (1227–63). Fifth regent in the shogunal government in Kamakura in medieval times.

Hokushi (Tachibana Hokushi 立花北枝; d. 1718); Togiya Genshirō 研屋源四郎. Born in Komatsu, Kaga Province; lived in Kanazawa. Sword sharpener in service to the Kaga Domain. Active in the Danrin school. Became a disciple of Bashō in 1689 along with his older brother Bokudō 牧童. Lived at Gen'ian (源意庵 or 立意庵) at the foot of Utatsuyama in Kanazawa.

Huang Tingjian 黃庭堅 (1045–1105). Chinese scholar, poet, and painter. His personal collection is titled *Huang Shangu* 黃山谷.

Ichibu 一無. *Haikai* poet in Nagoya.

Ichiei (Takano Ichiei 高野一栄, which Bashō writes as 鷹野一英, dates unknown); Heiemon 平右衛門. Rich merchant operating a marine warehouse business (*funadoiya* 船問屋) in Ōishida; also a tax collector.

Ihara Saikaku 井原西鶴 (1642–93). *Haikai* poet in the Danrin school and writer of popular fictions.

Ihei (Muramatsu Ihei 村松猪兵衛; dates unknown). A relative of Bashō—probably a nephew—from the town of Kamo in Yamato Province, who lived in Edo and sometimes took care of the nun Jutei.

Ikoman Manshi 生駒万子 (1654–1719). High-ranking samurai of the Kaga Domain. Common name: Manpei Shigenobu 万兵衛重信. Became a disciple of Bashō in 1689.

Ikkyū Sōjun 一休宗純 (1394–1481). Famous Zen monk and iconoclast.

Ippen Shōnin 一遍上人 (1230–89). Founder of the Time sect (*jishū*) of Buddhism.

Ishimaru Kentō 石村見桃 (precise dates unknown). The employer of Bashō's nephew Tōin in Edo.

Isshō (Kosugi Isshō 小杉一笑; 1653–88); Chaya Shinshichi 茶屋新七. Proprietor of a teahouse in Kanazawa. Disciple of Kigin and later Bashō.

Isshō (Yasukawa Isshō 保川一笑; precise dates unknown); Kamiya Yaemon 紙屋弥右衛門. Old friend of Bashō and poet from Iga Ueno who later lived in Naniwa. Paper merchant in Iga Ueno whom Bashō had known since at least 1664.

Isui 依水 (precise dates unknown). An Edo disciple of Bashō.

Izumi Saburō *see* Fujiwara Tadahira

Izumiya Shin'emon 和泉屋新右衛門 (precise dates unknown). Village headman in the area around Shitomae Barrier.

Jakushō *see* Chisoku

Jia Dao 賈島 (779–843). Chinese poet of the Tang dynasty.

Jian Zhai 簡斎 (1090–1139). Chinese poet. More properly known as Zhen Yuyi 陣与義.

Jianzhen *see* Ganjin

Jijun (Konishi Jijun 小西自準; alternatively, Jishun 似春; 1661–1704); Heizaemon 平左衛門. Disciple of Kitamura Kigin, Sōin, and later a friend to Bashō; *haikai* master in his own right. Originally from Kyoto, moving to Edo in the mid-1670s and to Gyōtoku in Shimōsa Province in 1682.

Jikaku *see* Ennin

Jikaku Daishi *see* Ennin

Jirōbei (次郎兵衛 or 二郎兵衛; precise dates unknown). Son of Jutei who was living with Bashō in Fukagawa in 1693, when he was perhaps sixteen or so; accompanied Bashō on his last journey west in 1694. Some scholars argue that he was Bashō's son by Jutei.

Jishō (Okajima Jishō 岡島自笑; d. 1713); Sasuke 佐助. A swordsmith and *haikai* poet in Narumi.

Jōbōji Zusho 浄坊寺 (or 浄法寺) 図書 (1661–1730); Kanokohata Takakatsu 鹿子畑高勝. *Haikai* names: Tōsetsu 桃雪 and Shūa 秋鴉. Son of Kanokohata Takaaki 高明; older brother of Toyoaki 豊明. House elder and deputy (*kandai* 菅代) in the Ōzeki clan of Kurobane Domain, with a stipend of 500 *koku*. Heir of the Jōbōji family, his mother's lineage. Became a disciple of Bashō in 1675. Father spent twelve years in Edo, where he and two sons became disciples.

Jokō (Kondō Jokō; 近藤如行; d. 1708?); Gendayū 源太夫. Samurai of the Toda clan in Ōgaki-han. Took tonsure before 1685, making a modest living as a *haikai* marker. Introduced to Bashō by Tōyō that same year. Hosted Bashō in his house at the conclusion of the journey of 1689. Dedicated to Bashō all his life and held memorial poetry gatherings in his honor.

Jokushi 濁子 (Nakagawa Morio 中川守雄; precise dates unknown); Jingobei 甚五兵衛. Samurai retainer of Toda-han with a stipend of 200 *koku*, later 1000 *koku*. Poet, painter, calligrapher; disciple of Bokuin. Met Bashō in Edo when in domain service there. Primary entrée into Ōgaki-han for Bashō. In Edo, Jokushi, Keikō, and Tōzan all became Bashō's disciples. Probably one of Bashō's patrons, along with Sanpū.

Jōshibō 丈芝坊; precise dates unknown. Bashō's disciple in Sendai.

Jōsō 丈草 (Naitō Mototsune 内藤本常; 1662–1704); Rin'emon 林右衛門. Originally a samurai in service to the Terao house in Inuyama; later, a *rōnin* in Ōtsu. Studied Zen from his mid-twenties; took tonsure in 1688 because of illness. Became a disciple of Bashō in 1689 at Rakushisha. Moved to Fukakusa and in 1693 went into Mumyōan at Gichūji. Died of illness in his early forties.

Josui 如水 (Toda Toshitane 戸田利胤; d. 1690); Gondayū 権太夫. House elder in the Toda clan, Ōgaki-han, with a stipend of 3,000 *koku*.

Jūgo 重五 (Katō Jūgo 加藤重五; 1654–1717); Zen'emon 善右衛門. A Nagoya merchant, friend of Etsujin and Yasui. Participant in the 1684 sequences that make up the anthology *Fuyu no hi* but beyond that not an important figure.

Jumyō 珠妙. Priest associated with the daimyo of Morioka Castle.

Jutei 寿貞 (d. 1694). Close to Bashō since his early days; perhaps once a common-law wife, probably the wife of his nephew Tōin. She had three children, probably none of them Bashō's: a son named Jirōbei and two daughters, Masa and Ofū. She and her two daughters moved into Bashō's house in Fukagawa after he departed for what would be his last trip in the summer of 1694, and she died there early in the Sixth Month.

Kaemon 加右衛門 (actually, 嘉右衛門; precise dates unknown). Proprietor of Kitanoya 北野屋 in Sendai, a woodblock carver. *Haikai* name: Wafūken Kashi 和風軒加之. Disciple of Ōyodo Michikaze.

Kaibara Ekiken 貝原益軒 (1630–1714). Famous scholar and educator.

Kakei (Yamamoto Kakei 山本荷兮; 1648–1716); Yamamoto Buemon Hirotomo 山本武右衛門周知; Ta'ichi 太一 or 太市. Physician; poet writing in both *renga* and *haikai*; resident first of Nagoya and later Kuwana. Initially a Teimon poet who became a disciple of Bashō in 1685, probably upon introduction by Bokuin or Tōyō. Opposed to Bashō's new style, while remaining on social terms with Bashō. After Bashō's death, ostracized; became *renga* master under the name Shōtatsu 昌達.

Kakinomoto no Hitomaro 柿本人麻呂 (fl. c. 680–700). Famous ancient Japanese poet and traveler.

Kamo no Chōmei 鴨長明 (1153–1216). Author of *Mumyōshō* and *Hōjōki*; prominent medieval poet and recluse. In Bashō's time believed to be author of the medieval travel record *Tōkan kikō*.

Kanefusa 兼房 (d. 1189). Retainer of one of Minamoto no Yoshitsune's women. After dispatching the woman, he died in the flames of the burning residence.

Kanokohata Takakatsu *see* Jōbōji Zusho

Kanō Tsunenobu 狩野常信 (1636–1713). Head of the Kanō lineage of painters, retained by Tokugawa shogunate.

Kansei (Tsutsumi Kansei 堤歓生; not Kansui 歓生, as Sora records it; also known as Kyōshi 亭子; precise dates unknown); Echizenya Shichirōemon 越前屋七郎右衛門. Rich merchant close to the Maeda house, daimyo of Komatsu. A disciple of the *renga* master Nōjun who was also active in *haikai* circles.

Kashō 何処 (d. 1731). A disciple. Traveling merchant of herbal medicines based in Osaka.

Ke Shi 可士. Chinese poet.

Keikō (Miyazaki Keikō 宮崎荊口; d. 1725); also known as Keihō 佳豊; Tazaemon 太左衛門. Samurai in service to the Toda house in Ōgaki-han, with a stipend of 100 *koku*. Student of Bokuin. Got to know Bashō when in service in Edo. He and his sons, Shikin 此筋 (1673–1735), Sensen 千川 (d. 1706), and Bunchō 文鳥 (d. 1743), became disciples in 1684.

Kenbutsu Hijiri 見仏聖 (or Kenbutsu Shōnin 見仏上人). A monk of the 1100s who spent twelve years in a hut at Matsushima (somewhere in the area of Ojima), reciting the *Lotus Sutra* sixty thousand times.

Kenkō 兼好 (1283?–after 1252). Medieval Japanese monk-poet; author of *Tsurezuregusa*.

Kenreimon'in 建礼門院 (Taira no Tokuko 平徳子; 1155–1213). The daughter of Taira no Kiyomori and mother of Emperor Antoku. When her son died a few years later in the sea battle at Dan no Ura, carried into the sea by his grandmother, Tokuko also jumped into the seas but was fished out and survived. Her entry into a retreat in Ōhara, a narrow valley just northeast of Kyoto, is the last sad story in *Tales of the Heike*, already a very sad tale.

Ki no Tsurayuki 紀貫之 (d. 945?). Prominent court poet and author of the first Japanese travel record, *Tosa nikki* (*Tosa Diary*) of the mid-tenth century.

Kifū 枳風 (precise dates unknown). Edo disciple. Appears to have been tonsured. Involved in arranging for the third Bashōan.

Kigin (Kitamura Kigin 北村季吟; 1624–1705). Common name, Kyūsuke 久助. Poet in all the major forms—*uta*, *renga*, and *haikai*; important scholar. Teacher of Bashō's samurai masters and of Bashō in his youth.

Kihaku 己百 (1643–98). Head priest at Myōshōji 妙照寺, a Nichiren-sect temple in Gifu.

Kikaku (Enoshita or Enomoto Kikaku 榎本其角; later, Takarai 宝井 Kikaku; 1661–1707). Physician under the name Juntetsu 順哲 in Nihonbashi. Became Bashō's disciple at about fourteen or fifteen. In 1686 became an independent *haikai* master. Among Bashō's first disciples. His father, Takeshita Tōjun 竹下東順 (1622–93), was samurai physician to the Honda clan of Zeze Domain, but serving in Edo.

Kinkō (Baba Kinkō 馬場錦江; 1801–60); Kotarō 小太郎. Samurai scholar-poet of the late Edo period.

Kinoshita Chōshōshi 木下長嘯子 (1569–1649). Former daimyo who became a recluse-poet.

Kiso Yoshinaka 木曽義仲 (1154–84). Famed Minamoto warrior.

Kiyowara no Motosuke 清原元輔 (908–90). Court poet.

Kohō *see* Ashino Suketoshi

Kōda Rohan 幸田露伴 (1867–1947). Prominent novelist and scholar.

Koeki *see* Takue

Kon no Kahei 金の嘉兵衛 (mistakenly identified as Imano Kahei 今野加兵衛 by Sora; precise dates unknown). *Haikai* name: Gyokuhō 玉芳. From a wealthy merchant house in Sakata.

Konohanasakuyabime 木の花さくや姫. Legendary cherry-blossom princess. Consort of Ninigi no Mikoto.

Koreyasu 惟廉 (1264–1326). An imperial prince who served as seventh of the Kamakura shoguns.

Kosai ㋑斎 (d. 1688); Ogawa Tokuemon 小川徳右衛門. Edo disciple.

Kosen *see* Fujimura Izu

Koshun (Kitamura Koshun 北村湖春; 1650–97). Son of Kitamura Kigin; scholar and poet.

Kōtan (Wakahara Kōtan 若原叩端; precise dates unknown); Sukezaemon 助左衛門. *Haikai* poet in Atsuta. Nephew of Tōyō.

Kōzan 工山 (precise dates unknown). *Haikai* poet in Atsuta; associated with Tōyō.

Kūkai 空海 (774–835). Also known as Kōbō Daishi 弘法大師. Founder of the Shingon sect of Buddhism.

Kumagae Naozane 熊谷直実 (1141–1207). Warrior who figures in a well-known episode of *Tales of the Heike*.

Kumenosuke 久米之助 (1676–1751); Jinzaemon 甚座左衛門. Son of Izumiya Matabei Toyotsure 和泉屋又兵衛豊連 (d. 1673). Proprietor of Izumiya bathhouse at Yamanaka Onsen in Kaga, assisted by his uncle, Jishō 自笑. Just fourteen years old when Bashō visited. *Haikai* name: Tōyō 桃夭 (or 桃妖).

Kūya 空也 (903–72); Kūya Shōnin. Founder of the Pure Land sect of Buddhism.

Kyohaku (Kusakabe Kyohaku 草壁挙白; d. 1696). Edo merchant, disciple from the early 1680s.

Kyōkei *see* Shōkei

Kyokusui (Suganuma Kyokusui 菅沼曲翠; d. 1717); Suganuma Geki 菅沼外記, Suganuma Sadatsune 菅沼定常. Prominent samurai in service to the Honda house in Zeze Domain, Ōmi Province, with a stipend of 100 *koku*. He was one of Bashō's benefactors and arranged for Bashō's stay at Genjūan.

Kyorai (Mukai Kyorai 向井去来; 1651–1704); Heijirō 平治郎. Samurai physician born in Nagasaki. Trained for samurai service but came to Kyoto and worked as an assistant to his older brother, Gentan. Met Kikaku in Kyoto in 1685 and began corresponding with Bashō, becoming a disciple formally in 1687 when he visited Edo. Never *tenja*. Considered a chief disciple in Kyoto and west. Hosted Bashō at his villa, Rakushisha, and in Kyoto.

Kyoriku (Morikawa Kyoriku 森川許六; 1656–1715); Gosuke 五介. Samurai in service to the Hikone Domain, Ōmi. Bashō's disciple and painting teacher.

Kyūzaemon 久左衛門 (precise dates unknown). The proprietor of an inn in Hachikenya 八軒屋, a town in the Yodo area, between Kyoto and Osaka.

Kyūzei 救済 (d. 1378). *Renga* master.

Lady Kogō 小督 (precise dates unknown). A concubine of Emperor Takakura (1161–81) who was forced by Taira no Kiyomori (1118–81) into retirement in Saga. Her grave marker stands near the north end of Togetsu Bridge in Arashiyama.

Lady Tamamo 玉藻. Figure from medieval folktales associated with Sesshōseki, "Killer Rock." A legend tells of one Lady Tamamo, a shape-shifter who took the form of a beautiful woman and seduced Emperor Toba. When her deception became known, she fled to Nasu Moor and was killed by an arrow, at which point she turned into the Killer Rock.

Lay Monk Nōin *see* Nōin

Li Bai 李白 (701–62). Chinese poet of the Tang dynasty.

Li Dong 李洞 (ninth century). Chinese poet of the Tang dynasty.

Li Han 李瀚 (mid-eighth century). Author of *Mengqiu* 蒙求.

Li He 李賀 (791–817). Chinese poet of the Tang dynasty.

Lin Hejing 林和靖 (Lin Bu 林逋; 967–1028). Song dynasty poet who, disenchanted with service in a corrupt regime, withdrew to the mountains in Hangshou with a crane as his child and plum blossoms as his wife. He spent forty years at Gu Shan (Gu Mountain).

Linji Yixuan 臨濟義玄 (d. 866). Chinese Zen priest; founder of the Rinzai sect. *Linji Lu* 臨濟録 (J. *Rinzairoku*) is a collection of his *kōan* (meditation exercises).

Lord Emino Asakari *see* Emino Asakari

Lord Regent *see* Fujiwara no Yoshitsune

Maiden of Toyooka 豊岡姫. The food goddess.

Makabe no Heishirō 真壁の平四郎 (d. 1189?). Buddhist name, Hōshin 法身 (or 法心). Head priest of Zuiganji.

Mangikumaru *see* Tokoku.

Masafusa *see* Shōbō

Masahide 正秀 (1657–1723); Mizuta Magoemon 水田孫右衛門. A merchant in Zeze. First a disciple of Shōhaku and later Bashō. Built Mumyōan cottage for Bashō.

Masumitsu (Nakatsu Masumitsu 中津益光; precise dates unknown); Nakatsu Chōzaemon 中津長左衛門. A travel agent and shrine guide (*oshi* 御師) in Ise Yamada.

Masuo Kanefusa *see* Kanefusa

Matsubaya Fūbaku 松葉屋風瀑 (d. 1707). An *oshi* in Ise Yamada/Ise Watarai. Also spent time in Edo, at the Iseya, an agency for pilgrims traveling to Ise. Studied under Haga Isshō. Bashō had written a farewell verse for the man when he left Edo for a visit to Ise in the Sixth Month of 1684.

Matsue *see* Dōetsu

Matsunaga Teitoku *see* Teitoku

Matsuo Bashō *see* Bashō

Matsuo Hanzaemon *see* Hanzaemon

Matsuo Yozaemon 松尾与左衛門 (d. 1656). Father of Bashō. Lived first in Tsuge 拓植, a village about nine miles southwest of Iga Ueno, but moved to Akasakachō 赤坂町 in Ueno to establish his own branch of the Matsuo lineage, probably before Bashō was born.

Michikaze (Ōyodo Michikaze 大淀三千風; d. 1707). A merchant of Izawa in Ise. At about thirty, became teacher of the Danrin school and spent about fifteen years in Sendai; also an important figure in places along the Japan Sea such as Kanazawa.

Minamoto no Nakakuni 源仲国 (precise dates unknown). In service to Emperor Takakura.

Minamoto no Sanetomo 源実朝 (1192–1219). Third Kamakura shogun; poet.

Minamoto no Shunrai 源俊頼 (1055–1129). Court poet.

Minamoto no Tōru 源融 (822–95). Heian-era courtier and poet.

Minamoto no Yorimasa 源頼政 (1104–80). Court poet and warrior who was obliged to commit suicide after losing in a conflict with the Heike.

Minamoto no Yoritomo 源頼朝 (1147–97). First Kamakura shogun.

Minamoto no Yoshitomo 源義朝 (1123–60). Father of Yoshitsune. After killing both his father and his younger brothers for political reasons, he fled but was assassinated for his involvement in the Heiji Disturbance of 1159.

Minamoto no Yoshitsune 源義経 (1159–89). Son of Yoshitomo and brother of Yoritomo. Died at Hiraizumi.

Mitsui Shūfū 三井秋風 (Mitsui Toshitora 三井俊寅; 1646–1717); Rokuemon 六右衛門. Rich connoisseur and amateur *haikai* poet. The Mitsui were a merchant family who ran one of the most prosperous stores of the time. Had a villa in the Narutaki area, near Rengeji Temple.

Mo Jie 摩詰 (699–759). More commonly known as Wang Wei 王維. Chinese poet and painter.

Mo Ye 莫耶 (precise dates unknown). Ancient Chinese swordsmith. Wife of Gan Jiang.

Moritake (Arikada Moritake 荒木田守武; 1473–1549). *Renga* master and early *haikai* poet.

Motohira *see* Fujiwara Motohira

Musashino Benkei *see* Benkei

Muso Sōseki 夢窓疎石 (1275–1351). Zen monk of the Rinzai sect, founder of Rinsenji in Saga.

Nagayama Shigeyuki 長山重行 (Shigeyuki also read Jūkō; precise dates unknown); Gorōaemon 五郎右衛門. A samurai of the Shōnai Domain, living in Tsurugaoka, with a stipend of 100 *koku*. A relation of Zushi Sakichi.

Nakakuni *see* Minamoto no Nakakuni

Nakatsu Hirokazu *see* Ajiro Minbu

Nakatsu Masumitsu *see* Masumitsu

Nasu no Yoichi 那須与一 (d. 1232?); Nasu no Yoichi Munetaka 那須与一宗高. A samurai on the Minamoto side during the Genpei Wars.

Ninkō Shōnin 任口上人 (also read Ninku; 1606–86). Head priest at Saiganji 西岸寺 in Fushimi, a branch temple of Chion'in, a great Kyoto temple of the Pure Land sect. Priestly name: Hōyo 宝誉. *Haikai* poet of the Danrin school; *renga* poet using the name Nyoyō 如羊.

Nōin 能因 (Tachibana no Nagayasu 橘永愷; b. 988). Late Heian poet, famous as a traveler.

Nōjo Daishi 能除大師 (correctly, 太子; d. 626). Prince Hachi 蜂子皇子, son of Emperor Sushun 崇俊 (553–92). Fled political conflict in the capital in the 580s and ended up in Dewa.

Nōjun 能順 (1628–1706). *Renga* poet; steward of the *renga* office at Kitano Tenjin Shrine in Kyoto and later director of the Komatsu Tenman Shrine in Komatsu.

The Nun Abutsu 阿仏尼 (d. 1283?). Court lady and wife of the famous poet Fujiwara no Tameie (1198–1275). Author of *Izayoi nikki* (Diary of the Sixteenth Night Moon, 1279–80).

The Nun of the Second Rank *see* Taira no Tokiko

Ōe no Asatsuna 大江朝綱 (886–957). Poet and scholar.

Ōnakatomi Yoshinobu 大中臣能宣 (921–91). Court official at Ise Shrine and important court poet.

Ōno Azumahito 大野東人 (d. 742). Imperial general who led campaigns against the *emishi*, a name given to eastern peoples who resisted the authority of the imperial government, into the late 730s.

Ono no Takamura 小野篁 (d. 852). Early Heian-era *waka* poet.

Otokuni (Kawai Otokuni 河合乙州; precise dates uncertain); Jirōnosuke 次郎助, Matashichi 又七. Probably son of Kawai Saemon, who was also father of Bashō's disciple Chigetsu. Merchant and warehouseman in Ōtsu. Entered the Kawai house as an adoptive child (*yōshi*), succeeded in 1686. Influential in Kanazawa *haikai*, where business often took him. Younger brother of Chigetsu and took over business from his brother-in-law (her husband) who died. One of the poet's benefactors.

Ōtomo no Yakamochi 大伴家持 (d. 785). Court official and poet, compiler of *Man'yōshū* (c. 759).

Prince Koreyasu *see* Koreyasu

Prince Yamatodake や ま と だ け. Son of Emperor Keikō and legendary military leader.

Qí Huangong 齊宣公 (precise dates unknown). King during the Spring and Autumn Period (771–476 BC) in Chinese history.

Qin Shaoyou 秦少游 (1049–c. 1100). More commonly known as Qin Guan 秦觀. Chinese poet of the Song dynasty.

Qu Quezi 瞿鵲子. Character in a story in *Zhuangzi*.

Rakugo (Yasukawa Rakugo 安川落梧; d. 1691); Suke'emon 助右衛門. A Gifu sundries merchant whose shop was named Yorozuya; also a calligrapher. Became a disciple of Bashō in 1684.

Ranchō (Kasai Ranchō 葛西嵐朝; precise dates unknown). Samurai of Ise Yamada. Disciple of Ransetsu. In Edo in the 1680s; later in Ise.

Ransetsu (Hattori Ransetsu 服部嵐雪; 1654–1707). As a youth, known as Kume-nosuke 久米之助; later, Magonosuke 孫之丞; still later, Hikobei 彦兵右衛 and Shinzaemon 新左衛門. As a *haikai* poet, also known as Rantei Harusuke 嵐亭治助. Father was a samurai from Awaji, but Ransetsu was born in Edo, Yujima. Samurai in youth. Became Bashō's disciple in 1675 and an independent *haikai* master in 1685. Strong supporter of Bashō and *karumi*.

Reizan 冷山 (d. 1674). Abbot at Konponji in Kashima before Butchō.

Rennyō Shōnin 蓮如上人 (1415–1499). Priest of the Jōdo Shinshū (Pure Land) sect. Abbot of Honganji.

Reverend Butchō *see* Butchō

Reverend Daiten *see* Daiten

Reverend Ganjin *see* Ganjin

Reverend Prince Shukaku 守覚法親王 (1150–1202). Son of Emperor Go-Shirakawa and major poet and patron of poets.

Rigyū (Ikeda Rigyū 池田利牛; fl. 1693–1708). Disciple of Bashō and contemporary of Yaba.

Rika 李下 (precise dates unknown). Edo disciple. Gave Bashō the *bashō*, or "plantain plant," that became his name. With Sanpū, assisted in rebuilding the Bashōan in 1692.

Risui 梨水 (precise dates unknown). *Haikai* poet in the Haguro area.

Riyū (Kōno Riyū 河野李由; 1661–1705). Head priest of Menshōji; close friend of Kyoriku. When Kyoriku became ill, he became leader of *haikai* circles in Hikone and continued so after Kyoriku's death.

Roboku 盧牧 (precise dates unknown). A recluse living in Ise.

Rochō 魯町 (1656–1727); Mukai Gensei 向井元成; Shōgenta 小源太. Samurai physician; Kyorai's younger brother.

Roku 六 (precise dates unknown). A servant that accompanied Bashō and Tokoku on their journey through Yoshino, on to the coast at Akashi, and on to Nara.

Rosen (Sawa Rosen 沢露川; 1661–1743); Ichirōemon 市郎右衛門. Native of Iga Province. Adopted into a merchant house in Nagoya. Student of Kigin and then Kakei; became a disciple of Bashō about 1691.

Rosenkō 露沾公 (1655–1733); Naitō Yoshihide 内藤義英. Second son of daimyo Naitō Yoshiyasu 義泰 of the Iwakidaira Domain. Born in Edo. Withdrew from worldly affairs in 1682 and dedicated himself to the literati life.

Rotsū (Inbe Rotsū 斎部路通, also written 露通 or 呂通; 1649–1738); Yajiemon 与次右衛門. Of the Yasomura 八十村 clan. Origins uncertain but seems to have been born in Mino; lived in Kyoto in his youth. Took the tonsure, living as a mendicant, studying at various places and giving lectures on classics such as *Tsurezuregusa*. In Edo about 1688–89. Probably became disciple around 1685. Accompanied Bashō to Ise, Iga Ueno, and Nara in 1690. Later, was ostracized by disciples and fell out with Bashō. Talented but willful and unstable.

Ryōbon *see* Tomoda Ryōbon

Ryūno Shōsha 竜野尚舎 (also read Tatsuno; d. 1693); Ryūno Hirochika 熙近; Den'emon 伝右衛門. Scholar of national studies at Ise Shrine.

Saigyō 西行 (1118–90). Japanese priest-poet of the late Heian era. Known as a traveler.

Saint Kūkai *see* Kūkai

Saitō Issen 斎藤一泉 (or Takayama Issen 高山一泉; precise dates unknown). Also known as Shōgen'an 松玄庵 (Bashō's 少玄庵 is a mistake), the name of his cottage close to the Sai River in Kanazawa. Retired samurai.

Saitō Sanemori 斎藤実盛 (1129–1183). Samurai in service to Taira no Munemori (d. 1183). Famous for dyeing his white hair black before going into battle. Subject of a famous Noh play.

Sakichi *see* Zushi Sakichi

Sakugen (Sakugen Shūryō 策彦周良; 1501–1579). A man of samurai origins who became a priest of the Rinzai Zen sect and had a career as a cleric, diplomat, and scholar. He traveled to China as an official envoy of the Ashikaga shogunate.

Sanekata (Fujiwara Sanekata 藤原実方; d. 998). Heian-era courtier-poet.

Sanpū (Sugiyama Sanpū 杉山杉風; 1647–1732); Ichibei 市兵衛. Pen name: Saitōan 採茶庵, which was also the name of his villa (別墅採茶庵) in Fukagawa. Contract provider of fish for the Tokugawa government. His business was named Koiya 鯉屋, located in Odawarachō, Nihonbashi District, Edo. Danrin poet who in the late 1670s became the first of Bashō's disciples, and a lifelong patron.

Satō Shōji 佐藤庄司 (precise dates unknown); Satō Motoharu 元治. Vassal of Fujiwara Hidehira at Hiraizumi.

Satō Tadanobu 佐藤忠信 (d. 1186). Son of Satō Motoharu. Samurai in service to Minamoto no Yoshitsune, who assisted him in escaping to the north country, but was found out while in hiding in Kyoto and committed suicide.

Satō Tsugunobu 佐藤継信 (d. 1184). Son of Satō Motoharu. Samurai in service to Minamoto no Yoshitsune who died defending him at the battle of Yashima.

Sei Shōnagon 清少納言. Heian lady-in-waiting in service to Empress Teishi (977–1000). Author of *Makura no sōshi* (*The Pillow Book*).

Seia 清亜 (or 清鴉; d. 1687). Priest in Ōtsu. Perhaps a disciple of Shōhaku; became a disciple of Bashō in 1685.

Seifū (Suzuki Seifū 鈴木清風; 1651–1721); Michisuke 道祐, Shimadaya Yaemon 島田屋八右衛門. Merchant based in Obanezawa who also maintained a residence in the Koishikawa district of Edo, where he met Bashō. Traditionally associated with rouge dye (*beni* 紅), but apparently involved more broadly in shipping and finance in Obanezawa, Dewa Province. Student of Shintoku and other Danrin poets of Kyoto and considered a master himself.

Sekidō (Hasegawa Sekidō 長谷川夕道; d. 1723); Magosuke 孫助. Proprietor of Shorin Fūgetsudō 書林風月堂, a Nagoya bookseller.

Sen no Rikyū 千利休 (1522–91). Tea master.

Sengin 蟬吟 (Tōdō Shinshichirō Yoshitada 藤堂新七郎良忠; 1642–66). Munemasa 宗正 (also read Sōsei) was another of his pen names. Son of Tōdō Yoshikiyo 良精 (d. 1674) and heir of the Shinshichirō lineage of the Tōdō Domain, residing in Iga Ueno, a castle town where Bashō was born and raised. Served as attendant to a warlord who was heir apparent to offices just under the acting lord of the castle. Disciple of Kitamura Kigin. Bashō did castle service as a young man, as a personal attendant of Sengin.

Senka 仙化 (precise dates unknown). Edo disciple. Close to Kikaku.

Senna (Mikami Senna 三上千那; 1651–1723). Head priest (法橋権律師) at Honpukuji 本福寺, a Shinshū-sect temple in Katada, Ōmi Province. Studied *haikai* under Takamasa and Shōhaku; Danrin poet who became a disciple of Bashō in 1685 but distanced himself soon after.

Sensen (Okada Sensen 岡田千川; d. 1706). Second son of Keikō. Adopted as heir of the Okada house in Ōgaki. Common name: Jizaemon 治左衛門.

Sensui 川水 (Takakuwa Kasuke 高桑加助; d. 1700); also known as Kinzō 金蔵. Village elder (庄屋) in Ōishida.

Sesshū 雪舟 (1420–1506). Zen monk and ink-wash style painter.

Shikin (Miyazaki Shikin 宮崎此筋; 1673–1735); Tazaemon 太左衛門. Oldest son of Keikō.

Shikō (Kagami Shikō 各務支考; 1665–1731). Born in Kitano, Mino Province, into the Murase 村瀬 house. Entered temple at age nine but returned to lay life at nineteen, although staying tonsured; studied Chinese classics in Kyoto. Became a disciple of Bashō in 1690, in Ōmi; lived with Bashō in Fukagawa for a time. Traveled extensively. Later moved to Ise Yamada.

Shintoku (Itō Shintoku 伊藤信徳; d. 1698); Sukezaemon 助左衛門. Kyoto *haikai* master associated with the Danrin school; friend of Bashō.

Shirin 翅輪 (precise dates unknown). Probably of the Tsukue 津久江 clan. Guided Bashō to the Nasu Kanamaru Hachiman Shrine and may have been a priest there.

Shōbō 昌房 (Kobayashi Masafusa 小林昌房 or Isoda Masafusa 磯田昌房; d. after 1729); Yojibei 与次兵衛. Had a tea shop named Chaya 茶屋 in Zeze, Ōmi Province.

Shōdō 勝道 (735–817). Founder of temples and shrines at Nikkō.

Shōhaku (Kōsa or Esa Shōhaku 江左尚白; 1650–1722); family name Shiokawa 塩川. Physician in Ōtsu. Student of Fuboku; became Bashō's disciple in 1685 but later fell away.

Shōheki 昌碧 (precise dates unknown). *Haikai* poet of Nagoya.

Shōkei 昌圭; Kyōkei 鏡鶏 (precise dates unknown). A Nagoya poet. Probably a *renga* master. Evidently a friend of Bashō's disciple Kakei.

Shōkū Shōnin 証空上人 (1177–1247). Also known as Seizan Shōnin 西山上人. Leader of the Pure Land sect.

Shōsai 笑哉 (precise dates unknown); Tawaraya Rokurōbei たわらや六良兵衛. Proprietor of an inn in Hatsusaki.

Shōshun 小春 (Kameda Katsutoyo 亀田勝豊; 1667–1740); Iemon 伊右衛門. Younger brother of Chikujaku. Kanazawa merchant and inn proprietor.

Shōya 笑也 (precise dates unknown); Ichikawa Ten'ya Yasōbei 市川天屋弥惣兵衛. Rich merchant and *haikai* poet in Kashiwazaki. Disciple of Kitamura Kigin.

Shōzaemon 庄左衛門 (precise dates unknown). Village head in Toima.

Shunjō Shōnin *see* Shunjōbō Chōgen

Shunjōbō Chōgen 俊乗坊重源 (1121–1206). Known primarily for his dedication to rebuilding of the Tōdaiji temple in Nara after it was destroyed during the Genpei Wars. He was honored with the title Shunjō Shōnin.

Sodō (Yamaguchi Sodō 山口素堂; 1642–1716); Yamaguchi Nobuakira 山口信章; Jinbei 甚兵衛. From Yamaguchi in Kai Province. Wealthy family of saké brewers. At twenty turned over house to his younger brother and went to Edo to study Chinese classics. Also studied *waka* in Kyoto. Friend of Bashō from the 1670s. Took the name Sodō about the same time as Bashō moved to Fukagawa. Lived at Shinobazu Pond.

Sōgi (1421–1502). Medieval *renga* master well known as a traveler and author of travel records.

Sōha 宗波 (precise dates unknown). Zen monk of the Ōbaku sect associated with Jōrinji temple in Edo. A student of Butchō's at the same time as Bashō. Lived near Bashō in Fukagawa at the time of the Kashima trip; close personal friend.

Sōin (Nishiyama Sōin 西山宗因; 1605–82). Prominent *haikai* master and leader of the so-called Danrin school with whom Bashō was associated early in his career.

Sōmu (Sugano Sōmu 菅野宗無; d. 1719). Third son of a rice dealer in Iga Ueno. Entered service in the Tōdō Shinshichirō house and spent time in Edo but took tonsure early on as a Zen priest.

Sora 曽良 (later, Kawai Sōgorō 河合惣五郎; 1649–1710); Iwanami Shōemon Masataka 岩波庄右衛門正字; Yozaemon 与左衛門. Son of merchant Takano Shichibei 高野七兵衛; born in Shinano Province, Suwa. Served as a samurai in Ise Nagashima, or perhaps trained there for service in a Shinto shrine. Left Nagashima and came to Edo around 1685 to study Shinto and devote himself to *haikai* and national studies. Lived near Bashō in Fukagawa. Studied Shinto under Yoshikawa Koretari 吉川惟足.

Soryū 素龍 (Kashiwagi Takemoto 柏木全故; d. 1716); Gizaemon 儀左衛門. Samurai of the Tokushima Domain who left official service and was active as a *waka* poet, scholar, and calligrapher, first in Osaka and later in Edo. Taught Bashō calligraphy and wrote up the fair copy of *The Narrow Road through the Hinterlands* that Bashō carried with him on his last journey.

Sōshichi (Kubota Sōshichi 窪田宗七; d. 1711). Owner of a saké brewery named Yamatoya 大和屋 in Iga Ueno. Relative of Ensui. One of Bashō's oldest friends, but not active in *haikai*.

Su Dongpo 蘇東坡 (1037–1101). Also known as Su Shi 蘇軾. Important Chinese poet, painter, and calligrapher of the Song dynasty.

Su Shi *see* Su Dongpo

Suitō *see* Tōsui

Sun Mingfu 孫明腹 (992–1057). Chinese poet of the Song dynasty.

Tachibana no Norimitsu 橘則光 (b. 965). Courtier who served as governor of Mutsu.

Tachibana no Tamenaka 橘為仲 (d. 1085). Courtier-poet of the mid-Heian era.

Taga 多賀. Wife of Kyorai's older brother, Gentan.

Taimu 大夢. Head priest at Tenrūji temple in Matsuoka. Had been at a temple of the same name in Shinagawa. He had trained under Butchō and may have been acquainted with Bashō through that connection.

Taira no Atsumori 平敦盛 (1169–84). Son of Tsunemori and the subject of a famous Noh play.

Taira no Kanemori 平兼盛 (d. 990). Court poet.

Taira no Kiyomori 平清盛 (1118–81). Warrior and politician.

Taira no Tokiko 平時子 (1126–85); also known as Nii no ama 二位の尼, "Nun of the Second Rank." Wife of Taira no Kiyomori (1118–81), the late leader of the Heike forces and upstart prime minister. At the final battle between the Minamoto and the Taira, she jumped into the sea with her grandson, Emperor Antoku, and drowned.

Taiso *see* Bokuhaku

Takeda Kuniyuki 竹田国行 (precise dates unknown). Heian-era government official.

Takemikazuchi 武甕槌. The mythological figure most associated with Kashima Shrine.

Takue 琢慧 (1643–1710). *Haikai* name: Koeki 古益. Head priest of Hontōji 本統寺, an Ikkō-sect temple in Ise Kuwana, the forty-second station on the Tōkai Road. Disciple of Kigin.

Takutai 卓袋 (1659–1706); Kaimasu Ichibei 貝増市兵衛. Wealthy merchant in Iga Ueno and friend/disciple of Bashō. Shop name, Kaseya 絈屋. Seems to have given financial assistance to the Matsuo house.

Tanganshi *see* Tōdō Yoshinaga

Tao Qian 陶潛 (d. 427). Also known as Tao Yuanming 陶渊明. Chinese poet.

Teiji 低耳 (precise dates unknown); Miyabe Yasaburō 宮部弥三郎. *Haikai* poet and merchant of Nagara in Mino Province who helped arrange for Bashō's lodging on the Hokuroku Road.

Teishitsu 貞室 (1610–73); Yasuhara Masaakira 安原正章; Kagiya Hikozaemon 鑓屋彦左衛門. Disciple of Matsunaga Teitoku; closely associated with Kitamura Kigin, Bashō's early *haikai* teacher.

Teitoku 貞徳 (Matsunaga Teitoku 松永貞徳; 1571–1653). One of the pioneers of the *haikai* tradition and still important in Bashō's day. Also a *waka* poet and scholar.

Tenya (Tenya Gorōemon 天屋五郎右衛門; precise dates unknown); also known by his *haikai* name, Genryū 玄流. Wealthy man in the shipping business in Tsuruga.

Terashima Hikosuke 寺島彦助 (precise dates unknown). *Haikai* names, Anshu 安種, Sendō 詮道, and Reidō 令道. A warehouseman and agent of the Tokugawa government in Sakata.

Tōdō Yoshinaga 藤堂良長 (1666–1710). *Haikai* name, Tanganshi 探丸子 (also read Tanmaru). Heir of Bashō's samurai patron Tōdō Yoshitada, head of the Shinshichirō branch of the Tōdō clan.

Tōdō Yoshitada *see* Sengin

Tōin 桃印 (1661–93). Bashō's nephew. His father died when he was five or six, and at sixteen he came to Edo and remained close to his uncle, although he was not active in poetry. Worked for one Ishimaru Kentō 石丸見桃, from whom he received the first character of his name. Sickly; died at Bashō's cottage, under his care.

Tokiwa Gozen 常盤御前 (1138–c. 1180). Mother of the famous samurai Minamoto no Yoshitsune. She was later in service to Taira no Kiyomori (1118–81), the notorious dictator whose rise and fall is one of the chief subjects of *Tales of the Heike*. Popular tradition says that in the end Tokiwa fled from the capital and was murdered not far from Fuwa Barrier.

Tokugawa Ieyasu 徳川家康 (1543–1616). Founder of the Tokugawa dynasty.

Tokoku (Tsuboi Tokoku 坪井杜; d. 1690); Shōbei 庄兵衛; adopted *haikai* name Nohito 野仁/野人 while under censure. Rice dealer in Nagoya and ward administrator (町代). Sentenced to death by the government for the crime of speculation in the rice market; sentence commuted; went into banishment in autumn of 1685, first at Hatakemura 畠村, then at Hobi 保美 in Mikawa Province, where he took the name Minami Hikozaemon 南彦左衛門 and practiced medicine.

Tōkyū 等窮 (actually 等躬; 1637–1715). Common name: Sagara Izaemon 相楽伊左衛門. Warehouseman in Sukagawa. *Haikai* names: Saitan 乍憚 and Tōkyū. Disciple of Ishida Mitoku 石田未得 (1587–1669) and *haikai* master in his own right. Referred to as station master (宿駅の長) in some texts, but without corroboration.

Tomiyama Dōya 富山道冶 (d. 1634). Physician and author of *Chikusai*, comic fiction about an eponymous quack physician that chronicles his travels on the Tōkaidō.

Tomoda Ryōbon 友田良品 (1665–1730); Kakuzaemon 角左衛門. A samurai of Tōdō Domain in Iga Ueno. A friend of Dohō who visited Bashō in Edo and was an important contact with the samurai leadership of his hometown.

Tonsured Emperor Kazan *see* Emperor Kazan

Tonsured Prince Shukaku *see* Reverend Prince Shukaku

Tōrin (Amano Tōrin 天野桃隣; d. 1719); Kahei 加兵衛. One of Bashō's nephews, who lived for a while in Osaka but in 1688 was in Edo, working as a *haikai* master, no doubt with Bashō's assistance.

Tōsai 等裁 (alternatively 等哉 or 洞裁; precise dates unknown). Many standard sources identify him with Kanbe Tōsai 神戸洞哉, whose *haikai* name was Kakei 筇景 (or 可卿), who was a major figure in local poetic circles who supposedly met Bashō while in service of Matsuoka Domain in Edo. Recent scholarship rejects this connection, and many scholars are dubious about his relationship with Bashō and the details of the episode related in *The Narrow Road through the Hinterlands*. The city of Fukui has placed a memorial stone at the supposed site of his hut in Sanai Kōen.

Tōsei *see* Bashō

Tōsui 桃翠 (Kanokohata Toyoaki 鹿子畑豊明; 1662–1728). Properly, Suitō 桃翠. Younger brother of Kanokohata Takakatsu (Jōbōji Zusho). Met Bashō in Edo in 1688. Since his older brother succeeded as head of the Jōbōji house, he became head of the Kanokohata lineage. Took the name Oka Tadaharu Toyoaki 岡忠治豊明 after his father was banished in 1667.

Tōyō (Hayashi Tōyō 林桐葉; 1653–1712); Shichizaemon 七左衛門. *Haikai* name: Mokuji 木示, then Tōyō. Lived just outside the main gate of Atsuta shrine in Narumi, fortieth station on the Tōkai Road; served as guide; his house served as an inn for pilgrims. Studied *haikai* under Bokuin. It was through Tōyō that Bashō met Chisoku.

Tōzan 嗒山 (precise dates unknown). Samurai in Ōgaki, or perhaps Shimozato Rokuzaemon 下里六左衛門, an Ōgaki merchant. He became a disciple of Bashō in Edo, probably under the auspices of Jokushi.

Ukō 羽紅 (precise dates unknown). Wife of Bonchō and a *haikai* poet. Lay name Tome (or Otome). Took tonsure in 1691, with the name Ukō.

Unchiku 雲竹 (Kitamuki Masazane 北向正実; 1632–1703); Hachirōemon 八右衛門. A priest at Tōji Kanchiin temple in Kyoto. One of the finest calligraphers of his day. Friend to Bashō, who may have studied calligraphy under him.

Ungo Zenji 雲居禅師 (b. 1582). Zen priest who studied at various prominent Zen temples in Kyoto, then traveled widely. Monk who became head priest at the temple Zuiganji upon the dying request of Date Masamune.

Wang Wei 王維 (699–761). Chinese poet, painter, and government official of the Tang dynasty. Particularly influential among Zen poets and artists in Japan.

Wang Xiang 王祥 (185–269). Chinese government official in the Eastern Han dynasty.

Wang Zhaojun 王昭君 (b. c. 50 BC). Known as one of the Four Beauties of ancient China. She was sent to Xiongnu.

Wumen Huihai (無門慧関; J. Mumon Ekai; 1183–1260). Chinese Chan (J. Zen) monk, author of *Mumonkan* 無門関 (C. *Wu-wen kuan*; *The Gateless Gate*), a thirteenth-century Zen *kōan* collection.

Xi Shi 西施. Legendary Chinese beauty of the Spring and Autumn Period.

Xie Zhaozhe 謝肇淛 (1567–1624). Author of *Wu zazu* 五雜俎, a miscellany.

Xu You 許由. Legendary Chinese hermit in the era of Emperor Yao.

Yaba (Shida Yaba 志太野坡; 1662–1740); Takeda Yosuke 竹田弥助. Edo disciple of Bashō and Kikaku.

Yan Guang 厳光 (39 BC–AD 41). Chinese poet of the Later Han dynasty.

Yang Guifei 楊貴妃 (719–56). Celebrated beauty of the Tang dynasty who was consort of the emperor Xuanzong.

Yanghu 羊祐 (221–278). A government official of the Chinese Jin dynasty.

Yasui (Okada Yasui 岡田野水; 1658–1743); Sajiemon 佐次右衛門. Disciple. Nagoya clothier, with shop named Bizenya 備前屋. Became a disciple of Bashō around 1684, with Tokoku and others; later, more interested in tea.

Yasunobu (Terashima Yasunobu or Anshin 寺島安信; d. 1722); Kaemon 嘉右衛門. Merchant, son of Bokugen and uncle of Chisoku; manager of daimyo lodgings (*honjin*) in Narumi. Disciple of Bashō.

Yohei 与平. Servant living next to Rakushisha. Caretaker and cook.

Yoichi Munetaka *see* Nasu no Yoichi

Yoshitomo *see* Minamoto no Yoshitomo

Yoshitsune *see* Minamoto no Yoshitsune

Yoshiyuki 由之 (Ide Yoshiyuki 井手由之); Chōtarō 長太郎. Samurai retainer to Naitō Rosen, Iwakitaira han 磐城平藩.

Yugyō the Second 遊行二世 (d. 1319). Also known as Taa Shōnin 他阿上人. Successor of Ippen Shōnin, founder of the Time sect of Buddhism.

Yūtō 游刀 (precise dates unknown). *Haikai* poet in Zeze.

Yūzan 幽山 (Takano Naoshige 高野直重; d. 1702). Common name Magobei 孫兵衛. Edo *haikai* master of the Danrin school. Bashō served as his scribe for a time when he was living in Nihonbashi.

Zaishiki (Noguchi Zaishiki 野口在色; 1643–1719); Jinhachirō 甚八郎.

Zen Master Dōgen *see* Dōgen Zenji

Zen Master Yuanmiao *see* Gaofeng Yuanmiao

Zensenshi 前川子 (Tsuda Zensenshi 津田前川子; precise dates unknown). Ōgaki samurai.

Zenzō 弾蔵 (precise dates unknown). A samurai in the retinue of Jōbōji Zusho in Kurobane.

Zhang Ji 張繼 (712–79). Mid-eighth-century Chinese poet.

Zhang Wuzi 長梧子. A character in *Zhuangzi*.

Zhuangzi 荘子 (also known as Zhuang Zhou 荘周; late fourth century BC). Fourth-century Chinese official and Daoist thinker; credited as author of a text of the same name that is one of the prime texts of the Chinese philosophical tradition.

Zōga 増賀上人 (917–1003). Priest of the Tendai sect who was associated with the temple at Tōnomine near Nara. *Senjūshō* contains a story of how on pilgrimage to Ise he removed his clothing and gave it to a beggar in order to rid himself of all signs of prominence.

Zushi Sakichi 図司左吉 (Kondō Sakichi 近藤左吉; d. 1693). *Haikai* name, Rogan (or Romaru) 呂丸. Leader of *haikai* in Tōge Village, at the foot of Mount Haguro. Dyer for *yamabushi*. Served as go-between to meet Egaku Ajari, with letter from Ichiei. Became a disciple of Bashō in 1689. Later traveled to Edo, saw Bashō, then went on to Ise, Kyoto, where he stayed with Shikō, dying there at age forty.

Places of Importance in the Texts

*Indicates prominent *utamakura*, a "poem words" or famous poetic place.

*Abukuma River 阿武隈川 runs from Fukushima Prefecture into Miyago Prefecture.

*Akashi 明石 is a coastal area in what is now Hyōgo Prefecture. It owes much of its importance to *The Tale of Genji*, as one of Genji's places of exile. Bashō visited here with Tokoku in *Knapsack Notes*. It is as far west as Bashō ever went.

*Arashiyama 嵐山 (Storm Mountain) is a mountainous area west of Kyoto, on the west bank of the Ōi River. It was already an important retreat from the city in Bashō's day and the location of many important temples and shrines.

Arima 有馬 is the name of a famous hot spring area in modern Kōbe.

*Asamayama *see* Mount Asama

*Asamuzu Bridge あさむづの橋 is now a train stop (Asozu) on the Fukui Rail Line. In Bashō's day it was a town on the Hokuroku Road.

Ashino 芦野 (Reed Field) is a district northeast of Ōtawara on the Nasu Moor. In Bashō's day it was a castle town and a stop on the Ōshū Road.

Atago Gongen Shrine 愛宕権現神社 is a shrine on the slopes of Mount Atago in Saga.

Atsuta 熱田 is now located within the city limits of Nagoya. In Bashō's day it was a town surrounding Atsuta Shrine 熱田神社 with a population of about fifteen thousand. It incorporated the forty-third stop on the Tōkai Road (called Miyajuku 宮宿 but also Atsutajuku).

Awanoshō 阿波の庄 was located in the mountains just east of Iga Ueno. It was the site of a temple, Shindaibutsuji.

Bashōan 芭蕉庵 was the name given to three different cottages where Bashō lived in Fukagawa. The location was near the modern Bashō Kinenkan (Bashō Memorial Hall) in Kōtō-ku, Tokyo.

Bodaisen Jingūdera 菩提山神宮寺, located at the northeastern tip of Isuzu Park, on the outskirts of Ise Shrine, is at present marked only by memorial steles.

Bukō 武江 (The Shōgun's City, The Shogun's Bay) is a name Bashō often uses for Edo.

Chion'in 知恩院 is now chief temple of the Pure Land sect in Kyoto. In Bashō's day it was a *monzekidera* 門跡寺 (imperial cloister) that enjoyed Tokugawa patronage whose abbot was a royal or court noble.

Chōkōan 長興庵 was the cottage of the Zen monk Butchō, located near Konponji in Kashima.

Chūsonji 中尊寺 is a temple complex located in Hiraizumi. Local traditions say the temple was founded in the ninth century by Ennin, but temple records indicate that it was founded by Fujiwara no Kiyohira and dedicated in 1126. Chūsonji fell into decline after the demise of the Northern Fujiwara but was restored by the Date clan as a subsidiary of the Kan'eiji in Tokyo.

Daikakuji 大覚寺 is a Shingon-sect temple in Saga. Originally an imperial residence, it became a temple in 876. In Bashō's day it was one of the central institutions of the area.

Daishōji 大聖寺 is now the name of an area in Kaga City, Ishikawa Prefecture. When Bashō visited it was a castle town in the Kaga Domain, boasting a stipend of 70,000 *koku*. The town took its name from a temple associated with Mount Hakusan and was adjacent to the temple Zenshōji. It served as a post station.

Dewa 出羽 was the general name in Bashō's day for the northern area that now includes Yamagata, Akita, and Aomori Prefectures on the Japan Sea coast.

Dewa Sanzan 出羽三山 refers to the Three Mountains of Dewa: Haguro 羽黒, Gassan 月山, and Yudono 湯殿. Into the early Edo period, the three peaks were associated with the Shingon sect, but by Bashō's time Gassan and Haguro were administered as Tendai temples. All were sites dedicated to mountain ascetic practices and the hosting of pilgrims, but there were numerous subtemples and shrines in the area as well. Gassan is the tallest of the peaks at 6,509 feet; Haguro is 1,358 feet, Yudono, 1,504 feet.

Dongting Lake 洞低湖 (Cave Lake) was located in Hunan Province, China.

Dōsojin Shrine 道祖神の社 (also known as Saeno jinja 佐倍乃神社) is located in Natori City, Miyagi Prefecture. There were other shrines to *dōsojin*, protectors of travelers and boundaries, in other places.

Edo 江戸is the old name for Tokyo. In the late 1600s it was an immense city, with a population approaching a million and over eight hundred separate districts (*machi*, aka *chō*). Nihonbashi, where Bashō lived in his first decade, was a thriving downtown area.

Eiheiji 永平寺 is now a major bastion of the Sōtō Zen sect. Established by the medieval monk Dōgen, it was already an important institution in Bashō's time.

Engakuji 円覚寺 is a Zen temple in Kamakura.

Fengxian Temple 奉先寺 is a temple complex in Luoyang, Henan Province.

*Fujikawa (Fuji River) 富士川 originates in the Kantō Mountains and flows to the west of Mount Fuji, on into Suruga Bay.

Fukagawa 深川, the area where the Bashōan was located, still survives in various place names in the Kōtō ward of modern Tokyo, located across the Sumida River from Nihonbashi. Now it is in the heart of the city, but in Bashō's time it was semi-rural. His house was located right on the river on a half-acre lot.

Fukui 福井 is now the capital city of Fukui Prefecture. In the seventeenth century it was a castle town in the Fukui Domain, Echizen Province, with a stipend of 520,000 *koku*. Ruled by a branch of the Matsudaira clan, it was a major post station on the Hokuriku Road.

Fukushima 福島 is now known for the triple disaster (earthquake, tidal wave, and nuclear meltdown) of March 2011 that afflicted the region (modern Fukushima Province). For Bashō it was a stop on the Ōshū Road. Another castle town, it was located in Iwashiro Province. The domain had a stipend of 100,000 *koku*.

*Furu Falls 布留の滝 is located in Nara Prefecture, near Tenri.

Furu Shrine *see* Isonokami Shrine

Fusa 布佐 is now a station on the Ueno Tokyo Rail Line just east of Abiko. In Bashō's day it was a river port.

*Fushimi 伏見 is now in the southern area of Kyoto. It was a commercial center on the shores of Lake Ogura (no longer extant) in Bashō's time.

*Futami Bay 二見ヶ浦 is now a train stop in Ise City. In Bashō's day it was a coastal area famous for its views.

*Fuwa Barrier 不破関 (literally, "the indestructible barrier") was an important fortress in ancient times but was abandoned early on and only a relic in Bashō's day. Close to the site of the battle of Sekigahara of 1600, which began Tokugawa Ieyasu's rise to hegemonic power.

Gannenji 願念寺 is a Jōdo Shinshū-sect temple in the Nomachi area of central Kanazawa.

Gassan *see* Dewa Sanzan

Genjūan 幻住庵 is a cottage in the hills behind Ishiyamadera in Ōmi where Bashō stayed in the summer of 1690. He later described the place in an essay of the same name.

Genyōin 玄陽院 was a subtemple of the complex at Minamidani, Mount Haguro.

Gichūji 義仲寺 is a temple of the Tendai sect located in Ōtsu.

Gifu 岐阜 is a major city (population of over 400,000) in the prefecture of the same name. In Bashō's day it was on the Nakasen Road, not far from Ōgaki.

Gohōzan Shindaibutsuji 護峰山新大仏寺 (Temple of the New Great Buddha at Mount Gohō), which still stands today, is a Shingon temple located in the hills just east of Iga Ueno.

Goten ごてん is an area along the Mogami River near modern Murayama, Yamagata Prefecture.

Gu Mountain (Gushan 孤山) is a mountain in Hangzhou, near Si Hu.

Gyōtoku 行徳 is now the name of a train station in Ichikawa City, Chiba Prefecture, just northeast of Tokyo. In Bashō's day it was a river port.

Haguro *see* Dewa Sanzan

Haguro Gongen *see* Dewa Sanzan

*Hakone 箱根 is the name of a mountain that stands at the base of the Izu Peninsula, inland from the coastal cities of Atami, Yugawara, and Manazuru. Today it is also the name of a tourist area on the shores of the lake Ashinoko. In Bashō's day, it was a station on the Tōkai Road, and a government checkpoint that stood there marked the entry/exit for the Kantō.

Hakuchōsan 白鳥山 was a hill west of Atsuta Shrine and the site of Hōjiji, a temple of the Zen Sōtō sect.

Hakusendō 泊船堂 (Harbor Hall) was the first name Bashō gave his first cottage in Fukagawa, which was later known as Bashōan.

Hasedera *see* Hatsusedera

Hatsusaki 鉢崎 is a small town on the Japan Sea that was near a government checkpoint in Bashō's day and had a number of inns.

*Hatsusedera 初瀬寺, more commonly known as Hasedera 長谷寺, is a Shingon-sect temple of ancient origins located in Hase, south of Nara City. In Bashō's day it was a major tourist and pilgrimage site.

*Hayabusa はやぶさ is an area along the Mogami River in Murayama, Yamagata Prefecture.

Hikaridō 光堂 (Shining Hall), also known as the Konjikidō 金色堂 (Golden Hall), is still a major tourist attraction at Hiraizumi. It was built in 1124.

Hina Peak 比那山 (now Hinoyama 日野山) is a mountain in South Echizen known as Echizen Fuji.

*Hinaga Village 日永 is in Yokkaichi, Mie Prefecture.

Hiraizumi 平泉 is a historic site in Iwate Prefecture whose glories came long before Bashō visited there. In Bashō's day it was known for the ruins of the fortresses of the Northern Fujiwara dynasty of the late 1100s. In 1689 he and Sora stayed in Ichinoseki, the nearest town, which also survives today.

Hirata 平田 is now a railway station in eastern Shiga Prefecture.

Hirugakojima 蛭が小島 is now the name of a park near Mishima on the Izu Peninsula.

Hiuchi Castle 燧が城 was located on Mount Fujikura in Fukui. In medieval times it was the fortress of Kiso Yoshinaka.

Hiyoshi Shrine (or Hie Shrine) 日吉神社 is in Komatsu City and is also called Motoori Hiyoshi Jinja 本折日吉神社.

Hobi 保美 is a small town near Tahara City on the Atsumi Peninsula in Aichi Prefecture.

Hōjiji 法持寺, a temple of the Zen Sōtō sect, is located at Hakuchōsan 白鳥山, a hill west of Atsuta Shrine.

Hokurokudō 北陸道 (also pronounced Hokurikudō) was the road that ran along the Japan Sea coast, from Echigo through Etchū, Noto, Kaga, and Echizen to Wakasa.

Honpukuji 本福路 is a temple of the Pure Land sect located in what is now Ōtsu City, on the western shore of Lake Biwa.

Honryūji 本隆寺 is a small Nichiren-sect temple located at Irogahama.

Hontōji 本統寺 is a Shingon temple in Kuwana affiliated with Higashi Honganji in Kyoto.

Hōrinji 法輪寺 (popularly known as Kōkuzō 虚空蔵) is a temple of the Shingon sect founded in the early 700s. It is located on a hill below Arashiyama. Kokūzō is the name of a bodhisattva (Skt. Akasagarbha), the titular deity of the temple.

Hoso Tōge 臍峠 is a mountain pass between Tōnomine and Yoshino.

Hyōchikuan 飄竹庵 was a cottage in Iga Ueno owned by Bashō's disciple Bokuhaku.

Ichiburi 市振 is now a train stop on the Echigo Miyagi line. In Bashō's day it was one of the stops on the Hokurokudō.

Ichinoseki 一関 is a city of about 120,000 people in Iwate Prefecture. In Bashō's day it was the castle town of a domain of the same name, under the control of the Tamura house but greatly influenced by the Date of Sendai. It was the closest town to Hiraizumi.

Ichinotani 一の谷 is a small coastal area near Sumaura Park on the coast of Osaka Bay. Bashō knew it as the site of a famous battle during the Genpei Wars of 1180–85.

Iga Domain 伊賀 was the name of the domain where Bashō grew up and his family lived. It is now part of Mie Prefecture.

Iga Ueno 伊賀上野 is Bashō's hometown. It was a subsidiary castle town with a stipend of 5,000 *koku*, administered by the Tōdō clan, the main bastion being the castle town of Anotsu 安濃津, in Ise Province. It had a population of perhaps ten thousand people in Bashō's day. For people traveling to Ise, the Iga Road led to Seki on the Tōkai Road and on to the shrine.

Iizuka 飯塚 (or Iizaka 飯坂) is now in Fukushima City. In Bashō's day it was a hot spring area.

Imasu 今須 is an area near Fuwa Barrier in Gifu Prefecture.

*Iragozaki 伊良湖崎 is a cape on the western end of Mikawa Province.

*Ironohama 色の浜 (Iro Beach, "Beach of Colors") still exists today on the western shore of Tsuruga Bay.

*Ise 伊勢 is the name of an ancient province that was the site of the Grand Shrines at Ise, the most important of all Shinto institutions since medieval times. Like many other people of his day, Bashō visited there often—a half-dozen times that we know of—and had a special affinity for a place that was essentially in his home province.

Ise Yamada 伊勢山田 is the area east of the outer shrine at Ise.

Ishinomaki 石巻 is now a city on the coast northeast of Shiogama. It is where the Kitakami River flows into the sea and was an important port in Bashō's day.

*Ishiyamadera 石山寺 is Shingon temple known for its Kannon image, located on the Seta River just south of Lake Biwa. In Bashō's time it was famous as a moon-viewing site and for its associations with Murasaki Shikibu, author of *The Tale of Genji*.

*Isonokami Shrine 石上神宮, also known as Furu Shrine, is located in Tenri, Nara Prefecture.

*Iwade Village 岩出の里 is now identified as Iwadeyamamachi 岩出山町, in Miyagi Prefecture, near Kurihara.

Iwanuma 岩沼 is a town in Miyagi Prefecture. In Bashō's day it was a post station.

Izumi Fortress 和泉が城 was the fortress of Fujiwara Tadahira at Hiraizumi.

Jōinji 浄因寺 is a Zen temple located near Numazu on the Izu Peninsula.

*Kaeruyama かへる山 (Return Hill) was a hill located near Hiuchi Castle.

*Kagenuma かげ沼 is located just east of Sukagawa City and is now known as Kawasakichō. In Bashō's day it was a marshy area.

Kamagainohara かまがいの原 is the name of an area in the Katsushika District of Chiba Prefecture.

*Kamo River 鴨川 runs north–south through the heart of Kyoto, much as it did in Bashō's day. Its wide riverbed was a recreation site.

Kanazawa 金沢 is the capital of modern Ishikawa Prefecture, a cultural center that boasts a number of famous parks and shopping districts preserved from the Meiji era. It has a population of over four hundred thousand. Bashō, who had many followers there, knew it as the chief city of the Kaga Domain, ruled by the Maeda lineage, who had an income of more than a million *koku*. It was a major stop on the Hokuroku Road. Among the most prominent of cities in Bashō's time, it had a population of perhaps fifty thousand and over thirteen thousand homes.

Kan'eiji *see* Tōeizan Kan'eiji

Kanmanjuji 干満珠寺 in Kisagata was a Tendai temple in ancient times but was revived by Jikaku Daishi as a Sōtō Zen temple.

*The Karasaki Pine 唐崎の松 is remembered now by a shrine by that name in Ōtsu, on the western shore of Lake Biwa. In Bashō's day it was one of the Eight Great Sights of Ōmi.

*Kasajima 笠島 (Rain Hat Isle) is in Natori City, on the outskirts of Sendai.

*Kashima 鹿島 (Deer Island) is the name of a city with a population of about 67,000 in Hitachi Province (now Ibaraki Prefecture) built around Kashima Shrine 鹿島神宮, which is now surrounded by a large deer park. The shrine was founded in the seventh century to honor the celestial deity Takemikazuchi, the god of thunder. Kashima Shrine was a prominent religious center and also an important military outpost. The shrine was badly damaged during the 2011 earthquake but has since been repaired. When Bashō visited his mentor Butchō there, the shrine was an even more prominent center for the area, owning much of the property around it.

Kashiwazaki 柏崎 is a small coastal city on the Japan Sea, just southwest of Niigata.

Kasukabe 粕壁 is now the name of a train station in Saitama Prefecture, northeast of Tokyo. In Bashō's day it was the fourth station on Nikkō Highway and essentially an inn town.

*Katada 堅田 is now a station stop on the Kōsei Line in northern Ōtsu City. In Bashō's day it was a separate city.

Katsuodera 勝尾寺 is a temple of the Shingon temple associated with Mount Kōya. It is located in Mino'o City, Osaka Prefecture.

Kei Jingū 気比神宮 (now pronounced Kehi) is located in Tsuruga. An ancient shrine, it is considered a premier Shinto site in the entire Hokuriku region.

Kei no Myōjin *see* Kei Jingū

Kinbu Shrine 金峰神社 is located in Nara Prefecture, south of Yoshino.

*Kisagata 象潟 is a small town on the Japan Sea in Akita Prefecture. In Bashō's day the bay there was full of small islands and rivaled Matsushima in reputation, but an earthquake in 1804 rearranged the landscape and destroyed the views.

*Kiso 木曽 is the mountainous area of Nagano Prefecture surrounding the Kiso River.

Kiso Road 木曽路 was a section of the Nakasen Road running between Ōtsu and Edo. Bashō uses it in reference to a section from Ōtsu to Zenkōji.

Kitakami River 北上川 is a major waterway that runs from Iwate Prefecture though Morioka and into the sea at Ishinomaki. It runs northeast of the ruins of Hiraizumi.

Kōfu 甲府 is a city of about 190,000 people in Yamanashi Prefecture, what used to be Kai Province. It was administered directly by the Tokugawa government in Bashō's day and was a post station on the Kōshū Road.

Kōfukuji 興福寺, a large temple complex in Nara City, was founded in the 600s as the headquarters of the ancient Hossō sect. In classical times, it was a rich landowner as well as the family temple of the Fujiwara clan and continued to be important in Bashō's day thanks to the direct support of the Tokugawa government.

Kokuzō *see* Hōrinji

Komatsu 小松 (Young Pines) is a city of just over 100,000 people in Ishikawa Prefecture. The town was a castle town of about 11,000 people in Bashō's day, close to Kanazawa but boasting a castle of its own.

Kōmyōji 光明寺 is now marked with a stele surrounded by farmland in the village of Otawara, Tochigi Prefecture. It began with a statue of Amida donated by Nasu no Yoichi.

Kongōbuji 金剛峰寺 is a center of Shingon worship at Mount Kōya, in the mountains west of Yoshino.

Kongōhōji gokokuin 金剛宝寺護国院 was a temple and pilgrimage site at Waka Bay on the Kii Peninsula. It is also known as Kimiidera 紀三井寺.

Konponji 根本寺 is a Zen temple located just to the west of Kashima Shrine whose origins date back to the 600s. Bashō's Zen teacher, Butchō, was head priest there.

Ko'ori 桑折 is now a district in Fukushima Prefecture. In Bashō's day it was a post station on the Ōshū Road.

*Koromogawa 衣川 (literally, "Robe River"; also called Kinugawa) is one of the tributaries of the Kitakami River, flowing into the latter near Hiraizumi.

Kumano 熊野 is a mountainous area in Wakayama Prefecture known as the site of several important shrines. In Bashō's day it was an important center of *shugendō* ascetic practices.

*Kurikara Gorge 倶利伽羅が谷 is located just east of Kanazawa, on the border between Etchū and Kaga Provinces.

Kurobane 黒羽 (or Nasunokurobane) is a small town in Tochigi Prefecture. In the late 1600s it was the castle town of the Kurobane Domain, with a stipend of 18,000 *koku*, administered by the Ōzeki clan.

Kurobe River く ろ べ 川 remains a river of many channels where it empties into the Japan Sea near Kotohira Shrine in Toyama Prefecture.

Kurozuka 黒塚 is a site located on the Abukuma River, east of Nihonmatsu.

Kuwana 桑名 is at present a small city in Mie Prefecture located between Nagoya and Yokkaichi. To Bashō it was a post station on the Tōkai Road, important as a port that transported travelers to Ise and the Kansai area across Ise Bay from Atsuta.

Kyoto 京都 was the imperial capital of Japan from 810 until 1869. Texts of Bashō's day refer to it variously as Kyō 京, Raku 落, and Miyako 都. When the Tokugawa established their offices in Edo in the early 1600s, the old city lost some of its cachet, but in Bashō's day it still had a population of approximately 520,000 and was of immense importance culturally and boasted an active cadre of *haikai* poets, among them Bashō's master and patron, Kitamura Kigin. Bashō spent a good deal of time in the area, which figures in *Bones Bleaching in the Fields*, *Knapsack Notes*, and *The Saga Diary*. He had only a few disciples there: Kyorai, Bonchō, and his wife.

Lake Biwa 琵琶湖, located just east and north of Kyoto, is Japan's largest freshwater lake.

Longmen 龍門 (Dragon Gate) is an area in Henan Province famous for its rocks and caves.

Longquan 龍泉 (Dragon Spring) is located in Zhejiang.

*Magaki Island 籬 が 島 is a small island off the coast at Shiogama.

*Manonokayahara ま の の 萱 は ら is an area east of Ishinomaki in Miyagi Prefecture.

Masshōzan 末松山 *see* Sue no Matsuyama

Matsuno'o Village 松尾 の 里 is on the Katsura River, in the Arashiyama area.

Matsuoka 松岡 (Pine Hill) is now an area of Eiheijimachi in Fukui Prefecture. In Bashō's day it was a domain of 50,000 *koku*, administered by the Matsudaira clan.

*Matsushima 松島 (Pine Islands) is a coastal area close to Sendai boasting a view of over two hundred islands. It was a tourist attraction already in Bashō's day.

Menshōji 明照寺 (Myōhōzan Menshōji 妙法山明照寺) is a Jōdo Shinshū temple in Hirata Village outside Hikone associated with the Nishi Honganji temple in Kyoto.

Minakuchi 水口 is a ward in Kōga City, Shiga Prefecture. In Bashō's day it was a station on the Tōkaidō and intersected with a road to Iga Ueno.

Minamidani 南谷 (South Valley) was the location of a subtemple in the complex at Mount Haguro, also known as Kōyōin Shionji 高陽院紫苑寺.

Minomushian 蓑虫庵 (Bagworm Cottage) is a cottage in Iga Ueno. It was owned by Bashō's disciple Hattori Dohō and was used by Bashō as a residence in 1688.

Mino'o Falls 箕面 の 滝 is located in Mino'o City, Osaka Prefecture.

*Miyagino 宮城野 is now the name of a ward in the city of Sendai. In Bashō's day it was a broad moorland.

*Mizunokojima 水の小島 is an area in Miyagi Prefecture between Ōsaki and Shinjō.

Mogami Estate 最上の庄 was already in Bashō's time an antique name for a district near modern Shinshō 新庄, which was on the Dewa Road.

*Mogami River 最上川 begins in southern Yamagata Prefecture, and flows north and then west from Shinjō and into the Japan Sea at Sakata.

Motoaikai 元合海 (本合海) is an area along the Mogami River in Yamagata Prefecture. In Bashō's day it was the port adjacent to Ōishida.

*Mount Asaka あさか山 (安積山) is located just north of Koriyama in Fukushima Prefecture.

*Mount Asama 浅間山 straddles the border between the ancient provinces of Shinano and Kōzuke and is a less than dormant volcano (with six eruptions since 1980, for instance).

Mount Atago 愛宕山 is a high mountain just northwest of central Kyoto that, along with Mount Takao, looms over the Saga Arashiyama area. It is the site of an important shrine.

Mount Chōkai 鳥海 is a high volcanic peak (7,336 feet) on the border between Yamagata and Akita and is also known as Akita Fuji because of its immense girth and symmetrical shape. It was a major center of *shugendō* in Bashō's day.

*Mount Fuji 富士山 is the highest peak in the Hakone area. Its peak could be seen from Edo on a clear day.

Mount Futagami *see* Taimadera

Mount Gassan 月山 (Moon Mountain) is the highest of the Three Mountains of Dewa and the site of a shrine. It is located south of Mount Haguro.

Mount Haguro 羽黒山 (Dark Feather Mountain) is one of the Three Mountains of Dewa. It is the site of the Haguro Gongen, a Shinto shrine, and an important pilgrimage site.

*Mount Hakusan 白山 (White Mountain) is located on the border between Gifu and Ishikawa Prefectures. It was a major site for mountain worship in Bashō's day.

Mount Itajiki 板敷山 is a mountain in northern Yamagata Prefecture.

*Mount Kaeru かへるやま is a mountain near Kinome Pass in Fukui Prefecture.

*Mount Kashima 鹿島 is a city in Ibaraki Prefecture. In Bashō's day it was known primarily for the famous shrine that gave the area its name.

*Mount Kazuraki 葛城 is a mountain in the Kongō Range standing between Nara and Osaka. Bashō's poem on the place shows that he knew the legend of the god of the place being so ugly that he avoided appearing in daylight.

Mount Kinkei 金鶏山 is a hill just southwest of Takadachi at Hiraizumi.

Mount Kōya 高野山, located in the rugged mountains of the Kii Peninsula, is the site of the Kongōbuji 金剛峰寺, a Shingon-sect temple of importance since the ninth century and still attracting pilgrims and visitors—Bashō and Tokoku among them—in the Edo period. The temple was a bastion of the ancient Shingon sect and a center of mountain rites.

Mount Kunimi 国見山 is located south of Iga Ueno in Mie Prefecture, on the way to Yoshino. In Bashō's day, it was widely believed that Kenkō, author of *Tsurezuregusa*, died there.

Mount Kurokami 黒髪山 (Black Hair Mountain), now known as Mount Nantai 男体山, is a volcanic peak just west of Nikkō.

Mount Lu 廬山 (C. Lushan), a favorite destination for poets and artists, is located in northern Jiangxi Province in central China.

*Mount Miwa 三輪山 is a mountain just to the east of Sakurai City in Nara Prefecture.

Mount Nikkō *see* Nikkō

*Mount Obasute (Obasuteyama 姨捨山) is a mountain in central Nagano Prefecture that is connected to ancient legends of senicide in China and India. The common name of the mountain now is Kamurikiyama. Bashō probably knew the stories from classical texts such as *Yamato monogatari* and the Noh play *Obasute*.

Mount Takao 高尾山 is a high mountain just east of Mount Atago at the western edge of the Kyoto basin. It is the site of Jingōji 神護寺, a Shingon temple.

*Mount Tsukuba 筑波山 refers to a mountain in Hitachi Province (now Ibaraki Prefecture) with two peaks, one figured as male and one as female. It had particular importance to *renga* and *haikai* poets because of a poem exchange that occurred there according to ancient records.

*Mount Unohana 卯の花山 is located just east of Kanazawa, close to Kurikara Gorge.

Mount Wu 巫山 (C. Wushan) is a picturesque range of mountains along the Yangtze River in China.

Mount Xianglu 香炉峰 (C. Xianglushan) is a mountain in Zhejiang Province.

Mount Yudono 湯殿山 is one of the Three Mountains of Dewa, located west of Gassan. It was known for its hot springs.

Mumyōan 無名庵 is a cottage in the precincts of Gichūji Temple in Ōtsu.

*Muronoyashima 室の矢島 is located near Ōmiwa Shrine 大神神社 in Tochigi Prefecture. There was a pond on the site with eight islands. It honors Hanasakuyahime.

*Musashino 武蔵野 (Musashi Moors) is now a city in the western area of the Tokyo metropolitan area. In classical and medieval times it was a moorland and in Bashō's day was still mostly open country.

Mutsu 陸奥 (also read Michinoku) was in Bashō's day the name for the area now encompassing Fukushima, Miyagi, Iwate, and Aomori Prefectures.

Muyamuya Barrier むやむやの関 (有耶無耶の関) is a name used in reference to three or four different places, and it is unclear which one Bashō had in mind. Bashō and Sora passed one such checkpoint near Shiokoshi, between Fukura and Kumano Gongen on the coast of the Japan Sea, when they were leaving Tsuruoka Domain.

Nagashima 長島 (Long Island) is a district in Mie Prefecture. In Bashō's day it was generally called Ise Nagashima, located where the Nagara River emptied into Ise Bay.

Nagoya 名古屋 is the capital of Aichi Prefecture and a major financial center with a population of over two million people. In Bashō's time it was the chief castle town of the Owari Domain, ruled by the Tokugawa, with a population estimated at sixty-five thousand.

Nakasen Road 中山道 was the name of one of the Five Roads established and maintained by the Tokugawa regime. It ran between Edo and Kusatsu, where it joined the Tōkai Road. The name Kisoji 木曽路 is sometimes used synonymously, although technically it refers to just one stretch of the Nakasen Road.

*Nakaso Barrier 勿来関 is in Iwaki City, Fukushima Prefecture. It was known as one of the Three Barriers (*sankan* 三関) of the northern provinces.

Nanbu 南部 is the name of the area north of Hiraizumi, otherwise known as Rikuchū. In Bashō's day it was the name of a domain.

Naoetsu 直江津 survives now as the name of a train station in Jōetsu, Niigata Prefecture. In Bashō's day it was a prosperous port city.

*Nara 奈良 was the capital of Japan in the eighth century and remains today a cultural center and the gateway to the mountainous regions of the Kii Peninsula. Bashō knew it as the site of religious institutions, such as Kōfukuji and Kasuga Shrine, and for the many cultural activities associated with them.

*Narugo Springs なるごの湯 is a hot spring resort between Ōsaki and Shinjō in Miyagi Prefecture.

*Narumi 鳴海 remains today as the name of a train station in the city of Nagoya. It was the fortieth post station on Tōkai Road.

Narutaki 鳴滝 is an area in western Kyoto, near Rengeji. In Bashō's day it was a district of elite retreats.

*Naruto 鳴戸 refers to the straits between the island of Awaji in the Inland Sea and the coast of Awa Province in Shikoku.

*Nasu 那須 is a moorland between Nikkō and Shirakawa.

Nata 那谷 dates back to the Nara period but was restored by the Maeda clan, daimyo of Kaga Domain, in the mid-1600s. The temple there has a famous thousand-handed Kannon statue.

Natori 名取 is now a midsize city in Miyagi Prefecture.

*The Natori River 名取川 runs through the Natori area and on through the southern area of Sendai City.

Nezu Barrier 鼠の関 (also written 念珠の関) is located in Yamagata Prefecture, on the border between the ancient provinces of Dewa and Echigo. It was known as one of the Three Barriers (*sankan* 三関) of the northern provinces.

Nigatsudō 二月堂 is a building at the great Nara temple Tōdaiji.

Nihonbashi 日本橋 is a major district of Tokyo still today, located east of Tokyo Station. In Bashō's day it was the first station of the Tōkai Road and a crowded urban commercial and cultural center. Bashō lived in the area from the time he first went up to Edo until 1680, when he moved across the Sumida River to Fukagawa.

*Nihonmatsu 二本松 (Two Pines) is now a small city in Fukushima Prefecture, located between Fukushima City and Koriyama. When Bashō visited there in 1689, it was in the Nihonmatsu-han and was administered by the Niwa clan, with a stipend of 15,000 *koku.*

Niigata 新潟 is now the largest city on the coast of the Japan Sea, a business and commercial center with a population approaching five hundred thousand. Bashō passed through there on his way through Echigo Province and on to Kanazawa in Kaga but said nothing about it. It was nonetheless a major stop on Hokuroku Road. The domain was administered by a magistrate (*bugyō*) from the Nagaoka-han, to the southwest.

Nijikō 西河 is also known as Ōtaki, located in what is now Kawakami Village, Yoshino District.

Nikkō 日光 is now a small city in Tochigi Prefecture that attracts large numbers of pilgrims and tourists. It is the site of a famous complex of religious buildings, the most important being Tōshōgū 東照宮, the mausoleum of Tokugawa Ieyasu, founder of the Tokugawa dynasty. Two hundred thousand cedar trees—donated by Kumano Shrines nearly fifty years before Bashō's visit—lined the roads leading to the shrine, and there were upwards of one hundred different buildings on the site.

*Nodanotamagawa 野田の玉川 is a river that runs east of Taga Castle in Sendai.

*Nonomiya 野々宮 (Shrine in the Fields) is a small shrine located in the bamboo groves of Saga, west of Kyoto. It was already an established tourist site in Bashō's day.

*Nunobiki Falls 布引の滝 is located in modern-day Kōbe.

Nyoirinji 如意倫寺 is a temple located in Yoshino. In earlier times it belonged to the Shingon sect, but by mid-Edo it was affiliated with the Pure Land sect. On its grounds was the tomb of Emperor Go-Daigo.

Obanezawa 尾花沢 is a small town in Yamagata Prefecture. In Bashō's time it claimed status as the regional office of the Tokugawa government. It was a post station on the Ōshū Road in Uzen Province and close to the Mogami River, the main artery of the heavily mountainous area through which it flowed. Nearby Ōishida, now an even smaller city, was right on the river and served as a port for its region.

Obasute *see* Mount Obasute

*Obuchinomaki 尾ぶちの牧 is a hill east of Ishinomaki in Miyagi Prefecture.

Ōgaki 大垣 is now a city of about 160,000 people located on the road from Hikone to Nagoya, near Sekigahara, site of a famous battle that paved the way for the establishment of a new government by Tokugawa Ieyasu. To Bashō it was a castle town on the Mino Road, which ran between Atsuta and Tarui. It was ruled by the Toda clan, with a stipend of 100,000 *koku*.

*Ogurozaki 小黒崎 still survives as a place name near Ōsaki, Miyagi Prefecture.

Ōi River 大井川 runs from the southern Japan Alps along the border between Suruga and Tōtōmi, flowing into Suruga Bay.

*Ōi River 大井川 is the name of the river that runs from the mountains in the Saga Arashiyama area of Kyoto. South of Togetsu Bridge it is called the Katsura River 桂川.

Ōishida 大石田 is now a small town in the mountains of Yamagata Prefecture. In Bashō's day it was an important port on the Mogami River.

*Ojima 雄島 is a small island in the bay at Matsushima. Bashō visited there because it had been the place of residence for several famous recluse monks.

Okinoishi 沖の石 (Rock on the Strand) is located just south of Sue no Matsuyama in Tagajō City. It is now surrounded by a moat and a fence.

Oku 奥 is a shortened form of Michinoku 陸奥, referring to the hinterlands north of the Shirakawa Barrier.

Ōmi 近江 (modern Shiga Prefecture) was the ancient name given to the land around the Ōmi Sea, now Lake Biwa, which is itself surrounded by some of Japan's most majestic mountains—the Hira Range to the west and the Ibuki Range to the east. After completing his journey to the hinterlands in the autumn of 1689, Bashō traveled all around this area over the next two years, where he had many disciples. He stayed for prolonged periods at a hut in the precincts of Gichūji Temple, at Genjūan behind Ishiyama Temple in Ōtsu, and in the home of his disciple Otokuni in Ōtsu. He visited Ōtsu and Zeze again, just months before his death.

Ōminesan 大嶺山 is a peak in the southern Yoshino area and another center of worship.

Osaka 大阪 was an important port in medieval times and continued to be so in the 1600s, boasting a population of about 350,000. Bashō died there, in what is now Chūo Ward.

Ōshūkaidō 奥州街道 was in the Five Road System, running between Edo and the northern cities of Utsunomiya and Shirakawa.

Ōtsu 大津 (population approximately 340,000) is one of the main port cities on the southern shores of Lake Biwa, just east of Kyoto. In Bashō's day it was the fifty-third station on Tōkai Road, a major crossroads for people traveling in and out of the Kyoto Basin. He had a number of disciples in the area, including Shōhaku, Otokuni, and the nun Chigetsu.

Oyama *see* Nikkō

Rakushisha 落柿舎 (Cottage of Fallen Persimmons) is the name of Kyorai's cottage in Saga. In Bashō's day, it was located closer to Nonomiya and Rinsenji than it is today. A building was built on the current site in memory of Kyorai by a *haikai* poet in the late eighteenth century and restored again in the Meiji era. It is now operated by a foundation and underwent major restoration once more in 2008.

Rinsen'an 臨川庵 was a small subtemple in Fukagawa close to Bashō's cottage, that served as the residence of Butchō when he was in Edo. Later it became a full temple named Rinsenji 臨川寺.

Rinsenji 臨川寺 (literally, "temple bordering the river") is a Rinzai Zen temple established by the Zen monk Musō Soseki in the 1330s as a subtemple of Tenryūji (located just to the west). It had begun as an imperial retreat named Kawabatadono, the Riverside Palace, at the time of Emperor Kameyama. The temple lot fronted on the Ōi River, just east of Togetsu Bridge.

Ryūmon (Dragon Gate) is the name of a peak and a waterfall south of Sakurai City in Nara Prefecture.

Ryūshakuji 立石寺 is a Tendai temple located on the outskirts of Yamagata City, founded by Ennin in 860. Also called Yamadera 山寺 (Mountain Temple), it sits high atop an outcropping of volcanic rock and offers breathtaking vistas. The original structure was destroyed in the early 1500s but was rebuilt several decades later and was a wealthy institution patronized by the Mogami clan.

*Sado 佐渡 is a large island off the coast in the Japan Sea. In Bashō's day it was known for its gold deposits and as a place of exile.

*Saga 嵯峨 (also called Sagano 嵯峨野, Saga Fields) is an area of the Nishikyō Ward in Kyoto, along the Ōi River. In Bashō's day it was already a lively tourist area known especially for the beauty of its cherry blossoms and autumn leaves.

Saiganji 西岸寺 is a branch temple of Chion'in, a great Kyoto temple of the Pure Land sect.

Saigyōdani 西行谷 (Saigyō Vale) is now memorialized with a plaque south of Mount Kamiji near the Ise Shrine. Saigyō lived there for a time.

Sakaida 境田 is now a district of Morioka City, Iwate Prefecture. In Bashō's day it was a tiny mountain village.

Sakata 坂田 is a medium-sized port city in northeastern Yamagata Prefecture. When Bashō visited it had a population of perhaps 2,250 homes and was a busy port, located at the mouth of the Mogami River.

Sangen Teahouse 三間屋 (properly, 三軒屋) was located just west of Togetsu Bridge, on the northern banks of the river in Saga. Photographs show that the teahouse was still there in the Meiji period. A grave marker for Kogō stands in a tiny grove in the same area today.

*Sarashina 更科 is the name of an area in modern Shinano Prefecture (premodern Nagano Province), on the outskirts of Nagano City. Nearby is a mountain identified as Mount Obasute.

*Sayononakayama 小夜の中山 is a mountain pass located in Shizuoka Prefecture.

Seba 洗馬 is a railway station in Shiojiri, Nagano Prefecture. In Bashō's day it was a stop on the Kiso Road.

Seimei Falls 蜻蛉が滝 is a waterfall in Kawakami Village, Yoshino.

Seiryōji 清凉寺 (also known as Saga Shakadō 嵯峨釈迦堂) is a Buddhist temple located in Saga, north of Rakushisha.

Sendai 仙台 is the capital city of Miyagi Prefecture, a political, economic, and cultural center that has a population of over 900,000. In Bashō's day it was the heart of the Sendai Domain in Mutsu Province, ruled by the Date clan, with a stipend of 620,000 *koku* and a population of 380,000.

Sengen Shrine 浅間神社 is now a tourist destination at the foot of Mount Fuji. In Bashō's day it was already a prominent institution.

Senju 千住 is an area of northern Arakawa Ward in Tokyo. In Bashō's day it was the first station on the Nikkō Road.

Sennindō 仙人堂 stands on the north bank of the Mogami River near Takaya.

Senoue 瀬の上 is a train station on the Abukuma Express railway in Fukushima Prefecture. In Bashō's day it was a post station.

Sesshōseki 殺生石 (Killer Rock) is an outcropping of rock located on a mountainside on the northern edge of the Nasu Moor. The area is famous for its hot springs.

Shihonryūji 四本龍寺 is a Tendai temple founded by Shodō in the mid-eighth century, the first of the many temples and shrines of Nikkō.

Shinjō 新庄 is a small city in Yamagata Prefecture. In Bashō's day it was a sizable castle town administered by Tozawa 戸沢, a daimyo lineage with a stipend of 68,200 *koku*.

*Shinobu しのぶ (信夫) is located in Fukushima City. In Bashō's day it was a small village.

*Shiogama 塩竃 is the name of the southern part of the bay at Matsushima and the site of the Shiogama Myōjin 塩竃明神, one of the most important shrines in Michinoku, dating back to the seventh century.

*Shiogoshi Pines 汐越の松 was located near Yoshizaki Inlet and is remembered with a monument today in Awara City, Fukui Prefecture.

*Shiraitonotaki 白糸滝 flows into the Mogami River in the Tozawa district of Yamagata Prefecture.

*Shirakawa 白河 is now a small city of about sixty thousand in Fukushima Prefecture. Its claim on Bashō's interest was the remains of the old Shirakawa Barrier 白河の関. It was then a castle town ruled by a branch of the Matsudaira clan, with a stipend of 150,000 *koku*.

*Shirane Peak 白根が嶽 (or Hakusan 白山, White Mountain) stands on the border between Kaga and Hida. It is often grouped with Mount Fuji among the finest of high peaks in Japan.

Shiroishi 白石 is a small city in Miyagi Prefecture. In Bashō's day it was a castle town in Natori district, administered by the Katakura 片倉 clan, retainers of the Date clan.

Shitomae Barrier 尿前関 had that name only beginning in the early 1600s. It was near Narugo Springs, on a hill at the border of Sendai Domain, going over into Shinjō Domain. It was established as a *sekisho* by the Date government.

Shōdaiji 招提寺 (formally, Tōshōdaiji 唐招提寺) is a temple of the Ritsu sect that is now a World Heritage site located in Nara City and one of that city's chief attractions. Founded by the Chinese monk Jianzhen (J. Ganjin) in 759, it was a major pilgrimage and tourist site in Bashō's day.

Shōgoin 聖護院 is an imperial cloister temple located in the Okazaki area of Kyoto. In Bashō's day the temple was the center of a village that was popular with artists and writers.

*Sode no Watari 袖のわたり is an area north of Ishinomaki, where a ferry once crossed the Kitakami River.

Sōka 草加 is a city of nearly 250,000 in Saitama Prefecture. In Bashō's day it was a post station on the Ōshū Road.

*Suenomatsuyama 末の松山 is located in Tagajō City. 宝国寺 Hōkokuji, the temple there—a branch of Zuiganji in Matsushima—was known by the Chinese reading of the place name, Masshōzan 末松山.

Sukagawa 須賀川 is now a city of about seventy-six thousand in Fukushima Prefecture. Originally it was a castle town, but the castle was destroyed by Date Masamune. For Bashō it was a post station on the Ōshū Road.

*Suma 須磨 is a coastal area just northeast of Akashi and is likewise of importance in *The Tale of Genji* and early Heian literature as a place of exile. Bashō visited there briefly in 1688. It impressed him enough that he mentioned it in *hokku* written later, most notably when he and Tōsai visited Ironohama, another sad shore, at the end of *The Narrow Road through the Hinterlands*.

Sumadera 須磨寺 is a Shingon temple complex (early on called Fukushōji 福祥寺) on the hillside in Suma that traces its origins back to the 800s but is associated with the Genpei Wars. The area around it was called Jōyasan 上野山.

*Sumida River 隅田川 runs through central Tokyo and empties into Tokyo Bay. In Bashō's day it was a major waterway, connected to numerous canals. Bashōan was located just to the east of the river, near the Konagi River, not far from the present-day Kiyosu Bridge.

Tada Shrine 太田神社 (more properly 多田神社 and also known as Tada Hachiman 多田八幡) is located in Komatsu City. It was founded in the sixth century. Dedicated to the God of War, Hachiman, it is associated particularly with the early scions of the Minamoto clan.

Tagajō 多賀城 is a city of around sixty thousand people immediately northeast of Sendai. It was a castle in ancient times but by Bashō's time the name of a town.

Tainohata 田井の畑, now written 多井の畑, persists in the name of an area just west of Kōbe Women's University in Suma.

Taichiin 大智院 is a Shingon temple in Kuwana City. It was a major stop on the Tōkaidō.

Taikōji 大江寺 is a temple of the Shingon sect located in Ise.

Taimadera 当麻寺 (later read Taemadera) is located at the eastern foot of what is now called Mount Nijō (another reading for Bashō's *futagami* 二上) in present-day Taimachō, Nara Prefecture, near Katsuragi City. It is also known as Zenrinji 禅林寺.

Takadachi 高館 was one of the fortresses of the so-called Northern Fujiwara at Hiraizumi.

*Takekuma 武隈 is an area in Iwanuma City, Miyagi Prefecture.

Takenouchi 竹内 is an area near Taimadera in Nara Prefecture.

*Tako Bay 担籠 (more properly, 多胡) no longer exists, but the area around Takonouranami Shrine, between Takaoka and Himi in the coastal area of Toyama Prefecture, was its past location.

The Tanba Road 丹波路 ran from Kyoto into Tanba Province.

Tenjin Shrine 天神の御社 (Tsutsujigaoka Tenmangū 躑躅が岡天満宮) is located north of Yakushidō in central Sendai City.

The Tenryū River 天龍川 runs from the Kiso Mountains into Tōtōmi Province, emptying into the sea at Hamamatsu.

Tenryūji 天龍寺 in Matsuoka 松岡 is a Sōtō Zen temple associated with nearby Eiheiji in Fukui Prefecture. It was the family temple of the Matsudaira clan, rulers of the Matsuoka Domain.

Tenryūji 天龍寺, a Zen temple, is now one of the main attractions of the Saga Arashi-yama area, as it was in Bashō's day.

Tōei Temple *see* Tōeizan Kan'eiji

Tōeizan Kan'eiji 東叡山東叡山寛永寺 (commonly called just Kan'eiji; literally, Hiei of the East) is a Tendai-sect temple in Daitō Ward, Tokyo. In the 1600s it received special patronage from the Tokugawa regime, hosting an imperial prince as an abbot and rivaling the Hieizan in Kyoto in prestige.

Togetsu Bridge 渡月橋 is a bridge across the Ōi River at Arashiyama.

Tōkaidō 東海道, the Tōkai Road, was the premier thoroughfare of the Five Road System (五街道 *gokaidō*), running between Kyoto and Edo. It had fifty-three post stations and was well maintained and policed.

Tōkōji 東光寺 is a Shingon temple in the Iwakiri district of Sendai City.

Tonase 戸難瀬 was apparently a rough stretch of water upriver from Tōgetsu Bridge in Arashiyama. Some sources seem to suggest it was a waterfall caused by a stream entering the current.

The Tone River 利根川 today follows a substantially different course than the river did in the 1600s. It was one of the great waterways of Bashō's day, flowing from the mountains of Echigo into Tokyo Bay.

Tōnomine 多武峰 is just southwest of Sakurai City.

Tosa 土佐 is the name for what is now Kōchi Prefecture on the island of Shikoku.

Tsu 津 (also known as Anotsu 安濃津) is a city of approximately 280,000 people located on Ise Bay, in Mie Prefecture. It was the domain seat of the Tōdō clan and an important port. The domain encompassing Iga and Ise was also referred to as Tsu.

Tsuetsukizaka 杖つき坂 (Walking Staff Slope) is now on the outskirts of Yokkaichii in Mie Prefecture. In Bashō's day it was a section of the Tōkai Road.

Tsukinowa Ford 月の輪の渡 is now marked with a stone monument just to the east of the Abukuma River in Fukushima Prefecture.

Tsuruga 敦賀 is now a port city in Fukui Prefecture. It still is and was in Bashō's day a port city and the location of the Kehi Shrine known for its scenic beaches.

Tsurugaoka *see* Tsuruoka

Tsuruoka 鶴岡 (also read Tsurugaoka) is a city of ninety-six thousand people in north-western Yamagata Prefecture. Bashō called it Tsurugaoka when he visited. It was a castle town of the Shōnai Domain, located on the Mogami River, and was ruled by the Sakai clan, with a stipend of 140,000 *koku.*

*Uguisu Barrier 鶯の関 (Uguisunoseki) was a barrier south of Nanjō, along the Hino River in Fukui. A stone monument at the roadside marks its location.

Unganji 雲岸寺 is a temple of the Rinzai sect of Zen located in the mountains just east of Ōtawara Village, Tochigi Prefecture. Initially, a temple on the site was founded around 1130 but was abandoned and established as a Zen temple in 1283. Bashō's Zen teacher, Butchō, had a retreat there.

Uraminotaki うらみの滝 is a site on the Arasawa River in Tochigi Prefecture.

Usui Pass 碓氷峠 was a mountain pass on the Nakasen Road.

Utatsuyama 卯辰山 is now a park on the eastern edge of Kanazawa City.

*Utsuyama 宇津の山 is an area near Mariko in Shizuoka. In Bashō's day it was a way station on the Tōkai Road.

*Waka Bay 和歌浦 is located on the coast near Wakayama City, in the prefecture of that same name. Bashō knew it as an *utamakura* of ancient origins and the site of a shrine to the god of *waka* 和歌, traditional court poetry.

Xihu 西湖 (West Lake) was located in Zhejiang Province, China.

Yakushidō 薬師堂 is located in Sendai and is also known as Mutsu Kokubunji 陸奥 国分寺.

Yamagata Domain 山形領 (or Yamagata-han) refers to the general area of Uzen Province. When Bashō visited there in 1689, it was a domain of 100,000 *koku* administered by the Hotta clan.

Yamanaka 山中 is an area near Fuwa Barrier in Gifu Prefecture.

Yamanaka 山中 is the name of a town at Yamanaka Lake in Yamanashi Prefecture.

Yamanaka Hot Springs 山中温泉, near Kaga City, is still a tourist destination with many inns, as it was in Bashō's day. Daishōji River ran through the area. It comprised about 142 houses in Bashō's time, a third of them inns.

Yamashiro 山城 was the name of the ancient province surrounding Kyoto.

Yamato 大和 was the name of the ancient province surrounding Nara City.

Yamura 谷村 survives now only as the name of railway station in the town of Tsuru, Yamanashi Prefecture. To Bashō it was a domain in Kai Province (also called Gunaihan), with a stipend of 18,000 *koku.*

*Yatsuhashi 八橋 (Eight Bridges) was located in Mikawa Province. It now remains only in the name of a railway stop in Aichi Prefecture.

Yawata 八幡 is the area around Katsushika Hachiman Shrine in Ichikawa City, Chiba Prefecture.

Yōsenji 養泉寺 is a Tendai temple in Obanezawa.

Yoshida 吉田 is now in the city of Toyohashi in Aichi Prefecture. In Bashō's day it was a major stop on the Tōkaidō.

*Yoshino 吉野 is the name of a mountainous area of central Nara Prefecture famous for its cherry blossoms and its many temples and shrines.

Yoze 余瀬 is a small town in Ōtawara City, Tochigi Prefecture.

Yuno'o Pass 湯尾峠 is located just south of Mount Hino, in Fukui Prefecture.

Zenkōji 善光寺 is the name of a temple in the modern city of Nagano (population approximately 375,000) in the province of the same name. Founded in the seventh century, it was a center of Amida worship affiliated with a number of different Buddhist sects and a major pilgrimage site in Bashō's day. The Zenkōji area was administered by the Tokugawa government. The town around it was a station stop on the Hokurokudō.

Zenshōji 全昌寺 is a Sōtō Zen temple in Daishōji, now a district of Kaga City. It was a castle town of the Maeda clan and a major institution in Bashō's day.

Zeze 膳所 is now an area in the city of Ōtsu. In Bashō's time it was the castle town of the Zeze Domain, with a stipend of 70,000 *koku*.

Zuiganji 瑞巌寺 is a Rinzai Zen temple in Matsushima, founded by Ennin as a Tendai temple but later reestablished as a Zen temple on the order of Hōjō Tokiyori, with the name Shōtōseiryūzan Enpukuzenji 松島青龍山円福禅寺. It was Date Masamune who added Zuiganji to the name and in 1673 made Ungo Zenji chief priest.

BIBLIOGRAPHY

The place of publication is Tokyo unless otherwise noted.

MULTI-VOLUME COLLECTIONS

BH	*Bashō no hon* 芭蕉の本. 1969–72. 8 vols. Kakokawa Shoten.
BK	*Bashō kōza* 芭蕉講座. 1982–85. 5 vols. Yūseidō.
KBZ	*Kōhon Bashō zenshū* 校本芭蕉全集. 1962–69. Ed. Komiya Toyotaka 小宮豊隆. 10 vols. Kadokawa Shoten.
NKBT	*Nihon koten bungaku taikei* 日本古典文学大系. 1957–68. Ed. Takagi Ichinosuke 高木市之助 et al. 102 vols. Iwanami Shoten.
NKBZ	*Nihon koten bungaku zenshū* 日本古典文学全集. 1970–76. Ed. Akiyama Ken 秋山虔 et al. 51 vols. Shōgakkan.
SBK	*Shin Bashō kōza* 新芭蕉講座. 1995. Ed. Ebara Taizō 穎原退蔵 et al. 9 vols. Sanseidō.
SKKT	*Shinpen kokka taikan* 新編国歌大観. 1983–92. Ed. Taniyama Shigeru 谷山茂 et al. 10 vols. Kadokawa Shoten.
SNKBT	*Shin nihon koten bungaku taikei* 新日本古典文学大系. 1989–2005. Ed. Satake Akihiro 佐竹昭広 et al. 106 vols. Iwanami Shoten.
SNKBZ	*Shin nihon koten bungaku zenshū* 新日本古典文学全集. 1994–2002. 88 vols. Shōgakkan.
SNKS	*Shinchō nihon koten shūsei* 新潮日本古典集成. 1976–89. 82 vols. Shinchōsha.

IMPERIAL POETRY COLLECTIONS

The following are imperial anthologies of Japanese poetry, all contained in vol. 1 of *SKKT*, with the exception of *Man'yōshū* (*MYS*)—technically not an imperial anthology—which is in *SKKT*, vol. 2.

GSIS	*Goshūishū*
GYS	*Gyokuyōshū*
KKS	*Kokinshū*
KYS	*Kin'yōshū*
MYS	*Man'yōshū*
SCKK	*Shin chokusenshū*
SKKS	*Shin kokinshū*
SKS	*Shikashū*
SZS	*Senzaishū*

Background Information on the Travel Writings

Bashō's travel writings circulated only in handwritten manuscripts during his lifetime. The first of his travel works to appear in print was *Nozarashi kikō*. It was included in a collection of Bashō's poetry titled *Hakusenshū* 泊船集 (gesturing back to his first days in Fukagawa) published in 1698 by Izutsuya, the Kyoto publisher of many of Bashō's poetic works during his lifetime, under the title *Bashō'ō michi no ki* 芭蕉翁道の記 (*A Travel Record by Bashō*). *Oku no hosomichi*, published by Izutsuya, followed in 1702. Next came *Sarashina kikō*, a version of which appeared in a collection of travel writings in 1704, and then again just five years later, in 1709, along with Otokuni's edition of *Oi no kobumi*. It was over forty years later that *Kashima mōde* and *Saga nikki* were published, in 1752 and 1753. Even early on, it was *Oku no hosomichi* that attracted the most interest, in the form of commentaries and as a guidebook for admirers who followed in his footsteps and made the trip through the hinterlands.

The order of publication would therefore be as follows:

1698	*Nozarashi kikō*
1702	*Oku no hosomichi*
1704	*Sarashina kikō*
1709	*Oi no kobumi*
1752	*Kashima mōde*
1753	*Saga nikki*

For my translations, I have relied most heavily on the editions in Imoto 1972 (in *NKBZ* 41), while also paying special attention to the 1997 Sakurai and Ueno edition of *Oku no hosomichi*, which many but not all scholars believe to be in Bashō's own hand. I have also consulted editions in the following collections: Sugiura and Miyamoto 1959 (*NKBT* 46); Akabane et al. 1967; Imoto and Yayoshi 1968 (*KBZ* 6); Akabane et al. 1968; Nakamura 1971; Toyama 1978 (*SNKS* 17); Yonetani 1985a and 1985b (*BK* 5); and Yokosawa 1995 (*SBK* 8).

Bones Bleaching in the Fields (Nozarashi kikō)

Early on, the text, or parts of it, seems to have been known as just *Nozarashi* 野ざらし (*Bones Bleaching in the Fields*) or as *Kusamakura* 草枕 (*Pillow of Grass*); other early names involve the term *kasshi* 甲子, referring to the elemental and animal figures of the Chinese zodiac for the year 1684: thus, *Kasshi ginkō* 甲子吟行 (*Record of Travel Poems*, 1684) or *Bashō-ō kasshi no kikō* 芭蕉翁甲子紀行 (*Travel Record of the Old Master*, 1684). It seems likely that the final manuscript joined together earlier texts with those names to produce what came to be known as *Nozarashi kikō*. However, it was only later that that title (*Travel Record of Bones Bleaching in the Fields*) gained ascendancy over earlier titles.

Bashō's illustrated text is referred to as *Bashō Shinseki emaki* 芭蕉真蹟絵巻 and Jokushi's as *Jokushihitsu Bashō okugaki emaki* 濁子筆芭蕉奥書絵巻 or *Jokushi seisho gakan* 濁子清書画巻. For selected photographs, see Okada 1972, plates 38–47. The fair copy with Jokushi's illustrations is favored as a basic text by most scholars, including Imoto 1972, who indicates where illustrations appear in his edition. In addition to the standard editions already noted, I have also consulted Yuzawa 1982 and Ogata 1998. All these scholars take as their base text Jokushi's illustrated manuscript, which boasts an afterword by Bashō's disciple Sodō and an *okugaki* (colophon) in Bashō's own hand. Sugiura and Miyamoto 1959 include material missing in this and other transmissions, such as two *hokku* after the *hokku* that begins *Karasaki no . . .* (see p. 21).

One feature of the text of *Nozarashi kikō* that is reflected in my translation has to do with format, which I have tried to represent by indenting prose passages and anchoring *hokku* on the left margin. As Yayoshi 1977, 212, argues, all the manuscripts of *Nozarashi kikō* that came through Bashō's hands are formatted the same way, with *hokku* in prime place and prose sections indented. If this makes the work seem more a collection of *hokku* (albeit one that follows a narrative order) with headnotes than a prose record, perhaps that is what came naturally to him at this point in his career. In subsequent travel records, *Oi no kobumi* and *Oku no hosomichi*, he did the reverse. Either way, the texts all remain hybrids.

A Pilgrimage to Kashima (Kashima mōde)

Received wisdom is that Bashō wrote up his account of the Kashima trip just after returning to Edo, around the 25th day of the Eighth Month of 1687. Early manuscripts of this text also have different names, some titled *Kashima mōde* (*Pilgrimage to Kashima*) and others *Kashima no ki* (*A Kashima Record*) or *Kashima kikō* 鹿島紀行 (*A Kashima Travel Record*). An early copy in Bashō's own hand, written up after the initial text he sent to Sanpū, bears the title *Kashima mōde*, which is the title used by Imoto 1972. Imoto relies on the *Shūkabon* 秋瓜本, which descends reliably from a copy in Bashō's hand passed down in the Honma house. I have followed Imoto's formatting of the text.

Knapsack Notes (Oi no kobumi)

This work began in fragments, some of the early ones being *Yoshino kikō* 吉野紀行 and *Yamato kikō* 大和紀行, which makes sense given the focus in the latter half of the text. We do know, however, that Shikō's edition—a highly boiled down version—was called not *Oi no kobumi* but simply *Kōgo kikō* 庚午紀行 (Travel Record of 1690; *kogō* corresponding to that year in the Chinese sexagenary cycle). Akabane 1970, 302, calculates that Bashō was working on the text at the time he stayed in Kyorai's villa in 1691, and sources indicate that Otokuni made a copy in the Ninth Month of that year. Ogata Tsutomu and others (see Uozumi 2011, 123–24, 135–36) reason that it was because of Tokoku's death in the Third Month of 1690 that Bashō decided to begin converting his travel notes into a true travel record that would function as a requiem for the demise of his friend and beloved disciple.

About its origins, we can say this much: (1) that Bashō kept poem logs (*kuchō*) on his journeys, (2) that he gave the notes (and later emendations) from his time on the road from the Tenth Month of 1687 to the Fourth Month of 1688 to his young disciple Otokuni, and (3) that it was Otokuni who had the text with its current title published in 1709. A more abbreviated version of the text, edited by another disciple, Shikō, appeared in a collection dated 1718.

In addition to the standard editions already noted, I have also consulted Yuzawa 1982 and Ueno 2008. All these scholars take as their base text the edition published by Otokuni in 1709.

In formatting I have followed the text of Ueno 2008, which does the best job of showing the separate *kobumi* that together make up the text.

A Journey to Sarashina (Sarashina kikō)

It appears that the writing of this short text was hurriedly done, probably back in Edo, as a sort of postscript to *Oi no kobumi*, with which it would appear in the 1709 edition of Bashō's disciple Otokuni. Muramatsu 1977 argues for the so-called *Sanpūbon*, but I follow Imoto 1972 and most other scholars in using the Otokuni text.

In addition to the standard editions already noted, I have also consulted Ueno 1985a and 2008.

The Narrow Road through the Hinterlands (Oku no hosomichi)

Working from notes of his 1689 journey and other documents, Bashō appears to have finished a draft of *Oku no hosomichi* in the autumn and early winter of 1693 (see Kon 2004, 19), then going on to produce a final draft by early in the Third Month of 1694 (see Uozumi 2011, 196–200). There are a number of manuscripts of Bashō's masterwork, most of which in one way or another descend from copies produced in 1694, by himself or disciples.

The differences between these texts are numerous but together reveal that *Oku no hosomichi* is the most complete and carefully written of Bashō's travel writings. (Most of the variations are in the nature of spelling and phrasing differences that do not even register in translation.) The following are the major manuscripts:

> The *Nakaobon* 中尾本, also called *Bashō jihitsubon* 芭蕉自筆本 or the *Yababon* 野坡本, which is accepted by many though not all scholars as in Bashō's own hand. It was originally in the hands of Bashō's disciple Yaba, and its existence was known as early as the time of the first publication of *Oku no hosomichi* in 1702, but it was only revealed to the world in 1996. It is now owned by Nakao Shōsen Shoten 中尾松泉書店, a rare book dealer. It shows interlinear corrections and also pastings that are said to show Bashō's last engagement with the text.
>
> The *Sorabon* 曽良本, which was thought to be Sora's handwritten copy of the *Nakaobon* but is now in dispute, some arguing that it is in Bashō's own hand and others that it was in the hand of Ikeda Rigyū.
>
> The *Soryūbon* 素龍本, or *Nishimurabon* 西村本, which is said to be a fine copy produced by Bashō's student, the Kyoto calligrapher Soryū, a disciple of Bashō's old teacher Kitamura Kigin, in the summer of 1694 at Bashō's request. It is believed to be the version Bashō carried with him on his last journey and left with his brother before his death. The title on the cover is thought to be in Bashō's hand. It was this manuscript that Kyorai arranged to be published by Izutsuya in 1702.
>
> The *Kakimoribon* 柿衛本, another manuscript said to be in the hand of Soryū, based on the *Sorabon*.

I cannot pretend to have the philological expertise to determine whether the *Nakaobon* is truly in Bashō's hand. (For a brief rehearsal of the many issues involved, see

Kaneko 2003.) However, I can say that I am impressed by the arguments of Ueno Yōzō, Sakurai Takejirō, Kon Eizō, and Tanaka Yoshinobu for the authenticity of the text. In particular, I am impressed by the explanations in Kon 2004, 16–20, and Tanaka 2002, 19–36, and 2009, 64, concerning the many typos and misspellings in the *Nakaobon*, which they attribute to the stress Bashō was under in the autumn and early winter of 1693 because of family problems, exhaustion, age, illness, and financial duress—factors that it is easy for modern scholars to overlook. For these reasons, I have chosen to use the *Nakaobon* as the basis for my translation. It is indisputably an early text that deserves as much attention as the Sora and Soryū texts used by prior translators.

In addition to the standard editions already noted, I have also consulted Ueno 1988; Sakurai and Ueno 1997; Ogata 2001; Horikiri 2003. Fukasawa and Kusumoto 2009 has been particularly useful because it offers a running digest of prior annotations as well as running texts of all the primary early manuscripts. For text and formatting, however, I have mostly followed Sakurai and Ueno 1997, which includes a photographic reproduction of the *Nakaobon* along with a full transcript in print.

The Saga Diary (Saga nikki)

Bashō probably wrote up his journal of his days at Rakushisha soon after his stay there. One scholar hazards that the text may have been written as a memento of sorts for Kyorai, which is plausible, and we know that Bashō's disciple Fumikuni treasured a copy of *Saga nikki* in Bashō's hand (see Okada 1972, *kaisetsu*, 115–16). In an era when the circulation of literary texts had not yet been completely absorbed into the commercial economy, a fine copy in the hand of an author had artistic, professional, and sentimental value.

In addition to the standard editions already noted, I have also consulted Ueno 1985a and Ueno 2008. As there is no sure evidence that a manuscript in Bashō's hand exists, scholars base their texts on Edo period copies, particularly the so-called *Nakamurabon* 中村本, which is generally seen as in Bashō's hand or at least a faithful copy of a text in Bashō's hand. Woodblock editions of the eighteenth century are generally thought to be unreliable.

JAPANESE SOURCES

The place of publication is Tokyo unless otherwise noted.

Reference Works

Haibungaku daijiten 俳文学大辞典. 1995. Comp. Katō Shūson 加藤楸邨, Imoto Nōichi 井本農一, Ōtani Tokuzō 大谷篤蔵, et al. Kadokawa Shoten.

Haikai daijiten 俳諧大辞典. 1957. Comp. Komiya Toyotaka 小宮豊隆, Aso Isoji 麻生磯次, et al. Meiji Shoin.

Nihon koten bungaku daijiten 日本古典文学大辞典. 1983. 6 vols. Comp. Noma Kōshin 野間光辰, Ōsone Shōsuke 大曽根章介, et al. Iwanami Shoten.

Sōgo Bashō jiten 総合芭蕉事典. 1982. Ed. and comp. Kuriyama Riichi 栗山理一 et al.

Primary Sources

Atsumori 敦盛. In *NKBZ* 33.

Bashō kushū 芭蕉句集. In *NKBT* 45.

Bashō o utsusu kotoba 芭蕉を移す詞. In *NKBZ* 41.

Fukuro sōshi 袋草子. *SNKBT* 29.

Fuyu no hi 冬の日. In *SNKBT* 70.

Genji monogatari 源氏物語. *NKBZ* 12–17.

Genjūan no ki 幻住庵記. In *NKBZ* 41.

Hachitaki no ji 鉢扣の辞. In *NKBT* 92.

Heike monogatari 平家物語. *NKBZ* 29–30.

Hōjōki 方丈記. In *SNKBT* 39.

Honchō ichinin isshu 本朝一人一首. *SNKBT* 63.

Horikawain hyakushu 堀河院百首. In *SKKT* 3.

Hyakunin isshu 百人一首百人一首. In *SKKT* 5.

Ise monogatari 伊勢物語. In *NKBZ* 8.

Ise sangū 伊勢参宮. In *NKBZ* 41.

Jōsō ga rui 丈草誄. In *NKBT* 92.

Kaidōki 海道記. In *SNKBT* 51.

Katsuragi 葛城. In *NKBZ* 33.

Kenkō hōshi shū 兼好法師集. In *SNKBT* 47.

Kinkaishū 金槐集. In *SKKT* 4.

Kotsujiki no okina 乞食の翁. In *NKBZ* 41.

Kurama Tengu 鞍馬天狗. In *NKBZ* 34.

Kyoraishō 向来抄. In *SNKBZ* 88.

Kyoriku o okuru kotoba 許六を送る詞. In *NKBZ* 41.

Kyoriku ribetsu no kotoba 許六離別詞. In *NKBZ* 41.

Makura no sōshi 枕草. In *SNKBT* 25.

Man'yōshū 万葉集. In *NKBZ* 1–4.

Miyako no tsuto 都のつと. In *SNKBT* 51.

Moritake senku 守武千句注. 1977. Iida Shōichi 飯田正一. *Moritake senku chū* 守武千句注. Furukawa Shobō.

Mumyōshō 無名抄. In *NKBT* 65.

Nozarashi kikō emaki batsu 野ざらし紀行絵巻跋. In *NKBZ* 41.

Obasute 姨捨. In *NKBZ* 33.

Rakushisha no ki 落柿舎記. In *NKBZ* 42. (By Bashō.)

Rakushisha no ki 落柿舎記. In *NKBT* 92. (By Kyorai.)

Saigyō monogatari 西行物語. 1981. Ed. Kuwabara Hiroshi 桑原博史. Kōdansha Gakujutsu Bunko.

Saigyō waka shūi 西行和歌拾遺. 1949. Ed. Itō Yoshio 伊藤憙夫. *Nihon koten zensho* 日本古典全書.

Sanka no ki 山家記. In *SNKBT* 67.

Sankashū 山家集. 1947. Ed. Itō Yoshio 伊藤憙夫. In *Nihon koten zensho series*. Asahi Shimbunsha.

Sanzōshi 三冊子. In *NKBZ* 51.

Sarumino 猿蓑. In *SNKBT* 70.

Senjūshō 選集抄. 1970. Ed. Nishio Kōichi 西尾光一. Iwanami Bunko.

Shirakawa kikō 白川紀行. 1976. In Kaneko Kinjirō 金子金次郎, *Sōgi tabi no ki shichū* 宗祇旅の記私注. Ōfusha.

Shitakusa 下草. 1977. In Kaneko Kinjirō, *Sōgi kushū* 宗祇句集. Kadokawa Shoten.

Sora nikki (or *Sora tabi nikki*) 曽良日記. In *SBK* 8.

Tōkan kikō 東関紀行. In *SNKBT* 51.

Tsukuba mondō 筑波問答. In *SNKBZ* 88.

Tsukubashū 莵玖波集. 1948, 1951. Ed. Fukui Kyūzō 福井久蔵. *Nihon koten zensho* 日本古典全書. Asahi Shimbunsha.

Tsurezuregusa 徒然草. In *SNKBT* 39.

Uda no hōshi 宇陀法師. In *KBZ* 7.

Wakan rōeishū 和漢朗詠集. In *NKBT* 73.

Yamato monogatari 大和物語. In *NKBZ* 8.

Yuki no kareobana 雪の枯尾花. In *NKBZ* 41.

Zoku gorin 続五輪. 1962. In Ogata Tsutomu 尾形仂 et al., eds. *Teihon Bashō taisei* 定本芭蕉大成.

Secondary Sources

Abe Kimio 阿部喜三男. 1970. "Bashō no tabi 芭蕉の旅," in *BH* 6: 89–123.

Abe Kimio and Asō Isoji 麻生磯次. 1964. *Kinsei haibun haiku bunshū* 近世俳文句俳文集. *NKBT* 92.

Abe Masami 阿部正美. 1965–89. *Bashō renku shō* 芭蕉連句抄. 12 vols. Meiji Shoin.

———. 1970. "Bashō denki no shomondai 芭蕉伝記の諸問題," in *BH* 2.

———. 1982, 1984. *Shinshū Bashō denki kōsetsu* 新修芭蕉傳記考説. 2 vols. Meiji Shoin.

Akabane Manabu 赤羽学. 1968. "*Oi no kobumi igo oyobi Sarashina kikō no ryotei* 『笈の小文』以後及び『更科紀行』の旅程," in Akabane et al. 1968: 105–26.

———. 1970. "*Oi no kobumi ron* 笈の小文論," in *BH* 6.

Akabane Manabu et al. 1967. *Nozarashi kikō, Kashima mōde: Bashō kikō shū I* 野ざらし紀行、鹿島詣：芭蕉紀行集 *I*. Meigen Shobō.

——— et al. 1968. *Oi no kobumi, Sarashina kikō: Bashō kikō shū II* 笈の小文、更科紀行：芭蕉紀行集 *II*. Meigen Shobō.

Arashiyama Kōsaburō 嵐山光三郎. 2000. *Bashō kikō* 芭蕉紀行. Shinchōsha.

Chōshōshi zenshū 長嘯子全集. 1972–1975. Ed. Yoshida Kōichi 吉田幸一. 6 vols. Koten Bunko.

Daiyasu Takashi 大安隆. 1994. *Bashō Yamatoji* 芭蕉大和路. Osaka: Izumi Shoin.

Danjō Masataka 壇上正孝. 1968. "*Oi no kobumi* no ryotei 『笈の小文』の旅程," in Akabane et. al.: 67–104.

———. 1970. "*Kashima mōde ron* 鹿島詣論," in *BH* 6: 227–44.

———. 1977. "Bashō Tōsei hyōtenkō 芭蕉桃青評点考," in *Nihon bungaku kenkyū shiryō sōsho, Bashō II* 日本文学研究資料叢書, 芭蕉 II, comp. Nihon Bungaku Kenkyū Shiryō Kankōkai 日本文学研究資料刊行会: 196–207. Yūseidō.

Eguchi Takao 江口孝夫. 1998. *Oku no hosomichi no tōsa kenkyū* 奥の細道の踏査研究. Musashino Shoin.

Fuji Masaharu 富士正晴. 1989. "Gendaigoyaku *Oku no hosomichi* 現代語訳奥の細道," in *Jitsuyō tokusen shirizu Oku no hosomichi* 実用特選シリーズ奥の細道, ed. Ogata Tsutomu 尾形仂 et al.: 111–58. Gakuken.

Fukasawa Shinji 深沢眞二. 2009. "Hagi no tabiji 萩の旅路," in Fukasawa and Kusumoto 2009: 365–401. Kasama Shoin.

———. 2016. "Bashō keikō no kuchō 芭蕉携行の句帳." *Kokugo to kokubungaku* 93–94 (April): 3–19.

Fukasawa Shinji and Kusumoto Mutsuo 楠本六男, comps. 2009. *Oku no hosomichi taizen* おくのほそ道大全. Kasama Shoin.

Fukasawa Tadataka 深澤忠考. 1997. "Bashō no shinkō no shinsō to hyōsō 芭蕉の信仰の深層と表層," in *Bashō kaitai shinsho* 芭蕉解体新書: ed. Kawamoto Kōji 川本皓嗣 et al.: 173–84. Yūzankaku.

Hama Moritarō 濱森太郎. 2016. *Matsuo Bashō saku Oi no kobumi* 松尾芭蕉作『笈の小文』. Tsu: Mie Daigaku Shuppankai.

Hisatomi Tetsuo 久富哲雄. 2002. *Oku no hosomichi no tabi handobukku* 奥の細道の旅ハンドブック. Sanseidō.

———. 2004. *Bashō to haikaishi no tenkai* 芭蕉と俳諧史の展開. Perikansha.

———. 2011. *Shashin de aruku Oku no hosomichi* 写真で歩く奥の細道. Sanseido.

Hori Mizuho 堀瑞穂. 1993. *Bashō Saga nikki no tabi* 芭蕉嵯峨日記の旅. Asahi Sonorama.

Hori Nobuo 堀信夫 and Imoto Nōichi 井本農一. 1972. "Hokku hen 発句編," in *NKBZ* 41.

Horikiri Minoru 堀切実. 1991. *Bashō no monjin* 芭蕉門人. Iwanami Shinsho.

———, comp. 2003. *Oku no hosomichi kaishakujiten* 『おくのほそ道』解釈事典. Tōkyōdō Shuppan.

Imoto Nōichi 井本農一. 1970. "*Oku no hosomichi ron* おくのほそ道論," in *BH* 6: 307–336.

———. 1972. "Kikō, nikki hen 紀行、日記編," in *NKBZ* 41.

Imoto Nōichi and Yayoshi Kan'ichi 弥吉菅一. 1968. "Kikō, nikki hen 紀行、日記編," in *KBZ* 6.

Inagaki Shisei 稲垣史生. 1993. *Nihon no kaidō handobukku* 日本の街道. Sanseido.

Inoue Toshiyuki 井上敏幸. 1982. "*Oku no hosomichi* made 「おくのほそ道」まで," in *BK* 1: 56–85.

———. 1992. *Jōkyō ki Bashō ronkō* 貞享期芭蕉論考. Kyoto: Rinsen Shoten.

Inui Hiroyuki 乾裕幸. 1982. "*Fuyu no hi made* 「冬の日」まで," in *BK* 1: 23–55.

Itō Yoshitaka 伊藤善隆. 2011. "Bashō no shōgai 芭蕉の生涯," in *Nijūisseiki nihon bungaku gaidobukku* 21 世紀日本文学ガイドブック 5, ed. Satō Katsuaki 佐藤勝明: 30–56. Hitsuji Shobō.

Kanamori Atsuko 金森敦子. 2000. *Bashō wa donna tabi o shita no ka Oku no hosomichi no keizai, sekisho, keikan* 芭蕉はどんな旅をしたのか『奥の細道』の経済、関所、景観. Shōbunsha.

———. 2013. *Sora nikki wo yomu, mō hitotsu no Oku no hosomichi* 『曽良日記』を読む、もうひとつの『おくのほそ道』. Hōsei Daigaku Shuppankyoku.

Kaneko Toshiyuki 金子俊之. 2003. "*Oku no hosomichi* no seiritsu to shohon ni kansuru shosetsu 『おくのほそ道』の成立と諸本に関する諸説," in *Oku no hosomichi kaishaku jiten* 『おくのほそ道』解釈事典, ed. Horikiri Minoru 堀切実: 10–21. Tōkyōdō Shuppan.

Kanzaki Noritake 神崎宣武. 2004. *Edo no tabi bunka* 江戸の旅文化. Iwanami Shinsho.

Kira Sueo 雲英末雄. 1985. *Genroku Kyōto haidan kenkyū* 元禄京都俳壇研究. Benseisha.

Kon Eizō 今栄蔵. 1989. "*Bashō no shōgai* 芭蕉の生涯," in *Jitsuyō tokusen Oku no hosomichi*, ed. and comp. Ogata Tsutomu 尾形仂 et al: 196–203. Gakushū Kenkyūsha.

———. 1992. *Bashō denki no shomondai* 芭蕉伝記の諸問題. Shintensha.

———. 2004. *Bashō kenkyū no shomondai* 芭蕉研究の諸問題. Kasumi Shoin.

———. 2005a. *Bashō nenpu taisei* 芭蕉年譜大成. Kadokawa Shoten.

———. 2005b. *Bashō shokan taisei* 芭蕉書簡大成. Kadokawa Shoten.

Kuriyama Riich 栗山理一 et al. 1972. *Kinsei haiku haibunshū* 近世俳句俳文集. *NKBZ* 41.

Kusumoto Mutsuo 楠本六男. 1994. *Bashō to monjintachi* 芭蕉と門人達. Nippon Hōsō Kyōkai.

———. 2006. *Bashō, sono go* 芭蕉、その後. Chikurinsha.

———. 2009. "Bashō no kikōbun 芭蕉の紀行文," in Fukasawa and Kusumoto 2009: 332–64.

Matsubayashi Shōshi 松林尚志. 2012. *Tōsei kara Bashō e, Shijin no tanjō* 桃青から芭蕉へ、詩人の誕生. Chōeisha.

Muramatsu Tomotsugu 村松友次. 1972. "*Bashō haibun hen* 芭蕉俳文編," in *NKBZ* 41.

———. 1977. "*Oku no hosomichi* tojō jinbutsu no kyōmei 『おくのほそ道』登場人物の虚名," in Nihon Bungaku Kenkyū Shiryō Kankōkai 日本文学研究資料刊行会, comp., *Nihon bungaku kenkyū shiryō Sōsho, Bashō II* 日本文学研究資料叢書, 芭蕉 II: 188–95. Yūseidō.

———. 1985. *Bashō no tegami* 芭蕉の手紙. Taishūkan Shoten.

Nakamura Shunjō 中村俊定. 1971. *Bashō kikōbunshū* 芭蕉紀行文集. Iwanami Bunko.

Narukawa Takeo 成川武雄. 1999. *Bashō to yūmoa* 芭蕉とユウモア. Tamakawa Daigaku Shuppanbu.

Ogata Tsutomu 尾形仂. 1977. "Chinkon no ryojō 鎮魂の旅情," in *Nihon bungaku kenkyū shiryō sōsho, Bashō II* 日本文学研究資料叢書, 芭蕉 II, comp. Nihon Bungaku Kenkyū Shiryō Kankōkai 日本文学研究資料刊行会: 122–33. Yūseidō.

———. 1989. "Oku no hosomichi no sekai 奥の細道の世界," in *Jitsuyō tokusen Oku no hosomichi*: 191–95.

———. 1995. "*Sora tabi nikki* 曽良旅日記," in *SBK* 8. 311–47.

———. 1998. *Nozarashi kikō hyōshaku* 野ざらし紀行評釈. Kadokawa Shoten.

———. 2001. *Oku no hosomichi hyōshaku* おくのほそ道評釈. Kadokawa Shoten.

———. 2002. *Bashō Handobukku* 芭蕉ハンドブック. Tokyo: Sanseido.

Okada Rihei 岡田利兵衛. 1972. *Zusetsu Bashō* 図説芭蕉. Kadokawa Shoten.

Ōtani Tokuzō 大田篤藏. 1962. "Hokku hen 発句編," in *NKBT* 45.

Ōuchi Hatsuo 大内初夫 and Wakaki Taiichi 若木太一. 1986. *Haikai no bugyō Mukai Kyorai* 俳諧の奉行. Shintensha.

Sakurai Takejirō 櫻井武次郎. 2006. *Oku no hosomichi angya, Sora nikki o yomu* 奥の細道行脚、『曽良日記』を読む. Iwanami Shoten.

Sakurai Takejirō and Ueno Yōzō 上野洋三. 1997. *Bashō jihitsu oku no hosomichi* 芭蕉自筆奥 の細道. Iwanami Shoten.

Satō Katsuaki 佐藤勝昭. 2014. *Bashō to Oku no hosomichi* 芭蕉と奥の細道. Tokyo: Yoshikawa Kobunkan.

———. 2018. "*Oku no hosomichi* no Echigoji zengo 『おくのほそ道』の越後路前後." *Kokugo to kokubungaku* 1032 (March): 3–17.

Satō Nobi さとう野火. 2014. *Kyōto, Konan no Bashō* 京都、湖南の芭蕉. Kyoto: Kyōto Shimbun Shuppan Senta.

Shibata Shōkyoku 柴田宵曲. 1986. *Bashō no hitobito* 芭蕉の人々. Iwanami Bunko.

Shimizu Motoyoshi 清水基吉. 1999. *Haikaishi Bashō* 俳諧師芭蕉. Seiabō.

Sugiura Shōichirō 杉浦正一郎 and Miyamoto Saburō 宮本三郎. 1959. "*Kikō, nikki, haibun* 紀行,日記, 俳文." *NKBT* 46.

Takahashi Shōji 高橋庄次. 1993. *Bashōan Tōsei no shōgai* 芭蕉庵桃青の生涯. Shunjūsha.

———. 2002. *Bashō denki shinkō* 芭蕉伝記新考. Shunjūsha.

Takatō Takema 高藤武馬. 1966. *Oku no hosomichi kasen hyōshaku* 奥の細道歌仙評釈. Chikuma Shobō.

Tanaka Yoshinobu 田中善信. 1998. *Bashō, futatsu no kao: zokujin to haisei to* 芭蕉二つの顔： 俗人と俳聖と. Kōdansha.

———. 2002. *Bashō no shingan* 芭蕉の真贋. Perikansha.

———, ed. and comp. 2005. *Zenshaku Bashō shokanshū* 全釈芭蕉書簡集. Shintensha Hankō.

———. 2008. *Bashō: haisei no jitsuzō o saguru* 芭蕉—俳聖の実像を探る. Shintensha.

———. 2009. *Bashō shinron* 芭蕉新論. Shintensha.

———. 2012. *Bashō no gakuryoku* 芭蕉の学力. Shintensha.

Toyama Susumu 富山奏. 1978. *Bashō bunshū* 芭蕉文集. *SNKS* 17.

Ueno Yōzō 上野洋三. 1985a. "*Saga nikki* 嵯峨日記," in *BK* 5.

———. 1985b. "*Sarashina kikō* 更科紀行," in *BK* 5.

———. 1988. *Shinchū eiri Oku no hosomichi, Sorabon* 新注絵入奥の細道曽良本. Izumi Shoin.

———. 1989. *Bashō, tabi e* 芭蕉、旅へ. Iwanami Shinsho.

———. 1992. *Bashō shichibushū* 芭蕉七部集. Iwanami Shoten.

———. 2005. *Bashō no hyōgen* 芭蕉の表現. Iwanami Shoten.

———. 2008. *Gendaigoyaku tsuki Oi no kobumi, Sarashina kikō, Saga nikki, Gendaigoyaku tsuki* 現代語訳付笈の小文、更科紀行、嵯峨日記. Izumi Shoin.

Uozumi Takashi 魚住孝至. 2011. *Bashō, saigo no ikku* 芭蕉、最後の一句. Chikuma Sensho.

Watanabe Nobuo 渡辺信夫. 1989. "Bashō no tabi to kaidō 芭蕉の旅と街道," in *Zusetsu Oku no hosomichi* 図説おくのほそ道. Kawade Shobō Shinsha.

Yamakawa Yasuto 山川安人. 2000. *Teihon shōmon no rokujūroku nin* 定本蕉門の66人. Fūjinsha.

Yamamoto Kenkichi 山本健吉. 2012. *Bashō zenhokku* 芭蕉全発句. Kodansha Gakujutsu Bunko.

Yamamoto Satoshi 山本侑. 1994. *Bashō Oku no hosomichi jiten* 芭蕉奥の細道事典. Kōdansha Bunko.

Yamamoto Yuiitsu 山本唯一. 1994. "Bashō no tabi 芭蕉の旅," in *Bashō o manabu hito no tame ni* 芭蕉を学ぶ人のために, ed. Hamachiyo Kiyoshi 浜千代清: 126–60. Sekai Shisō sha.

Yamane Tadashi 山根公. 2017. *Kaga no Bashō: Oku no hosomichi to hokurikuji* 加賀と芭蕉「奥の細道」と北陸路. Arufabeeta Bukkusu.

Yayoshi Kan'ichi 弥吉菅一. 1977. "*Nozarashi kikō* ron 野ざらし紀行論," in *BH* 6.

Yayoshi Kan'ichi and Nishimura Masako 西村真砂子. 1968. "*Oi no kobumi* ni tsuite 『笈の小文』について," in Akabane et al. 1968: 7–42.

Yokosawa Saburō 横沢三郎. 1995. "Kikōbun hyōshaku 紀行文評釈," in *SBK* 8.

Yonetani Isao 米谷巌. 1985a. "*Kashima mōde* 鹿島詣," in *BK* 5.

———. 1985b. "*Nozarashi kikō shō* 野ざらし紀行抄," in *BK* 5.

Yuzawa Kennosuke 湯沢賢之助. 1982. *Nozarashi kikō, Oi no kobumi* 野ざらし紀行、笈の小文. Shintensha.

English

Aitken, Robert, tr. 1991. *The Gateless Barrier: The Wu-Men Kuan (Mumonkan)*. San Francisco: North Point Press.

Aston, W. G., tr. 1972. *Nihongi: Chronicles of Japan from the Earliest Times to A.D. 697*. Rutland, VT: Charles E. Tuttle.

Carter, Steven D. 1987. *The Road to Komatsubara: A Classical Reading of the Renga Hyakuin*. Cambridge, MA: Council on East Asian Studies, Harvard University.

———. 1997. "Bashō and the *Haikai* Profession." *Journal of the American Oriental Society* 117.1: 57–69.

———. 2000. "Bashō and the Mastery of Poetic Space in *Oku no hosomichi*." *Journal of the American Oriental Society* 120.2: 190–98.

Graham, A. C. 1960. *The Book of Lieh-tzu, A Classic of Tao*. New York: Columbia University Press.

Heldt, Gustav, tr. 2014. *The Kojiki: An Account of Ancient Matters*. New York: Columbia University Press.

Keene, Donald. 1999. "*Haikai* Poetry: Bashō," in *World within Walls: Japanese Literature of the Pre-modern Era, 1600–1867*: 71–122. New York: Columbia University Press.

LaFleur, William R. 1983. "The Poet as Seer: Bashō Looks Back," in *The Karma of Words: Buddhism and the Literary Arts in Medieval Japan* 149–64. Berkeley: University of California Press.

Lau, D. C., tr. 1983 *Confucius, The Analects*. Hong Kong: The Chinese University Press.

———, tr. 1984. *Mencius*. Hong Kong: The Chinese University Press.

Mair, Victor, tr. 1994. *Wandering on the Way: Early Taoist Tales and Parables of Chuang Tzu*. Bantam Books.

McCullough, Helen Craig, tr. and ed. 1988. *The Tale of the Heike*. Stanford, CA: Stanford University Press, 1988.

———. 1990a. "An Account of a Journey to the East," in Helen Craig McCullough, ed. and tr. *Classical Japanese Prose: An Anthology*. 421–46. Stanford, CA: Stanford University Press.

———, tr. 1990b. "An Account of My Hermitage," in Helen Craig McCullough, ed. and tr. *Classical Japanese Prose: An Anthology*. 379–92. Stanford, CA: Stanford University Press.

Millett, Christine Murasaki 1997. "Bush Clover and the Moon" A Relational Reading of *Oku no Hosomichi*. *Monumenta Nipponica* 52.3 (Autumn): 327–56.

Miner, Earl. 1979. *Japanese Linked Poetry: An Account with Translations of Renga and Haikai Sequences*. Princeton, NJ: Princeton University Press.

Morris, Ivan. 1967. *The Pillow Book of Sei Shōnagon*. 2 vols. New York: Columbia University Press.

Prose, Francise. 2010. *Anne Frank: The Book, the Life, the Afterlife*. New York: HarperCollins.

Qiu, Peipei. 2005. *Bashō and the Dao: The Zhuangzi and the Transformation of Haikai*. Honolulu: University of Hawai'i Press.

Shirane, Haruo. 1998. *Traces of Dreams: Landscape, Cultural Memory, and the Poetry of Bashō*. New York: Columbia University Press.

———, ed. and comp. 2002. "The Poetry and Prose of Matsuo Bashō," in *Early Modern Japanese Literature: An Anthology, 1600–1900*. 178–232. New York: Columbia University Press.

Tyler, Royall, ed. and tr. 1992. *Noh Plays*. New York: Penguin Books.

———, tr. 2001. *The Tale of Genji*. 2 vols. New York: Viking Penguin.

Ueda, Makoto. 1965. "Matsuo Bashō: The Poetic Spirit, Sabi, and Lightness," in *Zeami, Bashō, Yeats, and Pound: A Study in Japanese and English Poetics*: 35–64. London: Mouton.

———. 1991. "Impersonality in Poetry: Bashō on the Art of the Haiku," in *Literary and Art Theories in Japan*: 145–72. Reprint edition. Ann Arbor: Center for Japanese Studies, the University of Michigan.

Waley, Arthur, tr. 1960. *The Book of Songs: The Ancient Chinese Classic of Poetry*. New York: Grove Press.

Watson, Burton, tr. 1993. *The Zen Teachings of Master Lin-Chi*. Boston: Shambhala.

INDEX OF FIRST LINES OF BASHŌ'S POEMS

GENERAL INDEX

Basic information about people and places appears in the appendices. Here the emphasis is on people and places of particular prominence in Bashō's travel and travel writing as well as important titles and terms. Italicized numbers indicate poems by the person in question.